E 2
DEC 91

PENGUIN BOOKS

Overtime

Georges-Hébert Germain studied at the University of Montreal and then spent several years as critic and reporter for the Montreal daily, *La Presse*, covering cultural events ranging from rock concerts to folksinging, theatre, film and literature. Since 1981, he has been a distinguished contributor to *L'actualité*.

Germain's articles have won numerous prizes and medals including the Brascan medal, prizes from the Order of Architects, Air Canada, the Judith Jasmin Foundation and prizes for excellence from the Canadian Magazine foundation in 1987 and 1988.

Germain lives with his family in Montreal.

D1092096

OVERTIME

The Legend of Guy Lafleur

Georges-Hébert Germain

Penguin Books

PENGUIN BOOKS
Published by the Penguin Group
Penguin Books Canada Ltd, 10 Alcorn Avenue, Toronto, Ontario,
Canada M4V 3B2
Penguin Books Ltd, 27 Wrights Lane, London W8 5TZ, England
Penguin Books USA Inc., 375 Hudson Street, New York, New York
10014, U.S.A.
Penguin Books Australia Ltd, Ringwood, Victoria, Australia
Penguin Books (NZ) Ltd, 182-190 Wairau Road, Auckland 10,
New Zealand

Penguin Books Ltd, Registered Offices: Harmondsworth, Middlesex,
England

First published in Viking by Penguin Books Canada Limited, 1990

Published in Penguin Books, 1991

1 3 5 7 9 10 8 6 4 2

Copyright© Art Global, Inc./Les Editions Libre Expression 1990
Original French language edition co-published by Art Global, Inc. and
Les Editions Libre Expression.
English translation copyright© Matt Cohen, 1990
Illustrations: Bellavance Photo, Jean-Louis Boyer, Denis Brodeur, Marc
Laforce, Jim Turner, Legaré et Kedl, Pierre Yvon Pelletier

All right reserved

Manufactured in Canada

Canadian Cataloguing in Publication Data
Germain, Georges-Hébert, 1944–
Overtime : the legend of Guy Lafleur

Also issued in French under title: Guy Lafleur :
l'ombre et la lumière.
ISBN 0-14-012924-3

1. Lafleur, Guy, 1951–   . 2. Hockey players —
Quebec (Province)—Biography. I. Title.

GV848.5.L33G4713 1991   796.96'2'092   C90-093604-5

Except in the United States of America, this book is sold subject to the
condition that it shall not, by way of trade or otherwise, be lent, re-sold,
hired out, or otherwise circulated without the publisher's prior consent in
any form of binding or cover other than that in which it is published and
without a similar condition including this condition being imposed on the
subsequent purchaser.

I owe a bright candle to
all the Québecois sports writers
whose innumerable articles have enlightened me.

I thank Francine Chaloult who,
because of this book,
will one day go to heaven.

And Stéphane Laporte,
without whom I still would not know
the right way to watch a hockey game.

I dedicate this book
to Lise Lafleur,
who believes that what is true should be said.

OVERTIME

Contents

Prologue

AT THIS EARLY hour of the morning the highway was deserted. He was driving slowly. In front of him was the pale November sun; in the distance, on the left, he saw the downtown buildings nestled into Mount Royal with their plumes of steam and white smoke. And in his mind he was going over and over the scenarios he had prepared the night before, when everything had seemed so simple and so clear.

He had repeated every word, every gesture, every look. He had found the exact stinging tone, the biting replies, and even the smile tinged with irony and contempt that he would soon be wearing as he calmly told them, looking them straight in the eye, what he was thinking.

Then he would slam the door in their faces. That would make a noise. A noise that would be heard everywhere — in Montreal, in Quebec, as far away as New York, Edmonton and Los Angeles. A big bang that would echo in every North American city with a hockey team. And people would say: "Guy Lafleur has walked out on the Montreal Canadiens."

As for himself, he would start all over again. A new life. Without them.

First would come the child—their second—that Lise would soon give birth to. Perhaps it would even arrive on Christmas Day, in exactly a month. They would buy a place in the country, a farm, somewhere in the Ottawa Valley or the Eastern Townships. He would get a tractor.

Lise could have horses. There would be a stream running near the house, and in the winter he would make a skating rink for the children on the pond, the way his father had when he was a boy, in Thurso. There would be a big garden, a swimming pool, trees surrounding the house. They would see no one except real friends. Finally they would have some peace and quiet.

For the moment, however, the dream darkened into an incomprehensible jumble, like mixed-up pieces of a puzzle. He could no longer get inside the skin of this hero—so sure of himself and of his future—that he and Lise had so brilliantly imagined the night before.

Lise had reassured him, saying that everything would go well, that he shouldn't make too much of it, that in any case there were other things in life than hockey; he, making his plans, had swung between anger and anxiety.

"You should demand a position in the organization," she had said. "It's your right. You gave them five Stanley Cups and they made a fortune with you."

"With Maurice Richard, too. And look how they treated him."

Just the same, he wanted to understand what had happened this past year, to know why they were so eager for him to go, why suddenly he was no longer given playing time and was no longer part of their plans, when everyone said he was still one of the best players in the whole National Hockey League.

What had happened to make his allies, his old companions in arms, turn so quickly against him and become enemies?

"Maybe I'm no good."

"That's what they'd like you to believe," said Lise. "That's what they'd like you to be, too—washed-up. But I know you're still a great player. And you can be sure that they know it. The problem isn't your game. What your father says is true—you talk too much, and you say what you think. You always question their authority. But unlike your father, I think it's good for you to do that. No one should ever blame you for telling the truth."

"I might be in the right, but I'm the one who's paying for it, I'm the one who's losing, and I'm the one who's leaving."

Driving into the city he told himself that from now on his family, Lise and Martin and this new son who would soon be born, would be the basis of his life. His career was over. In one hour, to be exact, when he walked out of the Forum for the last time in his life, it would be over forever. Perhaps he would even leave his skates in the locker room, his old leather Bauer antiques, the oldest skates in the whole National Hockey League.

Lise had got up at the same time as Guy. She had made him something to eat, even though he said that he wasn't hungry. "Eat a little," she'd said. "You're going to need it." Then he'd left to drive Martin to school. In the car he told his son:

"You know, Martin, Papa isn't going to play for the Canadiens any more."

"Who are you going to play for?"

"For no one. I'm going to play with you."

And suddenly, it was enough to break his heart. Now he wasn't sure of anything. He told himself that perhaps he hadn't made the right decision, that he would probably find his new life impossible. And of course he knew that Lise must be terribly worried, thinking that once again he would be going out and drinking. It wasn't normal that a thirty-three-year-old man, rich and in good health, would retire without any real plans. Moving, getting a new car, digging a garden, skiing, having a baby—that was well enough, but then what? What was he going to do then?

The future appeared to him as a cold and hollow abyss. His past accomplishments would slide into oblivion. Soon no one would remember him. No more attention, no more spotlight, no more anything. The emptiness made him afraid. Everyone knows a man without a future is a dead man. Or almost.

A terrible memory came to him, as it did almost every time in the past two years he had driven on Highway 20 outside Ville LaSalle. As usual he looked at the other lane, on the side of the Notre-Dame exit. There he had almost been killed, while driving back home to Baie d'Urfé in the spring of 1982. He had mowed down nearly two hundred feet of fence; a steel post, ramming through the windshield of his Cadillac, had skimmed along his right temple, cut the top of his ear, then lodged in the back of his seat. It was a miracle that he was still alive!

Slowly he went up Atwater, crossed Dorchester, then was faced with the imposing mass of the Montreal Forum. For a moment he saw himself on the ice at the height of his glory, with the immense roar of the crowd chanting his name: "Guy! Guy! Guy!" And he raised his arms high to celebrate his victory and welcome the homage that was being paid. It had been good. But it was over.

Nevertheless, somewhere deep inside himself he felt confusedly that sooner or later there would be something else. He knew that when he walked into the Forum he would be at home. One last time. And he would find the words and the ways to say what was on his mind. And afterwards, he would be free. Finally. Afterwards, he would start his new life. Trying to do better. One more time.

FIRST PERIOD

●

HE GROPED FOR his sweater, which was on the floor with its sleeves crossed, just beside his bed. After the sweater came his shorts and his stockings, carefully put in place so that his whole uniform was laid out from top to bottom. He dressed quickly in the dark, being careful not to wake anyone.

After the luxurious heat of the bed, he shivered in the cold air. The cloth of the shorts was icy, the thigh pads rigid, and the woollen stockings were coarse and scratchy.

He crossed the hall on tiptoe, skirting the hot air grill above the furnace. He went by the girls' room, then that of his parents and the baby. At the top of the stairs he heard his mother's voice whispering in the darkness:

"I've made you a lunch, Guy. In the refrigerator."

Below, in the kitchen, he lit the lamp on the counter. The window above the sink was always covered in frost, but he could see a weak light from the horizon where the sun was rising, and the field of snow glowed pink.

He opened the refrigerator door, frowning as if to hush the noises. He put his lunch in his blue cloth sports bag where his equipment, his helmet, his tape, his Canadian Army *Hockey Hints* manual, his puck, his clothes to change into and a windbreaker were already packed. He ate cereal and oranges. From time to time he would hear, from above, a creak, a sigh, the squeaking of springs, even the ticking of his father's alarm clock, which wouldn't ring today, because it was Saturday.

He picked up his bag and went into the sunroom where

he put on his shinpads, his shoulderpads, then his toque, some mittens and an old coat of his father's. Because of the shoulderpads, his own coat would have been too small. He took his hockey stick and went out into the night.

The sky was no longer pink, but blue, a deep, soft blue. During the night a light snow had fallen, dry and crystalline, which crunched under his boots. After crossing Rue Jacques-Cartier, he went back up Rue Bourget until he came to the vacant land behind city hall. He crossed the ditch, then the railroad line, and found himself behind the hockey arena. Its dark shape was silhouetted against the lightening sky, into which rose the smoke from the factory, a giant black plume hanging above the sleeping city.

The snow crunched more loudly as he approached the wall of the hangar adjoining the arena. In the old grey plank wall there was a narrow door that was always barred and padlocked. Every time he saw it, he wondered what purpose the door was supposed to serve. Just beside it, in front of the chute through which the old snow from the rink was removed, there were three boards that could be easily raised from the outside. He pushed his bag into the hangar and slid in after it.

It was completely dark. He could hear the clanking pipes of the heating and refrigeration systems. With a hand against the wall to guide himself, he went around the room until he reached another door. Through that he passed into an immense, shadowed emptiness. Once again he was aware of the comfortable damp smell, the almost animal smell of the ice, to which the nightlights lent a pearly glow. You would have thought the ice was a sleeping beast, bedded in its lair; the ice was alive and smooth, a beautiful, unmarked, virgin ice.

He leaned his stick against the boards and dug to the bottom of his bag for his battered puck, which he threw on the ice where it bounced and slid into the shadows. Carefully he laced up his skates. Then it was his turn to glide out onto the ice.

At first he skated easily, for the pleasure of it, to stretch his muscles and get warmed up. His skates traced giant arabesques on the new ice. Then he took the puck and began a spectacular rush towards the far net. He zigzagged, braked, reversed his direction, gave himself a pass off the boards, crossed the blue line, plunged into the left corner, came back towards the centre of the rink, eluded an invisible defender and found himself alone in front of the net: a fake to the left, a fake to the right, then he shot and scored.

And to mark his victory, he executed a series of shots against the boards. From twenty feet the puck made a loud solid thud, a big boom that echoed through the arena. He was warm now. He heard the sound of his breathing, of his skates on the ice. It was good.

He imagined that the invisible defender was waiting for him in the shadows, deep in the enemy zone. He charged at top speed towards him, carrying the puck. He could almost hear the crowd gasping. Once again he crossed the blue line, got away from the defence, skated in on the net, alone . . . Then the lights of the arena flashed on and he was stopped in his tracks. A loud, sleep-filled voice, edgy with impatience and surprise, called out to him: "Lafleur! What are you doing here?"

He stopped so suddenly that he almost fell over backwards. He turned around and tried to see where Ti-Paul was, but there was suddenly so much light that he was blinded.

"Do you know what time it is?"

Ti-Paul Meloche was the new manager of the arena. He seemed to be in a bad mood.

"First of all, what are you doing here at six o'clock in the morning? How did you get in?"

"I came through the wall."

"Ah! On top of everything else, you can pass through walls!"

Ti-Paul opened the gate beside the main entrance and advanced towards Guy. He was wearing his pyjamas, high rubber boots and an old soft hat. He was a wide, strong man, but not very tall. On his skates Guy Lafleur, who had just turned ten, was almost as tall as Ti-Paul.

"What are you doing here, Guy? Would you like to explain?"

"I'm playing hockey. I'm practising."

"At six o'clock in the morning!"

Guy stood in front of Ti-Paul, his stick resting on the ice. He looked at the puck, immobilized halfway between the blue line and the net.

"What else can I do? I have to serve the nine o'clock mass."

"Of course. But you know, the rest of us like to sleep on Saturday mornings. And we don't like you to wake us up."

Ti-Paul and his family lived in the small apartment beside the main entrance to the arena. Guy Lafleur often said to himself that it was as though Ti-Paul had a skating rink in his own house. If he wanted to, he could even get up in the middle of the night and go downstairs to skate.

Ti-Paul was a champion. He had played in the junior leagues. He knew important people. He had even met Maurice Richard, Jean Béliveau, Toe Blake. But this morning Ti-Paul had no desire to skate. He had gone to bed late after partying, as he did every Friday night that the good Lord provided, at the Hotel Lafontaine. For Ti-Paul, Friday nights were sacred. Therefore, Saturday mornings were too.

"I didn't mean to wake you up."

"How did you get in?"

"Through the hangar wall."

"Would you mind showing me?"

Guy led him to the hanger and showed him the three loose boards.

"How did you find these?"

"When I was cleaning the rink."

"You wouldn't have helped those boards get loose, by chance?"

"No! It happened by itself."

Ti-Paul looked contemplatively at the wall, perplexed but also amused. Bits of daylight filtered through the cracks between the boards. He could hear water bubbling through the pipes.

"Does your father know you come here in the middle of the night?"

"It's not the middle of the night. It's almost seven o'clock!"

"Seven o'clock on a Saturday morning — that's still the middle of the night."

"My father said to get your permission."

"Oh well! I spent some time with him last night. Seems to me he could have warned me!"

Ti-Paul was no longer in a bad mood, and didn't even seem to be sleepy. When they returned to the arena he picked up Guy's stick and played at shooting the puck into the left corner; each time the puck followed the curve of the boards, went behind the net, always halfway up, continued to the right corner of the boards. Ti-Paul would then run across the rink to pick up the puck at the blue line, as though he were playing with a boomerang. He seemed to have forgotten that Guy was there. He was running on the ice in his pyjamas and his felt hat, making the puck jump and dance. Then he stopped, came back to Guy, a little out of breath, and said to him:

"I'm going to make a deal with you. That place in the wall can stay open. But don't tell anyone about it. Only you are going to know. I don't want half the city bouncing around here in the middle of the night. Or robbers coming into our place. But you can come whenever you want—at three o'clock in the morning if you like. But make sure you don't wake us up. In other words, play at the far end of the rink. And try to avoid shooting against the boards."

Then he showed Guy how to turn on the spotlights. He explained the cooling system to him, took him into the little shop where he kept his tools, the cans of red and blue paints for the lines, the string for the nets, a small supply of wood for repairing the boards, the big barrel mounted on skates he used for watering the ice, the grinder for sharpening skates.

"I hope you understand why I'm showing you all this."

"So I can help you?"

"No, my boy. So you can earn your ice time. I don't ever want to hear that I asked you to help me. We're making a deal. You work for an hour, I give you an hour of ice time. If you don't work, you can't be here. Understood?"

"Understood."

• • •

When Guy left the arena to go to the church, the sun in the sky and the glare from the snow were blinding. The smoke from the McLarens plant rose high above the city. One day his father had told him that when the weather was good, you could see the smoke from Thurso as far away as Buckingham, Rockland and even L'Orignal or Ripon. When the wind, which usually came from the west, blew the smoke back down to ground level, the stink of Thurso carried all the way to Papineauville, and even beyond Montebello. It was an imposing mixture of the heavy acid smells of pulp, of burnt feathers and hides, of gases and of molten metals.

He let himself into the church by the door at the side, then when up to the sacristy where the curé, Arsène Hébert, was already preparing for mass. Like his house had been that morning, the church was warm, serene, silent. Over his hockey shorts and sweater he put on his soutane and his choirboy's surplice. The church smelled of incense, of melting wax, of polish.

Father Hébert was far from pleased that the Lafleur boy was one of his choirboys. Guy had never been able to memorize the Latin responses. He was so negligent and distracted that the officiating priest often had to prompt his replies and tell him what to do. The only job he could be trusted with was that of helping the priest don the sacerdotal garments. Those he always passed in the ritual order: the alb, the surplice, the chasuble, the stole. But after that he was incapable of staying attentive. He really didn't understand how the parish priest could have told his parents that their son might become a priest or a monk if only he took the trouble to study.

"He is an intelligent boy. He could enter the Church."

"But Father, we haven't the money."

"That can always be arranged. If you want to give your child to God, He will take care of his education."

But the boy didn't like to study. And the idea of being donated to the service of God terrified him. Like everyone else, he wanted to go to heaven — but only at the end of a long life.

While Father Hébert performed the ceremony, the choirboy thought of his agreement with Ti-Paul, of the possibility that from now on he could have as much ice time as he wanted. Looking after the rink wouldn't be work, it was a dream come true. Had he been given the choice between living in Ti-Paul's small place at the arena or the large and handsome presbytery, Guy would have immediately chosen the arena. In his eyes, Ti-Paul was a truly fortunate person, a lord of the manor.

At the offertory, the curé had to signal him to bring forth the cruets; at the *sanctus*, he reminded him he was supposed to ring the bell; and when mass was over he put a little anger in his voice to tell him to go get his biretta. When, a little later, he saw that Guy was wearing his hockey uniform beneath his soutane, he reminded him that that wasn't really good manners.

"I couldn't do anything else," said Guy. "I have a practice at eleven o'clock."

The curé smiled. The fanaticism of his young flock for the national sport sometimes frightened him a bit, and he thought that their mania for collecting pictures of National Hockey League players verged on idolatry. However, the sport was a healthy diversion. When Jean-Paul Meloche had become responsible for minor league hockey in Thurso, the curé had gone to meet him to assure him of his support, and had strongly encouraged him to enter his teams into the regional leagues.

After mass, while Guy helped him put back the sacerdotal garments and to clean the incense holder, the curé asked him: "What's happening with the Mosquito-age tournament at Rockland? Are you going to be playing?"

"We're supposed to find out today or tomorrow, Father."

"Tell Paul that the curé thinks you should go."

Ten minutes later, Guy was on his way back to the arena. A very unpleasant surprise awaited him.

• • •

Several of the players on the Pee Wee team were already in uniform and on the ice: Lalonde, Duguay, Payer, Jimmy Simpson. While waiting for practice to begin, they were skating in circles around the rink. In the middle of the rink, Ti-Paul was talking to Brother Léo. Brother Léo had opened up his little notebook, in which he had recorded the scores of every player; he seemed to be reading his notes to Ti-Paul.

Guy went to put on his skates, his shinpads and his shoulderpads. Then he came back and skated with the others until Ti-Paul blew his whistle. Jostling each other, they all skated towards their coach. Guy was about to tell Ti-Paul that Father Hébert wanted Thurso to go to the Mosquito tournament in Rockland but Ti-Paul spoke first:

"You, Lafleur. Go practise your backhand with Brother Léo while I work here with the others."

"What? My backhand? Can't I practise like everyone else?"

He wanted to add that there must be a mistake, to remind Ti-Paul that they had an agreement, that they were friends. But his voice caught in his throat. He didn't move. The other boys turned and looked at him.

"Listen, Guy, you might have a good slapshot, but you're the only one here who can't raise the puck on your backhand. Go practise. When you can do it, you can come back and work with the others."

Guy went to join Brother Léo, who was waiting for him at the other end of the rink. He was smiling and carrying a pail full of pucks. Brother Léo Jacques was the new director of the school, Sainte-Famille de Thurso. Energetic and authoritarian, Brother Léo was thin, tall and dry. He was a man who enjoyed stirring things up, and if a student misbehaved he was liable to get a slap on the back of the head or even a kick in the rear. He believed in the formative virtues of team sports, training and discipline.

Brother Léo would say that he didn't like followers, copy-cats or milksops, which was what he called those servile and submissive students who never took initiative and were content to follow the rules blindly. He preferred working with the harder cases, proud and autonomous individuals who were capable of self-discipline and even, when necessary, of rebelling against authority—whether that of the Church or his own.

Guy Lafleur had already had dealings with Brother Léo on several occasions, and they had not gone so well. First, right at the beginning of the season, when it was announced that hockey teams would be organized, Ti-Paul and Brother Léo had asked all the pupils who wanted to play to give their names, their weights and their ages. In theory the boys were free to choose, but to abstain they would have needed very good reasons. Thus almost everyone had registered: one hundred and sixty-eight boys, from which were made up several good teams at various levels.

The Brother had classed them according to skill and age. He had first summoned the youngest ones, the Mosquitos. Guy Lafleur fell into this class, and so one morning at the end of September, Guy Lafleur presented himself at the arena with his stick and his skates. Likewise most of the boys of his age, including Boulerice, Giroux, Berger, Meloche and the others.

One at a time Ti-Paul had sent them onto the rink and asked them to carry the puck, to shoot, to stop, to evade an imaginary defender, then a real defender plus a goalie. It was made more difficult by the fact that along the boards were all the other boys, even those large enough for Pee Wee or Bantam. They looked on and laughed every time someone made a mistake and fell.

Guy was ill at ease. He detested competitions. He didn't like to have to perform in front of everyone. But when his turn finally came and he found himself on the ice, he burst forward like a lion, shot, got around the defencemen and the goalie. Then he gathered the puck out of the net and started a rush in the other direction. Once again he faked out the defenders and found himself in front of an empy net. All along the boards the other players began clapping and calling out. Then Guy turned towards Ti-Paul and Brother Léo, who were both laughing and waving at him to let him know that they had been impressed.

They had given themselves until the next day to announce the results, but Guy stuck close to Ti-Paul, following him all around the arena and asking him over and over: "Are you going to take me, Ti-Paul? Are you going to take me?"

Following the rules, Ti-Paul didn't want to say anything. But by the time it was almost noon, and most of the boys had left, and since he really had been impressed by Guy, he finally said: "Of course you're going to be chosen. You're the best Mosquito I've ever seen."

And Guy Lafleur had gone back to his house for lunch in a state of total euphoria. He didn't say a word to his mother or sisters because he couldn't or didn't want to talk about such things.

In the afternoon he went back to the arena to see the try-outs of the older boys. He sat himself near Ti-Paul at the end of the players' bench and watched them as they performed. They had to pass a series of tests that seemed, to him, amazingly easy: carry the puck around the rink in less than a minute, shoot into the net from the blue line, make and receive passes while skating—nothing that he couldn't have done. So he went back home to get his skates and his stick. He mixed in with the boys of eleven and twelve. And when Ti-Paul yelled "Next" he leapt onto the ice.

He was just starting to skate around the rink when Brother Léo called out: "Hey, Lafleur! What are you doing here?"

But he continued to push the puck, went round the net, came back towards the centre of the rink, evaded two defenders, just as he had that morning, then buried the puck in the back of the net.

"Lafleur, you can't play Pee Wee. You're a Mosquito, Lafleur, you're only ten years old."

"What does it matter?" asked Ti-Paul. "There's a maximum age, not a minimum. According to the rules, there's nothing to stop us from registering a ten-year-old boy—or even a six-year-old or a three-year-old—in a Pee Wee hockey club."

"But Lafleur isn't big enough. He weighs less than a hundred pounds. And he skates on his ankles."

"We can fix that. And anyway, he already skates faster than anyone else."

"But he can't be on two teams at the same time."

"Why not? You're right, if you mean two teams in the same league who might play each other. But that's not the case. I really don't see the problem."

Guy had already noticed that Ti-Paul and Brother Léo never agreed on anything. They even seemed to enjoy their arguments. While they talked, he stood right in front of them—he wanted to tell them that he had just won the tennis championship playing against thirteen- and fourteen-year-old boys—but the two men paid no attention to him. It was as though he wasn't there, or the discussion had nothing to do with him. By the end of the argument Brother Léo had given in to Ti-Paul and Guy had been registered on the list of chosen ones. He would play for the Mosquitos and the Pee Wees at the same time, and Brother Léo had even congratulated him.

Two days later, when they were giving sweaters out to the Pee Wee players, Brother Léo gave Guy another taste of his unbreakable authority. All the boys wanted the famous number 9, which had belonged to Maurice Richard who had retired only a year before. Since Brother Léo had decided to give the first choices to the oldest players, number 9 went to the first-line centre, a big strong boy who was in grade seven. Many of the players had been deeply disappointed, but not Guy Lafleur: he wanted number 4, which belonged to his idol, Jean Béliveau. But number 4 was given to a boy who wasn't very fast on his skates, but was in grade six.

Guy, because of his age and weight, was on the last line. When his turn came, none of the numbers considered prestigious were left. Brother Léo offered him sweater number 10. Guy made a face. That was the number of Tom Johnson, a decent player, perhaps, but a poor scorer. Doug Harvey, number 2, would be okay; he was the Canadiens' best defenceman. He had won the Norris Trophy six times, and nine times he had been on the NHL first all-star team. But Tom Johnson! He'd only won the Norris once, and he'd only been on the first all-star team once.

"If you don't like it, Lafleur," Brother Léo had said, "the door is there. Take it and go home."

"I like it."

"In that case, change the look on your face."

These two experiences—the choosing of players and the distribution of the sweaters—had certainly not enhanced Guy Lafleur's esteem for Brother Léo. Although he had resigned himself to wearing number 10, he had done his best to let everyone know he deserved better. Since the season's start he had kept himself among the leading scorers, both as a Pee Wee and as a Mosquito. He was always at the arena, ready to play. Everyone, even Ti-Paul, said that he was the best player around.

And now he was being asked to go practise his backhand! The very day he had concluded an agreement with Ti-Paul that almost made him his assistant manager! He was humiliated and disappointed.

"Go on," said Brother Léo. "Shoot!"

But his backhand was weak and imprecise. At the end of half an hour he was almost crying with rage. While going to pick up the pucks he whacked his stick against the boards, cracking it. He was ready to give up.

"The door's there," said Brother Léo. "If you're not happy, you can go. I'll see you tomorrow with the Mosquitos."

He went back to the puck. Again and again.

"Don't strain. Wait until you feel the weight of the puck on the blade, slide your stick along the ice. Don't force it.

You'll see. The puck will end up in the air. It has to happen."

But it took a long time, too long. Furiously he threw his stick into the boards, crying:

"Damn puck! I'm going home."

This time Brother Léo ran up to him and grabbed him by the neck. "Listen, you. It's not the stick's fault, or the puck's fault, or my fault if you can't shoot like everyone else. It all depends on you, only you."

"You told me I could go home if I wasn't happy. I'm not happy, so I'm going."

"I've changed my mind. Pick up your stick and start over."

Guy hated Brother Léo. He hated hockey, the ice, the puck, the whole world. But, a little at a time, the puck began to lift off the ice. Soon, from the blue line, he could send it flying above the net. He was happy. Everyone else had left and he kept shooting, higher and higher, harder and harder.

"You see," Brother Léo said, "if you'd really quit . . . It's never a good idea to give up. Never forget it."

• • •

Rockland is on the Ontario side of the Ottawa River, across from Thurso and a little upstream. In 1962, the small, flat-roofed, cinder-block arena was already seventy-five-years-old, and secure in a hockey tradition that Jean-Marc Lalonde, its manager, had every intention of carrying on. In 1961 Rockland's Pee Wee club, the Boomers, had been good enough to participate in the most prestigious event in the world of minor hockey—the International Pee Wee Tournament in Quebec City. And now, Rockland was preparing for the intense rivalry of the second annual Mosquito tournament, to be held in February, 1962.

In the first tournament the Ontario clubs, led by Rockland, had dominated, easily overpowering the poorly coached, badly equipped and spiritless teams from Quebec. But this time was going to be different. It was unlikely that the tournament's Chamberland trophy would stay on the right bank of the Ottawa. In fact, even before the tournament began, the probable winner was known. Even the always-optimistic Jean-Marc Lalonde held out little hope for his own Mosquitos. During the regular season, Lalonde's Rockland team had played the Thurso Mosquitos, and his team had lost every game.

In Thurso, everything seemed to have happened at once. Only a year before, there had been practically no organized hockey. The arena, owned by the Singer company, had been used mostly for the Singer and Thurso Pulp curling leagues, and as a place where well-off young girls did their figure skating.

And then the city bought the arena from Singer and took on the task of renovating it. Jean-Paul Meloche, the best hockey man in the area, left his job at Singer to manage the coaching of the players. Brother Léo, the newly named director of the Sainte-Famille School, was a sports enthusiast, and did everything he could to encourage team sports. And then there was the incomparable prodigy, Réjean Lafleur's son, a ten-year-old boy who could play every position, left side or right, who skated like the wind, had a slapshot like a thunderbolt and an amazingly accurate backhand. In less than a year, Thurso had developed two excellent Pee Wee teams and a good Bantam team. And the Ontario teams were terrified to face the Thurso Mosquitos.

If only the Thurso club had, in the first round of the tournament, run into clubs strong enough to wear them down or shake their confidence. But there was no one to challenge them. The Merivale team, although well balanced, had been pitilessly crushed, 13 to 2. The next day, the second of the tourney, Thurso had to face a more difficult adversary, the club from Lake Placid, which was the only American team entered. They, too, had a formidable reputation. No one had ever seen them play, but everyone was afraid of them because they were said to be experienced and rough. This was a match everyone was looking forward to. At seven o'clock on Friday evening, twelve hundred spectators were crammed into the arena.

When the players leapt onto the ice, an immense clamour rose from the excited crowd.

Ti-Paul Meloche, with his gift for theatre, had started a rumour that the north end of the rink was better lit than the south. He claimed that the team defending the north end would have a definite advantage, and that therefore there should be a coin toss to see who would get the good end for the first and third periods. The two coaches met in the middle of the ice. Ti-Paul took a quarter from his pocket and said, flipping it into the air:

"Tails, you take the south end; heads, I choose. Okay?"

"Okay," said the other without thinking.

The coin bounced on the ice. It was heads.

"I won," announced Ti-Paul. "We'll start in the north end."

The American realized he had been tricked.

"Hey, it's not fair. You cheated."

"It was a deal, wasn't it?"

The Lake Placid coach couldn't say anything. In fact, both ends of the rink were lit the same way. Ti-Paul had invented the whole thing to upset his opponent, a tactic in what he used to call his "psychological warfare."

"Hockey," he told his players, "is not only played on the ice. A lot of the game is played between your ears."

In hockey, as in life, he believed that it was always necessary to arrange things to his own advantage, to pretend to be weak and timid when the other was busy boasting. Thus he had presented himself to the Lake Placid coach, oozing humility and trembling with fear.

"It's a rule, boys. Before an important match you have to bluff, one way or the other. If you're in good shape, pretend you're injured. If you're injured, make sure it doesn't show. And sometimes, just to confuse people, tell the truth."

Ti-Paul was a remarkable professor of duplicity. He taught his players the elementary principles of psychological warfare, the subtle game of feints and provocations that upsets and demoralizes the opposition.

"You have to break their concentration. Drive them

crazy. It's all part of the game."

In the Junior leagues, Ti-Paul had often had to play against Henri Richard. Richard was already a great player, "ticketed for the NHL" as they said. But Ti-Paul realized he could easily neutralize Richard. As soon as he found himself near him, and when he was sure the referee couldn't see, he would clear his throat and spit on Henri—a man who was always very proud, and careful to keep himself clean and well-dressed. Richard would usually crack. He'd jump on Ti-Paul and get a penalty, or he would lose his concentration, his ability to skate and stickhandle, and play like an idiot.

Ti-Paul had developed a whole series of this kind of trick that he used to deceive and frustrate and destroy the concentration of opponents who were bigger and stronger than he. And he taught these tricks to the Pee Wees and Mosquitos of Thurso.

"I can't say how much use you'll be able to make of them," he told Lafleur. "But I'm sure they'll help you understand something about the game of hockey. And you have to know the strategies others might use if you want to counter them."

And so, for the Mosquito tournament at Rockland, although he was confident of winning, he pretended to be weak and afraid in order to reassure the Americans. And he told his men to start the game cautiously, so that they could see how the Americans played.

It turned out that the reputation of the Lake Placid team had been blown out of proportion. The American Mosquitos were squashed by the Thurso team; by the end of the second period the arena had practically emptied. Guy Lafleur had scored ten goals and made five assists as well. Every time Guy got loose and skated in on the Lake Placid goalie, the goalie buried himself in the corner of the net, eyes closed, one glove in front of his face, the other over the family jewels.

Before the third period began, the American coach had a meeting with Ti-Paul: it was agreed that Lafleur would stop using his slapshot because it frightened all his players. It was a question of fair play, the poor man pleaded. Ti-Paul looked at him contemptuously. In his eyes, some-

one who begged for fairness and appealed to his opponent
for pity had a completely distorted idea of sport. But he took
Lafleur aside and told him of his agreement with the Lake
Placid coach.

"I promised him you wouldn't use your slapshot during
the third period."

The boy, not knowing how to respond, lowered his head,
deeply disappointed.

"You'll see," Ti-Paul added, "nothing will change.
When you get in front of their goal, just raise your stick as
though you are going to shoot as hard as you can. Then
shoot gently, just a wrist shot . . . "

Ti-Paul knew very well that the Lake Placid players, when
they saw Lafleur wind up for a slapshot, would scramble to
get out of the way. At the same time, he was keeping his
promise. As agreed, Guy Lafleur did not use his famous
slapshot. But he still scored another half-dozen goals.

Thurso won the game 21 to 1. The next morning they
were to play the Alexandria team. Its coach was a woman,
Mrs Howard Morris, who everyone called Gwen. She was
very nice, and well-liked by the players and their parents.
But among the parents of the Alexandria players was a tall,
strong woman with a flamboyant mane of red hair and a
deep voice that she used to terrorize opposing teams. She
had watched the defeats of Merivale and Lake Placid, and
had got the idea that Guy Lafleur, who had scored more
than two-thirds of his team's thirty-four goals, was not
within the Mosquito age limit. Even Gwen could not seem
to reason with her. An hour before the match she came to
speak to Ti-Paul:

"That boy is a Pee Wee."

Ti-Paul, amused, said, "He's ten years old."

"He's too big, too strong."

"He takes after his father. I can't do anything about that,
and neither can you."

"I don't believe you. He's a Pee Wee. I've already seen
him play at Buckingham and Grenville against their Pee
Wee teams."

"But that doesn't mean he's not of Mosquito age. He
plays in both our leagues."

"Just the same, we want to see his birth certificate."

Ti-Paul was so astounded that he couldn't get angry. Even after his whole team had sworn that Guy Lafleur was indeed the son of Réjean Lafleur, and he himself testified that he had practically witnessed Guy's birth, this woman continued to demand documentary proof. The game was postponed. The most scandalized of all was Guy Lafleur himself. Ti-Paul had brought him to the woman and asked him his date of birth, but Guy had been so intimidated and mortified that in replying he had started to stammer, lowered his eyes, and had the unbearable feeling of seeming to be a liar. He wanted to shout out:

"I've never told a lie in my whole life! Never! There is nothing in the world I hate more than a lie!"

But he was crushed by this woman's big blue eyes. She kept staring at him the whole time she talked to Ti-Paul and to the parents of the players on his team. Guy Lafleur went back to the bench, terribly upset. The evening before, the Lake Placid coach had asked him to play at half-speed. Now he was being asked to leave the rink.

While waiting, his teammates skated about and played in their own zone. But Guy didn't know what to do. Leaning against the boards, he could feel everyone looking at him. It was painful and uncomfortable, as though he were being penalized. But at the same time, deep inside, he felt a sort of pleasure that he could not define. He was the cause of all this controversy, and it made him feel ill at ease, but also happy.

Ti-Paul came to tell him that he had phoned his parents at Thurso, but there had been no answer.

"My mother is at my grandmother's house and my father is at the factory."

"On Saturday?"

"He's working overtime."

Finally, he got hold of Réjean Lafleur at the factory. He came to the telephone out of breath, convinced that some misfortune must have happened to his family. When Ti-Paul told him why he was calling, he couldn't suppress his anger.

"I should know the age of my own son, bonehead, I'm the one who made him!"

Ti-Paul let the parents of the Alexandria players know that he had Lafleur's father on the phone, but they refused to speak to him because they thought the call might have been staged. They demanded that the Thurso curé be called, and that he be asked for a copy of Guy Lafleur's birth certificate.

Finally, the notary public, Brunet, was presented with the irrefutable proof. Born September 20, 1951, Guy Lafleur, number 10 of the Thurso Mosquitos, legitimate son of Réjean Lafleur and Pierrette Chartrand, was indeed of Mosquito age in February 1962. More than two hours late, the match could finally begin.

Before the game began, Ti-Paul took Lafleur aside.

"This time, your slapshot is allowed. In fact, your favourite coach is strongly recommending that you use it as often as you like."

But as he leapt onto the ice, Guy found himself looking into the icy blue eyes of Gwen Morris. There he thought he saw such sadness, such resignation, that for a moment, afraid he would add to her pain, he lost all desire to win. He would almost have preferred her to continue being arrogant and unfair. After a few minutes of play, however, he began to score goals, one after the other. From time to time during the match, he would see Gwen's tearful face. How he would have liked to make her happy! But he couldn't be false to himself. The Thurso Mosquitos beat Alexandria 16 to 3.

• • •

That evening, when he went to have a drink at the Hotel Lafontaine, Réjean Lafleur met Jean-Paul Danis and his wife, who were back from Rockland where they had watched the Thurso Mosquitos win. When he saw Réjean, Danis parked his car against the sidewalk and practically threw himself on top of him.

"Réjean, you weren't at Rockland!"

"No. Why?"

"I think you'd better see your son play. Ti-Paul is right — he's a phenomenon!"

Réjean Lafleur had never seen his son play in a real game with a referee and spectators. And he wasn't really interested. That sort of thing was for children.

When he was young, Réjean had played hockey like everyone else. Two or three seasons, more or less regularly, he'd played defenceman or goalie. Strong as an ox, he had good stamina, quick reflexes, and was never afraid. But he had never been a good hockey player. Now, he didn't have the time. After putting in fifty or sixty hours a week on the job, a man has no desire to exhaust himself on the ice.

By 1962, Réjean Lafleur had lost almost all interest in hockey. Of course he watched the playoffs on television, but during the regular season he wouldn't watch the games unless there were visitors, like his younger brother Armand or his father-in-law, Léo Chartrand, a staunch fan of the Montreal Canadiens. He never set foot in the arena. There was always something to do at the house: repair the porch or the drainpipes, bring in wood for the furnace, put up or take down the storm windows. Or he would be working overtime at the factory.

Before the city had bought the Singer arena, he would make a large skating rink in his yard every winter. He had taught Guy how to skate, how to hold his hockey stick, how to shoot. But that was the extent of the sporting education that he provided.

He had just been served a drink when a group of parents, also back from Rockland, came into the Lafontaine and came up to congratulate him and buy him a beer, as though he himself were the hero of the day. And they couldn't stop talking about the exploits of his son.

The next afternoon, without even telling their son, Pierrette and Réjean Lafleur went to Rockland. The Thurso Mosquitos were about to play the Rockland Mosquitos, their natural rivals. This time, the contest would be closer than the evening before. The Rockland team was bigger and better coached than any of the other teams. In addition, they had the noisy support of their partisan crowd.

The Thurso players, and especially Guy Lafleur, found

themselves in a veritable lions' den. Every time a Thurso player got the puck he was loudly booed by the parents and friends—especially the mothers—of the Rockland players. Most of Ti-Paul's boys lost their heads. But the antipathy of the crowd had the opposite effect on Guy Lafleur, who seemed to have been galvanized. He was everywhere at once, piercing the enemy defences, scoring on end-to-end rushes during which none of the Rockland players could even touch the puck.

That day Réjean Lafleur got a double surprise. He was shocked to discover that what others had told him was not only true, but perhaps even an understatement of the truth. Guy was better than the others. A hundred times, a thousand times better than anyone. When he got the puck no one could take it away from him. He did whatever he wanted with it. But what amazed the Lafleur parents even more was that their son had always kept silent about his exploits, even about his enjoyment of the game. It was stunning to realize just how secretive he could be.

It wasn't until the middle of the third period that Guy saw his father and mother in the crowd, behind the players' bench. When, after scoring his fourth goal, he turned towards them, Réjean Lafleur gave him a broad smile and raised his hands victoriously above his head. Guy also smiled. After the game his parents were waiting for him in the dressing room; they didn't know what to say and neither did he.

They went to have dinner at the Castel Restaurant in Rockland. They still couldn't speak to each other. They were not in their natural environment and, in any case, people kept coming up to congratulate Guy, even people that they didn't know. Guy received this homage awkwardly. He was happy that he had won and that his father had seen him play, but he had nothing to say about it. In fact, left to himself he would not even have told his parents what had happened; he preferred to let others speak for him.

In the family, Guy was always said to be a pure Lafleur type, the spitting image of his father. Like him, he was secretive and self-effacing, and almost as reticent as his grandfather Damien, his godfather, whose name he had: Guy Damien Lafleur.

Everyone knew that if you didn't talk to Grandfather Damien, he simply didn't speak. Sometimes he came to dinner at the house; he would sit at the end of the table, eating silently, without uttering a single word through the whole meal. He was a locomotive conductor for the Thurso National Valley Railway, the private line of the pulp mill that kept half the village alive. In the summer he often took his grandson with him in his "kalamazoo," a type of big motorized railway car "made in Kalamazoo, Michigan." They would go along the railway track as far as Nominingue, a trip of three hours through forests, lakes and mountains. In the distance, in the hollows of some valleys, you could see small villages. Every now and then they would stop to gather raspberries, blackberries and blueberries. They would check the condition of the rails and the bridges. They hardly talked. The old man drove his strange machine, lost in his own thoughts. Sometimes he softly sang old songs. And Guy, comfortable in his armchair, watched the countryside roll by. He was happy. Often he caught a glimpse of wild animals, of eagles. He loved the peaceful silence of the wilderness.

With his maternal grandfather, Léo Chartrand, it was the opposite. Léo was an exuberant man, always ready with a trick or a joke. Every time he saw Guy he wanted to arm-wrestle with him, and of course he always let Guy win. Then he would lift him up onto his shoulders. He would play at boxing with Guy, always letting himself be knocked down. He had two passions: the woods and the game of hockey. He could talk for hours about either one of them.

He knew the woods intimately. He had been born there, he had lived there, he had raised his children there—in the north-eastern region of Ontario. Léo Chartrand was a true man of the woods—hunter, logger, one of those raftsmen of the Gatineau found in folk songs. Hockey was something totally different. He had never skated in his life, but he loved to watch the matches on television. He shouted, cheered, booed the referee, put down the enemy, sermonized at the Canadiens players when they played badly, and claimed all the time that if the great Maurice Richard were still playing, things like that would never have happened. When the Rocket retired during the Canadiens' training camp in September 1960, Léo Chartrand declared: "Hockey is half-dead. No one will ever take the Rocket's place. Unless Guy does something about it."

He laughed when he said that, but Guy took him seriously. And that evening in Rockland, even his parents began to believe such a thing might be possible.

The Thurso Mosquitos, having beaten Merivale, Lake Placid, Alexandria and Rockland (by a score of 8 to 4), were the winners of the Chamberland trophy for Category B. They had also won a weighty privilege—that night they were to meet the Category A winners, the Ville Saint-Laurent Combines.

In the minor leagues (Mosquito, Pee Wee and Bantam), the categories were set up according to the population of the towns and cities from which the teams were drawn. Category C teams, for example, included those clubs coming from centres with a population of less than seven thousand (Thurso, Rockland, Buckingham). Teams in Category A, including Ville Saint-Laurent, came from cities of more than fifteen thousand. The custom was that the winners in each category faced each other in a final match that was not part of the official competition.

Once again a problem presented itself, and once again Ti-Paul took care of it—in his own way. The two teams were wearing uniforms that were almost the same colour, royal-blue sweaters and white helmets. Jean-Marc Lalonde, whose club had been defeated, generously offered his team's green sweaters. But hockey players, even in the minor leagues, are terribly superstitious. Neither team wanted to change its sweaters. Everyone said that the club that didn't wear its own colours would be at a disadvantage, because it would be unlucky to play in someone else's clothes.

Ti-Paul, however, let the Ville Saint-Laurent coach know that he personally had no objections to his boys changing sweaters. He suggested that, just the same, they decide by a flip of the coin; then he played the same trick he had used on the Lake Placid coach.

"Take a quarter, flip it high in the air so that it touches the ceiling, then let it fall to the ice. If it's heads, you change sweaters. Tails, the choice is mine."

The quarter was still in the air when the Saint-Laurent coach realized he had been tricked.

"You cheated, Ti-Paul."

"I did not cheat. You should have thought before you agreed. A deal's a deal."

Two hours later the Combines were defeated by a score of 8 to 4; Guy Lafleur had participated in seven of his team's goals. The crowd was, however, much quieter than they had been. In regional solidarity, the people of Rockland had aligned themselves with the supporters of the Thurso Mosquitos. Guy Lafleur had become one of their own. After having booed him in the afternoon, in the evening they gave him a rousing ovation. The Chamberland Cup was no longer in Ontario but at least, thanks to Lafleur, it was still in the Ottawa Valley.

During the tournament the Thurso Mosquitos had accumulated, in five matches, the impressive total of sixty-six goals, of which forty-one had been scored by Guy Lafleur. In just a few days he had become an outstanding star in the small world of minor league hockey. In all the regional newspapers there were pictures of him receiving the "Boom Boom" Geoffrion trophy from Frank Wiechle, federal Member of Parliament from Kitchener, or shaking the hand of the Ontario Minister of Sports, or the mayor of Rockland, or Thurso, or even the Thurso parish priest.

He even had the signal honour of receiving a kiss on the cheek from the carnival queen, Miss Rockland '62, Madeleine Simoneau. Her lips were sweet and warm.

● ● ●

After the painful defeat of his Mosquitos at the hands of the Thurso team, and Thurso's equally definitive result against the Ville Saint-Laurent Combines, Jean-Marc Lalonde went to the bar of the Castel, where he was joined by two of his friends from the Ontario Provincial Police. In those days, provincial police officers from Ontario and Quebec often volunteered their services as drivers for minor league players in the Ottawa Valley, taking them to the arenas, then bringing them home after the games.

Jean-Marc was naturally a bit disappointed, a disappointment made worse by the fact that he was getting ready to take his Rockland Boomers to the International Pee Wee Tournament in Quebec City. Last year his team had placed among the ten best, behind Beaupré, Murdochville, Hershey and Pointe-Bleue, and he knew it would be difficult to improve on that result. His team worked smoothly together, it was very solid defensively, but it had no dangerous shooters or outstanding skaters.

One of the OPP officers suggested that Lalonde try to recruit Guy Lafleur.

"Otherwise, you'll be wiped out, just like last year."

It was an excellent idea. In spite of the tremendous progress it had made in minor hockey that year, Thurso didn't have the means to send a team to the international tournament. Surely Ti-Paul and Brother Léo wouldn't object to Rockland borrowing their best player for a few days.

Lalonde hesitated. Young Lafleur had shown himself to be an extraordinary Mosquito, but he was still very young and a little light for a Pee Wee tournament in which the best Canadian and American players were competing. Most of the players were a year or two older than Lafleur, and weighed ten to twenty pounds more. And it was also true that when Guy had played in the regional Pee Wee leagues, he had not been outstanding. Lalonde had see Guy play several times against the Boomers, or against the Buckingham and Brownsburg clubs. He was quick, he had a strong and accurate shot. But each club had some big defencemen capable of checking him.

"What you say was true at the beginning of the season," admitted one of the policemen. "But in two weeks, that boy has made more progress than any other player in a year. I tell you, Jean-Marc, you'll never come across a better Pee Wee than Guy Lafleur."

But perhaps it was already too late. The certificates and registration forms had to be in the mail before midnight of that very day. And the Lafleurs had just left Rockland in the car of Jean-Paul Danis, who always drove slowly. They had to make the detour through Ottawa, so they wouldn't arrive home until late.

Jean-Marc Lalonde and his OPP friends kept tossing the idea about. And the more they talked, the better it seemed. Lafleur had indeed gained a lot of experience in the Mosquito tournament at Rockland, and he had the ability to play in front of a crowd, even a hostile and aggressive crowd. This was an essential skill, according to Jean-Marc Lalonde. He had seen excellent players unable to play in front of a crowd, even when it cheered them on. Lafleur, on the other hand, was galvanized.

"In real life he might be a timid child," said Jean-Marc, "but on the ice I've never seen anyone so willing to make a rush."

Towards nine o'clock he called the Lafleur house. Pierrette answered. He asked to speak to Réjean and proposed his brilliant idea.

"And when does that tournament begin?"

"Two weeks Tuesday, the 27th. But he has to leave the Sunday before."

"How?"

"By car, from Rockland."

"And how long does it last?"

"Exactly one week. They'll be back the 3rd of March, in the evening. But I'll need Guy for the next two Saturday mornings, to practise with the Boomers."

"I'll have to speak to my wife."

"Okay, but please be quick. We only have three hours to fill in the papers and put them in the mail."

"She says that she'll have to warn Brother Léo that Guy will miss some school."

"I'll take care of that. Tell your wife not to worry about it. If necessary, Brother Léo can come with us. That way Guy wouldn't miss anything."

While Jean-Marc was talking to him, Réjean watched his son, who was waiting at the foot of the stairs. He must have been bursting with happiness, but his face gave nothing away. It was as though he were not the least bit interested in the conversation his father was having on the telephone.

"What will we do for the papers?"

"What papers are you talking about?"

"The registration forms. We need signatures from you and your son. We could send someone. If they cross the river, they could be at your house inside an hour."

"Wouldn't it be easier just to sign for us?"

"I didn't dare ask you."

At Rockland, they forged the signatures of Réjean Lafleur and Guy Lafleur. And the documents were mailed that evening. As of then, Guy Lafleur was officially a member of the Boomers from Rockland, the great rival of Thurso, the city where he had been born.

Between May and November, Rockland and Thurso were connected by a ferry. In the winter, the river could be crossed on foot or on skis. But if currents or thaws weakened the ice, it was necessary to take a detour through Ottawa, which extended the trip by fifty miles.

Réjean Lafleur had never owned a car. He had his licence, but he didn't like driving. Lafleur, so calm in everything else, became a nervous wreck behind the wheel. He went to work by bicycle when the roads were dry. In the winter, no matter what the weather, he walked back and forth. He loved to walk. This winter the ice on the Ottawa River was thick and solid, even where the current was strongest. Guy would have no problem crossing on foot.

At dawn the following Saturday Guy set his equipment bag on his sled and left the house. It was a cold, brilliant day. He took Rue Principale to the hill going down to the landing, then he knelt on his sled and glided down towards the river. At that point the river is almost a mile wide. In the middle are two long, flat islands between which you pass in order to keep the right direction for the Rockland landing. In the summer, the islands have trails where lovers can wander, masses of blueberries, muskrats and chipmunks; everything is pretty and alive. But in the winter the islands are sinister; their tall, naked elms sway and crack in the wind. Guy could see, on the Ontario side, the steep hill leading to the Rockland road and Jean-Marc Lalonde's truck, sending dark blue smoke into the icy air.

That first day, Guy had to get used to his new teammates. Some were Mosquitos he had defeated less than a week before, and who couldn't help still hating him for it. Then he had been Rockland's worst enemy; now he was to be its hero.

He fit into the Boomers' team without difficulty—and without speaking. Jean-Marc Lalonde had been correct; in the space of two weeks he had become a respectable Pee Wee. But he had not, personally, become any less timid. Not once, while they practised that Saturday morning, did he speak to anyone. And when he was spoken to, he replied in monosyllables without raising his voice. At the end of the practice he picked up his things, stuffed them into his bag and climbed into Jean-Marc's truck. He crossed the Ottawa River once more, climbed the hill dragging his sled behind him, then went straight to the Thurso arena.

"Have you eaten?" Ti-Paul asked him.

"No."

"Go get something. You can't play hockey on an empty stomach."

Twenty minutes later he was back.

"Did you have something?"

"Yes."

"In that case, walk around for a while. You can't play hockey on a full stomach."

Sunday, February 25, the day they were to leave for Quebec City, there was an enormous storm in the Ottawa Valley. Guy was supposed to meet the Boomers at the Rockland arena. From there, three cars carrying fifteen players and three chaperones, along with all their equipment, changes of clothes and hockey sticks, were to set out.

Towards the end of the afternoon, when Guy and his parents left their house to cross the river towards Rockland, it was almost impossible to see. In the middle of the river they stopped to make themselves a wind-shelter on one of the islands. Fortunately, it was mild. But they could no longer see the church, or the chimneys of Thurso Pulp, and on the Rockland side they could see nothing but an immense white and roaring wall of snow.

"There's no point continuing," said Pierrette Lafleur. "If the Rockland road is closed, Jean-Marc Lalonde won't be able to meet you."

"I can walk."

"You're not walking anywhere," said Réjean. "If Jean-Marc isn't there in three-quarters of an hour, by five o'clock—which gives him an hour extra—we're all going back home."

"If I can walk home, I can walk to Rockland."

"Rockland is twice as far."

"If I can go halfway, I don't see why I can't go the whole way."

"Because the storm is getting worse, Guy. Now stop arguing. You'll do what you're told."

Finally, at sunset, they saw headlights making their way down the Rockland side. Then there were signals from the bank.

"It's Jean-Marc. You can go, Guy. I'm going back to the house with your mother. Give us time to get there, then telephone so that your mother knows you're all right."

Guy kept on alone, walking into the wind, towards the blinding light that waited for him on the other side of the river. Jean-Marc saw him as he emerged out of the darkness, a snow-covered boy surrounded by a raging storm.

● ● ●

They didn't finally leave for Rockland until seven o'clock, after having being duly blessed by the curé and copiously embraced by their mothers—except for Guy Lafleur, the outsider, who stood to one side during all of these effusions.

Because of the storm, the trip took longer than it should have. The three cars drove slowly through the night, always within sight of one another. They glided along, drifting a bit on the heavy snow. They could hear the soft beating of snow against the sides of the cars. Inside it was warm. There were songs and laughter.

Guy Lafleur, in the back of Jean-Marc Lalonde's big Chevrolet, didn't unclench his teeth for the whole trip. Nor did he sing with the others. He barely even laughed when someone told a funny story. He looked through the window at the night. Sometimes, when they passed another car, he saw his reflection in the window. Then, once again, he would see lights in the distance, fields, woods, unknown cities—the wide world. The whole idea excited and fascinated him. He felt absolutely content. Only one thing bothered him. His mother had thought he should have new skates, new shinpads and shoulderpads. They were too new. He wished he had brought his old equipment. He had never liked using new things. Especially on strange ice. Fortunately he still had, at least, his old gloves and his old jockstrap. He woke up when Jean-Marc Lalonde stopped the Chevrolet in the parking lot of the Quebec City railway station. It was still snowing.

In principle, each team from out of town was supposed to be met by Quebec families who would provide places to stay for the players. But those who had been waiting for the Rockland Pee Wees, thinking they would never come, had all gone back home. The Boomers were put up at the Hotel Saint-Roch, just a few minutes away. Jean-Marc Lalonde was worried. The hotel was famous as a den of iniquity. From the bar downstairs came loud drunken conversation. Scantily dressed dancers laughed, sang and sat on the knees of the male customers. The celebrations continued all through the night. The young Pee Wees could hear the lascivious sighs, the crude laughter, the dirty songs. They were crammed like sardines into three small rooms where mattresses had been laid out on the floors.

Guy Lafleur could not sleep. It was the first time in his life that he had been in a hotel other than the Lafontaine, in Thurso, where he sometimes went to get his father. He found it both disturbing and exciting. He was afraid that the drunken men might come and hurt them. At the same time he was fascinated by the mysterious noises he was hearing. He wanted to get up, to go see; he listened carefully. And he wished the morning would arrive, so he could see the city and the arena, the famous Quebec Colisée.

The next morning, the members of the welcoming committee took charge of the Rockland Boomers and assigned them to families from Sillery and Sainte-Foy. Quebec was buried in snow, which only added to the magic and excitement of the Carnaval.

The International Pee Wee Tournament, taking place for the third time, had already become a phenomenal success. Many of those living in the area organized their vacations to coincide with it. The focus of intense media coverage, the tournament had strong local support, including the approval of the religious and political authorities, and enthusiastic backing from local businessmen and those involved in the tourist trade. Because its organization depended on hard-working volunteers, the people of Quebec City regarded the tournament as its own. They had even arranged for certain railway cars to drop off and pick up out-of-town spectators on a service track just behind the Colisée, while the telegraph services of the Canadian National Railway sent bulletins to radio stations and local newspapers.

There were clubs coming from everywhere: from the Beauce, from the Gaspé, from the Ottawa Valley, from Toronto, Don Mills, Peterborough, London, from the depths of Alberta and even from the United States, including the well-known Hershey club, which always got a loud ovation for distributing cartons and cartons of chocolate bars. All through the city, but especially in the area around the Colisée, roamed excited groups of happy Pee Wees.

In all that year, fifty-three clubs participated in the International Pee Wee Tournament in Quebec. Nearly ninety thousand spectators attended. The Colisée canteen was strained to the limit. From dawn until late in the evening, two teams of waitresses worked in tandem. They had to rent extra dishes, utensils, hire a new chef, an extra nurse, a second clean-up squad.

On Monday morning at ten o'clock, for the first time in his life, Guy Lafleur went to the Quebec Colisée. The Rockland players were stunned by the hugeness of the Colisée. They had two hours to wander about the huge arena, run on the ice, climb the stairway, even go onto the high-up gangways from which the rink looked like a lake of living light.

The Colisée was there for them, almost as legendary and magic as the Montreal Forum. It was in Quebec that Jean Béliveau, the greatest player of the era, had first displayed his talents playing for the Quebec Aces. Unfortunately, in the ten years since he had gone to Montreal, the Quebec Aces had almost totally collapsed. The advent of television, which broadcast the NHL games, had plunged them even deeper into the shadows. And the good people of Quebec, briefly distracted from the Montreal Canadiens by the feats of Jean Béliveau, had returned to their old favourites. In 1962, the Aces played in front of sad crowds of two or three thousand. The Colisée, so busy when Béliveau was there, now came alive only for the Pee Wee tournament.

At noon the Boomers were supposed to gather in the cafeteria. Half an hour later, Guy Lafleur had still not shown up. Jean-Marc Lalonde sent a group of Pee Wees out to look for him. They found him on the very last tier, on the west side of the Colisée. All alone, he was looking at the ice and the emptiness of the arena. Pulled out of his day-dreams, he came down to eat, but an hour later he had disappeared again. He was found in exactly the same place, watching the other teams practise.

Each club was given half the rink for half an hour. That way the players had a chance to get used to the ice before the official beginning of the tournament the next morning. When it was the Boomers' turn to try the ice, Lafleur seemed totally distracted; his shot was flaccid, he was hesitant on his skates. It was as though he were only half there. He spent the morning of the next day at his perch. Jean-Marc Lalonde and a few of the players joined him there and they watched the first games of the tournament. From where they sat, they were in a perfect position to observe the plays as they developed. Jean-Marc Lalonde called his players together and, from his place high in the stands, gave them a hockey lesson, commenting on each pass, pointing out every error.

Tuesday, February 27, Guy Lafleur played his first hockey game in the Quebec Colisée. The Rockland Boomers met the Pee Wees from Beaupré. They beat them easily, 9 to 2, and Guy Lafleur, the youngest player on the ice, scored three goals and got two assists. The next day, against Charny, he got five points again, leading Rockland to a 9 to 5 win. Thursday, March 1, in front of 13,800 spectators, he once more led his club to victory, this time in an 8 to 6 win over Murdochville.

Guy was now a personality in the small world of Pee Wee hockey. He was being talked about in the newspapers and on the radio; he was seen on television. Twelve hundred Pee Wees had come to Quebec City, and Lafleur was the best known, the star, the phenomenon. The coaches and players who knew they would have to face him in the days to follow came to watch him play. On each team a player was assigned the job of covering him, following him like a shadow, nullifying him, hating him.

"You'd better get used to it," Ti-Paul Meloche kept telling Guy. "They're going to harass you. They'll have someone on your back the whole time. Maybe two. You'll have to learn how to get rid of them without losing your concentration."

Jean-Marc Lalonde was amazed at the coolness, the ability to get things started and the maturity that the young Lafleur showed on the ice. Guy never hesitated, was never taken unawares. But he played his own game, alone. He intitiated his own plays and then executed them without anyone's help. In fact, there was no one on his team fast enough to keep up with him. Nevertheless, there were several times when, finding himself in front of the net with the goalie at his mercy, he chose to pass to one of his teammates rather than score himself. Which, again, amazed Jean-Marc Lalonde and the other coaches who were watching. Guy Lafleur, the star player, gave away goals to his companions. And doing this, instinctively, he affirmed his superiority and his power, not only over those he played against, but within his own team.

Once off the ice, he was his old self. He wouldn't talk. He was terrified of having his picture taken. One evening, just before the match against Murdochville, a photographer came unexpectedly into the players' room just as the Rockland Boomers were kneeling to say their prayers. He took a dozen snapshots. One appeared the following week in the *Star Weekly*. Fifteen smiling boys. Except for one, Guy Lafleur. He had hidden his face behind his gloves.

On Friday the Boomers wiped out Amos, 8 to 0. The boys from Abitibi had been unable to neutralize Guy Lafleur. Faster, more experienced, infinitely more talented than them all, he was becoming a master of evasion. With consummate ease he avoided bodychecks and kept possession of the puck, even when in the midst of a dense scramble.

The Rockland club, which had finished the tournament in tenth place the year before, was this year the easy winner of the Fernand Bilodeau trophy.

As always in this kind of tournament, the winners in each category had to play each other in matches outside the official competition. Saturday, March 3, in front of 14,640 people, the biggest crowd seen at the Colisée for ten years, Rockland (which was in Category C) met the Category A champion, Rimouski. Rockland won 4 to 3, thanks to Guy Lafleur, who scored two goals. But the same evening, the AA champions, Peterborough, crushed Rockland 12 to 0. There was nothing dishonourable in this loss—the Peterborough club was larger, older and more experienced—but Guy Lafleur took this first defeat very badly. All through the game he blindly persisted in his attacks against the Peterborough lines. Even after his own teammates had

given up and conceded to their more powerful opponents,
even when it was 10 to 0, 11 to 0, 12 to 0 and there was no
possible hope, Lafleur played as though the score were tied
and there was still a chance to win.

"Take it easy, Lafleur," the other players told him.

"You have to learn to lose," said Jean-Marc Lalonde,
standing behind the players' bench.

Guy did not know how to respond. Sometimes you lost,
true. But he didn't see why that meant you should stop
playing. Learn to lose? But why? He determined to talk to
Ti-Paul about it. Ti-Paul was a bad loser, and he boasted
about it. He often said to his players: "You have to hate
losing more than anything in the world. Be bad losers."

• • •

In Thurso, Guy Lafleur had become the centre of attention.
He didn't always know how to deal with other people. Of
course he was polite when spoken to; he even made an effort
to show everyone that he was like anyone else, an ordinary
boy, timid and shy, unsure of himself. But in this act there
was a kind of unconscious, instinctive trickery and
deception. A pious lie, the essential and spontaneous lie
common to all popular stars.

At ten years old, Guy Lafleur was no longer an ordinary
boy. For many people, he was the best Pee Wee hockey
player in all of Quebec, Ontario, Alberta, New England,
perhaps the whole world—even though he was only of
Mosquito age! "Ticketed for the NHL," as Ti-Paul
Meloche said. He was no longer "Réjean Lafleur's boy";
Réjean Lafleur was "Guy's father." At the Hotel
Lafontaine, Réjean was constantly congratulated and given
drinks because he was the father of Guy Lafleur, the glory of
Thurso. And he had instantly become someone magically
equipped with opinions and advice about everything.

"What do you think of Jean Lesage, of Diefenbaker, of
Toe Blake, of President Kennedy? Is it true, Réjean, that
it's going to rain tomorrow?"

Réjean Lafleur knew little about the coaching of
athletes. He never told his son how to play, or even how to
train. Guy instinctively knew what to do, and seemed to

have been born with a complete knowledge of the science of hockey. He knew what muscles he should be developing and how to do it, how to increase his skating speed, his stamina, his lung capacity . . .

His father had a watch with a second hand; Guy borrowed it and amused himself by holding his breath— sixty seconds, ninety seconds, two minutes—until his sisters, terrified, called out "Maman, Guy is killing himself!"

In magazines he had seen athletes and muscled body-builders brandishing enormous barbells. His father couldn't afford to buy them for him, but he could make them. He also poured steel into old boots so that Guy could strengthen the ankles Ti-Paul Meloche judged a little weak. Guy made himself a circuit through the fields, a bumpy path where he ran, good weather or bad, every day.

When he slept, it was only to gather strength in order to train the following day. And he ate even the foods he disliked if he was told they were good for his health. Soon he was eating, and even liking, everything. At the church he prayed first and above all that he would become better at hockey, faster, stronger. When he shovelled the driveway or stacked wood into cords for his grandparents or the neighbours, it was more to develop his muscles than to earn money. The same motivation made him get up early Saturday morning to go on the rounds (Thurso, Plaisance, Ripon, Masson) with the milkman: he ran, went up and down stairs, in the rain and under the broiling sun. All that just to make himself tougher, and for a pint of chocolate milk that he gulped down in the afternoon on his way back to the arena. When he ran to school, to the arena or to church, it wasn't to get there more quickly but to strengthen his lungs and circulate his blood. And why did he play Ping-Pong, tennis, tetherball, dodgeball? To sharpen his reflexes. Day and night, winter and summer, Guy Lafleur thought of only one thing: how to make his body stronger.

Ti-Paul said, "Réjean, your child is extraordinarily gifted. If he is well coached, if he doesn't do anything crazy, if he doesn't drink too much or smoke before he's eighteen, if he isn't badly injured, then I predict, Réjean, that Guy Lafleur will go to the NHL."

Réjean thought Ti-Paul was getting ahead of himself. After all, his son was only ten years old. How can you know what a child of that age might turn into? He could change his mind a hundred times. He could forget about hockey; he could take up some other passion.

"I'm not for pushing children into things," said Réjean. "It's a free country, even for them."

"It's not a question of pushing, Réjean. We should simply clear the way for him, the way the English do for their curling stones. We'll make sure he has every opportunity, then it will be up to him to decide."

During that summer of 1962, a stormy debate raged in the province of Quebec about minor hockey. Certain fashionable theories about sporting development were against highly competitive situations. Some of the directors of the Quebec recreation association publicly denounced the big Pee Wee tournaments which, they said, encouraged the cult of the superstar among impressionable children, and made some of them obsessed with the fear of losing. They worried that these competitions gave the children the wrong idea about participatory sports, and destroyed team spirit. And the moralistic theorists of education chastised certain parents for being too ambitious.

Some fathers, identifying with their children, pushed them to the limits of their strength, both physical and psychological, hoping to achieve, through them, their own childhood dreams. In their eyes hockey became the highest priesthood to which their child could aspire. Just as a good French-Canadian family used to dream of giving a son to the Church, certain parents of the sixties hoped one day to offer their well-loved son to Hockey.

In Thurso, rumours were already making the rounds. It was whispered that Réjean Lafleur was pushing his son too hard, that it was abnormal for a ten-year-old boy to be so consumed by ambition. It was said that Guy neglected his studies. Brother Léo was accused of exempting him too often from his homework and lessons. Even Ti-Paul was accused of giving him too much ice time.

These malevolent allegations were enormously painful to Réjean Lafleur. And they enraged Ti-Paul, who saw in this debate of bureaucrats and intellectuals pernicious ideas he thought children should be protected from. He didn't understand why they would want to forbid children to admire others and to want to succeed. Ti-Paul, emotionally and intellectually very American, was a go-getter for whom there was nothing dangerous or shameful about competition and success. On the contrary, he saw it as a mainspring, the sole truth of sport and of life. Without the prospect of success, what was the use of playing hockey? To go where? To win what? To become whom? In Ti-Paul's eyes it was totally legitimate to want to be the strongest and the best, even at ten years old. And the sooner you start to want, the better. That's what he told his boys. He also told them that the NHL was there for everyone, that it was just as accessible to them, nobodies from Thurso, as it was for big-city boys, and that it was not at all forbidden for them to take their chances seriously. He also told them that the NHL was more than just the Montreal Canadiens, and that they could also look elsewhere, including the United States.

Ti-Paul had always borne a grudge against the Canadiens, who he considered the club to beat, even though it had been two years since they had last won the Stanley Cup. And he also had something against Maurice Richard. In his iconoclastic fury, he claimed that Richard had finished his career on his knees, and that without his teammates (his brother Henri, Doug Harvey, Phil Goyette, Dickie Moore, Marcel Bonin) who set him up and opened the ice for him, he would hardly have scored. At the Hotel Lafontaine, the blasphemies of Ti-Paul started some magnificent debates. But at the arena, surrounded by his Mosquitos and Pee Wees, he demystified life and rendered everything possible and accessible.

• • •

After the many matches played at the Thurso arena during the day on Saturdays, the ice had to be refurbished, because during the evenings there was free skating to the music of Strauss waltzes and Guy Lombardo's Royal Canadians. As Ti-Paul worked, he played the music that he liked: Paul Anka, Elvis Presley or Jerry Lee Lewis. And he always provided a beer for himself and a Coke for Guy Lafleur, his trusted assistant.

First they scraped the ice. Then they dragged the barrel onto the rink and filled it from the hose. Guy loved to manipulate this gigantic watering can, a dead weight of five hundred pounds. To get it moving, he had to push against it with all his strength; then, bit by bit, it got lighter, until finally, almost weightless, it could be controlled by just his fingers. When the tap was opened the water squirted out from the perforated pipes, making a pleasant tinkling sound as it hit the ice. Then Guy would lead the barrel around the ice on its leash, like an enormous meek lamb.

But who was going to come to the arena on a Saturday night, when the Canadiens were to be seen on television? It was the only moment of the week when Guy Lafleur could have wanted to be somewhere other than the arena. Especially in April, during the playoffs.

Just the same, towards six o'clock as he inspected his work, he felt a twinge of regret: in front of him was a beautifully remade ice, a perfectly smooth and shining surface that mirrored the ceiling of the arena. If Ti-Paul hadn't been there, busy putting away the barrel, the hoses, the scrapers, the bucket, the nets, he would have put on his skates and, with a few cuts of the blades, put his signature to this ice.

But he had to go home. The sun on this mild spring evening was setting at his back, behind the heavy columns of smoke from the McLarens plant that swirled in from the west. He had been shut up in the arena for almost twelve hours. He had participated in two practice sessions, beaten the Pee Wees from Buckingham and the Gatineau Mosquitos, watched a Bantam match and worked on the ice. He was exhausted, empty, famished. As on every Saturday night, his mother had made spaghetti, loaded with meat, vegetables, herbs. As soon as he came into the sunroom, the odours surrounded and invaded him. He would eat like a starving dog, take his bath, then come down in his pyjamas to the living room.

While his mother and sisters did the dishes and cleaned the kitchen, he and his father would wait for the hockey game to start. And while he waited he would let his fatigue creep up on him until he was dozing. He would close his eyes and remember himself, just a little boy, skating on the round rink his father used to make in the yard. It was late afternoon, when the light was heavy and grey. And suddenly he couldn't find his puck anywhere. Desperately, he looked all over, for hours, days, but the ice was empty as far as the eye could see. And he skated so far, hoping to find it, that he could no longer see his house, or the plume of smoke from McLarens, or the clock atop the church, or the mountains behind the village. He was lost in an infinite desert of ice, blue with cold, his stick useless in his hands . . .

He woke up at the sound of the musical introduction to "Hockey Night In Canada," and his father's voice calling everyone to watch.

Réjean Lafleur, caught up in the passion of his son, had become a devoted hockey fan. In the living room, just beside the television, he had put up a shelf on which he aligned the numerous trophies won by his son: a "Boom Boom" Geoffrion, a Red Storey, several Robin Hoods. Pierrette kept them dusted and polished, but Guy almost never looked at them. Each time he was given a new trophy, he took it home and left it in a corner. He had even forgotten one at the Rockland arena.

He couldn't have said why, but he didn't really like his trophies and never talked about them. He treated them with total nonchalance and an ostentatious lack of tenderness, as if it would have been shameful or out of place to show his joy at having won them. On the other hand, he was always delighted to see that, thanks to his exploits, Thurso's Pee Wee team, the Idéal, and the Thurso Mosquitos filled the town arena when they played. There were always lots of people to watch them play, sometimes even at practices, but especially for the Sunday afternoon game.

In fact, the weekly Sunday game had become a local event not be missed, and all of Thurso was there. The most eminent citizens and town councillors sat beside the players' bench. There was Father Arsène Hébert, the Member of Parliament Gaston Clermont, the Mayor, Rodolphe Pelletier, Fernand Lafleur, president of the Board of Education, and Brother Léo Jacques, director of the Sainte-Famille School. "O Canada" was sung by the choir while the first-line players stood at the centre of the ice with the referee in the middle and the defencemen and goalies of both teams at attention near their nets. All eyes were turned towards the crucifix and the photograph of Queen Elizabeth that were hung above the main entrance. Thurso existed. The newspapers were talking about it. Thurso finally had something all its own, which pleased Father Hébert very much.

No one was exactly sure by whom, or how, or where, it had been decided that Thurso could afford to send their Pee Wee club to the fourth annual International Tournament in Quebec City, but thanks to the Thurso Idéal, Thurso was going to be put on the map of the Pee Wee world. No question this time of lending Guy Lafleur to the Rockland Boomers. And who cared about the mumbling and complaints! Something was finally happening in Thurso.

The idea hadn't come from above, from the parish priest, from the factory boss or the school director, although they were all in favour of it and they had approved of and supported it in every way. It was the ordinary citizens of Thurso who had set themselves the challenge, and who sought out the means to meet it.

An agreement had been made with Valiquette Sports in Hull. Credit had been extended for ten thousand dollars' worth of equipment (shinpads, gloves, shoulderpads, jockstraps, sticks, pucks, masks, helmets). Réjean Lafleur, Ti-Paul and some of the other parents had signed a note to guarantee payment of the debt.

"We're just a gang of beggars," said Ti-Paul, "but

Valiquette trusts us. He knows we'll find a way to pay everything back."

"Oh, sure. How?"

"The gate receipts from the arena could bring us seven or eight thousand, if we put on a good show. As for the rest, we'll have to see. If we have a good club, Thurso won't let us down."

"And if we don't?"

"We will."

In a small working-class town, the hockey or baseball club is often the glue that holds the community together. The club becomes the identity of the city, its ambassador, its soul and its most important product. Thus the Idéal had become the passion of the people of Thurso, and their hero was Guy Lafleur.

Guy had been set apart: distinguished, unique and therefore isolated. Without his opinion or permission, a mission had been entrusted to him. At the Rockland tournament he had won the Chamberland trophy; now his duty was to win the Bilodeau in Quebec.

When Ti-Paul came to watch the Saturday night hockey game at the Lafleur household, he would sit in the big rocking chair beside the fire. Pierrette and Réjean sat on the corduroy-covered sofa. Guy and his sister Suzanne would be on the floor, close to the black-and-white screen beside the trophy shelf. At the between-period commercials, Guy would jump up, get an orange for himself and beer for Ti-Paul and his father, sometimes also for his uncle Armand, his grandfather Chartrand, or even for Brother Léo, who occasionally came to visit. During the intermissions they would listen to Gerry Trudel, Jean-Maurice Bailly, Charlie Maillé, the wise men of the Hot-Stove Lounge. Ti-Paul never failed to criticize their commentaries, accusing them of being completely mad, or at least totally illogical.

In those days, the Canadiens were going through a bad period. From 1956 to 1960, five years in a row, they had been easy winners of the Stanley Cup. But for two years, since Maurice Richard had left, although they were still a powerful, well balanced team with the best players in the world (Jacques Plante, Bernie Geoffrion, Jean Béliveau, Henri Richard), and a genius for a coach (Toe Blake), something was wrong with them that even Ti-Paul could not diagnose. And that worried him, especially since he had been the one to say "good riddance" when the Rocket retired, and had even bet that the Canadiens would play better hockey without him.

None of this stopped Ti-Paul from adding his own observations and scolding the players and the coaches of both teams when they made a mistake. The only times he kept silent, along with everyone in the house, were when the great Jean Béliveau leapt onto the ice. Bewitched and trembling with excitement, they watched him. Every movement was delicate, perfect, effortless.

Béliveau gathered in the puck at the red line; he went back into his own zone to give his teammates time to regain their positions. For a moment, no one moved. The twelve men on the ice seemed to have been frozen. The Forum crowd held its breath. All across Canada, six million viewers also watched, silent, on the edges of their seats. Then, with slow, long slides, as though in slow-motion, Béliveau circled his net, passed his defenceman, then skated at full speed towards centre ice. The first thing you knew, he no longer had the puck. He had dropped it behind to Jean-Guy Talbot, who had passed it to Gilles Tremblay on the left wing, who had pushed it to Béliveau, already at the enemy blue line, at the other end, the other side of the rink. Béliveau swept around the enemy defence (how? impossible to see or know), moved in on the goalie, faked a shot to the left, then to the right, then to the left again, and then he shot it hard into the pads of the goalie, who couldn't trap the puck. Then Béliveau got the rebound and, with a powerful backhand, buried it deep in the net above the shoulder of the unhappy goalie. The entire drama had unfolded in just a few seconds. Then the cheering mob at the Forum was on its feet.

"The most complete player you'll ever see is Gordie Howe of the Detroit Red Wings. But, Guy, the most rewarding to watch is Jean Béliveau. When Béliveau is on the ice, he always makes things happen. He's not just a goal scorer like Maurice Richard. Richard couldn't put things into motion, he wasn't even able to avoid being checked, which meant he was often injured. And an injured player is no use to his club. But Richard's greatest flaw was that he couldn't control his emotions. Anyone at all could make him fall apart just by calling him a 'frog' or a 'pea-souper.' Not Béliveau. You have to wake up early in the morning to ruin that man's concentration. Take it from me, Béliveau is a true master. Watch Béliveau play, because he is the best model you could ever have."

Brother Léo, when he was there, protested vehemently. To give his words more weight, he would rise to his feet in the small room to point out that Richard had something Béliveau never had and never would—an aura, a mythic presence, charisma. Ti-Paul was absolutely opposed to such ideas. He repeated to Guy that if he had any serious intentions of making hockey his career, he should not let himself be impressed by auras or legends or the charisma in which certain players wrapped themselves.

"When you're in front of some guy on the ice, don't take him for more than he is. Even if he has scored a million goals, even if he's a friend of the prime minister, don't worry about it, and never think about his goals or his records. Just take care of him. Play as though you're seeing him for the first time in your life. Don't say to yourself that he's better or faster or bigger. If you make him into a monument or a mountain, you'll never outplay him. He'll have beaten you before you get near him. Tell yourself that on the ice everyone is equal, and that no one is better than you."

What Ti-Paul said, Guy remembered.

• • •

Brother Léo Jacques wrote a small book about Guy, in which he is held up as a model for Christian youth.

"These modest notes written in haste, and without pretension, reflect the desire to pay homage to a young man who does honour to the city of Thurso, to his family and to his early coaches who taught him the elements of the game of hockey."

Brother Léo went on to show how, by his courage, his tenacity, his self-confidence and, of course, with the grace of all-powerful God, this young man had succeeded in breaking out of his background and achieved full self-realization. In this, Brother Léo saw, first and foremost, an excellent example of good old-fashioned Christian faith. But Guy Lafleur also presented an excellent and impressive model of social success, of perfect conformity to the post-war North American dream.

Obviously the Brothers were proselytizing, but their point of vew, in common with religious thinkers such as Brother Marie-Victorian, Canon Lionel Groulx, and later Brother Untel, was deeply nationalistic. They had a well-defined social project; a good part of the ideas from which today's Quebec was born derived from their teachings and reflections.

Brother Léo may not have had the intellectual scope or rigour of Canon Lionel Groulx or Brother Untel, but he was aware of the nationalist thought of his time, and therefore persuaded that the French-Canadian people were blessed, singled out and destined for great things. In his pamphlet he even went so far as to explain the immense talent of Guy Lafleur by the fact that he was French Canadian, and therefore one of God's elect, and had received from Him a faith capable of moving mountains, extraordinary strength and an irresistible will to succeed.

"One of the best things about him," he wrote, "is that he is French Canadian, and when he gets an idea in his head, he succeeds. Guy is a young man laden with talent and goodwill. He listens to the advice of his teacher and scrupulously tries to follow it to the letter. At first he might seem stubborn, but he understands an argument when he knows where it is leading!"

Thus Brother Léo set up Guy Lafleur as a model of generosity, tenacity and patriotism, attibuting to him all sorts of talents, virtues, moral doctrines, symbols and ideologies.

Guy Lafleur was already, more or less in spite of himself,

a kind of icon, a carrier of diverse messages, an official
star, a salesman of ideologies who would become, later, a
spokesman for the giant sports equipment and automobile
manufacturers.

• • •

At the 1963 International Pee Wee Tournament, Guy
Lafleur of the Thurso Idéal wore the captain's sweater and
the number 4, sought-after number and title of his idol
Jean Béliveau. That year, when the sweaters were handed
out, the first choice was his. Because he was already a star,
he knew it and he accepted the accompanying privileges
and responsibility, just as he found it normal that he be
consulted in the planning of plays, the choosing of the
players and the lines of attack.

He was then eleven years old. He was tall and strong for
his age. His shot was so powerful that, when he aimed at the
enemy net, players got out of his way. At the Quebec
tournament, 1963 edition, he would once more set new
records and harvest trophies.

But things had begun poorly. In fact, during the practices
at the Colisée, Ti-Paul had noticed that Guy was playing
with less intensity and forcefulness than the year before.
And he was continually being harassed by his opponents,
which made his work more difficult. Almost all the clubs,
knowing Guy's feats, assigned him two checkers so he could
never move freely.

Ti-Paul was disappointed. When he left Thurso he told
everyone that he was going to get the Fernand Bilodeau
trophy. The third day of the tournament he happened to
run into Jean-Marc Lalonde, who had coached Lafleur on
Rockland's team, and he explained his problem to him.

"I'll give you a trick," Jean-Marc said to him. "When I
saw he was slowing down, I put him on the defence. A
defenceman is always more difficult to cover. You never
know when he is going to leave his zone, or from which
side."

This extremely magnanimous piece of advice from
Jean-Marc Lalonde to Ti-Paul was going to cost the
Rockland coach dearly.

On Friday, February 22, Guy Lafleur confronted the
Rockland Boomers, who he had led to victory the preceding
winter. It was a rough and spectacular game. Jean-Marc's
players knew Guy well; they could predict his moves,
counter some of his feints and check him. During the first
two periods they almost succeeded in neutralizing him; he
scored only one goal. At the beginning of the third period,
the Ontarians led 2 to 1. Ti-Paul then decided to put the
advice of his generous rival into practice, and placed Guy
on the defence.

There Guy's checkers lost him, and he scored the tying
goal three minutes before the end of the match, sending it
into overtime. Five minutes later, Jacques Massie from
Thurso scored the winner. The Thurso team, who had not
even been in the race the year before, returned home with
the Fernand Bilodeau trophy for 1963. Guy Lafleur had
accomplished the mission with which he had been
entrusted. If, from the score of each of the tournament's
games, his goals had been subtracted, his team would not
have won a single contest.

Guy Lafleur had become the man to beat for all the Pee
Wees, even those who had never seen him play. In
Marvelville, half an hour south of Ottawa, the boys were
obsessed with him. They made him into a terrifying legend
that grew in strength and stature. On the one hand they
were afraid of him; on the other hand they couldn't wait to
play against him. Even Larry Robinson, who was also tall
and strong, was worried. When Marvelville finally played
Thurso on its own rink, in the autumn of 1963, the players
were half paralysed with fear. They wouldn't stop looking
at Lafleur, even when he was on the players' bench.

Ti-Paul said, "Did you see those idiots? They lost before
they even got here. Just thinking about you, Guy. Do you
remember what I told you? When you let yourself be
impressed by someone, you've lost."

Very frequently during this time, the sporting press,
instead of writing that the Pee Wees of Cornwall or Amos or
Petawawa had been defeated by those of Thurso, would
give the cutline "Guy Lafleur Crushes Petawawa" or

"Lafleur Leads Thurso Into Hockey Final." Exactly the way, twenty years before, during the Second World War, the Canadian newspapers would say "Richard Defeats The Rangers 5–3" or "The Hawks Unable To Contain Richard."

But Richard had not been talked about in the newspapers and over the radio until after his debut in the NHL, at the age of twenty-one. Never before had the public heard his name or seen his face. Guy Lafleur, at the age of twelve, was already a highly publicized star. Red Storey, the famous former NHL referee, had twice given Guy Lafleur the trophy bearing his name for being the top Pee Wee scorer.

In 1964, Lafleur played for the third consecutive year in the International Pee Wee Tournament in Quebec City. He was such a celebrity that his visit to the carnival village and the ice palace was an event to be recorded in the newspapers. He had become a personality; his every act held the public eye, his every movement created a stir.

He was compared to Jean Béliveau, who was still his idol. And the real, the one and only Jean Béliveau, then at the very height of his glory, had come to be present at the Quebec tournament. He had affirmed, impressed by the young prodigy, that the young man he had watched was indeed "a true Maurice Richard." It was also written that Guy Lafleur was the young Canadian most likely to inherit the nickname "Boom Boom." He was similarly compared to Bobby Hull for the power of his shot and for the force of his acceleration.

Along with Guy Lafleur, there were other young players who were starting to show that they, too, might become stars in the NHL—players like Gilbert Perrault, Jacques Richard, Marcel Dionne. Dionne, who had been born in Drummondville, was a good-natured and cheerful young man, remarkably comfortable around the press. Jacques Richard was also a real firecracker, instantly making friends with all the journalists. Every time he scored a goal, he showed how happy he was by waving to the crowd and showing off like a clown. He was irresistible; he was loved and applauded.

But Guy Lafleur, in all his photographs, continued to show a closed and severe face with, from time to time, only a trace of a smile. He was happy to have won; otherwise he found nothing else to say to the journalists who surrounded him after the games. When he was on the ice, in motion, it was different, though: Guy Lafleur was still the one who always stole the show and brought the crowd to its feet.

His shot was so strong that it terrified all the goalies. To play the Thurso Idéal, several of the goalies wore two chestpads and other extra pads as well. With this heavy shell they were better protected, but they were also dangerously weighed down. And the protection didn't help much.

"The astonishing and talented Guy Lafleur of Thurso stunned the South Durham goalie yesterday when he let go a formidable slapshot that hit him on the chest. The young goaltender had to be carried off the ice, but he came back a few minutes later to congratulate Guy Lafleur, who had just eliminated his club."

The papers of the following day published a photograph showing the poor little goalie extending his hand to the conqueror. In his look was admiration, his smile was warm. But Guy was still not smiling.

During the Thurso–Petite Rivière game, young Réjean Sansfaçon aroused the admiration of the crowd. Although he was so short he could stand straight up inside the net, he had the audacity to confront Lafleur, whose bullets had already sent two players to the infirmary. He didn't do much better than the others, but he was warmly applauded for his courage and tenacity.

Many of the mothers who had come to see their cherished children play that day despised Guy Lafleur. Not only was he destroying their hopes of seeing their offspring among the best, but he terrified and injured them. Guy was carrying the puck along the boards when he distinctly heard a woman shout, "Guy Lafleur, unholy devil!" The cry gave him wings. He swept like a whirlwind into the enemy zone and shot so hard that the goalie was knocked over backwards and the puck trickled into the net. Lafleur didn't even look towards the woman who had sworn at him. He skated back toward the bench while the crowd cheered and booed—without, of course, the slightest smile. He thought he heard the same woman call out again. She didn't have the right. He had always played fairly, never resorting to low blows or cheating. It wasn't his fault that he was better than the others!

The next day, February 5, 1964, the Thurso Idéal once again met their beloved enemies, the Rockland Boomers, who had given them so much trouble the year before. But this time, Guy Lafleur scored seven goals. Never before had he felt so much in possession of himself and the game. Throughout the match he had the exalting impression of knowing in every detail what was going to happen in the next few seconds. Everything was magic, everything was perfect: the weight of the puck on his stick, the temperature, the shouts from the crowd, the texture of the ice, the position of the other players on the rink. He played without thinking of his game, without plan, as though in a dream, carried along by a force to which he had entirely abandoned himself.

Seven goals in one game. They spent a long time searching the archives for an equivalent, not only in minor or junior hockey, but even among the professionals. The statisticians finally discovered that on January 31, 1920, the star of the Quebec Bulldogs, Joe Malone, had beaten Howard Lockart, the Toronto Maple Leaf goalie, seven times. He had thus broken the record of six goals in one game established twenty-one days earlier by Newsy Lalonde of the Montreal Canadiens. But in the forty-four years since that time, no player had ever scored, in any major or minor league of organized hockey, seven, or even six, goals in one game. Seven black velvet pucks were immediately sewn onto the sweater of the Thurso Idéal's number 4, and Guy Lafleur proudly posed for the photographers. For once, finally, he wore a large, satisfied smile.

Guy was happy, not only because he had accomplished

an almost incomparable feat, but also because he had discovered this mysterious force that gripped him. He knew that he was now acquiring a true mastery of the game.

That same day, Guy met Paul Dumont for the first time. Bachelor and civil servant, Dumont devoted his free time to Quebec's junior hockey teams. He had made it his mission to revitalize junior hockey in Quebec City. He knew that it would be difficult, and that he would have to plan for the long term. But Paul Dumont was well suited to carry out his project. Everyone agreed he was the strongman of hockey in Quebec, a sort of benevolent godfather, an intelligent and well-organized planner, a visionary. He also knew how to recognize talent and how to exploit it.

He said to himself that, among the fifteen hundred players who were at the Colisée during the tournament, there must be the material to put together, in five or six years, a good Junior A club. That is why, every winter, he took time off to be able to watch all the Pee Wee matches played at the Colisée. He prepared file cards on those players who seemed most interesting.

Like everyone else, he had noticed Guy Lafleur at the 1962 tournament. He had often observed equally talented Pee Wees who, after one outsanding season, completely lost interest in hockey. But it seemed that the young Lafleur was determined to become a hockey player. The day Guy scored seven goals, Paul Dumont went to the players' dressing room, beneath the stands, on the east side of the Colisée. He congratulated Guy and said, "If your father is in Quebec with you, I would be pleased to meet him."

"I'll go get him for you."

Thirty seconds later, Réjean Lafleur was in the players' room, his hat in his hand, totally intimidated by the elegant Paul Dumont.

"When Guy is fifteen," said Dumont after the usual introductions, "I'd like to see him in Quebec, in our organization."

Addresses and telephone numbers were exchanged. When he got home that night, Paul Dumont, who had a mania for keeping things in order, filed Guy Lafleur's address and the notes he had taken on his play.

"I'll be looking at those again," he said to himself.

Guy Lafleur, at twelve, had been entered into the hockey system. It was already certain that it would be a long time before he escaped.

• • •

When school opened in the fall of 1964, there was a new mathematics teacher at the Saint-Famille School in Thurso, a young man from Montreal. His name was Normand Chouinard. He was cheerful and shy, twenty-four years old, his teeth were crooked and his hair tousled. Soon he was nicknamed "Chouine."

Chouine was the best friend of Brother Léo Jacques. One day when Chouine had come to visit, Brother Léo had taken him to the arena to see a young hockey player he described as "absolutely phenomenal." At that time Normand Chouinard had no interest in hockey, and would have preferred to go for a walk in the countryside. But he was fascinated by what he saw that day at the Thurso arena—not by the show on the ice, about which he didn't understand much, but by everything that it generated, especially the vibrant enthusiasm that the people of Thurso had for their Pee Wee Club and its best scorer, a little blond boy who was everywhere at once on the ice and who seemed to have magnetized both the puck and the crowd. It was moving and exciting.

Normand Chouinard, a product of the rough and commercial big city of Montreal, had never seen a crowd filled with so much passion, warmth, pleasure. He was seduced by the people of Thurso. And a few months later, when he learned that a teaching position was open, he applied, telling himself that he would even learn to ignore the disgusting smells of the city's industries.

He took a room at the Malette house, on Rue Bourget, which was very close to the Lafleurs. The following spring the Malettes acquired a trailer into which they intended to move that summer. There would be no room there, of course, for Chouine. One fine evening, while he was taking his after-dinner stroll, Chouine passed in front of the Lafleur house. Pierrette was busy working on her borders

and flowerbeds. When Chouine told her his problem she
said:

"You can move over to our place."

"But there are already seven of you with the
children!"

"We'll be eight, if you're willing."

A few days later Normand Chouinard moved to the
Lafleurs. He had few possessions: no more than one leather
suitcase for his clothes and a box of books. With Guy he
shared the long narrow room on the south side of the house.
At each end of the room was a window and a narrow bed;
against the windowless wall was a small table, two
straight-backed chairs and a large commode. The pale-blue
walls were undecorated save for a crucifix and a palm
branch above the door; there were no posters, no pictures of
hockey players, of racing cars or shining motorbikes or wild
beasts that you might expect to find on the bedroom walls of
a thirteen-year-old boy.

Guy Lafleur was a well-behaved young man, extremely
orderly and disciplined, driven by a determination equal to
any challenge, but he was so unforthcoming that Chouine,
himself so talkative, was at first taken aback. He even
wondered if his presence was unwelcome, and if Guy
might not have preferred to remain alone in his room. He
confided this to Pierrette, but she could offer no explanation. She often said that her son wasn't much of a talker,
while her four daughters were veritable motor-
mouths, even Lucie, who didn't go to school yet.

"But in the end, you always know what he's thinking,"
she said to Chouine. "Wait, you'll see."

A few days later the Lafleurs, in their private train with
their private chauffeur, Grandfather Damien's "kalamazoo," left for their hunting camp, which they held on a
ninety-nine-year lease from the government. They were
going to spend a week fishing for grey trout and pickerel.
Only Guy, who was studying for his exams, and Chouine,
who was marking papers, stayed home. Tuesday afternoon, duties accomplished, they decided to join the rest
of the family. First they took the road through Ripon,

Montpellier, Chénéville—an hour's drive through densely
wooded mountains with few houses. Then they had to walk
through the woods on a bumpy and tortuous corduroy road
that was always branching off. Chouine was amazed at the
sense of direction and the confidence of his companion.

It was pitch black when they arrived at the camp, tired
and chilled to the bone. They were also a little nervous
because they had seen a bear with its cubs travelling
through the woods. Chouine claimed that Guy had been
afraid. Guy said that Chouine was always seeing threatening shadows. It seemed that the walk had made them
friends.

The next day the sun was dazzling. They left at dawn so
they could get back to Thurso in time for school. This kind
of impromptu hike was Chouine's speciality. He loved
being on the road, especially when he had no particular
destination. Over the summer, Guy, and sometimes
Suzanne, spent hundreds of hours with him travelling the
roads of the Gatineau Hills, sometimes pushing as far as
Temiskaming, or the plateau of Mont Tremblant, to the
parkland of La Vérendrye, of Kipawa . . . Guy discovered
in himself a veritable passion for road-maps and topo-
graphical maps, which he could read with amazing speed.
He always wanted to plot their position, to know exactly
where they were in relation to Thurso, Ottawa, Montreal.
Chouine bought him an atlas, the first book that Guy
Lafleur used carefully and with pleasure.

Chouine quickly became an integral part of the family.
When the teachers went out on strike, Pierrette made an
arrangement with him that satisfied them both. He would
stop paying room and board, and instead would take on a
share of the familial responsibilities. The question of money
was never again raised between him and the Lafleurs.

One of his tasks was to be the driver. He also became the
children's tutor, going over their lessons with them,
sometimes giving them special review lessons. He also made
arrangements with the other teachers so that Guy, when he
had an important match to play, could be excused from his
homework or classes.

In September 1965 Guy entered the eighth grade and had Chouine as his classroom teacher. Chouine, who had practically never seen Guy except at the house or the arena, where he was always the centre of attention, was amazed to find him so self-effacing, so timid, so undemonstrative. He felt he hardly knew him. In class, Guy never raised his hand to ask or answer a question. He followed what was happening, but at a distance, with a sort of indifference or polite detachment. He didn't like school because he didn't believe in it. For certain things, he had extraordinary powers of concentration, but for his studies . . .

But when he had to and wanted to, Guy could be very disciplined and serious. What bored or discouraged him in class he could always—with Chouine's help—assimilate in a few minutes in the evening after supper.

Sometimes Chouine had no choice and was forced to give Guy a detention. One evening Réjean Lafleur asked his son why he had come back so late from school.

Guy kept eating his supper. Chouine lied:

"I needed him to help me clean the classroom windows."

Guy immediately raised his head and said it wasn't true, that he had been given a detention. He had an almost pathological fear of lying. He could be quiet and keep his feelings and his thoughts secret. But he could never bring himself to lie, or even to let someone else do it for him.

Chouine became a kind of interlocutor between Guy and his parents—a counsellor and sometimes a referee. When Guy wanted to follow the current fashion and let his hair grow and Réjean Lafleur was utterly opposed, Chouine intervened as mediator.

"Let him, Réjean. Long hair never hurt anyone."

"No. It's ugly and it's dirty."

"Not when it's washed."

"I don't want my son to look like a girl."

"If I were you, Réjean, I wouldn't worry about that."

Sometimes Guy talked to Chouine about the girls at school, who he admired but didn't dare approach. Chouine had noticed that Guy fascinated many of the students, boys and girls. His athletic accomplishments with the Idéal, but also with the baseball team and on the tennis courts, had given him a certain prestige. He was physically stronger, taller, faster, more agile than anyone else. But there was also something else, a kind of mystery with which, more or less consciously, he surrounded himself. Despite his shyness, he always knew exactly what he wanted—a fact that made him different from other boys his age. He was a public figure. The entire city had been mobilized, three years in a row, so that he could go to Quebec and to Rockland to win trophies for Thurso. The town had banked on him, and in doing so burdened him with responsibilities.

Systematically, Chouine pushed him to develop his talents. He had heard Jacques Plante, the famous Canadiens goalie, "the all-time greatest" according to Ti-Paul, recommend playing Ping-Pong to sharpen the nerves and the reflexes. As there wasn't room in the house to set up a Ping-Pong table, Chouine had the idea of making Guy play against the wall that separated the kitchen from the living room. Every night after supper, sometimes for hours, he would play . . . toc, toc, toc . . . with his back to the window, standing between the table and the refrigerator . . . toc, toc, toc . . . while his sisters did the dishes or their homework . . . toc, toc, toc . . . until Pierrette Lafleur couldn't stand it any more and said:

"Guy, for the love of Heaven, can't you stop for a while!"

And Guy, without stopping, would say, "If I stop, what am I going to do?"

To have nothing to do terrified him. It made him feel disarmed, threatened, all alone in the world. He only felt truly good when he was in the midst of battle.

One day when it was raining heavily, during the spring, Chouine found Guy in front of the kitchen table. He was covering page after page with his name, his signature, his flourish, dozens and dozens of times. He signed and signed again: Guy Lafleur, Guy Lafleur, Guy, Guy, Guy.

This little game went on for days. Even in class, on his schoolbooks, he practised his signature. Chouine and everyone else said to him:

"Guy Lafleur, you're practising signing autographs! Have you decided to become famous?"

In a few weeks his signature had entirely changed.

According to graphologists, your signature reveals what you would like to be, while your handwriting reveals the person you really are. One is dream, the other reality. With certain people, sometimes the two get mixed up. In the spring of 1966, Guy Lafleur created a signature that was vigorous and energetic, projecting an image of himself as a determined man who knew how to assert himself and did not fear the future. A man who, at the same time, with his attractive arabesques, wanted first and foremost to seduce.

• • •

Every year Paul Dumont, in his capacity as director of the Quebec Junior As and person responsible for the recruiting and training of players, used his summer vacation to organize his files. In the summer of 1966, while surveying the notes he had written on the best Pee Wee and Bantam players during the preceding years, he came to "Lafleur, Guy, 20 Sept. 1951, Thurso, excellent skater, strong and accurate right-handed shot, interesting style of play, can fake right or left. Excellent forward. Can also play defensively."

"And he'll be fifteen years old in September! Tomorrow I'll call his father in Thurso."

The next day, late in the afternoon, just as he was coming home from a golf game, Dumont's own telephone rang. It was the father of Guy Lafleur, reminding him that his son was turning fifteen and that they were ready to meet him if he still wanted to.

"Of course I still want to!"

"In that case, I'm going to give the telephone to a family friend, you can arrange everything with him."

The family friend was, of course, Normand Chouinard. To the great relief of Réjean Lafleur, Chouine had decided that he would act on their behalf with the Junior A organization. That day, on the telephone, he asked Paul

Dumont for details about how junior players from outside
Quebec City would be housed, to what schools they would
be sent, how they would be supervised . . . almost nothing
about hockey, which made a favourable impression on Paul
Dumont. He had too often had his ear talked off by
parents who were overly involved in the coaching and
instruction of their sons, demanding for them a certain
minimum ice time, this or that position and a guaranteed
career in the major leagues.

Dumont invited the Lafleurs and their adviser to come
down to Quebec to get to know the people in the Junior A
organization—all expenses paid, of course, and rooms
reserved at the Sainte-Foy Motel Universel. Guy and his
parents were not at all used to this kind of place. Getting up
the next morning, Pierrette had to stop herself from making
the beds and cleaning the rooms. Chouine, however,
was perfectly at ease. As regional representative of his
teachers' union, he often went to Quebec City for meetings.
It was at this very motel that he would meet his colleagues
and the bureaucrats of the Ministry of Education. He knew
Quebec City well. He loved to bargain and negotiate. The
Lafleurs put themselves entirely in his hands.

They dispatched with the question of education: Guy
would be registered in the ninth grade of the
Jean-de-Brébeuf School, which had a good reputation. As
soon as the hockey season was over, he would go back to
Thurso to finish his school year under Chouine's supervision. Aside from room and board, he would receive eight
dollars a week as pocket money. All of this was most
agreeable to Guy and his parents. They were categorically
opposed, however, to his accepting a long-term contract
with the Quebec Junior As. He was too young. Quebec,
though a Pee Wee paradise, offered little future to an
ambitious junior. The minor leagues were very well-struc-
tured, but major junior hockey floundered in total
disorganization.

"But this way we'll never set things right," pleaded Paul
Dumont. "So long as the good juniors continue to ignore
us, we can't put together good clubs. It's a vicious circle.

We approach promising young players like Guy because we hope they will stay with us and help us build something."

"A worthy project," Chouine said, "but we don't want Guy to finance it."

Paul Dumont understood. In any case, he had no choice. In Quebec, a player of the calibre of Guy Lafleur, even in minor hockey, could set his own conditions.

"We want him on the Junior A team right away," said Chouine. "Not on the B."

"If I understand you right, you want him to skip a year."

"That's about it, yes."

"You think he can?"

"Positive."

"He is very young to play Junior A, you know. I can't remember another fifteen-year-old boy playing Junior A."

"Perhaps, but that doesn't change anything. He's too strong for the B, you'll see."

"In that case there shouldn't be any problem."

But there was.

Guy was well prepared for his first season of real hockey. He had followed a strict and intensive program of conditioning. Moreover, he had spent three months working on the farm of Jean-Marc Perras. He enjoyed farm work: making fences, cleaning the irrigation ditches, digging out old stumps and especially taking in the hay. Haying is one of the most enjoyable activities on a Quebec farm. First, it happens only when the weather is fine, under a clear summer sky, with a small breeze rising gently from the river. The smells are sweet. It is physical, mystical, melodic, poetic.

Guy developed a true passion for the earth. He decided that if something were to happen to him—you never know, a broken ankle or ruined knee—and he were forced to renounce his career as a hockey player, he would become a farmer. In any case, when he retired he would buy himself a farm, somewhere in the Ottawa Valley or the Laurentians, with animals and a big woods, perhaps a maple grove. He knew that attachment to the land would never desert him. In the meantime, he would use it to strengthen his muscles.

On weekends, when the weather was good, he would go swimming in the Ottawa River. With some friends he would collect pulpwood that had escaped from the paper mills and sell it back to the company. It hardly paid—two or three dollars a cord—but it was a game and, for Guy Lafleur, a way of building up his lungs and his stamina, quickening his reflexes, making himself more supple.

In mid-August he took a ten-day course at the Modern Hockey School in Montreal. There were already several institutions of this type in Quebec. Most of them were directed by physical education teachers, theoreticians and technicians with diplomas and experience, who called on NHL players to animate the workshops and the practical courses. This school, directed by Gaston Marcotte and Jean Trottier, was undoubtedly the most prestigious and sought-after.

Attached to the University of Montreal, and using its facilities, the school was attended by the best of the minor league hockey players. Every morning they had to train for two or three hours on the ice. Then they would do series of exercises, either inside or on the mountain, which was just behind the university's athletic centre. In the afternoons there were theoretical lessons on offensive and defensive play, physical conditioning, exercises for developing muscles, nutrition, and so on.

Henri Richard, who like Guy Lafleur shot from the right, gave lessons on stickhandling and taught the technique of passing. Jacques Plante revealed his goaltending tricks. Jean-Claude Tremblay helped the young players work on their defensive games. And from time to time, a young player from the Junior Canadiens of Verdun, Jacques Lemaire, came to give demonstrations of the slapshot, a shot that was as debated as it was effective. Lafleur especially liked to work with Lemaire. For hours the two men took turns bombarding the net and the boards with powerful bullet shots. Lemaire was impressed. Certain coaches still disapproved of slapshots because they were supposed to lack accuracy, and it *was* difficult to control them. But the young Lafleur could hit his targets with amazing regularity.

Thus Guy found himself at the controls of the most marvellous possible machine: a smooth-running, high-performance, powerful athlete's body. And the machine seemed to be racing. Guy was no longer able to stop himself: he ran, skated, worked without rest. It might be said that he had completely inverted certain biological functions: sleep seemed to make him tired, activity made him rested and relaxed.

When he arrived at the Quebec Junior A camp in September, he was in peak condition. However, it was easy to see that, despite his extraordinary talent, his physical conditioning and his exceptional strength, he was still lacking the experience and weight (he was barely 135 pounds) to play in the Junior A league. Clearly, he should spend a year or at least several months in furthering his training at the Junior B level.

This backward step did not please Guy. He still believed the only way to get better was to play against players better than himself. Consequently, he was afraid he would get weaker playing with those at his own level, or worse. Paul Dumont, a good teacher, explained to him that he had no choice.

"Trust us a little. Everyone in the organization wants you to become a great player. We wouldn't take the risk of keeping you back in the B team if we weren't sure there are still things you have to learn there. Understand one thing, Guy Lafleur: good as you are, it's very unlikely that anyone with the slightest intelligence would want to compromise your career in any way. Get it into your head. You are in no danger, here or anywhere else. Your talent will protect you. So respect it, and develop it as you should."

The young Lafleur was so gifted and played so well that there were many things he had neglected to learn. Playing with the Pee Wees or Bantams, he could easily get hold of the puck as soon as he leapt onto the ice, and he would shoot from the blue line with amazing force and accuracy. The other players were so afraid of his shot that most of the time they left him to it, practically making a guard of honour for the puck, which went straight to the back of the net. Thus he had never had to learn to elude the defence, to stickhandle or to develop complicated moves.

But in the Junior A, there were some boys who were much bigger and stronger. Whereas Guy was just fifteen, on the ice there were boys of eighteen and nineteen, weighing up to two hundred pounds. Lafleur himself realized that he would no longer be able to get control of the puck, and that he would no longer be left a clear field.

It was decided that Guy would begin the season in the Junior B league, with the Canadian Tire and Repair Club, the CTR. Although he understood the situation, he felt cruelly disappointed, which, according to Paul Dumont, proved that he was truly a good player, ambitious and intelligent.

On September 20 his parents telephoned to wish him a happy birthday. Only then did Réjean Lafleur learn that his son had been put back. He was appalled. Ordinarily shy with cultivated and important people like Paul Dumont, Réjean immediately decided to call and tell him that there was no way Guy Lafleur would stay in Quebec simply to waste his time.

"I promised you, you're right," admitted Dumont, when Réjean Lafleur finally gave him a chance to speak. "But you have to understand that I'm thinking of Guy first. If he's left in the A, he'll be wiped out. He's much too young and too light. He's enormously talented, I've already told you, and he could become a player of the calibre of Béliveau or Bobby Hull or Gordie Howe. He is probably the best junior I have seen in my whole life. But he must learn the fundamentals. If you want to make him into a great player, he must learn the fundamentals."

Réjean Lafleur was still on the telephone, standing against the kitchen counter near the door, when Chouine came home from school. He understood right away that something important was happening.

"Paul Dumont wants to demote Guy to the B," said

Pierrette. "And as you can see, Réjean won't hear of it."

"I think Dumont is probably right," said Chouine. "It's just like school. It's not always good to have students, even the best ones, skipping grades."

But Réjean Lafleur, still on the telephone, continued to explain that his son had become an outstanding player because he had always played with boys who were older and bigger than he was.

"Did you see him play when he was a Pee Wee, Monsieur Dumont? Yes or no? The first year he was Mosquito age, but he won the Red Storey trophy. He was the club's most valuable player. And he was also the youngest!"

Chouine waved at him.

"Calm down, Réjean. Say that you'll call him back."

Finally Réjean hung up, got himself another beer, sat at the table and let himself be convinced by Pierrette and Chouine that Paul Dumont was probably correct. He accepted finally, not without rancour, that his son could be pushed back to Junior B. Chouine called Paul Dumont the same evening. It was understood that Guy would play ten or so games with the Junior A during the regular season and that, if all went well, he would be put on that team during the playoffs in the spring.

In the meantime, Guy Lafleur, aware of his gaps and his weaknesses, threw himself into his training. But even in Junior B, the year started poorly. Despite his enthusiasm, he clearly was not in his element. Not yet. One day, a month after the beginning of the season, Paul Dumont called Réjean Lafleur to tell him that he thought his son was having problems.

"What do you mean, problems?"

"I think he's afraid."

"Guy? Afraid of what?"

"I don't know. You would think he was afraid to play."

"I'm on my way."

The next day, Réjean Lafleur travelled to Quebec with Normand Chouinard. It was raining heavily, an icy November downpour. They went to Limoilou, Rue La

Sarre, to the modest house where Guy was staying.

The families that agreed to lodge the players from September to May clearly did so not for the love of hockey, but for the sixty dollars a month paid to them by the Quebec hockey organization. So it was often the less affluent families who took in the schoolboy players.

That first year, Guy had been placed in a family of good people, but they had two players in a small and overcrowded apartment. Guy and his companion, Dave Boidas, slept in the living room on two broken-down sofas arranged in an L. They did their homework along with the four children from the family on the rickety kitchen table. Sometimes in the evening, when the father and his friends decided to have a few drinks, going to sleep required formidable powers of concentration.

Réjean Lafleur took his son to a restaurant—just the two of them, father and son.

"What's wrong with you, Guy? Are you afraid?"

"The coach says that I'm too cautious."

"Are you afraid of the other boys?"

"No, but I'm afraid of making mistakes and taking penalties."

"I think it's okay to take a penalty sometimes. Remember what Brother Léo used to say. The perfect players, who respect the rules too much, go absolutely nowhere. Nothing ever goes their way. In hockey, as in life, you have to accept a few penalties and know that you deserve them. Do you understand?"

That same evening, Guy played with the CTR against a club from the Beauce. He had two minor penalties. He also scored two goals and got an assist. He had just learned that, in life, you can't always give only the best of yourself. You have to give everything—the best, and sometimes the worst.

At the beginning, too eager to do well and to follow to the letter all the rules of this unfamiliar new world, he had found himself imprisoned by a host of prohibitions. He no longer knew how to behave on the ice. In order to play well, he needed time to adapt, to get used to the place, to get to know his teammates, and even the spectators, who were different in every place. In fact, Guy Lafleur was, first and foremost, a seducer and charmer of crowds. So long as he was unsure that his charm was working or could work, he played coldly and nervously. At the beginning he had the impression that the scanty crowds who attended CTR games were indifferent to him, and that froze him. But as soon as he felt that he had won the esteem and sympathy of the public, he started to play with all his heart and strength.

Playing in Junior B is playing in the shadows. It's not too serious when you are fifteen years old and have your whole life ahead of you, but nevertheless Guy Lafleur was nostalgic for his Pee Wee years. During the Christmas holidays, despite their remarkable performances, the Junior B clubs played in front of a few hundred—sometimes a few dozen—mostly mothers and fathers, brothers and sisters, close friends of the players.

It was scarcely better in Junior A, where Guy made his debut on November 25. Paul Dumont wanted to test his courage. That night he made him play against the Sorel Éperviers, masters of bodychecking and cheap shots. For the first time in his career, Guy Lafleur found himself in a truly violent game. He had often been present at or participated in Bantam and Midget battles, but never anything so violent, and pointlessly so. The Éperviers played the man, that is, they declared war against the man carrying the puck.

In sending Guy into this free-for-all, Paul Dumont and his coach, Martin Madden, understood that they were putting him to a test, a sort of obligatory initiation for the serious player of junior hockey. One of the unwritten laws of hockey requires that each player establish himself among his peers, not only by the skill and artfulness of his hockey, but by his audacity and his ability to keep his head. That evening they were submitting Guy to a test of strength, a baptism of fire. Like everyone else on both teams, Guy knew what was happening. He wasn't there to score but to fight.

He did not get a goal or an assist. Nonetheless, he shone. Not once during the ten minutes he spent on the ice was he effectively bodychecked. Though he often carried the puck, he succeeded in sliding away from all the hits. At least twenty times, players from the other team charged him, trying to crush him, but every time they ended up crashing into the boards or swinging at empty space. When he saw them coming, Guy would accelerate, put on the brakes, suddenly change direction. Several times his fakes and his side-stepping aroused the admiration of the small crowd at the Sorel arena. During the third period, one of Sorel's proudest warriors charged him. Guy leaned over, draped him over his back, then stood up and sent him spinning off behind him. Test perfectly passed.

As had been agreed, during the regular season he played ten games in the Junior A. He scored two goals and got seven assists.

"Good," said Paul Dumont.

He gained a lot of weight, almost fifteen pounds. And not an ounce of fat. Only muscle—young, flexible, strong.

"That's even better," said Paul Dumont. "Now you're ready for Junior A."

Was this good news? The Junior As were going from bad to worse. At Christmas they had been in last place, far behind the Drummondville Rangers, the Sorel Éperviers, the Shawinigan Bruins, and they kept this position until the playoffs. The season ended with a spectacular victory for the Junior Bs and an equally spectacular defeat for the As, in which Guy now played. He had improved almost as fast as the Junior As had declined. By the end of the season he was one of their best players, but that wasn't saying much. What was to be gained by playing for a mediocre team?

Guy adored Quebec, but he wouldn't hesitate to go live elsewhere if the quality of hockey did not improve. There were plenty of good junior clubs all over Ontario.

As soon as the hockey season was over, the same day as the spectacular opening of Expo 67, in Montreal, Guy went back to Thurso. There he fell again under the iron rule of Chouine, who had registered him at the Buckingham

High School, where he was to finish grade nine. Every evening after supper, Chouine reviewed the day's school-work with him, pointing out his weaknesses and giving him exercises to do.

Pierrette had set them up a sort of study in the basement: a table, two backless benches, a small lamp, an old radio.

"Test in half an hour. If you pass, you can go twice around the block."

Guy stayed alone in the basement. From above he could hear the television, footsteps, laughter. His sisters chattered and squabbled. He was bored to death. But he studied as hard as he could, because he was anxious to be ready for the test.

Chouine had found a method to motivate his pupil. While in Quebec City, Guy had conceived a passion for cars. Every day since his return he had been asking Chouine to teach him how to drive. Chouine owned a magnificent beige Chevrolet Impala convertible. A dream!

"Okay. You do your homework and learn your lessons. I'll give you a test. If you pass, I'll let you drive."

Chouine was inflexible and incorruptible. When Guy failed his test, the Impala stayed in the yard. But when he passed, the two of them set out, Guy proud as a peacock at the wheel, and they would drive around the block. After having bought ice time from Ti-Paul Meloche, Guy was now buying road time from Chouine. And with Chouine, as with Ti-Paul, he was paying with hard work.

At the end of May, when the light lingered until nine o'clock, they would drive on the roads above the city, towards Ripon. The girls would sit in the back and sometimes even Réjean and Pierrette would come along. There would be eight in the car, the whole family. The weather was mild, the top down, the radio playing. Guy was driving. He was happy.

He was looking forward to summer. And the NHL hockey season was going to be the most exciting ever. Six new teams were being allowed into the league: the California Seals, the Los Angeles Kings, the Minnesota

North Stars, the Philadelphia Flyers, the Pittsburgh Penguins and the St Louis Blues. The regular season schedule would now have seventy-four games.

The purists were worried. They predicted that the hockey would be inferior. Before 1967, the NHL and its six clubs (the Montreal Canadiens, the Boston Bruins, the Toronto Maple Leafs, the New York Rangers, the Chicago Black Hawks and the Detroit Red Wings) had the 125 or 150 best hockey players in the world. Henceforth, it would be the 300 or 500 best who would be playing. According to the hardliners, the quality of hockey was bound to be affected.

But a young player of the age and ability of Guy Lafleur couldn't keep himself from seeing the possibilities. Twelve teams, seventy-four games—that represented a fantastic amount of ice time per season. And everyone said that expansion had only begun, that one day there would be sixteen clubs, or perhaps even eighteen or twenty or more.

Never in the history of hockey had there been so much ice as in 1967. For a young and brilliant player like Guy Lafleur, all hopes were allowed.

FIRST INTERMISSION

●

TODAY, ON RUE BOURGET in Thurso, where the skating rink Réjean Lafleur made every winter used to be, is a gigantic parabolic antenna turned towards the United States. Guy had it installed so that his parents could follow him on the rinks of New York, Chicago, Los Angeles. It was also Guy who arranged the monumental electronic altar in the living room—forty-five-inch giant screen, VCR, turntable, cassette players, sophisticated speakers—that Réjean Lafleur stubbornly refuses to learn how to use. Every time he wants to record or see something, he has to ask for help from his wife or one of his four daughters, who all live in the area and often come by to visit.

The wall against which Guy used to play Ping-Pong for hours has been replaced by a big archway joining the kitchen to the living room—another of Guy's ideas, because he likes big rooms. When he buys himself a house, he almost always starts by taking down walls.

Réjean Lafleur knows nothing about gadgets, but he is an orderly man. In an old bureau he has carefully stored the videocassettes on which, with the help of Suzanne or Lucie, he has recorded some of the highlights of his son's career—the lightning rushes of the "Blond Demon," his hundredth goal, his five-hundredth, his last match with the Canadiens on November 24, 1984, his return to hockey four years later in New York, his inauguration into the Hall of Fame. That unforgettable moment at the Forum, on December 17, 1988, when he wore the Rangers' sweater in

73

front of an ecstatic crowd, many with tears running down their faces. It was a gesture many found overly provocative, but Réjean Lafleur loved it.

That day he had been truly proud of his boy. He and Pierrette had watched in the living room, in front of the television. Guy had asked them not to go to the Forum, because, with all the journalists around him, they wouldn't be able to see him. They didn't know what he was going to do there. No one knew.

Other videos Réjean Lafleur especially likes include one of a hunting party on the island of Anticosti. In another, Guy is on his big Harley-Davidson, bareheaded in the streets of Montreal. Or signing autographs at the Forum exit. Scoring a goal at the Forum. Driving a Formula One on the Mont Tremblant circuit. Holding the Stanley Cup high in the air. And the crowd everywhere, a mob chanting his name: "Guy! Guy! Guy!"

In his small living room in Thurso, Réjean Lafleur looks at it all, perhaps for the hundredth time, always as proud as ever, each time a little more nostalgic. These images are almost all that remain to him of his son whom he sees so rarely, who lives in the big world now and no longer needs or consults his father.

When he was fourteen, Réjean Lafleur started working at the Singer plant. There he learned how to be a welder, and that was the job he had all his working life. Almost half a century in the midst of screaming metal in a big iron and cement factory. That's enough to destroy your hearing, your lungs, your nerves, your back—even your soul.

Today Réjean Lafleur is a worn-out, tired man. His bones hurt, his confidence is shaken. In the morning, when he swings onto his bicycle to go to the plant, he can hear his joints creak. He has to ride for a few minutes to get himself going. His big callused hands are no longer sure, and they are often numb. He used to devour whatever was put in front of him, but now he eats sparingly. In the summer of 1969, a few days before his sixtieth birthday, the doctor told him to stay at home for over a month, and told him to start thinking seriously about retiring.

"In my case, I'm really going to retire. Not like Guy. In my case, there's no choice. This is the end. He was just making a change. He had somewhere to go to. Not me."

He smiles sadly, as though expecting you'll contradict him, say, "But no, Monsieur Lafleur, it's not so bad, everything will be all right, you'll see." But you feel that in his heart he has already quit. He has worked too hard and too long for too little: a small house it took him twenty years to pay for, a bicycle, not even a car, a canoe, a hunting camp up north that's not quite his, the television—no more than anyone else might have.

In spite of everything, Réjean Lafleur is content with his life. He has a son who is celebrated, rich and fulfilled; his son is his joy, his passion, his avocation. On one finger he wears an enormous signet ring. On the setting, surrounded with precious jewels, is engraved a coat of arms and *Coupe Stanley Cup, Canadiens de Montréal Canadiens, 1972–73*. It is one of the five Stanley Cup rings Guy won with the Canadiens. He still keeps one that he sometimes wears. Jean-Yves Doyon, his longtime friend, has one. Jerry Petrie, who used to be his friend and business agent, had one, too, but he seems to have sold it since he and Guy lost touch. The fifth seems simply to have disappeared.

"Guy has so much to take care of," says his father, "he doesn't have time to worry about that."

Guy no longer has any of the souvenir watches given to members of the NHL first all-star team, of which he was five times a member. And his trophies—the Art Ross scoring trophies, his Lester B. Pearson, his Seagram's Seven Crowns Sports Award, his Red Storeys, his Victors, his Harts, his Conn Smythe and all the others, the dozens and dozens of little statuettes and bronzed, chromed and gold-plated trinkets—he long ago left all of them with his parents.

"You would have thought you were in a museum," his mother says. "They took up almost half the living room. One day, I said to Guy: 'All this junk is yours. I'm sick of dusting it—take it back to your house.' He threw it all into boxes and I don't think he even knows where it is. He's given them away or thrown them out or lost them. Anyway, if there's anything in the whole world he doesn't care about, it's his trophies."

Réjean Lafleur had been particularly fond of the little Robin Hoods, the first trophies his son had won, when he was still an Atom or a Mosquito. In those days, the Robin Hood flour mills financed minor hockey and amateur sport. For three years Guy Lafleur won all their trophies, little red-and-green Robin Hoods with boots, a cap and a bow, and they were kept on top of the refrigerator.

"I don't know what happened to them. He must have made sure they got lost, like the rest."

Guy Lafleur's father has surely been his most faithful and creative fan. And his first and greatest biographer. He has amassed monumental archives: thirteen bulging albums, twenty-four by eighteen inches each, and each weighing about twenty pounds. They contain thousands and thousands of clippings and press photos, everything that was to be found in Canadian, American and even European magazines. Everywhere, they talked about his son: in French, in English, in Swedish, in Russian, in Czech, in Italian. "Guy is a global phenomenon," he says.

For almost thirty years Réjean Lafleur has been carefully and patiently reading, collecting, cutting out, classifying, assembling, pasting all these articles, photos, headlines, elegiac commentaries, critiques, poems, statistics. He has laboured like a medieval monk, one of those copyists ceaselessly copying and recopying the Holy Book.

During the past eighteen months, because of fatigue and illness, but also because he doesn't really understand his son's career these days, he has fallen behind.

"That child is not so easy to follow."

In July 1989, when Guy signed with the Quebec Nordiques, his father had not yet finished categorizing the hundreds of clippings that he had gathered or that had been sent to him from New York, Quebec, Sherbrooke, Trois-Rivières, Toronto or Los Angeles, about his return to hockey in August 1988 with the New York Rangers.

Today, when he thinks about the albums he put together,

Réjean Lafleur sometimes asks himself what he got from all
that work, from those thousands of hours spent reading and
re-reading in the most minute detail about the life of his
son, and then carefully arranging each of the episodes. Of
course Guy still occasionally visits his parents. Or he
telephones when he can't come. But he no longer consults
them when he has a serious decision to make, scarcely talks
to them about what he is doing. In November 1984, it was a
neighbour who told Réjean and Pierrette that their son had
quit playing for the Canadiens. A few months later, when he
left the organization, they first discovered the fact in a
newspaper. And it was on the Radio-Canada "Téléjour-
nal" that they learned Guy Lafleur was coming back from
New York in order to play for the Quebec Nordiques.

Their feelings and their pride have suffered from the
indifference that Guy shows towards them now—especially
when journalists call them to hear what they have to say
about some decision their son has made, or some twist in his
career or his life. Now they don't know any more, and often
a lot less, than the journalists themselves.

In the first of the enormous volumes in his parents' home
are the carefully preserved images of Guy's early years.
When Guy Lafleur comes back to Thurso or goes to spend a
couple of days at the hunting camp on Lac Simon, the first
things he seeks out are the landscapes and faces of his
childhood. Then, he says, he was happy and fulfilled. He
never tells his parents what he's doing now, because he
doesn't want to worry them. And he doesn't want to disturb
the happy memories of his childhood with his contract
problems, his domestic squabbles, his investments, his
career, his triumphs or his reverses. He wants to leave the
beautiful dream of those first few pages in his album
undisturbed and pure.

Often crumpled and brittle with age, the newspaper and
magazine clippings are not perfectly chronological. But as
you go through them, the saga of Guy Lafleur moves into
focus and reads like a novel.

Hockey is a literature in itself. It has its laws, its heroes, its
critics. The sporting press, especially in Quebec, is prolix

and prolific. It sees all and says all, what is true and what is false; it extrapolates, interprets, confesses, praises, invents intrigues and provokes all kinds of dramas. It plays an important role in professional hockey because the coaches and the players must come to terms with it and constantly feed it new material. And sometimes also obey it. The press devours everything that is put in front of it—scandals, misunderstandings, trifles, falls from grace, victories. It is as interested in the players' moods as in their physical condition. It is as interested in the causes of defeat as those of victory. The press is hockey's parallel government; it has great power which, unlike that of the owners, is practically impossible to overturn.

Reading the albums of Réjean Lafleur, it is striking to note just how much, over the past twenty years, the sporting press has matured. The headlines are more gripping, the writing and the photographs are better, the interviews and reporting have vastly improved.

Réjean has also gained experience; he has mastered his art. He uses higher quality paper and a special paste that his wife makes from a mixture of flour, vinegar and water that she cooks over a low heat. By this method she gets a very white paste that spreads well, stays flexible and never yellows, unlike most of the glues available in stores.

The first picture in the first album dates from 1962. Surrounding the ten-year-old Guy Lafleur are all the figures symbolizing prestige and authority in French Canada at the end of its period of darkness, the historic epoch preceding the Quiet Revolution. French Canada is still in shadow, and the photo is, of course, in black and white, now a little yellowed and crumpled. Here, and elsewhere in these early pictures, are to be found the Brother-director of the Sainte-Famille School, almost always wearing a bulky fur hat, the mayor, the member of Parliament, the chief of police, the parish priest, the English bosses of Thurso Pulp and the Singer Factory. They all wear long black coats and are usually either dropping the puck for the opening face-off or handing out a trophy.

Monsieur and Madame Lafleur are also present. And, of

course, the Queen of the Rockland Winter Carnival 1962, the curvaceous Madeleine Simenon, with her provocative smile, her crinoline and her rabbitskin muff. In the midst of all these people, arms full of trophies, is the young Guy Lafleur, always looking complacent, but never smiling.

"He always kept things to himself," his father says. "He hardly talked in those days. Even to us. When he came back from the arena we always had to ask him if we wanted to know what had happened.

" 'Guy, did you play well?'— 'Yes.'

" 'Did you win?'— 'Yes.'

" 'Did you score?'— 'Yes.'

"With Guy, if you didn't ask, you didn't find out."

It's still true. Guy Lafleur has remained a secretive man who never spontaneously says what he's thinking. If you want to find out something from him, you have to ask. But then, without holding back or being evasive, he will reply to even the most embarrassing or penetrating questions.

"Guy is a little shy, like me," Réjean Lafleur adds. "But with the life he has lived and all the people he has met, he's had to overcome it. Now he can talk to anyone. When a man succeeds, he has no more reason to be embarrassed. He can say whatever he wants to whomever he wants. But I'm not sure it's always a good thing."

The only fault Pierrette Lafleur finds with her son is that he doesn't talk enough. The only fault his father finds is that he talks too much: "He always says what he thinks. In my opinion, that got him into a lot of trouble with men like Savard and Lemaire. He would have been better to keep his mouth shut."

But Guy learned, first from Ti-Paul Meloche and later from Henri Richard—a man he both liked and admired—not to let himself be overly impressed by "important people." Or, rather, to see in them not what distinguishes them from ordinary mortals, but rather what they have in common. Guy would, like his father, remain essentially shy—but no more so with the prime minister than with his hairdresser or garage mechanic. With all of them he talks in the same way about the same things. He has a very sharp sense of class, and where people belong, but in his eyes a person's real worth has nothing to do with how rich or successful he is. In the same way, a player's reputation is not what makes him good; it is what he can do on the ice.

In 1978, Réjean Lafleur put his name to a book entitled *Guy Lafleur, mon fils*. The idea came from Russian-born photographer Michel Ponomaref, who wrote it based on a series of interviews with Réjean Lafleur. He gives a few anecdotes about Guy Lafleur's childhood and the first few years of his professional career. At times the book is simply an uncritical tribute, but Ponomaref also throws new light on Guy Lafleur's childhood and the milieu from which he emerged. Ponomaref was the first to understand the extent to which Guy Lafleur's life was shaped and influenced by his father.

"Every man wants a son, it's only normal," says Réjean Lafleur, dreamily caressing his Stanley Cup signet ring. "Me, I had four daughters. But if I hadn't had a son, I would have believed that God was testing me."

Guy Lafleur was born on September 20, 1951. It was a Thursday, a few hours before the autumnal equinox and under the sign of Virgo—order and calm. In Chinese astrology his sign is the cat, which stands for flexibility and cunning. He was a big baby, almost ten pounds.

"I had five babies," says Pierrette Lafleur. "They were all big, well-behaved, easy to take care of and healthy."

She, too, personifies health, stability, youth and good humour. This petite and active woman—curious, cheerful, shy—is almost sixty but seems at least ten years younger.

Réjean and Pierrette Lafleur are a typical French-Canadian working-class couple of their generation. The man is tired, silent and closed in on himself, stubborn ("I'm not sick, I don't want to see the doctor") but no longer very sure of himself. At the factory and sometimes at the tavern, he is practically cut off from everyone else. As retirement approaches he feels diminished, lonely, without resources or plans. The wife is better educated and better informed. For years and years she has done the housework, the laundry, the ironing, and prepared tens of thousands of meals. Like her husband she has worked hard. But unlike her husband, who worked for a master, she has been the absolute mistress of her universe, autonomous, independent and free. So, unlike her husband, she has kept up with the times. With each child, helping with homework, she has re-educated herself. And with them she has followed the restructuring of the educational system and the great social changes of the Quiet Revolution.

Pierrette Lafleur talks easily, but without looking at you. From time to time, however, she gives you a worried glance, as though to see what effect her words are having. Guy resembles her. Most of the time he talks and listens while looking elsewhere. That way he dominates the conversation, just as on the ice he dominates the puck, because he knows, better than anyone, how to control it by stealing it away. But when he has just said something important, he looks you straight in the eye; that means he's just confided something to you, given you a pass. Don't miss it, because he can't and won't repeat it.

In the kitchen of the little house in Thurso, there's a big poster of Guy with Martin, his oldest son, both in the Canadiens' uniform. On the refrigerator, where the red-and-green Robin Hoods used to be, is now a tiny figurine of a Canadiens player, number 10. On the living-room wall is a photo of Guy in action—hair blowing in the wind, skating at full speed, the puck glued to his stick—and a dedication: "For Pierrette and Réjean. From your son with much love. Guy." In this house, Guy is everywhere.

Pierrette Lafleur has taken out her boxes of photographs. They cover the whole kitchen table. Here is to be found, pell-mell, the whole story of Guy Lafleur, and the stories of the men and women he's known. Brother Léo Jacques is there. Also Paul Dumont, Martin Madden and Maurice Filion—the coaches of the Quebec Junior As and the Quebec Remparts. It must be the night of a big win; they are smiling broadly. Here is Maurice Richard with Guy, then Toe Blake, then Gordie Howe. Here is Chouine's

Chevrolet Impala, the car in which Guy learned to drive. Here is Pierre Trudeau shaking Guy's hand. And then Jean Trottier and Gaston Marcotte of the Modern Hockey School where he took courses for several summers.

Guy can be seen as an Atom, a Mosquito, a Bantam, a Midget, then in the uniforms of the Canadiens, the Nordiques, the Remparts, the New York Rangers. There is a picture of him as a Junior A, with a broken tooth and a nasty bruise beneath his right eye. The one with the cigarette in his mouth is Ti-Paul Meloche. And then Guy with Lorne Greene, with Mireille Mathieu, in Las Vegas, in Paris, in New York, in Saint-Tropez, in Moscow with Lise, in Los Angeles with Steve Shutt and Jacques Lemaire, with Claude Quenneville when they used to fish together. Guy, again, with his wife and two sons in front of the enormous chalet he had built two years ago at Mont Tremblant and where he has almost never had the time to go. Here are the houses he has had—the one in Baie d'Urfé, in Verchères, in Kirkland, their apartment in Sanctuaire. That one is the Beaver, Narcisse Charette, a close friend of Guy's from his days in Baie d'Urfé.

These three albums commemorate his wedding. Here he is kissing his wife, Lise Barré. Jean Béliveau was there, and Henri Richard, Jacques Laperrière and Yvon Lambert—almost two complete generations of the Montreal Canadiens. That man is Roger Barré, his father-in-law, a charming gentleman even if he has a lot of money. When he died, Guy suffered. Look! There's Yoland Guérard—she sang at the wedding. And the buffet was fantastic! Mountains of lobsters, a Stanley Cup made of ice, a huge cake with the Canadiens' logo. It was June 1973. All the men in those days wore long hair (except for Jean Béliveau, of course), flowered shirts and wide ties. On the day of the wedding it was cold, and raining cats and dogs. You would have thought it was November.

Madame Lafleur has gone to look for a big colour photograph. Guy and his father are posing in it, laughing, probably a bit drunk, in front of the Knights of Columbus Hall, which is just across the street. In their hands is the

Stanley Cup, the real Stanley Cup that Guy, one night when he was partying, "borrowed" from the Montreal Canadiens and brought for the night to Thurso. In the photo he is wearing the sweater his friend Gilles Villeneuve gave him, a saffron-yellow sweater on which is written, in big black letters, "World Champion, Ferrari." Guy is looking at his father. His father is looking at the camera. His eyes are shining with pride and success. These two men bear a striking resemblance to one another, though their lives do not.

Guy Lafleur belongs to the powerful baby-boom generation, the largest in demographic memory ever to be let loose on humanity. During the fifties, all across North America, the way was opened for them, and all obstacles to their growth and happiness were removed. For them, schools, arenas, playing fields, swimming pools and more were specially constructed.

These children were the best equipped, the best educated, the most loved, pampered, listened to and applauded in the history of the human race. This generation of baby-boomers was the proud masterpiece of the generation of Pierrette and Réjean Lafleur, who were the workers and the builders, the humble generation of sacrifice and duty.

Their children would frolic and enjoy; they would play hockey, strum the guitar, tour the world. Unlike their parents, their priorities would not be duty, but pleasure, leisure and recreation. For them, first and foremost, life would be a game.

Pierrette and Réjean Lafleur believe that their lives have been a success and that their plans have been fulfilled. They created a star, a Guy Lafleur, whose life has been nothing like their own.

SECOND PERIOD

●

THAT SUMMER, WHILE he was haying, or milking cows on Jean-Marc Perras's farm, Guy Lafleur ceaselessly replayed his favourite day-dream. He walks into the Saint Francis of Assisi Recreation Centre in Limoilou, like a man returning from afar, a man who has seen life. He is tanned, muscled, his hair is a bit too long; he is wearing a flowered shirt, jeans and a big silver-studded leather belt. He sits down alone at the counter of the snack bar, nonchalantly orders fries and a Coke. He seems almost absent. Then he swings on his stool towards the bowling lanes and lets his eyes wander, his elbows propped on the counter, his Coke in his hand.

And there she is, bathed in the pearly light of the jukebox, her smile enticing, her eyes . . .

Which one of them will it be? The blue-eyed blonde— Suzanne—or Roxanne? The pale brunette, the sister of his friend Lépine? Or the other one, with the big sexy breasts and velvet lips? It doesn't really matter. One or another. She's there, in front of the jukebox. Their eyes meet, and it's like an electric shock. He smiles, a little nothing of a smile, just enough to make her ask herself if he really did smile, to make her ask herself a thousand and one questions, imagine all sorts of things . . .

Then he'll go join the boys around the billiard table. He'll play an incredible game. More than once he'll feel her eyes on him, burning and disturbing. Poker-faced, he'll keep playing, as though nothing were happening, as though he were the only person in the world. But at the end,

85

after sinking the eight-ball, he'll go straight to her—the blue-eyed redhead or the black-haired one who's always laughing, or the tall, misty blonde—and in his soft voice will talk to her. But about what?

From that point on, the scene gets foggy and so complicated that he has to abandon it. Anyway, he knows the whole thing is terribly dangerous. He's been told often enough that a good athlete should stay away from girls, that a career and love don't go together. It is necessary to live like a monk, no drinking or smoking or thinking too much about women. He should especially avoid falling in love, even in his dreams, before he's finished his training and has fully mastered the game.

If he can't forget his dangerous day-dream, he will have to stop going to the Saint Francis of Assisi Recreation Centre and never see them again, any of them. But even at the wheel of Chouine's Chevrolet Impala, driving to Quebec at the end of August for the Junior A training camp, Guy was still dreaming.

This season's beginning was less worrisome than last. First of all, he was now absolutely certain to be playing Junior A. Everyone said so, and he'd been promised by Paul Dumont and Guy Rouleau, the Junior A coach. He was ready—strong, heavy, tall. No longer would he be the lonely little boy, far from home and his mother; finally he knew where he was going. He had made some friends in Limoilou, some teammates he would be happy to see again. And there would be the exciting atmosphere of the arenas, the parents and friends of the local players who followed them everywhere, encouraged them, cheered them on. There would be a few fans, too, and especially those two or three girls he hardly knew but whose faces had haunted him the whole summer long.

He felt in perfect form. He had taken a second course at the Modern Hockey School, after working hard the whole summer. He had trained well. Guy and Chouine had devised a new training method they called "water-pulling." Chouine, at the wheel of his seventy-five-horsepower outboard, took Guy out for hours on the Ottawa River. It was like water-skiing, but Chouine drove at a low speed. The water came half-way up Guy's calves, so that to avoid falling he had to lean back with all the strength of his knees, his thighs, his back, his shoulders. He really felt as though he were pulling all the water in the river. It was painful and difficult, but remarkably efficient. And it was also the new price to be paid for the privilege of driving the Impala.

Guy's only worry was about where he would live. The year before he had stayed in a small, overcrowded house on Rue La Sarre, a small street steps away from the recreation centre and the Colisée. The people were nice, and he loved the working-class district, full of children. He wanted to stay there, but he dreamed of having a room of his own, like some of the other players.

Chouine had decided to make this a new element to be negotiated with Paul Dumont. He knew Dumont and the whole organization were extremely impressed by Guy's performance, and they were anxious to keep him.

"We're not asking you for more money," said Chouine. "But Guy should have a better place to stay. It's not just a question of comfort, he also needs a proper place to do his homework."

"We'll offer him the best we have," Dumont replied. "He can make his own choice."

In fact, Dumont had found him a huge house, clean and quiet, but it was at the opposite end of the city from Limoilou, where he had started to find friends and feel at home. Guy was shattered.

"Do you want to come back home?" his mother asked.

"No. I have no choice. I'll get used to it. Don't worry about me."

But he was almost in tears when his parents started back for Thurso.

That night, after his parents left, Guy called Dumont, his voice breaking, to tell him that he didn't want to stay in the new place. Paul Dumont knew him well enough to understand he was angry.

"Take a taxi and meet me at the Colisée."

On the way to the arena, Guy began to day-dream. He asked Dumont to set him up somewhere in the Colisée. There must be some place in the building that could be turned into a bedroom! Paul Dumont found the idea appealing, but made Guy understand that it wasn't possible. Instead, he arranged for Guy to go back to the house on Rue La Sarre in Limoilou, with its familiar snack bars, restaurants and the Saint Francis of Assisi Recreation Centre.

One Sunday afternoon Guy went into the recreation centre, sat down at the counter and ordered fries and a Coke. He swivelled his stool, and with his elbows on the counter and his glass in his hand, he gazed distractedly towards the bowling lanes.

And suddenly she was there, bathed in the pearly light of the jukebox, Roxanne, the blue-eyed blonde, smiling broadly as she came towards him.

"Hey, you're back!"

Soon they were good friends. She invited him to her place, introduced him to her mother, her father, her brother, her cat. Guy became one of the family—he ate at their table, watched hockey in their living room, played in their bowling league, helped shovel their driveway, even went out with them, as though he were one of their sons.

One evening, during a bowling game, Roxanne's mother, Madame Côté, introduced him to Eva Baribeau, a small, cheerful woman who liked sports. She was a widow in her early sixties and she lived alone at 238 Rue Benoit XV, near the house where Guy boarded on Rue La Sarre. Eva Baribeau owned a nine-room apartment, but now that her three sons had married and gone she found it much too big to live in alone.

"Why don't you take a boarder?" suggested Roxanne's mother.

"I've thought of it, but I don't really need the money. And you never know who you're going to get."

Madame Baribeau was probably the first person Guy had ever met who didn't intimidate him at all. With her, everything seemed simple. Surprised by his own boldness,

Guy decided to present himself to her as a boarder. He told her that where he lived, it was difficult for him to concentrate on his schoolwork. He slept poorly. He was afraid that his studies would go badly, that his career would suffer.

"My dream is to have a room all my own."

"First you'd better see the place," said Madame Baribeau. "Drop by tomorrow morning and I'll show you the room."

The next morning, at the agreed time, he rang the doorbell at 238 Rue Benoit XV. He was carrying his suitcase.

"But you haven't even seen the room! You make up your mind too quickly!"

"I've seen you, that's enough. I know I'm going to like it here."

The room was clean and bright with handsome, well-polished old furniture, a large, comfortable bed, and even a bedside rug, a wardrobe, a desk and a bedside lamp. Guy Lafleur had never had the luxury of so much space, peace and order. He slid into it the way you slide into a hot bath.

What Guy liked above all was the good-natured warmth of his landlady. In her company, Guy Lafleur—who the whole world, even his own family, had always considered closed-in and taciturn—began to talk. He talked as he had never talked before in his whole life, with anyone else. He talked about everything, he talked about nothing, he talked all the time. He talked about Thurso, about Lac Simon, about his sisters, his plans, Jean-Marc Perras's farm.

Madame Baribeau cooked him good meals, made sure that his laundry was always impeccably clean and neatly put away in his dresser or wardrobe. In the evenings after supper he did his homework and his lessons in his room, with the radio turned down low. She read in the living room or entertained her sister or friends. On Sunday mornings they went to mass at the Saint Francis of Assisi Church, where they would meet the rest of the Baribeau family, and they would all go back together to eat at Madame

Baribeau's apartment. Guy had found a second family, in which he was the cherished and pampered child.

Eva Baribeau started going to watch her adopted son play hockey whenever the Junior As had a game in Quebec or nearby. The morning after, over breakfast, she would comment on his performance and give her analysis of the game. Her observations were generally very acute. The night before an important match she would cook special dishes for him, "full of vitamins," and send him to bed early so that he would be well rested. And when he was setting off for his classes at Jean-de-Brébeuf School, she would inspect him from head to foot.

"You can't wear that jacket with your blue sweater. The colours don't match!"

When he came home, he'd find that she had bought him a more becoming sweater.

The Quebec Junior As were having their highs and their lows. Mostly lows. They had become the laughing-stock of the league. At the Colisée, the attendance was never more than eight hundred. This vast, empty space, echoing dismally with a few sparse shouts, was terribly oppressive.

Nonetheless, Guy Lafleur had some very good moments: four goals in the game of October 7, five on January 28. In all, over the 1967–68 season, he managed to score thirty goals and nineteen assists in forty-three games. By spring he had become a star in junior hockey circles. When he came back to Thurso to finish grade ten, he was welcomed as a real hero, "ticketed for the NHL." Chouine would worry every time he saw Guy setting out at the wheel of his most recent car, a Rambler convertible.

"If anything ever happens to him, I'm the one who's going to be blamed."

Now Guy was being courted by the powerful Ontario Junior Hockey League. Representatives from four teams (St Catharines, Kitchener, Ottawa and the Junior Canadiens) met with Guy and his parents and offered very attractive proposals. They couldn't offer more money than he was already getting from Quebec—that would have violated hockey's code of ethics. What they could offer was the chance to play on the best Canadian junior teams, in a much more efficiently structured league, one infinitely more dynamic than the poor Quebec Junior Hockey League.

But Guy refused all the offers, despite pressure from his father and Ti-Paul Meloche who, not without reason, believed he would learn more in Ontario than Quebec. Guy didn't dare admit it, but he feared the unknown. He was afraid to move again, into a strange new environment, where he would have to find new fans and new friends, and one that was, moreover, anglophone. He had grown deeply attached to the city of Quebec, Madame Baribeau, Roxanne, his fellow players, Paul Dumont . . . In fact, he was a prisoner of the affection and admiration that people had for him. Finally, because Quebec loved him, he wouldn't leave. Chouine alone agreed with him, arguing that Paul Dumont had been straight with them, and that they owed him a chance.

Guy's second season with the Quebec Junior As, now coached by Martin Madden, was pretty much like his first—a few highs, many lows. But one thing was changing: because of Guy Lafleur, the people of Quebec were beginning to take an interest in their junior team. Paul Dumont, recognizing the importance of the media in the success of a hockey campaign, had made a pitch to Quebec's journalists. As a result, they gave good coverage to all the activities of the club, and even managed to create an air of suspense every time the As played, making even the worst defeats interesting, or at least amusing. "How low will our As sink?" "Will the Junior As play even worse this evening?" "Will they succeed in breaking the string of seven (or eight or ten) consecutive defeats?"

Before going to school in the morning, Guy would read the articles from *Le Soleil* or *L'Action* aloud to Madame Baribeau, and even when the headlines were devastating, she could always make him laugh. Guy realized that people were beginning to talk about and like the As, despite their weaknesses. He sensed that the people of Quebec had faith in the team, and wanted it to succeed. With so much intelligent, enthusiastic support from the fans, he knew that, sooner or later, the dream would have to come true.

On October 30, 1968, luck was on the side of the Junior As. There were more than two thousand people to watch them play at the Colisée—the biggest crowd they'd seen in nine years. By the next day, the end of the As' long slump was being talked about all over the city.

"Are we going to relive the great days of the Quebec Citadelles?" the journalists wondered in full-page articles. In the newspapers and on the radio they recalled the exploits of Gilles Tremblay, André Lacroix, René Drolet and Jean Béliveau.

But at the end of November, the As began to lose again. By Christmas they were in next-to-last place, ahead of the unlucky Trois-Rivières Maple Leafs, but far behind the leading Shawinigan Bruins, with their top scorer Michel Brière. The Drummondville Rangers held second place, thanks to Marcel Dionne and a coach, Maurice Filion, who was clever, demanding and inspiring. In third place were the hard-hitting Sorel Éperviers, and the Thetford Mines Canadiens seemed to hold fourth place by luck alone.

Lafleur continued to be talked about. Even when the As lost, he managed to make himself noticed.

On December 2, 1968, the Quebec Junior As were crushed 13 to 3 by the terrifying Sorel Éperviers. But in the papers the next day, no one talked about the defeat. Instead, they concentrated on the fact that Guy Lafleur had participated in all three of the As' goals, scoring twice unassisted and assisting on the third. Paul Dumont was fascinated.

"Every time that boy touches the puck, it's an event."

Even when he didn't touch it, he could get himself talked about. In February the Junior As were again humiliated by the Sorel Éperviers. The headline? "Guy Lafleur, with an ankle injury, did not play in last night's defeat."

Dumont felt almost remorseful. He was fully aware that this immense talent that he was watching bloom before his eyes could not fully mature under these conditions. Perhaps, in the long run, Guy's talent would be stifled by the mediocrity of the teams he played against. If he could just get a few other good players, a decent goalie, a couple of solid defencemen and one or two fast, aggressive wingers, capable of combining with him to make plays; if only the team had more energy, more inspiration, a coach who was strict and able to inspire the players. Martin Madden was a good coach but not a tough one; the players saw him more as a "good guy" than a leader. He could teach the players skills, individually, but he couldn't make them into a team.

"A good coach, a few good players, they can be found, they can be found," Dumont kept repeating. In a few months, a few weeks, he would locate them. It was a promise! He already had some good prospects: Jacques Richard, perhaps Michel Brière and a few others. Thanks to them he would finally create in Quebec an environment in which Guy Lafleur could blossom.

"Otherwise," he told Martin Madden, "following my conscience and my soul, I'll have no choice but to let him go, even if it breaks my heart. We can't ask Guy to compromise his career just to launch a strong league in Quebec."

No one, not even Paul Dumont or Martin Madden, was surprised to see, on January 28, 1969, a four-column article in *Le Soleil*: "Guy Lafleur is interested in pursuing his career in Ontario next year."

Lafleur finished his second Junior A season with fifty goals and sixty assists, an impressive team record. How much better would he have done if he had played with a good team? Malicious tongues said that he had been a standout only because the other players were so bad; in the Ontario Hockey League, he would simply have been one of many good players, not a star. Paul Dumont and Martin Madden thought otherwise: in their opinion Lafleur, if he had been surrounded by competent players, would have exploded and beaten out the league scoring champion, little Michel Brière of the Shawinigan Bruins.

Paul Dumont was juggling some very exciting ideas.

They were risky, perhaps mad, filled with ifs and maybes, but they might work. And they depended, above all, almost entirely, on Guy Lafleur. They had to do with keeping him in Quebec. Paul Dumont was going to set a trap, and it would be more attractive than any a brilliant young hockey player could ever imagine.

• • •

Quebec's two A-level teams, the senior Quebec Aces of the American Hockey League and Quebec's Junior A team, the Citadelles, had been the exclusive property of the Philadelphia Flyers since 1967, purchased for the exorbitant price of $600,000. Like all the NHL expansion clubs, the Flyers needed to develop reserves of players if they ever wanted to be able to rival the Montreal Canadiens, the Boston Bruins or the Detroit Red Wings, and buying clubs like the Quebec As was the way to do it.

It hadn't worked out. Their Quebec teams were costing the Flyers $50,000 a year, and it looked like it would be a long time before they would be able to get a single worthwhile player from their investment. Moreover, new rules regarding recruitment had been established. The NHL clubs were no longer allowed to establish private domains. In the good old days, the great teams used to have farm teams on which they kept and trained promising young players. These players they could, when needed, draft, sell or trade at will. This feudal system was abolished at the beginning of the sixties, just a few months after the Flyers acquired Quebec's teams, and was replaced by a universal draft. Each club then had to assemble a commando team of scouts who covered the rinks from coast to coast, spying out the good players. These were the players that they would then try to pick up at the annual draft, held at the NHL headquarters in Montreal every June.

The Flyers no longer had any motive to support junior clubs that couldn't pay for themselves. So, like fishermen at a fished-out lake, they had become totally uninterested in the fate of their Quebec teams. Paul Dumont, however, figured that he had a large fish indeed. The best way of holding him, he knew, would be to buy the Quebec teams, junior and senior. Then he could rebuild junior hockey in Quebec from the ground up by creating a new team around Guy Lafleur. In essence, the plan was to create a sort of showcase in which Guy Lafleur, the finest jewel in Canadian hockey, could be seen at his true value.

Dumont began by convening about twenty Quebec businessmen; together they founded the Colibec Corporation. Each of the twenty shareholders invested a thousand dollars: five hundred towards the costs of establishing the company, five hundred more to be paid at mid-season. It was a considerable sum of money for the time, and a real gamble. In April, Colibec met with the director-general of the Flyers, Bill Putnam. He agreed to hand over the Quebec teams to Colibec at no charge, and also promised to help wipe out the team's debts by acquiring for the Flyers, at least during the first year, some of the better players.

The gamble paid off. Soon Colibec had wiped out the debt and began to make money, lots of it. In less than a year, thanks to Guy Lafleur, they would completely re-arrange the geography of Canadian Junior A hockey.

For years the Quebec teams, much too weak, poorly coached and unmotivated, had been systematically crushed by teams from the Ontario Hockey League during the playoffs. The Memorial Cup had not crossed the Ottawa River for nine years. The Quebec clubs played among themselves, among losers, among the excluded, and they grew progressively weaker. For nine years not a single player from the Quebec Hockey League had been drafted by the NHL. The Montreal Canadiens supplied themselves mainly from their own club, the Junior Canadiens, which was part of the Ontario league, the real breeding ground of the NHL.

Dumont was entirely aware of the fact that he could not realize his dream of mounting a truly good Quebec Junior A club if the other clubs in the league remained weak and impoverished. To succeed he needed worthy opponents, a strong league, challenging competition. Junior hockey would have to be restructured province-wide. At that time, there were three leagues in the province: the Quebec hockey

League, the Metropolitan and the Saguenay–Lac-Saint-Jean. Dumont arranged a merger between the first two in order to form the new Quebec Junior A Hockey League, which would henceforth have twelve participating clubs.

Once the circuit was restructured, he started the overhaul of the broken-down machine he had inherited from the Philadelphia Flyers. It was decided that the As, whose very name recalled such terrible memories, should have a new name. In a competition, a new name was found, one much more suitable to North America's only fortified city—the Remparts—and a marketing plan was developed.

Dumont, who already had the cooperation of Quebec City's sports journalists, launched himself into an extensive press campaign that quickly generated excitement, not only on the sports pages, but also among businessmen, the municipal authorities, the tourist trade and the general public. There was soon a new emblem, a new name, new colours, a new uniform and a new logo.

Now a good coach was needed.

Everyone was talking about Maurice Filion, who had proved himself with the Drummondville Rangers, the team that had dominated the provincial league over the past few years. Filion immediately accepted Paul Dumont's proposal. Jean Sawyer, a linotype operator from Drummondville, decided to follow Filion to Quebec and take care of the new club's promotion. The journalists had nicknamed Filion "Monsieur 100,000 volts," the name originally given to French singer Gilbert Bécaud, who at that time had a big hit song on the radio, *"L'important, c'est la rose."* The song inspired the new slogan for launching the campaign to resurrect junior hockey in Quebec: *"L'important, c'est Lafleur."*

In fact, the first job of the new coach was to secure Guy Lafleur. Without this outstanding player, Paul Dumont's project would make no sense. It was for and around Lafleur that the entire operation had been mounted: the creation of Colibec, the purchase of the teams, the restructuring of the junior leagues, the formation of the Remparts, the hiring of

Maurice Filion . . . By May everything was in place, the showcase was ready. All that remained was to persuade the jewel.

Everyone knew how attached Guy Lafleur was to the city of Quebec. He was totally charmed by the people of the Old Capital, by Limoilou, by his friends at the recreation centre, by Madame Baribeau. All this was favourable to Colibec. Lafleur, they hoped, would also respect a man like Maurice Filion. Although he didn't know him well personally, he'd played against his players, seen him work with his team and knew he was the best coach in the province.

In the spring Guy left the city, impressed by the enormous project taking shape around him and practically convinced that he couldn't do otherwise than accept Colibec's offer. But by the time he got back to Thurso—to his parents, Ti-Paul, Chouine—he began to have doubts. Bit by bit, Quebec's charm lost its hold on him. During the month of May he changed his mind hundreds of times.

Those who were advising Guy were divided. Of course Dumont's plans were impressive, but nonetheless most people still considered Quebec one of the worst hockey cities in all of Canada. There was nothing to prove that the NHL scouts, who had ignored all junior hockey in the province for ten years, would overnight develop an interest in the players of a new team that might or might not live up to its promises. Heartsick, Guy Lafleur began to think that if he took his future seriously he should get ready to say goodbye to Quebec.

The Ontario clubs continued to court him assiduously. The Ottawa 67s, the Junior Canadiens and the St Catharines Black Hawks of the OHL had already let him know that they would be making him offers before the end of the summer. It was both exciting and completely overwhelming. He felt trapped, pursued by all these people who were badgering him. In his heart, he wanted to go back to live in Quebec. It presented a frightening challenge, and one that was extremely tempting. Quebec was asking him to bring back the Memorial Cup, the way Thurso had expected him, six years ago, to get the Chamberland trophy from Rockland, then the Fernand Bilodeau from Quebec.

At the end of April he began work as a labourer on the construction of the Ottawa-Montreal pipeline. Eight hours a day, shirtless, in good weather or bad, using pick and shovel, he would dig through rock, break stones, move earth. He loved this work. It was very demanding, but left him feeling relaxed. The first hour in the morning was always difficult, but once his muscles were stretched and warmed up he let himself be carried away by the rhythm of the work. For long periods he thought about nothing. Around seven in the evening he came back to Thurso, starved, happy, worn out. While he ate, Chouine told him of the latest developments. Dumont had telephoned again; Guy was supposed to call back the 67s, arrange a meeting with the Junior Canadiens organization; the Black Hawks coach was still waiting for his response. What was Chouine supposed to say?

"Guy, what are you going to do?"

Chouine wanted Guy to learn to decide for himself, so he did not try to influence him. But he did reproach him for always expecting others to make the choices and take the risks in his place. Guy met with Ti-Paul and let himself be convinced to play in Ontario. After seeing his Uncle Armand he said he was ready to leave for Ottawa. When Paul Dumont telephoned, he swore his fidelity to Quebec.

So, when Marcel Dionne and his coach came to Thurso on Mother's Day to try to convince Guy to play for St Catharines, Chouine arranged a little drama, in order to prove to Guy how easily influenced he was. In principle, Réjean, Pierrette and Chouine were supposed to have been at this meeting, but instead they went to the Hotel Lafontaine, leaving Guy alone to deal with the enticements of Dionne and his coach.

"And I bet when we come back an hour from now, you'll be announcing that you're going to sign with St Catharines."

Guy knew Dionne from the old days of the Pee Wee tourneys in Quebec, and he had played against him several times in Junior A. Dionne had just made the jump to the

Ontario league, and Guy was impressed and reassured by him.

"If you come to St Catharines, with the two of us our team will be unbeatable. We'll wipe out everyone. The Ontario players will have to stop saying that we Québecois are useless players."

Dionne talked to Guy about the races on Lake Ontario, the extraordinary girls and the warm climate.

"And English is easy, you'll see."

The coach explained to him that he would receive better training on an Ontario team, where the hockey was high calibre, tough, intelligent, professional.

"Within two years you'll be in the NHL for sure, making big money."

When Chouine and Lafleur's parents came back, the three men, sitting on the swings, glasses in hand, seemed to have become fast friends.

Guy got up and said, "Listen Chouine, I know you're going to be angry, but I honestly think I'd be smart to go to St Catharines."

He had let himself be persuaded and he wanted them to know it. He had spoken loudly so he'd be sure that Marcel Dionne and his coach could hear him clearly. He wanted them to know that if he didn't come to play for them, it was because the choice was out of his hands. He always put himself into the role of the nice guy, easy-going and willing to do what was asked of him.

"I always get the impression that I'm negotiating with you," Chouine would say. "As though you yourself had become the St Catharines Black Hawks' or Quebec Remparts' representative. You should start working for them!"

Guy met Ti-Paul, who was of course in favour of the Ontario teams.

"If Filion couldn't keep Marcel Dionne, his best player, when he coached the Drummondville Rangers, then I figure he doesn't really believe in this business."

"But Dionne signed with the Black Hawks before we had the Remparts!"

"The Remparts are nothing more than the As. Never forget that."

"The Remparts are the As plus Maurice Filion, plus me, maybe, and other guys too."

"Do you want me to tell you something? If Maurice Filion was in your place, he would choose to play in Ontario, with the good players. Like Dionne. In the Bible it says you don't hide your light under a bushel. You have a duty, which is to develop the talent the Good Lord gave you. In Quebec you risk burying it."

When Ti-Paul starting talking about the Bible and the Good Lord, it was a sure sign that the situation had got out of hand!

The Junior Canadiens were also in hot pursuit of Guy Lafleur, and by the end of May, their campaign had reached its peak. This was a serious matter. For all sorts of reasons, the appeal of the Junior Canadiens was stronger than that of all the other Ontario teams put together. Because of the immense prestige of the sacrosanct Montreal Canadiens organization, for any young hockey player, to grow up in the heart of the junior club of this venerable and all-powerful institution was the cherished dream, the entrance into the priesthood, the ultimate consecration. Thus Roger Bédard, the Junior Canadiens' coach, possessed a large advantage over the others.

But the Junior Canadiens organization had both advantages and disadvantages, as Chouine explained to Guy. It was so rich and powerful, and boasted so many talented players, that it had become difficult for a young player to stand out, even one as gifted as Guy Lafleur.

"I don't mean you won't play well," Chouine explained to him. "But you'll get a lot less ice time than anywhere else. You'll get fewer shifts, and each one will be shorter. The end result will be that you'll score fewer goals. In that environment you'll be under a lot of pressure. You have to obey, and you have to warm the bench when you're told to."

At the end of May, at the Meridien Hotel on Rue Sainte-Catherine in Montreal, Guy had his first meeting

with the management of the Junior Canadiens. It was the
first time Guy had dealt directly with such important
people from the world of hockey. Not only had Coach
Bédard come to see him, but he was accompanied by two of
the people who, in Guy's eyes, represented supreme
authority in the hockey universe.

The first was Claude Ruel, who had succeeded Toe Blake
as coach of the Montreal Canadiens. Ruel and his
Canadiens had just won the 1968–69 Stanley Cup by
crushing the Saint Louis Blues in four straight games. It was
said of Claude Ruel that he was the best man in the business
for training players. A longtime scout in the Canadiens
organization, he knew every rink in the country, and had an
incomparable flare for spotting good players. He was a
small, sturdy man with an enormous head, immense jowls,
one glass eye and a soft, feeble voice. Through the whole
meeting he hardly opened his mouth, except to talk with
Réjean Lafleur about things that had nothing to do with
hockey.

Also present was Ronald Caron, the man responsible for
recruiting players for the Montreal Canadiens organization. Everyone called him Professor Caron, because he
had taught English at Saint-Laurent College. Eloquent,
cheerful and a flatterer, he was the complete opposite of
Ruel. He had an extraordinary memory and was a natural
storyteller. He started talking to Pierrette about the first
times he had seen her son, at the Modern Hockey School in
August 1966. Of course he claimed to have immediately
picked Guy out from the others. He had understood at first
glance that here was an elite athlete who, aside from having
exceptional physical gifts, was determined to overcome all
obstacles. According to Caron, this quality was even more
rare and precious than Guy's athletic talents. Of course
Pierrette Lafleur already knew this, but hearing it put so
beautifully gratified her mother's pride.

In spite of Ruel's shy approaches—he seemed to be
interested in Réjean's work as a welder—Guy's father was ill
at ease in the luxurious suites of grand hotels. He was likely
to trip over the flowers in the rug, too thick and too soft for

his taste. The armchairs were too deep. And it was cold. Every time he wanted to make an observation or pose a question, he timidly addressed himself to Chouine, who transmitted his comments and questions to the others.

Réjean found himself unable to trust Roger Bédard. Chouine also found Bédard both arrogant and crafty. The year before, Bédard had sat Réjean Houle and Marc Tardif on the bench for whole games, so that both players had fallen out of the public eye and were no longer talked about. It was said that his job in the all-powerful Canadiens organization was to break the spirits of the good players so that eventually they would fit into the mould and be obedient.

That day at the Meridien, Bédard listened carefully to the demands of Chouine, who, among other things, wanted guaranteed ice time for Guy.

"Don't you worry. The good players get to play. I promise you that."

"We'd like it written into the contract."

"I'm sorry, but that's not possible—it's never been done and I doubt it ever will be. In any case, not in our organization."

"If you intend to keep your word, you shouldn't be afraid to write it down."

"It's not the same thing. And it's not only up to me."

Ruel and Caron said nothing. The negotiations were broken off.

A few days later, Ronald Caron telephoned the Lafleur house. He had noticed that no one there seemed to have warmed to Bédard. He suggested to Pierrette that perhaps they could make an agreement without Bédard present. A meeting was set up for the following Monday, June 23, at the Forum.

"Come through the small side entrance, Rue Lambert-Closse, on the east side of the Forum. I'll be there, with Claude Ruel if he's free."

That day, Chouine was in Hull at a teachers' union meeting. He was summoned to the phone; it was Paul Dumont calling from Quebec.

Dumont and Chouine liked and respected one another. They talked for a good hour on the telephone. Chouine, standing in the hall of his hotel, listened while Paul Dumont, for the hundredth time, described his beloved project, aligned his battery of arguments, appealed to Chouine's reason, his heart, their friendship. Out of respect for this intelligent and passionate man, Chouine agreed to meet. They settled on Sunday, June 22, at the Sainte-Foy Motel Universel, as always.

Since they would be away for two days—in Quebec on the 22nd and Montreal on the 23rd—Réjean Lafleur called his boss and arranged to take the following Monday off. Saturday afternoon, Pierrette made an enormous pot of spaghetti sauce. Chouine bought soft drinks, cold cuts, fruit, everything necessary to feed the Lafleurs' four daughters for at least a week. The care of the house was entrusted to Suzanne, the eldest. But Pierrette was still worried.

"Lock the door, put out the stove the way you're supposed to after you use it, don't leave the little one alone. If something happens, call Grandfather Chartrand or your Uncle Armand."

"Maman, I'm almost nineteen years old. And the little one is almost as big as you!"

"I don't want any boys here while we're away. Understand?"

A few days earlier Chouine had traded in his Rambler, prematurely worn out, for a Javelin, a more responsive car. Guy was delighted. Saturday afternoon he washed and waxed it, and wiped it carefully with a shammy. Sunday morning he filled it with gas and checked the oil. Over Réjean's fearful objections, Chouine had promised to let Guy drive as soon as they were on the highway, on the condition that he go no faster than seventy-five miles an hour and that he give back the wheel before the Quebec Bridge.

At the Motel Universel, Maurice Filion, Paul Dumont and Doc Massicotte, one of the Colibec shareholders, waited for the Lafleur clan with big smiles and attractive proposals.

At the time Colibec was established, the directors had set strict regulations that gave them little room to bargain. The players' salaries were not to exceed $2,500 a year. The Ontario clubs, however, could offer three times as much to their best players. Dumont argued for a bending of the rules. Guy Lafleur, like Jacques Richard and a few of the other players, was, after all, no longer a newcomer in the organization. He proposed that Guy Lafleur be offered a higher salary. No one could say that was unfair. Accordingly, he was offered the considerable sum of $7,500. And of course he would be fed and housed. In addition, he would be eligible for bonuses to be awarded at the end of the season if he broke records or—touch wood—if the Remparts won the Memorial Cup.

But money wasn't enough. The others had also offered money. And they, too, could offer various supplementary financial incentives. Other arguments were necessary.

"If all the good players of your calibre refuse to come to Quebec," said Paul Dumont, "it's certain that it will never be tempting for anyone. You have the chance to be in on the beginning of something. You have a historic role to play. Anywhere else, you'll just be a very good player. In Quebec, you'll be someone important."

Guy understood that a challenge was being offered. In Quebec he would be king. Elsewhere, a nobody. But he wasn't crazy enough to compromise his career just for the pleasure of responding to a challenge.

Chouine, afraid that his protégé might commit himself to Quebec on the spot, demanded that Guy's contract stipulate he would become a free agent if, after a year, it appeared that the Colibec project wasn't working—that is, if the Colisée was still three-quarters empty and the NHL scouts were still uninterested in the Remparts.

"We can't do that," Dumont replied. "Our whole plan is based on the long-term presence of Guy Lafleur. We can't make this kind of investment in a player unless we are certain of keeping him for at least two years."

Once again, negotiations were broken off. Sunday evening, June 22, the Lafleur clan set out for Montreal—a little worried, of course, even though they knew it was still possible, if worst came to worst, to go back to Colibec. They stayed in a little hotel on Sherbrooke, and the next morning they met Ronald Caron and Claude Ruel in the Forum offices.

Caron had done his homework and knew exactly what the Lafleurs wanted. He promised that the contract with the Junior Canadiens would stipulate that Guy had a lot of ice time. As for the salary, he had thought of a clever strategy. A league regulation prohibited paying players more than $5,000 a year. To get around the rule, Caron proposed that Guy's father get an equal salary as a scout, which was, after all, well deserved.

The deal was in the bag. Or almost. The contract was sent out to be prepared and in the meantime everyone went to dinner at the Texas Restaurant, near the Forum. Thick steaks, red wine. Caron led the conversation brilliantly. Everyone was happy, although vaguely worried just the same.

Back at the Forum, around three in the afternoon, there was trouble with the contract. Sam Pollock, managing director of the organization, had refused to authorize the clause concerning ice time. Back to zero. Once more, negotiations were broken off, and Pierrette and Réjean Lafleur, Chouine and Guy, were out on the street again.

Chouine said, "Réjean, he's your boy, you decide. If you want my opinion, I wouldn't go with the Canadiens. It's a matter of principle. But you should do as you see fit."

Guy was no longer talking. All this was starting to weigh on him, to irritate him and make him angry. So this was hockey! Meetings, discussions, negotiations, bargaining that never ended!

Réjean Lafleur paced back and forth along Rue Lambert-Closse. At this hour, the small street fell under the heavy shadow of the Forum, but each end of the street, from Rue Sainte-Catherine and from Boulevard de Maisonneuve, they could see the bright summer sunlight. Where to go? What to do?

"Réjean, you have to decide. He's your son."

"Do you think there would be a chance of reopening negotiations if we called Paul Dumont?"

"I'll tell you something. Right now Paul Dumont is glued to his phone and waiting for our call."

"So what are you waiting for?"

"For you to give me a dime."

From the street-corner telephone booth, Normand Chouinard made a collect call to Paul Dumont. He answered on the first ring.

"Paul, it's Normand."

"You changed your mind?"

"Yes and no. It depends on you."

"How's that?"

"If you want Guy to play for the Remparts, you'll have to start by buying us two airplane tickets to Quebec."

"That's all?"

"Are you ready to take a step or two in our direction?"

"Perhaps. It depends. But I think so."

"Good. I think things will work out."

"Can you buy the tickets?"

"I have enough for that."

"We'll reimburse you for them. There's a plane leaving from Dorval at about four o'clock. You should arrive at the Ancienne-Lorette airport a little after five. I'll be there."

Guy's parents could not go to Quebec. The next day, Tuesday, Réjean had to work, and Pierrette didn't want to leave the girls alone at the house any longer. They were to drive the Javelin back to Thurso. Even though he had a driver's licence, Réjean Lafleur had almost never been behind the wheel of a car. But he had no choice. This would be his first long drive, at the same time as his son's first airplane flight.

In the plane Guy was very excited. "You'll see," he said to his friend, "you'll end up making money with me."

"You're mistaken, Guy. Our time together is almost finished. You know very well I can't follow you where you're going. I am no hockey man. At the next stage, I'll have to get off. I can't be your agent or your manager.

When this business is settled, our paths will separate. You'll make your life, and I mine. We'll be in different worlds."

"But I want you to keep taking care of me!"

"There's no choice, Guy. You'll see. There will be plenty of people around you who will want to take care of your affairs, and who will also want to use you. You will have to be very strong. Up until now you have learned to play hockey. Now you have to learn to survive by yourself in that world."

"But why can't we do it together?"

"Because there's no place there for someone like me. I told you that. I don't know how to lie. I'm not slick enough. I have none of the skills of a real hockey man."

"Who will help me?"

"You know very well that I won't just drop you. I'll always be there if you need me. But I want to be sure you understand one thing. When you decide to drop me . . ."

"Chouine! I would never do that!"

"Guy, let me talk. When you take on a professional agent I want you to remember what I'm telling you today: that I won't be angry at you for doing it. All I want is for you to conduct yourself properly and honestly. And for that, no one can be your agent."

Paul Dumont and Maurice Filion were waiting for them at the Ancienne-Lorette airport. They went straight to the Motel Universel, where the Colibec board of directors was already gathered. These were successful businessmen, cheerful and friendly professionals, less intimidating, less coarse, less hurried than their Montreal counterparts.

The suite had been supplied with snacks, fruit, drinks. Guy didn't talk much; he listened carefully. He didn't speak unless he was questioned. A remarkable but predictable thing: he had spontaneously sat down on the same side of the room as the men from Colibec, so that Norman Chouinard found himself all alone on the other side of the negotiating table.

Chouine felt he had no need to come back to the clause about ice time. In Quebec, Guy would have as much as he wanted. Moreover, he knew that Colibec didn't have the financial resources to get into a bidding war. Just the same, he wanted to be sure that if the project didn't work out, Guy would be able to leave.

"I have confidence in your plans. But we can't sacrifice Guy's career to the hope that sooner or later the Remparts will be a success. He needs an escape clause."

It was finally decided to make up a contract for two years that would include a cancellation clause in the event that the Colisée didn't attract spectators. Instead of negotiating about ice time, they were bargaining about the size of the crowd.

Towards ten o'clock in the evening, just as they were about to put the details of their agreement onto paper, the secretary-treasurer of Colibec realized that he didn't have a copy of the official contract of the Quebec Junior A Hockey League. Nor could they find anyone in the city who did. Finally they located someone in Montreal who agreed to come down to Quebec with a blank contract. It was three in the morning when he arrived. Guy Lafleur's contract was made up and at four in the morning, June 24, 1969, the two parties signed the agreement: Paul Dumont and Doc Massicotte for Colibec; Guy Lafleur and Normand Chouinard for the Lafleur family.

Someone noticed that Guy was not yet eighteen, and that therefore his signature had only symbolic value. This irritated Guy, who frostily replied:

"My signature is my word. You can trust it."

The sun had long since risen when he was finally able to go to bed. Before going to sleep, he telephoned his father.

"Papa, I'm staying with Quebec."

"Are you happy?"

"I think so. I'll tell you tomorrow."

Then he tried to sleep. He knew that by signing he had just put enormous pressure on himself. This time, unlike when he was Mosquito and Pee Wee, he knew what was happening. They had bet heavily on him, and he was expected to produce. For the first time, he was afraid.

Paul Dumont and his colleagues had already started to alert the media and to organize a press conference. There would be no newspapers that day, but just the same, according to Dumont, the timing was excellent. The people of Quebec would see something highly symbolic in this contract negotiated, made out, signed and ratified on Saint-Jean-Baptiste Day, Quebec's national holiday.

In Thurso, Réjean Lafleur couldn't go back to sleep. He went downstairs to make himself a cup of coffee and took it outside to drink while he watched the day grow brighter. He thought about his son, who had just started on his road to fame and success, and about himself. He would soon be forty. And he told himself that in this world filled with children, forty was truly old. But to be young in 1969, he thought, that must be wonderful because everything was possible and everything permitted.

He listened to the six o'clock news on the radio. The announcer said that Guy Lafleur had signed with the Remparts and during the course of the afternoon would be holding a press conference at the Dow Brewery in Quebec. Réjean Lafleur felt that his son was already a man, yet still a little boy.

He got his lunch box from the refrigerator, climbed on his bicycle and, as he had every weekday for almost a quarter century, he rode to the factory. He was always a good half hour early. He liked to have the time to get changed without hurrying, then sit in the cafeteria and look at the paper or just do nothing while waiting until the clock marked 6:55. Then he punched his time card. When the siren went off at seven o'clock he didn't hear it; he was already at work. His helmet on his head, his mask on his face, his acetylene torch in one hand and his hammer in the other, he stepped into the enormous machine that swallowed him up with its raucous noise and toxic fumes. He knew that *his* life would never change. That morning, despite his joy for Guy, there was sadness in the air.

• • •

In Quebec they say that it was Jean Béliveau who built the Colisée, and Guy Lafleur who made it grow. Even though

Béliveau left almost forty years ago, he is still a Quebec City boy, a great hero, born in Trois-Rivières, raised in Victoriaville, but discovered and invented in Quebec by the people of Quebec, their well-loved creation. Like Guy Lafleur.

The people of Quebec City are extremely proud of their Colisée. The Montreal Forum is incontestably the most prestigious hockey rink in the world, from Los Angeles to Moscow. Vladislav Tretiak, the great Soviet goalie, tells the story that when he was a small boy in Dmitrov, north of Moscow, he covered the walls of his room with posters of players from the Montreal Canadiens, especially his idol, Jacques Plante. The Forum is the mecca of hockey. But the Quebec Colisée is even more fiercely loved. The city built it, then had it completely renovated at the beginning of the eighties. The Colisée is still managed by the city, which acts as producer and promoter of the shows and hockey games that take place there. The Colisée truly belongs to the people. Not to a Protestant brewery or an anonymous and heartless multinational or some rich businessman, like the other NHL arenas. The Colisée is a sacred temple.

It is situated well away from the centre of the city, near the working-class district of Limoilou, in a vast complex of huge buildings devoted to sports and recreation: the Colisées (the big new one and the small old one), the Hippodrome, the exhibition grounds and parking lots so vast that the wind is always whistling across them. There are also some handsome red-brick buildings put up in the years when art deco was fashionable; these house the offices of the Ministry of Agriculture. Looking north you see a tangle of highways and in the distance the Laurentians; towards the south, Cap-Diamant and the Upper Town hide the river.

When it was small, the Colisée had the shape of a vault. To increase its size (from ten thousand to fifteen thousand seats), the lateral arches had to be broken, so that today you no longer see, from the outside, anything of the original vault except for the peak, which scarcely emerges from the new quadrangular structure. It has an austere and perfect symmetry. From the outside the design appears banal and functional, but inside it is immense and magical.

The skating rink is a lake of light. The boards that surround the ice are covered in multicoloured logos and advertising slogans. Beyond are the red, blue and white rows of seats. Above, straight up, is the permanent shadow that is found in all amphitheatres. But in the shadows can be seen the movement of banners, streamers and flags, pennants that illustrate the history of hockey in Quebec, signifying its greatest moments and most prestigious figures: the two Stanley Cups won by the Quebec Bulldogs in the 1910s; the Memorial Cup of the Citadelles, and that of the Remparts in 1971; the Avco Cup won by the Nordiques in the days when they belonged to the now-defunct World Hockey Association. And in this glorious firmament four names: Joe Malone, Jean Béliveau, Jean-Claude Tremblay, Guy Lafleur.

When Béliveau played here at the end of the 1940s with the Quebec Aces of the American League, the Colisée had only ten thousand seats, and it was always jammed full. Of course the people of Quebec City listened to NHL games on the radio and, like everyone else, they adored the Montreal Canadiens. But the Aces were the true passion of the people of Quebec, their pride, their heroes. Through their hockey team they affirmed themselves, declared their existence, they were unique. For once.

Quebec has always been only too aware of the dominance of Montreal in the arts, sports, fashion, industry, even politics and intellectual life. The power, the big show, the real excitement has always been located in Montreal. But for two years, those two unforgettable hockey seasons during which Jean Béliveau played there, the action was in Quebec. At the same time, the Montreal Canadiens, despite the electrifying presence of Maurice Richard, were in a terrible slump, unable to win the Stanley Cup a single time from 1946 to 1953.

In those days the Quebec Aces had the wind in their sails

and went from triumph to triumph in the American Hockey League. Everywhere it was agreed that there was nothing finer in the world of hockey than to watch Jean Béliveau as he got hold of the puck, then, skating the length of ice while easily evading the defence, buried it in the net of the Shawinigan Cataractes, the Ottawa Senators or the Montreal Royals.

When Béliveau left, the spell was broken and the charm gone. Gradually the Colisée emptied. Television didn't help. Thanks to the small screen (which didn't arrive in Quebec until 1954, two years after Montreal) the Canadiens regained their prestige of earlier days, not only at home but throughout the province of Quebec and in hockey cities all over North America. Maurice Richard scaled hitherto unknown peaks of glory, and Quebec was left foundering . . .

Even Roger Lemelin's "The Plouffe Family," the first of the great popular serial dramas to be shown on French-Canadian television, favoured Montreal over Quebec. The action took place in Quebec, at the bottom of the Pente Douce, right near the Colisée. Nevertheless, the family's youngest son, Guillaume, dreamed of playing for the Montreal Canadiens and his father, Théophile, who was a plumber, dreamed of capturing the extremely profitable plumbing contract for the Montreal Forum. Thus, even in fiction, the people of Quebec City were dispossessed. For twenty frustrating and bitter years they had been no more than an extension of Montreal. Of course there had been a few good moments since Béliveau's departure, with the Aces or the Citadelles, a few good players (Jean-Claude Tremblay, among others), but the love affair was over. In any case, as soon as a player began to show some promise, he was snatched up by an NHL club.

By the spring of 1969, hockey in Quebec was on the road to financial disaster. So few people attended the games that a crowd of two or three hundred was considered good.

The challenge facing Guy Lafleur and the Remparts was enormous.

• • •

By giving Guy Lafleur sweater number 4, the number of the incomparable Jean Béliveau, the team was announcing to the world that Guy Lafleur would take up the torch that Béliveau had passed. Paul Dumont was worried that this mission might be too heavy a burden. He begged the journalists to stop comparing him to Jean Béliveau, and to allow him to become Guy Lafleur. But Maurice Filion, the coach, had an entirely different view of the matter. He sensed that Guy Lafleur liked this challenge, and that he always worked better under pressure. He said to the journalists:

"You've been dreaming of a Jean Béliveau. Now you've got one. Watch him."

But Guy was still a bit nervous and worried. He couldn't help but wonder if he had done the right thing by signing with the Remparts instead of the Junior Canadiens or the St Catharines Black Hawks. Marcel Dionne and Gilbert Perrault had joined Ontario teams and everyone kept saying, even in Quebec, that they had promising careers. This talk angered him, and made it hard for him to put his heart into his work.

"You can't go back now," Madame Baribeau said. "You signed with the Remparts and you must play for them, a hundred and twenty percent. And stop asking yourself if you did the right thing."

October 2, a few days before the beginning of the regular season, the Remparts played a match against the Saint-Hyacinth Gaulois of the Quebec senior league. The Gaulois were terribly rough, ten times worse than the Sorel Éperviers, heavier, older, meaner. There were endless fights. The Remparts lost 13 to 3, Lafleur having scored two goals and set up the third. He had established himself, right from the first game, as a solid and talented player.

On the TransCanada highway that evening, in the bus taking them back to Quebec, the Remparts elected their captain for the 1969–70 season. Not surprisingly, Guy Lafleur, the candidate of Maurice Filion, won easily.

Maurice Filion was a tough man, a man of principles, paternalistic and authoritarian, with a pedagogue's view of hockey. According to him, a coach, especially at the junior level, should play a formative role, not only directing the players on the ice and teaching them the techniques of hockey, but also imbuing them with team spirit, and with the skills, attitudes and mentality of winners.

On December 30, 1969, the Remparts were playing at the Paul Sauvé Centre in Montreal against the Rosemont National, owned by Johnny Rougeaud, a famous boxer. Filion had promised his players two days off if they won. In Thurso, where everyone believed the Remparts couldn't lose, a big New Year's Eve party had been organized, with Guy Lafleur as the guest of honour. All of Thurso would be there. Chouine and Réjean Lafleur had come to watch the game, with the plan of going home with Guy. But the Remparts, whose play was apathetic and random, were flattened 8 to 1.

After the match a furious Maurice Filion decreed that the entire team would return to Quebec, Guy Lafleur included. Réjean Lafleur, rendered less timid than usual by his anger and a few beers, decided that this was unacceptable. There was a heated exchange between the two.

"You told my son that he would have a holiday."

"If the Remparts won, I said."

"I never heard that, I swear to you. In my mind, Guy was having a holiday, whether or not he won. So he'll come to Thurso with us."

"In that case, he can stay in Thurso with you for as long as he likes. If he's not at the Colisée for tomorrow afternoon's practice, we'll get along without him. And not only tomorrow. We'll do without him for the rest of the season. The coach of the Quebec Remparts is me, not Guy Lafleur. Good evening!"

Guy, his father and Chouine got into the Javelin and left for Thurso. But on the road, remorse, worry and guilt gradually crept into them. Réjean Lafleur thought that perhaps he had gone a bit too far. Guy, sitting in the back seat, was depressed, apathetic, exhausted by the defeat.

Meanwhile, aboard the Remparts' bus as it drove through the night towards Quebec, Maurice Filion was terribly depressed. Sitting alone at the front, to the right of the driver, he watched the road as it disappeared under the wheels. His whole strategy was in danger of falling apart. Even though the Remparts had lost badly that night, they were turning into a very good team, perhaps the best in the new Quebec Junior A league. The boys had just played a bad game, but normally they were filled with team spirit.

The Quebec public and the media had truly taken to their new team. For the first time in ten years, the Colisée was a place for people to go: four thousand a game in November, nearly five thousand as the holidays approached. Without Guy Lafleur, this audience would quickly evaporate. Lafleur was not just an extraordinary and electrifying player, he knew how to communicate his passion for the game, both to his teammates and to the crowds.

"What will you do if the Lafleur boy doesn't come back tomorrow?" the driver asked.

"We'll try to fix something. I can't destroy the career of a player just like that, especially not a player like him. But I have to teach him a lesson. I think he needs it."

"With everything that's happened, perhaps he's getting a swollen head. Everyone keeps saying how fantastic he is."

"Maybe he is getting a swollen head. Personally, I have nothing against it. In fact, I think that for a player to be great, he has to see himself that way. But he also has to realize that in life there are some things that you can't do—like thinking, when you're part of a hockey team, that you can get personal favours. You can think you're better than the others, that's fine—if you are. But you still have to follow the same rules as everyone else, and put the team before yourself. Especially when you're the captain."

Back in Thurso, Guy, his parents and Chouine were sitting around the kitchen table waiting for Maurice Filion and the Remparts to arrive in Quebec so they could phone him.

"By now, they must have reached Saint-Apollinaire,"

said Chouine. "In about three-quarters of an hour the bus will be at the Colisée. Ten minutes later Maurice Filion will be home. I'll call him at two."

At two o'clock in the morning, when Maurice Filion's phone rang, he knew it was the Lafleurs. For a second he was tempted not to answer and to let them worry until the next morning. But his wife and children were sleeping.

"Hello."

"Maurice, this is Normand Chouinard."

"How are you?"

"What time do you need Guy tomorrow afternoon?"

"Who told you I need him?"

"Good! Listen. Guy regrets not having taken the bus with the team. He apologizes. His father takes the whole responsibility for this business. But he thinks there's no reason for you to punish his son."

"There will be no reason if he's on time for practice tomorrow."

The next morning, New Year's Eve, 1970, Chouine drove Guy to Quebec. As always, Guy was the first to arrive in the dressing room.

Maurice Filion congratulated him but also scolded him.

"You've just proved to me that you have what it takes to become a great athlete. But never forget that you'll never get anywhere alone. Hockey is a team sport."

• • •

Madame Baribeau went out often. She went bowling, played bridge and bingo, did volunteer work, went to vespers and the movies, had many "girlfriends" she saw frequently, and enjoyed visiting her sons and shopping for her grandchildren and daughters-in-law. But she never left 238 Rue Benoit XV without preparing her boarder's meal. All he had to do was heat it up and help himself. But since Guy hated eating alone in the house, and hated kitchen chores even more, he would often go out. He would wander about the streets, sometimes going as far as the Upper Town and the Plains of Abraham. On his way back to Limoilou, he would stop at his favourite restaurant, the

Cendrillon. It was two minutes from his place, at the corner of 3rd and 11th Streets, right across from the old movie house. He always made sure to go there when it wasn't crowded. He would sit in a corner with his *Road & Track* or *Automobile Quarterly* or *Yachting* and look at the cars, tractors, motorcycles and boats while eating a huge platter of spaghetti with meat sauce, the specialty of the house.

In those days, nothing bored Guy Lafleur more than talking about hockey. If he preferred to come to the Cendrillon outside of its busiest times, it wasn't only out of shyness, but also to avoid having to talk to all the strangers who would come up to praise him, then force him to listen to all their theories on the national sport, ask his opinion on this or that player and make him say that he would or would not stay in Quebec the following year. Everyone he met seemed to feel obliged to talk to him about his exploits and his career, so that he often had the impression that he was no longer a person but simply a hockey player.

As in every restaurant, the staff at the Cendrillon ate while business was slow, and so did the two brothers who owned the place, Jean-Yves and Lorenzo Doyon.

Jean-Yves, the younger, was two or three years older than Guy, and the owner of a red Mustang. He had been born in the district and knew everyone. He wasn't particularly interested in hockey.

He talked about what was happening in the world, about everything and nothing, about girls, the Beatles, Jimi Hendrix and Janis Joplin, who had just died of an overdose in California, about cars, motorcycles, about fashion, about the weather. He liked to laugh. He dreamed of having a sailboat, a racehorse, and children—lots of children. With Jean-Yves Doyon, Guy discovered that there was more to life than hockey. Doyon treated him not like a star but like a friend, like a real person. With him, Guy had the reassuring sensation that he actually existed, even outside the hockey rink.

One fine January day, when Jean-Yves Doyon had gone to a wedding with one of his girlfriends, Guy found himself alone in the city. The prospect of passing two long days alone terrified him. He decided to leave town. It would be a serious offence for which he could get into trouble if the Remparts' informers ever found out. But it was unlikely that Filion's spies, knowing how serious and well-behaved was Guy Lafleur, would bother to check his whereabouts with Madame Baribeau. Anyway, they were busy enough with players like Jacques Richard, who spent their time in bars or chasing girls.

Madame Baribeau tried to dissuade Guy from going, but finally agreed to cover for him. If they came to see her, she would say that Guy was in bed, asleep. And if they wanted to see for themselves?

That exact thing had happened to Jacques Richard. The Remparts' police had gone to his parents' home one evening at ten o'clock. One of his brothers, who was doing his homework at the kitchen table, said that Jacques was asleep.

"Can we see?"

"There's nothing to see. I tell you he's sleeping."

"We'd like to see, just the same."

"You'll wake everyone up. My mother is in bed."

The two informers went in regardless and peered into each of the rooms. There were eleven people in the Richard family: the father (a taxi driver), the mother, and their nine children. The boys slept two or three to a room. In one room a young man was sleeping, his face in the pillow. He had longish brown hair.

"Who's that?"

"That's him, my brother."

"Are you sure?"

"Positive, I swear it. The other bed is mine."

Like everyone in Limoilou, Madame Baribeau knew this anecdote; it was part of the growing legend of the mischievous Jacques Richard. Unaccustomed to lying, Madame Baribeau nevertheless assured Guy she would say whatever was necessary.

"You won't have to."

"I hope so, for your sake."

The next day, at six in the morning, Lafleur took the bus to the railway station on Rue Saint-Vallier; he took the train to Montreal and Chouine met him at the station. At ten-thirty they were in Thurso.

That evening it began to snow heavily. And it kept snowing all night and all the next day. Over the radio, people were told they should stay home. Those highways still passable would probably be closed to traffic by nightfall.

This was enough to get Chouine going. He, Réjean and Guy left Thurso in the late afternoon. It took them almost three hours to get to Montreal. Crossing the city took another hour. At the entrance of the Lafontaine Tunnel, a Quebec Provincial Police patrol advised them to turn back. Highway 20 was snowswept, and the visibility poor.

They had a good car, a snow shovel in the trunk, and all three of them were physically strong. And although Réjean didn't like fast driving, he had no fear of wind or snow. So they drove into the blowing snow, into the heart of the storm. It was magical, like something out of a fairy tale. The only other cars they saw along the road were parked on the shoulders, their lights off, empty. They tuned in to an American radio station and listened to Réjean Lafleur's favourite Big Band music. At about five in the morning they arrived in Quebec City, exhausted and famished, but excited.

"In the midst of a storm, we crossed the whole inhabited part of the province, from one end to the other," Chouine said proudly.

Guy, the stray returned to the fold, was playing that evening. After having slept for a few hours, eaten a big steak with eggs, shovelled the front steps, the entrance to the house and the sidewalk, he arrived at the Colisée at about five o'clock, as usual, just as though nothing had happened.

When he was playing in Quebec, he always started out for the arena two or three hours before the game. It wasn't only to get himself physically ready or to practise, but because he needed to take possession of the place, establish his presence, like a wolf marking off his territory, like actors who pace the corridors before a performance or walk in circles around the set before filming.

He loitered for a while in the players' rooms, chatted with the janitors, went to see what was happening in the empty kitchen, got a coffee, smoked, went into the corridors, lay down for a while in the dressing room, telephoned Doyon to see if it was still snowing, called his friend Roxanne to see if she would like to go to the movies with him the next evening, called Madame Baribeau who was waiting to hear from Thurso . . .

He felt as though he were on another planet, in a sort of cave apart from the rest of the world. And, in a way, he was somewhere else, in his own country—the ice. Often he would climb up to sit in one of the last rows of seats on the west side of the Colisée, in the shadows, the same place he had found when he was a Pee Wee. From there he looked at the ice. Sometimes, without moving, he would sit alone for more than an hour.

"Be sure not to disturb him," Paul Dumont instructed the maintenance workers.

Lafleur went over his plays in his mind, as though they were mantras. When the other players arrived they were in Lafleur's territory, and he was its master.

By November 11, 1969, he had already scored twenty-eight goals in fifteen games for the Remparts. There was no doubt that at this rate he would keep his lead in the scoring race, far in front of all the other Quebec Junior A league players. By the end of February he had already broken the league record of seventy-five goals, held by Michel Brière. Brière, formerly of the Shawinigan Bruins, was now playing in the NHL for the Pittsburgh Penguins. Everyone agreed that if he could finish the season without being injured, Guy Lafleur would pass the hundred-goal mark by end of the regular season. Everything was going perfectly. Filion and Dumont were delighted to see how well their prodigy bore the pressure.

And then, suddenly, Guy went into an inexplicable slump. Having amassed more than ninety goals in fewer than fifty games, Lafleur could no longer find the net. Grace, strength and magic seemed to have abandoned him, as though he had suddenly been unplugged. He played without energy, listlessly. All great players live in fear of these periods of drought, of these unpredictable deserts they will have to cross. Several times Maurice Filion had spoken to Lafleur about them.

"When it happens to you, you can't get discouraged. You just have to keep playing. It always ends sooner or later, you'll see. Everyone has these droughts, even Jean Béliveau. Talk to him about it. He'll tell you that the only cure is time."

But despite the fact Filion gave him more ice time, kept telling him not to worry, every time Lafleur leapt to the ice he was suddenly unable to play. He felt it physically; it was as though some malignant force had sucked out all his energy. He no longer understood the plays. Sometimes he even lost sight of the puck for long periods. It was like the sad dream he used to have when he was young, the dream in which he was lost on the big skating rink his father used to make in the yard, and he looked for his puck in the immense ice desert, depressed, discouraged, his stick useless in his hands . . .

He would have liked to have been able to wake himself up, as before. He would have pulled the covers up to his neck, burrowed into the warm bed and gone back to sleep. But this time it wasn't a dream. It was, unfortunately, reality. He could no longer see the puck. And when, by a fluke, he got hold of it, he didn't know what to do with it. He could no longer free himself to get in position to receive good passes. And the regular season was almost over.

In Quebec, the suspense had become intolerable. Every day in the newspapers, on radio and television, everywhere, they talked of nothing else. They had written new words to the tune of a folk song, and would sing whenever Guy came onto the ice:

Oh, if Guy would only score here
I'd give him a fine hat

Score, Guy, score
Don't you hear the people?
Don't you hear your fans?

The song encouraged him, but didn't really help. On the contrary, so much solicitude could only add to the terrible pressure he was under. He wished only to be forgotten, wished that people would stop talking about him, stop observing him, so he could just play in peace.

By mid-February, two or three matches before the end of the season, everyone had lost hope. They knew it wasn't going to happen; Guy wouldn't reach the magic hundred-goal mark. He'd run out of gas and was hopelessly blocked at ninety-four goals. Everyone felt as though this was a terrible failure.

That Lafleur couldn't score a hundred goals in a season was no big thing. But that he be revealed as so susceptible to pressure, that he could let himself be destroyed by it—that was worrisome! The best hockey player in the world would never get anywhere if he couldn't overcome nerves and pressure. But Guy Lafleur, the hope of Quebec junior hockey, seemed unable to pass this test. He had become paralysed and thrown off the track. The more the newspapers questioned and criticized his apathy, the deeper he sank, the more he closed himself off in silence and solitude, in a sort of chilly indifference even Madame Baribeau and Jean-Yves Doyon couldn't really penetrate. He spent hours shut up in his room, doing nothing, listening to the radio.

Maurice Filion believed in the hard-line approach. He didn't try to lessen the pressure by denying it—just the opposite. Every day he reminded his player that he would have to learn to deal with it if he wanted to become great.

"Knowing how to skate or score—that's one thing. But you have to be able to skate and score under all circum-stances. It's like singing. You can sing like Caruso in your shower, but if you can't do it on a stage, no one will ever say you're a great singer. You'll always be a shower singer."

Filion finally discovered that Lafleur was preoccupied by, among other things, the record of Luc Simard of the Trois-Rivières Ducs. In a formidable sprint, Simard had considerably narrowed the gap between himself and Lafleur in the league scoring race. It was practically impossible for Simard to catch up before the end of the season, but during the last month he had scored a lot more than Lafleur. Now Simard was the league sensation, the player the media were talking about. After being the centre of attention for months, Lafleur now felt pushed back into the shadows. And in the shade Guy was cold, paralysed. He wanted both to escape his slump and to have peace and quiet. But celebrity and peace, he would discover, don't go together.

Strangely, contrary to what Paul Dumont and many others had thought, he had not been worried or burdened by the comparisons made between him and such great hockey players of the preceding generation as Jean Béliveau, Maurice Richard or "Boom Boom" Geoffrion. What worried and weighed heavily on him were the comparisons made with his teammates and with other players of his own age. He felt he was in the position of the challenger, the person who must at any cost prove something, beat someone. Or be beaten.

Tuesday, February 17, there were only two matches left in the season. It was a magnificent winter day, brilliant white with a sparkling blue sky and a shining sun, a cool fresh breeze; it was the kind of day, sky, light, that Guy Lafleur, who had always loved winter, adored. That morning he had walked alone through the streets of Limoilou, dropping in at the Cendrillon, the recreation centre, Roxanne's house. He felt free, and as if by magic relieved of an enormous weight. He had decided to forget the record of a hundred goals. He would simply play his best, for the pleasure of playing.

After he'd had a short nap in the afternoon, Madame Baribeau prepared his meal for him. As always he had his choice: chicken, meatloaf, steak, pasta, stew . . .

"I'll have eggs, if you have any."

"How many?"

"Four. Turned over, please."

When he'd finished, Madame Baribeau asked him, as always, if he was still hungry.

"I'd like some more, if it's no bother."

"More eggs?"

"Two more, please."

That evening, playing against the Sherbrooke Castors, Guy Lafleur scored six goals. He was the first player in the history of junior hockey to do so, and the first to break the barrier of a hundred goals in a season. The crowd was ecstatic, wild with delight. By the third goal, they were already at their limit. At the fourth, it was a matter of collective hysteria. After the fifth, the crowd noise was so loud you could no longer hear the puck ricocheting off the boards, or the referee's whistle. And when, with less than three minutes to play in the game, Guy Lafleur scored his sixth goal, everyone was crying, punching their neighbours, laughing insanely, kissing each other, throwing their hats onto the ice. Ten thousand Québecois had just experienced an unforgettable event.

The hero was carried about in triumph. He was happy, but also serious, hardly smiling, dazzled, stunned. Long after the match was over the crowd, usually in such a hurry to leave, stayed in their seats joyfully singing "*Il a gagné ses epaulettes*," the French-language equivalent of "For he's a jolly good fellow."

Madame Baribeau, filled with pride, mixed in with the fans waiting for Lafleur at the dressing-room door.

"Six eggs, six goals! The Castors are lucky I didn't cook you a dozen!"

From that day on, Guy Lafleur made a cult of eating eggs. He ate them in omelettes, scrambled, fried sunny-side-up or turned over. He ascribed almost magical qualities to them. He had always said he wasn't superstitious, but like all hockey players he believed in rituals and spirits.

Two days later, the Remparts were playing their last game of the season, against Laval. Lafleur scored three more goals, bringing his total for the season to 103.

The failures he'd experienced at times during the winter did not tarnish his glory in the least. On the contrary, he emerged even stronger; he had overcome the pressure, he was better loved, more adored than ever. In Quebec, everyone was talking about Guy Lafleur and Guy Lafleur alone.

That same day, in promoting to the position of magistrate Gaston Michaud, the lawyer who had given legal counsel to the Remparts, the Treasurer of the Quebec Provincial Bar had said to him: "I hope you will be the Guy Lafleur of the Quebec bench." In Quebec, Guy Lafleur had become a model, a metaphor and a symbol for intelligence and power.

There were many who attributed the immense success of the Remparts almost exclusively to Guy. Businessmen of all sorts began to take an interest in him. Prospective advertisers paid him constant court. Makers of skates, sticks, helmets, pads all offered to pay him enormous sums to wear their labels or logos. Everyone told him that his name was a veritable gold-mine, and that he should be taking full advantage of it. He was also made to understand, more or less subtly, that he was being underpaid and that he should demand a new contract from the management of the Remparts.

Among those offering to be his agent were Gilles Tremblay (a former Montreal Canadiens left-winger who had just retired the year before), Roland Mercier, then agent for Jean Béliveau and vice-president of the Canadian Amateur Hockey Association, and Ronald Corey of the Carling O'Keefe Brewery.

The businessmen of the area had understood that Guy Lafleur could be worth a fortune to them, and that he had to be treated well if he were to remain in Quebec. The big service clubs invited him to their dinners, congratulated him, showered him with honours and gifts. Les sportifs de Quebec, an association dedicated to economic regional development, even organized a subscription campaign to finance a big celebration at which Lafleur would be given a Corvette. As soon as he found this out, Paul Dumont had the individual concerned come to his office and told him that the management of the Remparts and Colibec were strictly opposed to this project.

Lafleur was stunned. A Corvette. The most perfect symbol of success, the most extraordinary toy a young eighteen-year-old could dream of having.

"I know it's hard to swallow," Paul Dumont told him, "but you have to understand, I can't permit it. No more than I can allow you to do advertisements for hockey sticks or skates."

"I'm ready to understand, but you'll have to explain a little."

"First, it goes against the regulations of the league, of the club, and of all amateur sport. Also, you're our captain. Your role isn't limited to making plays and scoring goals, you also have to contribute to the creation of a team spirit, and to serve as a model for it. You don't have the right to play the lone horseman, if you understand me. I want you to refuse to accept the Corvette, and I want you to tell your friends that you've done so. Otherwise I will be obliged to intervene, and I won't be able to do so nicely."

Evidently, Dumont was anxious that the team regulations be respected. But his decision was motivated by something else. He knew the danger complacency represented for a young athlete. "An athlete who is sated and content is always in danger," he used to say. And, according to him, the Corvette was a kind of mortgage drawn on the talent of the young prodigy.

"I'm not saying that you don't deserve it. You do. But I want you to deserve it more—ten or a hundred times more. For an athlete of your age what's important is not to have things, but to work towards them."

Lafleur, although he was visibly very frustrated, forced himself to say that he understood. But he couldn't keep from feeling resentful and angry. He had delivered the goods. He had even gone beyond what had been asked of him. Now he was being asked, in the name of so-called principles, to refuse all reward.

"I want to make a bargain with you," Dumont said. "At

the end of your final year with the Remparts, *we* will give you a car."

So Lafleur gave up his Corvette. But the voices he heard around him were disturbing. He had filled the Colisée, they said, and the Colibec owners were making a fortune with him; he should have a bigger piece of the cake. Finally, one March evening, he called Chouine at Thurso. Awkwardly, he told him he was going to have to get a professional agent. He was anxious not to hurt Chouine; he tried to explain to him that the stakes had risen and that now he needed advice from someone who knew the business side of hockey.

But Chouine was upset. He didn't mind Guy taking away duties that no longer interested him and that he'd always known he'd eventually have to give up. What bothered him was that he could feel Guy's embarrassment at the other end of the line, and that he was sure he had once more allowed himself to be manipulated.

Chouine was tempted to remind him of the conversation they'd had a few months ago while flying from Montreal to Quebec. When Chouine had said their paths would soon be diverging, Guy had replied that he would never get rid of him. But Chouine kept silent. Knowing Guy, he could be sure that Guy was also remembering that conversation. He wished Guy could have waited until his junior career was over to do without his advice. He knew that Guy must be getting a professional agent because he intended to demand that his contract be renegotiated, and he feared for his reputation.

For a while Chouine refused to go to Guy's games. Every time the Lafleurs decided to go to see the Remparts, he would make sure he was otherwise occupied. Guy, worried and hurt, would ask his mother, "Where is Chouine? Why didn't Chouine come? Is he angry?"

It wasn't until the playoffs, in April, that Pierrette Lafleur managed to convince Chouine to go watch the Remparts play at Sorel. It was an unexciting game, dominated by the Quebec team.

During the second intermission, Roland Mercier, Béliveau's agent, introduced himself to Chouine and smilingly announced to him that he was Guy Lafleur's new representative and that they were ready to go on strike to force Dumont to reopen his contract and give him the salary he deserved. But there was a snag. As vice-president of the CAHA, it wasn't easy for Mercier to represent a player who was a member of a junior league. So he had come to ask Normand Chouinard to work with him—in other words, to be his front man.

Chouine refused, and furthermore told Mercier that he found him in a situation of serious conflict of interest. He also denounced the idea of going on strike. In the circumstances, he believed it would be a dishonourable and dishonest step. During the third period, he was incapable of paying attention to the game.

The next day, without telling Guy's parents, Chouine notified the school that he would be absent, went to the Ottawa airport and flew to Quebec. At eleven o'clock he was in Paul Dumont's office, where he informed him of Mercier's plans.

"I'm the one who negotiated this contract with you, last summer. And I don't want this business to go badly for Guy. Of course, he is free to do what he wants, but I want you to know that I am opposed to the idea of a strike. I think the contract should be reopened."

It was agreed that the contract would be rewritten in June and that Guy's salary would be raised substantially. Moreover, he would be given a car at the end of his second year with the Remparts. If he accepted these terms, Guy Lafleur would become the best paid junior in Canada.

The next morning Chouine called Guy at Madame Baribeau's.

"I'm at the Motel Universel. I'll expect you for lunch."

He started by reminding Guy of the circumstances under which he had signed with the Remparts.

"Someone said that your signature was meaningless because you weren't yet eighteen . . ."

"I remember."

"And you replied that your signature was like your word. Might you have forgotten that?"

To Chouine's amazement, it turned out that Guy had no idea that his new representative was planning a strike.

"I don't want you to think that I'm trying to meddle in your affairs. But it's important to me that I finish properly what I started. I'm the one who negotiated your contract. I know Paul Dumont, he's an honest man. If anyone else had been acting for you, he never would have agreed to reopen your contract. That's why I went to meet him. He will offer you new terms. If they suit you, you can sign a new contract at the end of the season, in June. But I don't want to hear you moaning about it afterwards. If you sign, you sign. And you play."

Lafleur read the proposals. He was entirely satisfied. At eighteen, he was already making more money than his father had ever earned. And in a little more than a year, he would have his Corvette. And he would play in the NHL.

Meanwhile he had to deliver the goods. In the following weeks Lafleur would learn that it wouldn't always be easy.

• • •

Guy Lafleur made a point of pretending not to pay attention to his critics. But he always managed to know what people in Montreal were thinking or saying about him, what sorts of comparisons were being made between him and Marcel Dionne of the St Catharines Black Hawks, or Gilbert Perrault or Richard Martin of the Junior Canadiens.

He was especially interested in Dionne's totals. During the 1969–70 season, Dionne had been the top scorer in the Ontario league, with 55 goals and 77 assists for 132 points. Perrault had scored 121 points with 51 goals and 70 assists.

Now Guy Lafleur, with his 103 goals and 67 assists, had the impressive total of 170 points in 56 games. Mathematically, he had wiped out Dionne and Perrault. But for the analysts and statisticians of junior hockey, his record was

marked with an asterisk that pointed out the pitiful quality
of Junior A hockey in Quebec. It was claimed that had he
been playing in the Ontario league, the Remparts' brilliant
number 4 would certainly not have done as well, and that
therefore his records, all things taken into consideration,
didn't mean much. Even worse, some NHL scouts couldn't
be bothered to go see him play, since they were convinced
that Quebec junior hockey was inferior.

All this hurt Lafleur. A few days before the playoffs, it
was being openly said that he wasn't really a good hockey
player, and that there was nothing exceptional in what he
had accomplished.

He began to regret bitterly his decision to play in Quebec
rather than St Catharines or Montreal. He was being paid
well, but his hopes of a great career seemed doomed. And in
spite of himself, for a few days he was angry with everyone, including Filion and Dumont, and even Chouine and
his father, who had let him put himself in this position.
Maurice Filion noticed his sour mood. He listened to Guy,
who told him what he was thinking and voiced his
frustration.

"You have to straighten out your head, my boy. In a week
the playoffs begin. If your mind isn't right, you won't play
well, and the whole team will suffer. You most of all."

Lafleur was experienced enough to know that the
psychological condition of an athlete is almost as important
as his physical condition. He had to regain his equilibrium.
He forced himself to be happy, telling everyone how
pleased he was to be in Quebec. Bit by bit his bad mood
lifted. With his soul finally at peace (or almost), he began
the long and difficult playoffs.

The first task was to beat Drummondville. In spite of the
departure of Maurice Filion and Marcel Dionne, the
Rangers were still powerful and solid, a well-balanced
team. Next they had to overcome the Sorel Éperviers, a
painful and miserable task, and after them the Saint-
Jerôme Alouettes. By the end of March the Remparts were
the champions of the Quebec Junior A league. But the
hardest task lay ahead.

The ultimate goal of Junior A hockey in Canada is to win the Memorial Cup, for which the champions of the leagues in Quebec, the Maritimes, Ontario and the West compete. After having beaten the Port-Alfred National, champions of the Saguenay league, the Remparts had to face the Maritimes champion, the Charlottetown Islanders. Their players were known as fearless and terrifying fighters, whose bloodthirsty supporters had a passionate hatred for "frogs" and "stupid Frenchmen."

In all the North American junior leagues, play tended to be excessively violent. Fights would break out before, during and after the games, on the ice and in the stands. It wasn't unusual for spectators to throw coins, eggs, marbles, apples, boots, even chairs at the opposing players. The rivalries were often traditional and intense. The approach to the sport was very Manichaean: the home side was good; the other side was the evil invader, the outsiders who must be defeated. When, as in Charlottetown, ethnic rivalry was mixed in, the game became truly barbaric and merciless. On the ice, the players lived dangerously.

Rare was the player who managed to get through junior hockey without having all his front teeth and his nose broken, along with several fingers, a leg, an arm, some ribs. Guy Lafleur had already lost some teeth, and he earned his annual share of cracks, fractures and bruises. But, strangely enough, every time he was hit, his determination and daring only grew, as though his injuries were his weapons and his protection. Many players reacted in the same way, especially at the end of the long, embattled season. They threw themselves at the enemy lines, covered in cuts and bruises, practically unaware and unconscious of danger.

However, on April 12, intimidated by the loud and hostile crowd at the Charlottetown Forum, the Remparts lost the first game of their series against the Islanders. The arena was old and run-down, badly lit and poorly equipped. Though it held only 2,700 seats, 8,000 people were packed in like sardines. The second game was so violent that the referee, Jack Johnson, cut the match short by five minutes, called in the police and arbitrarily awarded the victory to the Islanders. Maurice Filion, the Quebec coach, had objected so strongly to the referee's partiality (fifty-nine minutes in penalties against the Quebec team) that he was thrown out of the game. One very good player, André Savard (who would later play in the NHL) was even jailed for a few hours.

In Quebec, these skirmishes heightened the interest and emotion surrounding the series. The three following games took place at the Colisée. On April 17, more than 14,500 spectators (in an arena that should only have held 10,000) awaited the Islanders in a state of near hysteria. Insulting banners were waved in the air and the crowd chanted, "Stupid spuds!" For the occasion, a song had even been composed to a popular tune:

> They are golden, they are golden!
> Hold on to your hats! Here come our Remparts!
> There's no one in the game who can frighten our
>   players!
> They are golden, they are golden!

Marcel Gagnon, the Colisée organist, had a repertoire of French songs that the public knew by heart and that he used as a sort of code. "*Y a des loups, Muguette*" (or "Here come the wolves, Muguette") meant an opposing player was approaching the Remparts' zone; "*J'ai pas tué, j'ai pas volé*" ("I didn't kill, I didn't steal") was played when a penalty was imposed against a player from the Quebec club.

The game turned out to be a heated battle, violent and hard-fought. The Islanders were soundly defeated, then beaten twice more in Quebec and finally definitively eliminated at home. Nonetheless, Guy Lafleur wasn't at his best during this series, even if he had made a large contribution to his side's victory. He was strained, tired, weighed down by the brutality and violence of these hockey rivalries.

Champions of the Quebec junior league, the Saguenay and the Maritimes, the Remparts now advanced to meet the winners of the powerful Ontario league, the Junior

Canadiens. This team had some excellent players, notably Richard Martin, Jocelyn Guèvremont and Gilbert Perreault, all players of brilliant promise who were "ticketed for the NHL."

For hockey connoisseurs, this series possessed a special attraction. It was once again Quebec versus Montreal and especially Guy Lafleur versus Gilbert Perreault. Their true mettle would finally be tested. For the first time, in a best of five series, the two heroes would be confronting each other.

The first two games were to take place in Quebec. The day that the tickets were put on sale, the Colisée was besieged by a crowd of more than three thousand who, while waiting for the box office to open, played chess, knitted, slept, read and practised their battle songs. Never, even during the reign of Jean Béliveau, had Quebec experienced such a passion for hockey. Never had a match raised so much expectation.

Perreault, dazzling, scored four goals and got an assist. Lafleur, playing well, registered two goals and two assists. In the following match, the Remparts began to falter. With the Remparts leading 6 to 3 at the beginning of the third period, it looked as though they might win, but they lost the game 9 to 7. In fourteen minutes the Junior Canadiens had scored six goals. Guy Lafleur, suddenly seized by total lethargy, was unable to gather himself. Once again the play slipped away from him. He was totally incapable of concentrating, of anticipating, of knowing the direction the play would take. He hated this trial by comparison that had been imposed on him. His limbs felt heavy and awkward. He wanted to do well, he thought of nothing else. But the player who thinks too much is paralysed.

The third game was in Montreal, May 3, 1970, in front of the most discerning and demanding hockey public in the world. That evening, the jam-packed Forum was more than ever charged with excitement. Summer was on its way, the weather was good, the game promised to be a battle.

Maurice Filion, heartbroken, could see before the match that Lafleur had been undone by his own nervousness. It was impossible to do anything for him. That evening he had to play one of the most important games of his young career. The Forum boxes were filled with NHL scouts, managing directors, coaches. They had come from everywhere to watch the best Canadian junior players, those who, in principle, would soon be playing in the NHL.

The Quebec Remparts lost 7 to 1. Guy Lafleur got only one assist. He made no notable checks, grave errors, spectacular plays. He didn't even receive a minor penalty. Every time the puck came to him he quickly got rid of it by passing it weakly to one of his teammates. The Forum crowd was puzzled and disappointed. Where were the uncanny fakes the Quebec writers had bragged about? Where were the thundering shots, the spectacular rushes? Where was the worthy successor of Jean Béliveau?

The only Rempart to sparkle was Jacques Richard. Several times he roused the crowd to loud ovations. But what could he alone do against Roger Bédard's team and an unleashed Gilbert Perreault? The huge Forum crowd chanted: "*Québec Pee Wee! Québec Pee Wee!*"

For the Remparts the game was a total, painful and unforgettable humiliation. Especially for Guy Lafleur who, like all the others, had to go to centre ice to congratulate the winners. The next day the newspapers carried a magnificent picture of Lafleur and Perreault shaking hands, heads bowed as though they were exchanging Japanese-style greetings.

Afterwards, going back to the dressing room, Lafleur, for the first time in his life, began to doubt his ability to play hockey. He had let himself be defeated by the pressure. He had played badly. On the ice, he had been unable to play his normal game. His mind had been elsewhere, up with those who were watching him from the boxes above. He hadn't been able to keep himself from imagining the thoughts of Roger Bédard and the others from the Junior Canadiens organization, who last summer had proposed that he join them: "Too bad for you, Guy Lafleur! If you wanted to learn how to play hockey, you should have stuck with us!"

Camille Henry, former husband of the famous Quebec show business star Dominique Michel, and once a brilliant, spectacular and admired player for the New York Rangers and St Louis Blues, was also at the Forum that night, as a scout for St Louis Blues coach Scotty Bowman. In the report he gave to his employer a few days later, Henry spoke almost exclusively of the Canadiens' centre, the extraordinary Gilbert Perreault. Like Jean Béliveau, Perreault was a native of Victoriaville and, also like Béliveau, he skated well and played intelligently.

"All of us, even old pros, can learn from this boy. He has developed a series of extraordinary moves. But don't dream about him too much, Scotty. He is so good that I would be surprised if you could afford to get him. And I'm not the only one to have seen him. Everyone here agrees he will be the hottest and most expensive player in next June's draft."

Not a word about Guy Lafleur.

A few days after the cruel defeat, before he had really recovered, Guy Lafleur met the directors of the Remparts to conclude the renegotiation of his contract. He was so depressed and demoralized that he would have agreed to anything, even a cut in salary. But Paul Dumont, a man of integrity, reminded him that even though he'd had some bad moments during the season, he was still the best player in the league. Thanks to him the Colisée was filled, and the Colibec shareholders were making healthy profits.

"All in all, I'm not upset that you're having problems. Up till now, everything's been too easy for you. You have to learn to deal with defeats. That's part of the game. Just yesterday Maurice Filion was telling me that you now have all the skills you need on the ice. Now you have to start working on the mental side of the game. You have to learn how to do everything, under any kind of circumstances. It's like singing. You can sing in your shower . . ."

"Yes, Monsieur Dumont, I know. I can sing like Caruso in my shower, but if I can't do it on stage, no one will ever know I'm a great singer. I'll always be a shower singer. You already told me that. Maurice Filion, too."

"You are a great player, Guy. But professional hockey is played in front of thousands, tens or hundreds of thousands of people. And where you're going, the NHL, you'll be watched by millions. You'll be constantly observed. Every time you make a mistake or hesitate, people will talk about it. You have to get used to it. The spotlight will always be on you, more than anyone else, because you are the best."

As agreed with Chouine a few weeks earlier, he offered Guy a much improved contract for the following year: a salary of almost $8,000, with possible bonuses of up to $4,000. And finally, a car of his choice, with a minimum value of $6,500, which he would receive in a year at the conclusion of the contract.

A few days later, Guy Lafleur went to the annual sports gala at the Château Champlain, presided over by Roland Michener, the Governor-General of Canada. The cream of French-Canadian sport, from the worlds of hockey, racing, boxing, skiing, was in attendance. Eddie Merckx, the great Belgian cycling champion who had won the Tour de France and the Tour d'Italie on several occasions, was named the outstanding francophone athlete of the year 1969–70. Serge Savard, the Montreal Canadiens defence-man, got the medal for the best professional French-Canadian athlete. And Guy Lafleur was proclaimed the outstanding amateur. Many, including Guy, were surprised that Gilbert Perreault, the brilliant Junior Canadiens centre who had single-handedly undone the Quebec Remparts, was not the winner of this award.

But Perreault, a good sport, had come to congratulate his rival. Engaging and curious, Perreault was genuinely interested in other people. He questioned Lafleur at length about his plans, the way he prepared himself for games. They talked about their craft as though they were old pros. Lafleur felt his confidence returning. The fact that this great player, this opponent who had dominated him, was now showing such interest and respect reassured him. When they parted, they each knew that they would soon talk again.

In the June draft, Perreault was taken by the Buffalo

Sabres. He was very pleased to be going to the United States to play. And he said so openly, which some considered blasphemy against the sacrosanct Canadiens organization that had nurtured him.

"I'll never forget what I learned here," he told the journalists, "but I prefer going to the States, because there I'll get plenty of ice time right from the beginning. Here I might have to warm the bench for two or three years, and that doesn't interest me."

As for Lafleur, he knew he wouldn't be spending much time on the bench during his next season with the Remparts. Everyone expected great things of him. Paul Dumont had warned him. For fame and glory he would have to pay the price.

• • •

Guy Lafleur was often called on to act as an official representative of the Quebec Remparts at formal dinners, charity campaigns, openings. He would be seen smiling at the side of carnival queens, members of Parliament, patrons of the arts; shaking hands with all sorts of dignitaries; having his picture taken with the mayor, a minister, a singer, an industrialist, a high-ranking Church official. At his request, his friend Jean-Yves Doyon almost always accompanied him. Though Lafleur protested that he hated these official excursions, he would always, with the help of Madame Baribeau, ready himself with the utmost care.

Everywhere they went, Jean-Yves Doyon noticed how skilfully his friend attracted and held people's attention, as though he'd been doing it all his life.

"Guy has a magnetic personality," he would reply when people asked him what sort of man the Remparts' star was.

Guy and Jean-Yves had become inseparable. During the hockey season they saw each other almost every day, listened to the same records, saw the same girls, and every now and then drove together to Thurso. If he was free, Doyon even went with the Remparts when they played away from home.

The first time he saw his friend's powerful magnetism in action was on the occasion of a sort of powwow organized in the Huron village of Ancienne Lorette by the promotion people from the Molson Brewery. Everything flowed towards Lafleur. Everyone wanted to be photographed with him—the chiefs, the children, the attractive young girls, the fat, middle-aged mothers, the visitors. And the photographers had eyes only for him. Every time he opened his mouth, everyone else stopped talking and listened. He had become a public personality. When he spoke, people laughed heartily at the least of his jokes. And Lafleur seemed to enjoy his position, while pretending not to notice what was going on.

The Doyon brothers had made a sort of tacit agreement with Guy. He could have his meals free, at any time. He could even occasionally invite guests to the Cendrillon. What did they ask of him in return? What you ask a magnet to do: to attract. The Remparts players, and also the players' parents when they were visiting Quebec, got into the habit of eating at the Cendrillon, not because Guy Lafleur had in any way solicited their presence, but simply because he was there. His presence alone had made the Doyon brothers' restaurant the Quebec meeting place for all the young athletic set and the Remparts' fans—it became the fashionable place, at the other end of the spectrum from the hippie cafés of Rue Saint-Jean and Old Quebec. Writers from *Le Soleil* or *L'Action*, broadcasters from CJRP or CKCV, got into the habit of interviewing Remparts' players or members of the organization at the Cendrillon.

"You don't really know your own power," Jean-Yves Doyon sometimes told him.

Lafleur was perfectly aware both of the importance of his image and of its vulnerability. For example, he was very careful never to be seen smoking or drinking a beer. If a journalist came into the restaurant, Lafleur was quick to stub out his du Maurier or pass it to Doyon or a waitress.

He always kept a very low profile and projected the modest image of a young man who respected law and order and was aware that he should set a good example. His task was all the more difficult because the times were completely opposed to such values. In the universities of Europe and America, students were giving themselves body and soul to the battle against the Establishment. The hippie era was in full swing. Common sense, popular wisdom, all the current ideologies were in favour of breaking down the traditional order and established authority, overturning the old values, breaking rules and taboos, questioning absolutely everything, including the changes that were already happening!

More or less consciously, Guy Lafleur had in this context developed an image and personality that were conservative, even reactionary. Of course he followed what was happening, but from a distance, cautiously. His hair was just a bit long. Jeans, which his generation wore on every occasion, almost as a uniform, Guy wore circumspectly. Especially since the day when he'd been wearing his jeans to go to an official Remparts dinner at the Château Bonne-Entente, and Madame Baribeau had told him to come back and dress like everyone else.

He had always liked fine clothes. As soon as he could afford it, he started dressing himself as he wanted, as a proper young man, in a classic style. Madame Baribeau, who shared his tastes, went with him to the stores on Rue Saint-Joseph or the shopping centres in Sainte-Foy. Benôit Boilard, owner of a haberdashery in Limoilou called Le Marquis de Brummel, came to meet Lafleur at the Cendrillon and got him to agree to make his first television commercial. Dressed like a fashion plate, Lafleur strolled through the store, smiling tensely and proclaiming that at Le Marquis de Brummel, the man of good taste always found what he needed to dress himself from head to foot. Boilard paid him in suits, shirts and ties.

Hockey players, unlike entertainment and film stars, didn't set fashion trends, though they did their best to follow them. But should a hero not himself oppose to the manners and morals of those around him? Should a hero not, above all, set himself apart? Lafleur, a conformist in his clothes as in his ideas, went counter to the iconoclastic ideology of his times and generation. Of course, the circles in which he moved were infinitely less progressive and reformist than the student world. Just the same, in hockey, as elsewhere, this was a time when everything was being questioned. Even those who ran junior and professional leagues had to adjust to new ideas.

Hierarchical direction was now disapproved of, and so coaches became more flexible and began to listen to their players. Gradually they relaxed their strict supervision and talked, instead, of self-discipline. Paul Dumont, who was extremely irritated by these changes, one day said to Maurice Filion, who was the target of the anti-authoritarian struggles of his players:

"We talk to the boys about self-discipline, self-this and self-that—they aren't even capable of behaving like human beings!"

The new demands began to have serious budgetary repercussions. All the players started to want personalized sticks, with this or that curvature of blade, a certain colour or brand. They demanded hairdryers in their dressing rooms. The paltry lunch once served in the bus after road games no longer satisfied them: now they wanted to be able to choose—ham or chicken or cheese sandwiches, apple or orange, Coke or 7-Up, Caramilk or Oh Henry! It was the triumph of unbridled individualism; the ego was king. The concept of team spirit, so important in hockey, was being seriously undermined.

In the middle of this psychedelic tornado, Guy Lafleur continued to demonstrate an almost servile respect for authority. Just as he had renounced the Corvette that Les sportifs de Québec wanted to give him, he sacrificed the privileges that his star status could have provided, and put his trust in men like Dumont and Filion, whose ideas he defended to his teammates. He appointed himself as champion of the established order, a position that sometimes drew sarcastic remarks from his fellow players.

For example, Jacques Richard informed Guy that he didn't know how to enjoy life. Richard was a decent and honest young man, but he smoke, drank, had the occasional joint and slept with women. That year, he had got one of his girlfriends pregnant. His pranks and adventures fascinated the other players. He presented himself as a hero—resourceful, hedonistic, seductive—the opposite of Lafleur. Lafleur fled from anything that belonged to the fashionable ideologies of the counter-culture, starting with drugs. Several times, in spite of himself, he'd caught their bitter fragrance at the entrance to the recreation centre or the cinema's men's room. Jean-Yves Doyon would say, "Do you smell that? That's pot." For Lafleur, such things were dirty, a bit frightening and to be avoided.

Occasionally he smoked a du Maurier or sipped a beer. But he never touched marijuana, or girls. His relationship with Roxanne Côté had become a chaste friendship. He had a sort of timidity or mistrust of the world of bars and night people. He might sometimes have liked to possess the elegant assurance of a Jacques Richard, but at the same time he was nervous of it.

Richard was not as prolific a scorer as Lafleur, but he was equally talented at setting up plays. He gave the Colisée crowd some moments of sublime artistry. And he had one thing Lafleur almost never had: contentment.

"That's what will finish you," Maurice Filion would tell him. "You're too easily satisfied with what you've got. Not Lafleur. Keep your eye on him. He's never satisfied."

When Guy had scored three goals, he wanted four. When he got four, he wanted a fifth. He never stopped. One day, five minutes from the end of a game against Trois-Rivières, when the Remparts were leading 8 to 1 and all the players and their coach had shifted into neutral, waiting for the game to finish, Guy Lafleur was still throwing himself at the enemy lines like a madman, as though they were playing overtime. Jacques Richard said, "Take it easy, we've won." But Lafleur didn't seem to understand why he should take it easy. He didn't play only to win, he played to score goals, as many goals as possible, and so he was never truly happy. Jacques Richard, on the other hand, like many players, lost all motivation as soon as the outcome of the match was settled.

Lafleur always showed up for practice before any of the others. If someone had observed a little mistake, or mentioned that he had a weakness somewhere in his play or skating, he would work to correct the fault, improve himself. There was never an end to it. If someone said he turned more sharply and quickly to the right than the left, a month later he would be turning better to the left than to the right.

This intensity and perseverance couldn't fail to impress the coach, who had never seen their equal in another player. And Filion was also pleased to discover that Lafleur was a team player. Sometimes, though, he went too far. How many times had he seen Lafleur reach the net with Brière, little Michel Brière, and pass to him instead of shooting? Filion had finally wondered if Lafleur wasn't just trying to make his teammates think he was a generous player. It was almost as though he were afraid of finding himself all alone, far in front of the others.

Some days, when Lafleur passed rather than shot, Filion angrily shouted:

"Guy, for Heaven's sake, stop diddling with the puck and making passes. For the love of God, shoot!"

Much was said about the speed of Guy Lafleur. In fact, he was both fast and elegant on the ice. There were others on the team who skated as well, but no one had his acceleration or his incredible ability to suddenly change speed. He would seem to be skating as hard as he could. Then, suddenly, with an amazing burst, he would skate even faster. That way he could get free of any defenceman in the league and almost always slide away from bodychecks. The players would charge him by evaluating his speed and aiming towards a place a bit in front of where he was headed, the way a hunter shoots a bit ahead of a duck or a rabbit in full flight. But Lafleur, seeing them on their way, would suddenly speed up or stop—the other player would find himself alone or crashing into the boards, in front of Lafleur or behind him.

The Remparts' team was much better balanced than it had been the year before. Maurice Filion had reinforced the lines of defence by taking on some big players. He had created a long-term plan for his team, the way they do in the good NHL teams. That way Colibec hoped the team would be able to survive the eventual departure of Guy Lafleur.

Guy had finally caught the hungry eyes of the NHL scouts. But he didn't like these experts watching him. The big crowd of hockey lovers—yes, any time. He knew how to excite them and bring them to the edge of hysteria. In the presence of his fans he was always happy and played well. But in front of the pundits, the strategists and the bigwigs, in front of the big league scouts and buyers, he felt totally awkward. He would soon have to get used to it. In September 1971 he would turn twenty, the age of eligibility for the NHL. During this second and last season with the Quebec Remparts, the NHL big-shots would be coming from everywhere to watch him at work. He would be judged, measured, compared with former and current players; reports would be written about him giving his statistics, analysing his assets, his faults, his style. Just the idea of all this examination horrified him; he didn't like to be watched this way.

"You have to get used to it," Filion kept telling him. "These things are part of your job. You have to be able to play naturally, even when you feel that people are watching you. You can do it. It's a matter of concentration."

Easy to say! Lafleur was always easily impressed and destabilized by the outer world. But Filion would not spare him. Ever faithful to his Spartan principles, Filion had decided never to make a secret of the presence of important people. He knew that the scouts would show up sooner or later, so he wasn't surprised when, on March 22, Punch Imlach, the Buffalo coach who had directed the Quebec Aces when Béliveau was there, dropped in to the Colisée. At the time, the Sabres were in the Third World of the NHL. Imlach desperately needed good players to compete against the old clubs who, despite the new regulations regarding recruitment, still had the best teams. Gilbert Perreault had strongly recommended to Imlach that he go watch Lafleur play in Quebec.

"He came to see you," Filion told Guy before the game. "Try to play well."

But Lafleur played badly, getting only an assist against the Drummondville Rangers. At least five players outshone him, skated better, played more energetically.

A few days later the American network, CBS, came to Quebec to do a documentary piece on the Lafleur phenomenon. In front of the cameras, Guy was paralysed. Jacques Richard stole the show. The CBS team went home to New York without any convincing images of number 4, but with explosive footage of his teammate, who performed so well that he became the focus of the show.

Claude Ruel said to Sam Pollock, managing director of the Canadiens, "The secret is to see without being seen. Like when you're hunting. If the deer spots you, he disappears. Same thing with Lafleur. He hasn't yet got used to civilization. If he knows you're out there, he's just a shadow of himself."

It was known that the stalwart Ruel, who had just ceded his place as head coach of the Montreal Canadiens to Al MacNeil and, with relief, had returned to his post as scout, considered Guy Lafleur the best prospect in junior hockey. Ruel often came to Quebec to see him play. Timid and ill at ease with the press, awkward with the players who derived a wicked pleasure from making fun of him, Ruel hadn't been able to establish his authority as coach. However, in finding and training young players he had no equal. And he had made up his mind about Lafleur. Now he had to sell him to his organization.

Of course, when Lafleur was told Ruel was there, he slowed down, made mistakes, skated poorly, scored little or not at all. Ruel took to arriving unannounced, without even telling his good friend Paul Dumont. He had thus seen Lafleur at his best several times, and was his ardent defender to Sam Pollock, the boss of the organization and the man reponsible for acquiring new players.

But Sam Pollock was slow to agree. He had carefully collated all the reports, rumours, observations and diverse opinions then circulating on the two big hopes of junior hockey, Guy Lafleur and Marcel Dionne. The members of his organization were still divided. Ronald Caron, having failed the previous year in his attempt to woo Lafleur, was now on the side of Marcel Dionne.

Dionne was a brilliant centre, intelligent, robust and well-balanced. He knew how to set up fantastic plays and had an impressive repertoire of moves and fakes.

Taller and sturdier than Dionne, Guy Lafleur had a thundering shot, a remarkable sense of anticipation, and also knew how to set plays in motion, how to make or gather in a pass while skating at full speed. But he had difficult periods; several times he had slid into deep and inexplicable slumps. He also sometimes seemed to be incapacitated by nervousness. Thus he was psychologically more complicated, perhaps more fragile, more introverted than Dionne.

Every time Ruel managed to convince Ronald Caron or Sam Pollock to come see Lafleur play, Lafleur would trip over his own feet at the blue line or stumble over his shadow.

One evening at the Forum, the Quebec juniors were playing a team of American all-stars. Pollock, Caron, the entire management of the Montreal Canadiens were there. Lafleur, informed by Filion that he would be keenly observed, was, as usual, frozen to the ice. It was as though, at some level, he didn't want to be drafted.

He was so happy in Quebec! He could almost have wished that the rest of the world didn't exist. The NHL was a North American league. It was huge, tough, violent. Everyone spoke English. It seemed to lack heart.

One day, in April 1971, just half an hour before the beginning of an important match against the Trois-Rivières Ducs, Paul Dumont spotted Sam Pollock in the hall of the Colisée, squeezed into the dense crowd, his ever-present felt hat on his head and his white handkerchief in his hand. At his side was Brian Travers, his chauffeur in those days.

Sam Pollock, a fervent Scottish Catholic, dreaded flying. So he spent his time with Brian, who drove him as far as Chicago, Buffalo, New York, Minneapolis, all the hockey cities of the continent. Pollock was the true presiding spirit of the Canadiens, without doubt the most powerful man in hockey, not only in Quebec but throughout the NHL. He was terrifyingly intelligent, an acute strategist. Shy and reserved, he was also a connoisseur and collector of Canadian landscape paintings and a confidant of the wealthy Bronfman family, owners of the Montreal Canadiens. It was said by those who knew that there was no negotiator more clever than Sam "the Trader" Pollock, also sometimes called "the Fox."

Brian Travers was the exact opposite. He was a lion, an exuberant, big-jawed Irishman who got along as well with the Rue Sainte-Catherine scalpers as with his friends in the police. Jack-of-all-trades for Maislin, the big trucking firm with close ties to the Forum, Brian knew all the backroom secrets of the Canadiens organization, while Sam knew the boardroom. Between them they saw all, knew all, could pull all the strings. Nothing escaped them.

Paul Dumont waved and started towards them, making his way through the crowd so he could give them tickets. Without saying a word Sam took a ticket out of his pocket and showed it to him. He rolled his eyes at Dumont, whose intervention had caused a stir in the crowd. Everyone was whispering Pollock's name and craning their necks to see him. Dumont finally understood that he'd just made an error. Pollock had wished to watch the game incognito, in order not to frighten off the prey named Guy Lafleur.

That evening, unaware that Pollock was there, Lafleur played a brilliant game, scoring three goals and getting three assists. But Paul Dumont saw little of it. He had positioned himself to be able to observe Pollock without being seen, in order to know his reaction to Lafleur. But Pollock, as always, was impassive. At the end of the second period he got up and walked straight towards Dumont:

"Paul, my decision is made."

With Brian at his heels, he left without staying for the third period. Sam Pollock was interested in junior players, but he didn't want to know anything about junior hockey. Paul Dumont was left perplexed and worried. The Fox had decided, but what?

He was 99 percent sure that Pollock had decided to draft Lafleur, but in this kind of game could you ever be certain? And there was nothing to ensure that when the next draft came, the Canadiens would be in a position to pick first and thus get Lafleur.

In fact, that evening Sam Pollock had been absolutely dazzled. Lafleur had played like a god. Stretched out on the back seat of the limousine, Pollock turned things over in his mind and congratulated himself.

Sam Pollock, the great artist, had no equal when it came to selecting, buying or trading players, the noble materials of the living sculpture that is a hockey team. At the controls of the Canadiens since 1964, he had won four Stanley Cups with them, and the way things were going, would probably have a fifth within a few weeks.

Nevertheless, his team was in a period of transition, an exciting but dangerous phase. This year there had been too many changes. According to the cagey Fox, success could only be assured by stability. A team that constantly changed its coach or owner, or who lost its experienced players too quickly, couldn't win. A new coach, Al MacNeil, had just succeeded Claude Ruel, right in the middle of the season. The players, as fragile and nervous as prima donnas, were undoubtedly much more upset than they appeared. Jean Béliveau, the captain and pillar of the team, would soon turn forty and couldn't be kept playing much longer. He had been wanting to retire for at least two years. Henri Richard had just turned thirty-five; his best years were behind him. John Ferguson was also talking about leaving. It was time their successors were in place.

Of course Sam had foreseen this crucial turning point, and during the past years had acquired some rookies who would be excellent players. But he lacked a really great player, someone who might be the heir to Jean Béliveau, an athlete who could shine not only on the ice but off it, someone of mythic stature, like Maurice Richard.

The sixties, otherwise so colourful, had been dull for hockey. The Canadiens had dominated the NHL, as much if not more than during the very exciting fifties. But they no longer had that flare, that irresistible passion that a man like Maurice Richard had been able to give them. That spring evening in 1971, at the Colisée, Sam Pollock had felt passion and electricity, and they had been unleashed by a nineteen-year-old player with an instinctive dislike of authority. Anyway, that is how Pollock explained his attitude. Lafleur played like a god in front of and for the crowd. But more or less consciously, he refused to do so in front of the big bosses when they came to observe him. The crafty Fox liked the deep-seated and innate rebellion that he had perceived in Lafleur. It made him likeable, sympathetic.

"We need someone like him. A player who plays for the people."

He had seen how the Quebec fans were captivated by Lafleur. The first thing that Maurice Filion had ever said to Pollock about Lafleur was, "You'll see, Sam, that boy will never do anything like the others." It was true. When he leapt onto the ice there was electricity in the air, magic.

"These things have no price," Pollock mused. "It's a gift from God. What do you think, Brian?"

As always, Brian took his time in replying.

"Me? I think you can't pass him up. You have to show him to Toe Blake."

"Toe Blake has seen him, believe me. Can you name a good hockey player Toe Blake hasn't seen?"

"What did he say about him?"

"The same as Ruel. That he's a complete player with a genius for playing hockey and for playing the crowd."

"And he's damned smart. Did you see what he was doing? He scored goals, but he also made unbelievable passes, even when he could have shot himself. That's what I call a generous player."

"Better than generous. I think he chooses to pass rather than shoot because he thinks it's the better option. In a fraction of a second he evaluates all the possibilities open to him, as if he saw the whole play at once. It's as though he has the whole rink in his head, knows every player and what he's going to do. I don't call that generosity—that's genius."

"If you want Lafleur, Sam, there's nothing in the world to stop you."

"But we're going to have to play it very carefully."

In principle, the Canadiens, the NHL's most powerful team, should not have had access to the best players in the next annual draft. The chances of Pollock acquiring Lafleur or any other of the most-desired players should have been infinitesimal. However, Pollock had thought ahead, and if everything went according to his plans, his club—the strongest, the richest, the best supplied with players—would have the first draft pick.

Two or three small points continued to bother him. In Quebec, where he was such a star, Guy Lafleur had fallen into the habit of using the media to express himself. He would talk about his problems, his expectations, his plans. He was often quoted, interrogated, polled by the journalists. He had got used to reflecting aloud and speaking very freely. Perhaps too freely!

Questioned about his plans for the future, he had declared that he had nothing against going to play for Montreal, but that he would not easily accept, as had Réjean Houle, Marc Tardif or Pierre Bouchard, all two or three years older than him, spending his first seasons warming the bench.

In fact, it was a Canadiens' tradition that rookies be pitilessly broken in so that they would fit the mould.

"I've spent ten years learning how to play hockey," Lafleur said, "not how to be a bench-warmer."

In short, he had allowed himself to publicly criticize the all-powerful Canadiens organization. He had said that he understood the choice Gilbert Perreault had made the summer before in going to play in Buffalo. Moreover, he was absolutely sure he would get a lot more ice time playing for an NHL club other than Montreal. Perhaps he would drink less often from the Stanley Cup, but his point totals would be higher and so would his salary.

The fact that Lafleur expressed his fears and let it be

known he wouldn't accept having his ice time constrained was enough to cool the ardour of certain members of the Canadiens' management. Like Ronald Caron, for example. But Sam Pollock liked Lafleur's show of impatience and his need to play.

In April, the Canadiens organization was still divided. If Marcel Dionne had been two inches taller, he might have had the clear advantage. He had been trained in Ontario junior hockey, which had the reputation of being much stronger than Quebec's. Lafleur, with his beginnings on the impoverished Quebec circuit, had demonstrated that he could be a big fish in a small pond, but how would he perform against the truly good players? That would be revealed during the playoffs.

On April 18, following the last game of the regular season, Guy Lafleur was given the car Colibec had promised him when his contract was renegotiated. A few days earlier, Paul Dumont had the cold sweats rereading the contract. It had stipulated that the car must have a minimum value of $6,500, but no maximum had been established, so that in principle Lafleur could have demanded a Rolls-Royce or a Lamborghini, which would not have pleased the owners of Colibec.

But Guy chose his dream car, the Corvette, a car that was responsive and symbolized the star or the playboy. Things got complicated, however, when Réjean Lafleur spoke out against it.

"I don't want my son hurting himself in an accident. Give him something else."

Reluctantly, Guy opted for a Buick Riviera, more conventional and a safer choice. On the evening of April 18, it was presented to him in the centre of the Colisée rink. It was a handsome, flaming red, as he had asked. Its licence plate was 4G4 444—his number and his initial.

This car was destined to cause him innumerable frustrations. Since the team rules didn't permit players to drive, Lafleur had to park his car in front of the house on Rue Benoit XV for almost a month, until the end of the playoffs. Eventually Paul Dumont weakened and allowed him to use his Riviera to get to the Colisée, three minutes away. Of course, Lafleur would take long detours. Sometimes Dumont would hear through the grapevine that the famous red Riviera had been seen near the Quebec Bridge or on Boulevard Tabot or the Grande-Allée. But he turned a blind eye. The series had begun and the Remparts had the wind in their sails.

They easily won the Quebec Junior A championship, then defeated the teams from the Saguenay and Maritimes, sweeping the opposition aside. In the Memorial Cup final they were pitted against the Ontario league junior champions, the St Catharines Black Hawks, whose team included the well-liked and celebrated Marcel Dionne, Guy Lafleur's main rival in the eyes of the Canadiens organization.

During the regular season, Guy Lafleur had shattered his own records: 130 goals and 79 assists in 62 games. Such statistics had never been recorded anywhere in organized hockey. With the series he would add 22 goals and 21 assists, for a total of 252 points in 72 games, an average of exactly 3.5 points (2 goals, 1.5 assists) per game. In two seasons with the Remparts he would have 233 goals and 146 assists, plus the points he would earn during the playoffs. This was clearly superior to Dionne's totals. But people kept saying the two records couldn't be compared, because they had been established in leagues with different levels of play. Finally, in these playoffs, the two players could be judged against each other.

On May 8, when each of the teams had already won two games in the best of seven series, the St Catharines Black Hawks came to the Colisée, where they were crushed 6 to 1. A brutal fight broke out following the game. One of the Ontario players injured a security guard. The crowd attacked the bus where the unfortunate losers had taken shelter, and the police, although reluctantly, had to protect them. During the following days, the Ontario newspapers talked about the brawl. The people of Quebec were called savage brutes, racists and bloodthirsty.

The Black Hawks, terrified, refused to return to Quebec

to finish the series. The Edmonton Oil Kings agreed to substitute for them. The crowd was civil to the Edmonton players, even applauded them when they first came onto the ice. Nevertheless, they were also demolished: 5 to 1, and 5 to 2.

For the first time in nine years the Memorial Cup returned to Quebec. It was one of the most rewarding evenings of Guy Lafleur's career. He had accomplished his mission. Just as he had once set out to get the Chamberland and Bilodeau trophies for his home town, he had now captured the Memorial Cup for his much-loved adopted city.

Lafleur had emerged victorious against Marcel Dionne. It seemed obvious to everyone that he would be the most sought-after player in the June draft. Everyone would want him—but who would get him?

• • •

June 10, 1971, a bright cool Thursday, was a day Réjean Lafleur would not forget. That day he took a holiday from his job at McLaren's, from his welding torch and his steel-toed boots, to go to Montreal with his son— the two of them wearing ties and in their Sunday best. Pierrette would be with them, but Chouine couldn't come; he had to be at school for final exams. But that was okay—on this trip there was nothing for him to do, say or negotiate.

They hadn't slept much, the three Lafleurs and Chouine. They had talked for hours, sitting around the kitchen table, drinking beer and coffee, until the girls, kept awake in the rooms above, shouted down that they'd like to get a little sleep. The sky was already growing pale when they went to bed. Four hours later, everyone but Guy was awake. Réjean Lafleur and Chouine took up the conversation exactly where they had left off, repeating the same things for the hundredth time—just what had to be said to Claude Ruel, what they should have replied to Ti-Paul, who was against the Canadiens, how they would negotiate with Sam Pollock, what sort of man Scotty Bowman was—nothing that wasn't about hockey and, more particularly, Guy's career.

From time to time Réjean went to the foot of the stairs

and shouted, "Guy, are you coming?" And groans and
squeaking springs were heard from above. "Guy, do you
want your mother to make you some eggs?"—"Guy, you
bonehead, it's going to be seven o'clock, will you get down
here?"

Finally Guy made his appearance, dressed only in jeans.
Without saying a word he pushed the screen door and went
out into the yard to stretch, bare feet in the wet grass.

"Guy, where are you going dressed like that?"

"Breakfast."

"Pierrette, make four eggs. Do you want ham, Guy?
Pierrette, give Guy three slices with his eggs. Do you want
potatoes? Suzanne, make your brother some orange juice.
Lucie, make the toast."

"I don't want toast, Papa. I never eat toast with eggs, you
should know that. I don't like bread."

"Don't worry. Lucie, make the toast anyway. I'll eat it for
him."

That morning of June 10, 1971, Réjean Lafleur was in a
dangerously good mood, happy, even though he had slept
little. The weather was fine, he was feeling good, he was on
holiday, he was going to Montreal to give his son to the
NHL. What more could a father want? Years ago, families
were proud to give their boys to God. The Lafleurs were
doing almost the same thing today. Their only son was not
putting on a robe, the way Brother Léo and the parish priest
might have wanted. Instead he would wear the uniform of
the Montreal Canadiens, the greatest club in the whole
history of hockey. It was a great day!

"Guy, this is the greatest day of your life, do you know
that?"

But Guy, never talkative in the morning, was even more
silent than usual. When his father or Chouine asked
whether he agreed with them about Pollock, Ruel, Jean
Béliveau or Scotty Bowman, he just nodded absently.

On the radio everyone was talking about Jean Béliveau.
The night before he had announced his retirement after
almost twenty years with the Canadiens. And about Scotty
Bowman, the team's new coach. Al MacNeil, Claude Ruel's
replacement, had barely lasted two months. Henri Richard

had forced him to resign by saying in front of the players that he was incompetent to coach the *"Tricolore,"* the Canadiens, because he didn't speak French. That was a few days before the playoffs began. Richard's diatribe had been followed by an unbearable silence. Even Jean Béliveau, who normally could calm people down and appeal for moderation, had not known what to say. MacNeil had understood Richard's accusation, because Richard had taken care to express himself in both languages. The players, heads lowered, avoided looking at poor MacNeil, who, not speaking French, could of course not reply. Despite this disruption the Canadiens had once again won the Stanley Cup, thanks to Richard, who scored in overtime of the final game. The next day Al MacNeil submitted his resignation, and Sam Pollock approached Scotty Bowman, who agreed to take the helm of the Canadiens.

It was an eventful spring for the Montreal Canadiens. A putsch, a resignation, retirements . . . and that was just the beginning. There were shake-ups to come, starting with those that would surely come from Scotty Bowman. A new coach has to establish his authority.

"Ti-Paul Meloche used to know him well," said Réjean Lafleur. "He's been in the Canadiens organization for a long time."

"What does Ti-Paul say about him?"

"Not much that's good."

"Yeah, but Ti-Paul has always had something against the Canadiens . . ."

"Anyway, the Canadiens are so strong that it would take a really bad coach to make them lose the Stanley Cup next year."

On the radio, they were talking about NHL expansion, with two new clubs in Long Island and Atlanta.

"Where is Atlanta, Chouine?"

"In Georgia. That's where Martin Luther King came from, the black preacher who got himself killed two or three years ago. Have you seen *Gone with the Wind*?"

"No."

"It takes place in Atlanta."

"And what does Atlanta have to do with hockey?"

"Nothing. But it's possible Geoffrion will be the coach of the new club."

" 'Boom Boom'?"

"Yes, monsieur. 'Boom Boom' Geoffrion."

"What a great idea! But I thought he lived in New York."

"Perhaps. But a man isn't a tree, he can move. You never thought of that?"

They wanted to leave early, but Guy dawdled. He changed his clothes three times. Then he put his jeans back on to use his shammy to wipe the dew off his Buick Riviera. He said there would be spots if he let the water dry by itself. Then he changed again. He had more coffee. Then he went up to his room, wondering if he had chosen the right tie. He tried on three or four others, then put the first back on again. His mother and sisters, whose advice he kept asking, didn't know what to say any more. Réjean started getting upset.

"Bring them all, you can decide on the way. Guy, are you trying to be late on purpose?"

Finally, at eight-thirty, they managed to get on the road—Guy at the steering wheel, his father beside him, Pierrette Lafleur in the back.

They were approaching Plaisance when Guy said, "I forgot my sunglasses." The sun, still low in the sky, was blinding. They went back to Thurso to look for his sunglasses.

Guy wanted to put on a different suit, but his mother told him, "Guy, that will do. We're already late. You're perfect as you are." It was after nine when they were again on Highway 148, heading for Montreal. The sun was already high. Guy pushed his sunglasses up on his forehead. At Plaisance he took them off and slid them behind the visor. Watching him, his father murmured sardonically, "Good thing we went back for them, eh Guy?"

Usually, when Réjean Lafleur drove with his son, he kept telling him, "Not so fast, Guy, look, slow down a bit, there's no rush." But this morning his warnings were unnecessary.

Guy was driving slowly, and let himself be passed by everything on the road—trucks, Volkswagens, motorcycles. It seemed that he really wanted to be late.

At Montebello his father asked him to stop so he could buy the newspapers. He came back to the car with *La Presse*, *Le Droit*, *Le Journal de Montréal*, the *Gazette*, the *Montreal Star*, *Montréal-Matin*, and three coffees, which they drank while Réjean read the sports pages aloud. Of course there was much discussion of the event of the day, the NHL draft at the Queen Elizabeth Hotel. There were long commentaries on Jean Béliveau's retirement. They said he had been one of the greatest players in the history of hockey, that he would probably stay with the Canadiens organization, that it was an enormous loss for the team, but that perhaps he would be replaced by the young Guy Lafleur, who would probably be drafted by Sam Pollock that very day. Marcel Dionne was also mentioned, and the strong points of both players were compared. While his father read, Guy wedged himself in his seat, behind the steering wheel, day-dreaming.

So, in a few hours he would be in the National Hockey League. The dream would finally become real. In other words, there would be no more dream—only reality, pure and simple. With more or less ice. And his friends would be far, so far away.

Réjean Lafleur and his wife were well aware that their son was nervous and upset. In a few hours he would be taking the most important step of his life. Réjean Lafleur, himself timorous by nature, instinctively understood his son's anxiety. At the Queen Elizabeth Hotel there would be too many people, cameras, microphones, spotlights, over-excited journalists who would throw themselves at him. And nothing was certain yet. Guy had an excellent chance of being drafted by the Canadiens, but so far they had nothing more to go on than the hypotheses, extrapolations and deductions of the journalists. Obviously Ruel and Pollock and all the Canadiens' scouts had seen Guy play dozen of times over the past years, but no doubt they had paid equal attention to Dionne. It was still possible that Caron had carried the day and that the Canadiens had decided to draft Dionne rather than Guy. That was one problem. And the draft was now surrounded by all sorts of new rules. Would the Canadiens be able to draft him? In principle, the strongest clubs weren't supposed to have the first choices, in order to allow those in need the chance to draft the best players.

But something else was on Guy's mind. He was feeling a wave of panic. Was this what he really wanted? Of course he was aware of his value; even if he was not drafted by the Canadiens, another club would take him. He wondered if that might not be better for him. The Canadiens organization, he knew, everyone knew, was a real grind. The army. Rookies were chopped into mincemeat, and after having been reduced to mush they were shaped into obedient slaves.

Now they were driving east on Highway 640. The traffic was unusually heavy for ten o'clock on a Thursday morning. For a good quarter hour it was bumper-to-bumper. Same thing on the Métropolitain. Decarie was even worse. There was road construction and a detour. Guy decided to take Rue Sherbrooke—like hundreds of other drivers. No one in the car was talking any more. At the Queen Elizabeth, the draft would soon begin. NHL President Clarence Campbell must already be making his annual speech on the state of the league.

"Guy, you'll have to speed up. We're going to be late."

"So what?"

"What do you mean, so what? What do you think the journalists will say when they see you're not there?"

"They'll write what they want, whatever. As always."

"Guy, it makes me angry to hear you talk like that."

"It's a farce."

"You'd better get one thing straight, my boy. You're going to have those journalists on your back your whole life. And if you don't treat them well, they'll get you back. They're powerful, they can hurt you."

For ten years Réjean Lafleur had been collecting and filing in his albums all the articles written about his son. He understood the growing importance of journalists to professional sport, and had developed a great respect for them. He wasn't well educated, read slowly and with difficulty, and his own writing was very awkward. But he had an intuitive appreciation of the power of the media. He could never bring himself to throw out the newspapers, even after he had clipped everything that had to do with Guy or hockey. It was his wife who had to gather them up and make them disappear. ·

While Guy looked for a parking spot, his father finished folding the morning papers. He had sorted the sports pages into a separate pile.

"Guy, open the trunk for me. I want to put my papers inside."

"Are you afraid they'll get stolen?"

"Guy, don't be stupid. I don't want the sun to turn them yellow."

The Queen Elizabeth Hotel was jammed with photographers. Guy and his parents were still on the sidewalk of Dorchester Boulevard when they started to shout: "There he is, there he is, that's Guy Lafleur." And they pounced on him, on the whole family, surrounding them and taking pictures from every conceivable angle. Guy, moving towards them, felt as though he were on the ice in front of a wall of defencemen. As the Lafleurs went into the hotel, the photographers moved with them, still taking pictures. They were all around them as they climbed the monumental stairway to the salons and meeting rooms. The tension that had been strangling Guy since the morning, since the day before, dissolved as though by magic with each step he took towards the main hall from which he now heard the sound of voices. He was walking towards the photographers, increasingly at ease, his mother and father behind him. And suddenly he felt good again, powerful, sure of himself, of his luck, of his future.

They were almost at the top of the stairs when they heard his name spoken in a loud voice—"Guy Lafleur"—with a slight English accent. There was a commotion from the hall, then the sound of clapping.

"The first choice of the Montreal Canadiens, Guy Lafleur."

It was the voice of Sam Pollock, whom they couldn't yet see. He repeated himself in English, then again in French. And Clarence Campbell added, in both languages: "The Montreal Canadiens have chosen Guy Lafleur." The people at the top of the stairway began to shout: "He's here, Guy Lafleur is here, look, he just arrived." Guy kept moving forward, the crowd opened before him, the welcoming crowd, which he penetrated slowly, with a kind of sensual pleasure of intense relief. As soon as he could see the entire room, and knew that he could be seen from everywhere, he stopped and waved. For a moment, he became the centre of attention. Then he noticed that he was alone. A space had opened up around him. His father and mother had stayed far behind, invisible in the crowd. Then he understood that from now on this was how it would be, that he had entered another world.

Gradually the attention turned away from him. Left to himself he could look around and take in what was happening around him.

There were fourteen numbered tables in the middle of the room, one for each of the clubs in the NHL. The New York Islanders and the Atlanta Flames, whose formation had just been announced, were not yet included. Above each of the tables had been posted the club emblem—the maple leaf of the Toronto Maple Leafs, the Indian in feathered headdress of the Chicago Black Hawks, the winged wheel of the Detroit Red Wings, the tricolour emblem of the Canadiens. The top management and scouts of the teams were sitting at these tables: hard, mature men, dressed in dark, conservative suits.

Guy saw a tall redhead he'd played against in Ontario during his Pee Wee, Bantam and Midget days. He nodded to him. Larry Robinson was also eligible for the draft. Like Guy Lafleur and many of the others, he was accompanied by his parents, country people who felt lost when they came to the big city. Larry turned to his father and said, "It's like a livestock auction, don't you think?" And everyone around burst out laughing, because Robinson's comment was on the money.

In the middle of the room were the buyers, the serious and anxious businessmen who surrounded the auctioneer, Clarence Campbell. Campbell ordered the herd to file past a group of attentive "farmers," the team spokesmen. And what Larry had jokingly called the "livestock" were stationed outside the enclosure. They were amateur players eligible for the draft, robust young men, still pimply, cramped by their muscles and their brand new suits, sweating, nervous, absorbed in their invocations and prayers:

"God, make them take me. I'll do anything they want. I'll go to bed at nine o'clock weekdays and Sundays. I won't drink, I won't smoke. I'll play with the heart of a lion."

The room was dotted with flowered shirts and gaudy ties. Long hair, which had been forbidden by most of the clubs, was gaining ground this year, along with moustaches and sideburns. Flower power was at its height.

In the big hall of the Queen Elizabeth, other general managers were announcing their choices. As soon as a player was drafted, a clerk wrote his name on a piece of cardboard which he dropped into a slot under the big board, opposite the logo of the appropriate club. The Philadelphia Flyers chose a couple of unknown players— Larry Wright from the Regina Pats, Pierre Plante from Drummondville. Then the New York Rangers took Steve Vickers. When it was Sam Pollock's turn again, he chose Chuck Arnason from the Flin Flon Bombers (right wing, shooting from the right side, like Guy, and born in the summer of 1951, also like Guy).

Six clubs hadn't yet had a chance when Trader Sam, the crafty Fox, was making his third choice of the first round: Murray Wilson of the Ottawa 67s (right or left wing, same age as Guy). And he still had three choices in the second round, which would mean that six of the first twenty-eight chosen were going to him. He picked up Larry Robinson along the way, and then eight lesser players, small fry he had no intention of putting on his team but who would be useful for trading. Not only had he succeeded in drafting the most desired players, but he had also harvested the greatest number, twelve altogether. All the other clubs had fewer than ten each. It was an injustice, totally unethical. The club that had the most and best players in the NHL, winner of the 1971 Stanley Cup, winner of ten cups in the past fifteen years, had just further enriched and reinforced its position. But it had done everything according to the rules.

The drafting of Guy Lafleur is one of the most extraordinary episodes in the history of the buying and selling of players within the NHL. It was not the first time the Montreal Canadiens had gone to great lengths to assure themselves of a player. In 1950, to obtain Jean Béliveau, they had bought the entire Quebec senior hockey league and integrated it into their network of farm teams. But to get Lafleur, Pollock had to work in the dark and prepare his trap without others knowing. It was only on June 10 that the businessmen and players of the NHL found out what had happened.

The preceding year the Canadiens had lost their traditional right to have the two best French-Canadian recruits. This step had been taken as part of a program to assure a better balance between teams, to give them all more depth, so that each would have a few solid defencemen and some good forwards. These steps were considered necessary to assure hockey's future as a North American sport.

Among the big team sports, hockey was then the poor cousin. The big leagues of baseball, football and basketball were much more competitive and infinitely better organized. They provided more drama, more exciting rivalries, and as a result had been able to make extremely lucrative deals with the television networks. The strategists of the NHL had therefore decided, in order that hockey not be left behind, that from then on the weakest clubs would choose first at the annual draft. This led to a strange race for the bottom of the standings, the big loser being assured of having the first choice when the following summer's draft was made.

In principle, at the June 10, 1971, draft, Sam Pollock, holder of the Stanley Cup, should have been the fourteenth to choose. But he had foreseen the problem. Two years earlier, in 1969, he made a deal with the Oakland Seals, a young, poor club, desperate for players. He had given them his first choice in the 1970 draft in exchange for their first choice in 1971.

In spite of this transaction, the Seals had remained weak, and Pollock was sure to be among the first to pick in 1971. But to be the very first, it was necessary for the Seals to finish the season at the very bottom, and the Seals no longer had any real interest in finishing last, since they had traded away the privileges involved.

To Pollock's dismay, they played quite well until Christmas, and it looked as though the Los Angeles Kings would finish last. That was when Pollock intervened. He lent the Kings three players in order to reinforce them. And so, three months later, the Kings having improved, the Seals again finished the NHL season dead last.

So, on June 10, 1971, Sam "the Fox" Pollock was the first to speak and was able to choose Guy Lafleur. That day everyone, even his victims, had to recognize Pollock's genius. But many hockey lovers were disappointed. The powerful players the Canadiens had just acquired threatened to upset the precarious equilibrium that had been preserved since the NHL's expansion. Without real rivals, the Canadiens might become monotonous and boring. The suspense and the battle for supremacy would be gone.

The management of the Canadiens wasn't worrying about such problems. Claude Ruel, standing up beside the Canadiens' table, waved at Guy and lifted an empty chair above his head. Guy Lafleur slid between the tables and came to sit with his new owners.

He had just made his entrance into a grand institution, and a magnificent story, of which he was already the hero.

SECOND INTERMISSION

●

FOR MORE THAN three-quarters of a century, an army of statisticians has, with fanatical care, maintained the immense edifice of statistics in which can be found the undeniable and eternal truths of the Montreal Canadiens. Everything is there: number, height, weight and age of the players; their records; the frequency and duration of each of their appearances on the ice; the number of shots, points, goals; number and length of the penalties against them; the injuries they have suffered. All the individual or collective exploits, victories and defeats have been duly recorded, dated, timed and ratified, and compared to those of other teams and other players.

There exists, therefore, in these figures, a perfectly objective history of the Canadiens in which everything is rigorously precise. And then there is the legend—unique, incomparable, a media masterpiece, an impressive collective creation.

The Canadiens date from 1910, the year of Halley's Comet, whose passage that year—as in 1986—created a sensation. It was the epoch of the last geographic conquests and of the great sporting exploits that enthralled the public. The American explorer Robert Edwin Peary planted the "star-spangled banner" on the North Pole, reached after four attempts. Robert Scott, the Englishman, and the Norwegian Roald Amundsen set out for the South Pole, which would take them a year to reach. The French aviator Louis Blériot crossed the English Channel, from Calais to

Dover, in thirty-seven minutes. In England, work on the *Titanic* was begun. In the streets of large North American cities, the first Model-Ts were appearing. In Canada, mainly in Quebec and Ontario, great fortunes were being made from the exploitation of our natural resources, especially mines and forests. The future was radiant, the present fascinating and exciting.

At the time there was the Ontario Professional Hockey League (OPHL), which included teams from Toronto, Guelph, Brantford and Berlin (renamed Kitchener after the Second World War). There was also the ECHA (Eastern Canadian Hockey Association), which had a varying number of professional clubs. In northern Ontario and western Canada there were, in addition, a good number of very active clubs, subsidized by big mining or forestry companies, or even the railways. Some years there were as many as twenty clubs from different leagues competing for the Stanley Cup, including the Kenora Thistles, the Renfrew Millionaires, the Dawson City Klondikers and many more. Cities that today would have trouble putting together a decent Bantam team were then enjoying a boom in lumber, silver or gold and found themselves playing for the famous trophy.

Montreal already had four professional clubs: the Shamrocks, the Nationals, the Victorias and the Wanderers. The Wanderers had dominated the eastern league for years and pitilessly crushed the clubs from the other leagues that had the misfortune to confront them. In 1909, they won the already well known Stanley Cup for the third consecutive year. That was when everything began to go badly for them, not because the team faltered, but because the hockey money-men could no longer agree.

There were then two arenas in Montreal, the Jubilee (with 3,500 seats) located in the east end of the city at the corner of Moreau and Sainte-Catherine, and the Westmount arena (6,000 seats) at Wood and Sainte-Catherine, quite near the present Forum.

The small Jubilee arena belonged to a man called P.J. Doran, who was also the owner of the powerful Wanderers.

Because the owner of the arena got 60 percent of the gate receipts and the teams divided the rest, Doran, of course, wanted the Wanderers to play in his own arena. It is also easy to understand why the owners of the other teams of the eastern league—the Ottawa Silver Sevens, the Quebec Bulldogs and the Montreal Shamrocks—wanted nothing to do with this small arena. The larger Westmount arena was more profitable for them. In addition it had heated dressing rooms, a good restaurant and a better ice surface.

When the 1909–1910 season began, there was an impasse. On November 25, in the face of Doran's refusal to have his club play at the Westmount arena, the owners of the three other clubs met at the Windsor Hotel and decided to dissolve the eastern league as it was constituted and found a new league, the Canadian Hockey Association (CHA). The CHA took in two new teams, the All-Montreal and the Montreal Nationals, but refused to allow in the Wanderers. The Wanderers, who currently held the Stanley Cup, now found themselves all alone without a league to play in.

That same evening, Ambrose O'Brien, son of the wealthy M.J. O'Brien who owned railways, lumber companies and two hockey teams in the Ontario league, went to the Windsor Hotel hoping to get a CHA franchise for the mining town of Renfrew. The CHA owners laughed in his face. Furious, O'Brien was leaving the hotel when he met Jimmy Gardner, one of the Wanderers' directors. Bitter, disappointed and humiliated, Gardner had just found out that his club had been excluded from the CHA. Gardner and O'Brien decided right there and then to found a new league. They already had three clubs: two in Ontario and one in Quebec.

"Also," said Gardner, "we could have a fourth made up exclusively of French-Canadian players. That would create a good rivalry. And we would have a league that was truly national in scope."

This idea of racial rivalry in sports was in the air. The same year, on July 4, 1910, in Reno, Nevada, Jack Johnson became the first black world boxing champion when he knocked out Jim Jeffries. By boosting the enthusiasm of black fans, his victory unleashed a series of violent racial confrontations, some of them leading to deaths. Boxing became widely popular; it became more than just boxing, more than just a sport.

O'Brien and Gardner got together with Jean-Baptiste "Jack" Laviolette. Born in Belleville, Ontario, Laviolette owned a tavern called Jack's Cage on Rue Notre-Dame. This tavern was a gathering place for Montreal's francophone hockey players. Excluded from the professional leagues, they had made up an excellent team of amateurs who played exhibition games all around the Montreal area.

A few days later, on December 2, 1909, the three men met at the St Lawrence Hotel on Rue Saint-Jacques, and there they founded the National Hockey Association (NHA), which would eventually become the National Hockey League. Two days later they announced that a franchise had been granted to a new Montreal team, "the Canadiens." Jack Laviolette, who was well known in French-Canadian hockey circles, was given the task of recruiting the players and organizing the team. The Montreal Canadiens were born. They were given blue and white as their colours. January 5, at the Jubilee arena, they played their first match, against the Cobalt Silver Kings, and were badly beaten.

O'Brien and Gardner had let it be understood that as soon as the arrangements could be made, the direction and ownership of the club would be handed over to French Canadians. However, since the Canadiens quickly showed themselves to be very profitable, no one was in a hurry to make the switch.

During the early years, 80 percent of the players had francophone names. On the souvenir photos, however, everything was in English. At the museum of the Montreal Forum is displayed a mosaic of photos showing the 1915–1916 club: "The Canadian Hockey Club Incorporated. The Stanley Cup Champions. Champions of the World. Montreal, Canada." Sixteen players, of which twelve were francophones. Four owners, all anglophones.

The team itself anglicized rapidly, but the idea of its distinctive character persisted. The strategy of the club, which seemed to have an innate sense of marketing, always insisted on the ethnic particularity of the Canadiens, on the fact that this team's players weren't like the others. During the thirties and forties, when the outstanding star was Howie Morenz, an anglophone born of Swiss parents in Mitchell, Ontario, his bosses asked him to speak with a French accent to the American journalists, and let it be understood that Morenz was a typically French-Canadian name. This was meant to add fuel to the legend of the Canadiens, the only NHL club that still has a name designating a nation, a race, an ethnicity.

The recipe has proved itself in other domains. The greatest club in baseball history also has an ethnic name—the New York Yankees. And basketball's most prestigious club calls itself the Boston Celtics. At the time the team was established, and until it was replaced by the word "Québecois," the word "Canadien" designated the whole of the French race in Canada, the "Canayens." And the H within the C on the club's logo was a reference to the "Habitants," the French-Canadian settlers and farmers.

In fact francophones were gradually being excluded from the team. The Maroons, Montreal's other NHL team, had just been dismantled and the Canadiens obtained their best players. In addition, the almost exclusively anglophone directors did not maintain contact with Montreal's francophone community. And unlike today, there weren't scouts who kept track of every minor or junior player.

At the beginning of the forties Paul Stuart, a francophone Montrealer, was in charge of Montreal's junior leagues. They played on the rinks of Parc Lafontaine. He was offered the position of coach with the Junior Canadiens, the farm club of the Montreal Canadiens, and was prepared to accept, but on the condition that the club encourage the development of young French-Canadian athletes. He was refused. So Stuart stayed at Parc Lafontaine, in minor hockey. Nevertheless, he did manage to draw attention to a young player of exceptional talent, a boy from the north of the city, the ferociously tough Maurice Richard.

As soon as the bigwigs saw him at the Verdun arena, they understood that here was their chance to make themselves a lot of money while returning some lustre to the Montreal Canadiens who, despite the players acquired from the Maroons, hadn't won a Stanley Cup for twelve years. The Canadiens played poorly and had no French-Canadian stars with which the public could identify. When Richard started to play regularly, in 1943, there were many more English players than French on the team.

In 1944–45, as Hitler's Reich foundered, Maurice Richard made his sensational entrance into the legend of the Montreal Canadiens. There he would shape for himself one of the great roles of French-Canadian mythology. During that whole first season he shared page one with the Allies. As they liberated Europe, Richard was establishing an incredible record: fifty goals in fifty regular-season games. Richard was burning up the league.

Maurice Richard had always dreamed of playing for a hockey team made up exclusively of French-Canadian players. He carried this imposing and disturbing vision with him all his life, an impossible dream that he couldn't give up: an army of twenty players (six heavy and sturdy defencemen, twelve speedy and clever forwards, two unshakeable goaltenders) trained and driven on "Canayen" principles, a feudal host surging out from Montreal and crushing everything in its path, from the Atlantic to the Pacific, from the St Lawrence to the Rio Grande.

What a magnificent and outrageous notion. This tribal and primitive idea of hockey is somewhere in the heart of every Québecois fan. A dream in reserve. A dream on ice. They know it's crazy, racist, that it will never happen, that it's just a dream of going on the warpath . . . but, in the end, isn't war what hockey is? Or isn't it what we have in the place of war?

Like the rest of his generation, Richard had a Manichaean vision of the world, and an ethnic vision of hockey. He never would have played for the Toronto Maple

Leafs or the New York Rangers or the Chicago Black Hawks. He had entered the NHL at the height of the Second World War, when the idea of patriotism was not to be laughed at. He didn't distinguish between life and hockey, between asphalt and ice. He was the first hockey player whose art went beyond the arena and whose deeds became, especially in the heart of French Canada, symbolic and allegorical.

In 1953, in the column he wrote for *Samedi-Dimanche*, Richard openly accused Clarence Campbell, the NHL president, of partiality and racism with respect to French Canadians. No one, even professional journalists, had ever dared to state such brutal truths.

But Campbell had all the power. Richard had to apologize and give up his Sunday column. The French-Canadian people's champion was defeated by the WASP in the most public way. A *Toronto Telegram* cartoon pictured him as a schoolboy writing on the blackboard, under the furious eye of a fat monocled teacher: "I will not call Mister Campbell a dictator."

Two years later, on the eve of the 1955 playoffs, Campbell got his revenge. Following a brawl during which Richard hit a referee, Campbell suspended him for the rest of the season (as had been expected) and also for the entire playoffs—a move that had not been expected, and was never accepted as just. The Montreal fans saw this presidential gesture as an unacceptable insult.

Thanks to Richard, the pride and soul of French Canada had become identified with the Canadiens. By going against them and taking from them any chance of winning the Stanley Cup, Campbell had placed himself on the side of the enemy. He was seen as the *de facto* spokesman of WASP Canada, in all its arrogance and contempt. Throughout French Canada the reaction was extremely violent. On March 17, while the Montreal Canadiens, without Richard, were playing the Detroit Red Wings at the Forum, the angry crowd went on a rampage, breaking store windows and destroying cars and buses.

That night, it is said, marked the beginning of the Quiet

Revolution, the movement that, during the sixties and seventies, would turn every institution—social, cultural, religious, political and economic—inside out.

Five years later, when Richard left the club, 60 percent of the players were francophones. And they were the best, the "Flying Frenchmen": Jean Béliveau, Bernie Geoffrion, Jacques Plante, Claude Provost, Maurice and Henri Richard, Jean-Claude Tremblay, Jean-Guy Talbot, Marcel Bonin, Armand Pronovost, Phil Goyette, Albert Langlois. The French-Canadian people saw themselves reflected in these men. They had faith in them. They were aware that with them, due to them, something unique was happening. A story, their own story, was being written. A conquest was beginning. And it was being spoken about all through North America; it was visible, victorious, vengeful. Richard's dream had never been so close to being realized as in 1960, and it never would be again.

Richard's rebellion had been broken. First by Clarence Campbell, then by the organization of the Canadiens themselves who, later, excluded him from all the club's activities and decisions. The people of Quebec discovered that their greatest hero was powerless and had been accorded no respect, that, in the final analysis, the Montreal Canadiens did not belong to them.

Jean Béliveau knew, better than Richard, how to keep the peace with the powers that be. There was nothing in him of the rebellious hero or the man in conflict with himself. He was content to be a great hockey player, an elegant man, a pure sportsman. His actions and gestures never created social upheavals comparable to those that Richard could unleash. On the contrary, he was always the epitome of law and order, a centre on the ice and a man of the centre, the agreeable and reasonable man in charge of public relations for the Montreal Canadiens organization. In the history of hockey, Béliveau's period of supremacy, the 1960s, is one of the more colourless chapters.

Nevertheless, throughout that decade the Canadiens dominated the NHL, winning the Stanley Cup one year out of two, which is just as often as during the intense and exciting 1950s. But they had become merely a hockey team, certainly the best in the NHL, but without the emotional and mythic charge Maurice Richard had given them. Everything ran smoothly, with no conflict, no drama and little passion.

That was the situation when Guy Lafleur arrived, June 10, 1971.

THIRD PERIOD

●

HE HAD WOKEN up at dawn and couldn't go back to sleep. Too much was swirling about in his mind: dark forebodings, regrets, worries. The Canadiens' training camp was two days away. He would have to be in good condition, not only physically but also psychologically. He had to get rid of these feelings of sadness and nostalgia that had been weighing on him since he'd left Quebec two weeks ago.

They had thrown a wonderful party for him at the Cendrillon. It had been a beautiful summer evening, warm and soft. For the first time in his life he had got drunk and, though he was normally timid and awkward with women, he had flirted with every woman there, spoken openly to all of them, said over and over again to his Quebec friends that he would never forget them, that there was no one in the world he loved more than the people of Quebec and that the prospect of leaving them was breaking his heart. All night he had wallowed in his drunken sadness.

He had even come close to making a terrible mistake. At two or three in the morning he'd wanted to telephone Eve, beautiful Eve. Jean-Yves Doyon had talked him out of it. Eve was married. For several months she and Guy had been having a dramatic and complicated affair. She had taught him beautiful things: how to speak of love, how to make love. Some days she told him that, if he wanted, she would leave her husband for him—he had only to "say the word." But he kept silent. He was afraid. He liked her well enough—"yes, maybe I love you"—but there was something else in his life, hockey, and it was more important and more demanding than love. The great career waiting to be filled with fantastic deeds seemed more of a challenge than an adventure of the heart. Guy tried to explain but Eve, obviously, was in pain. And the pain of a woman terrorized Guy. So he distanced himself even further.

But the night of the party at the Cendrillon, he felt he was ready for anything. He wanted to call her, to tell her that he loved her, that he needed her. They would have gone to a hotel somewhere in Old Quebec and they would have made love all night.

They had never managed to spend a night together. Eve didn't want to. As she said, "If I leave for the night, I leave for good." Guy, also, was unable to stay out all night. Madame Baribeau had often warned him: "Never force me to lie." He himself had such a horror of lying and such a great respect for this lady, his "second mother," that he never wanted to embarrass her in any way. But on that evening all of these problems were far from his thoughts. He didn't want to be alone. He needed to have a woman with him, to have Eve at his side.

"Be careful, Guy. Think about what you're about to do. That woman loves you for real. You could destroy her life."

That had cooled him off, because deep down he knew that he did not want to spend his life with Eve. Moreover, he was no longer his own man. Having signed with the Montreal Canadiens, he had to be serious and prepared, to be in control of himself, mind and body.

A few days later he left for Thurso. He knew that he would probably never see Eve again, but he had convinced himself that this was the right thing, that the affair couldn't continue. The idea that he could destroy the lives of this woman and her husband was unbearable to him. He envied men who went to bed with women casually. His own affairs were always so torturous and complicated. Perhaps it was because, in a way, he didn't really want them. Love represented an inconvenience, a distraction that might prevent him from realizing his dream of becoming a great player. Or maybe it was just because he didn't know how to take the first steps.

Eve had come to him, she had taught him the acts and words of love. He had only to let himself be taken. He had made no promises, but he had never said no. He had let Eve think what she wanted, day-dream about trips they would make and their life together. Gradually he had come to feel imprisoned in his own silence, in a future that she was invading and furnishing to her taste. He began to wonder if all women inhabited the lives of their lovers in this way, taking possession in the name of love, making their plans, planting their dream gardens, building their houses, imposing a new order.

By leaving Quebec, he was putting an end to this doomed liaison. He would never forget the beautiful Eve, and he was filled with remorse, but it was finished.

He spent two weeks in Thurso. Two weeks of doing nothing. He would do a little jogging in the morning, find a partner for tennis in the afternoon, or drive alone through the sparkling Laurentian summer. Everyone in town was glad to welcome their hero. He couldn't go out onto the streets of Thurso without hearing his name called out. He could almost have gone into the corner grocery or the hardware store or the pharmacy, helped himself and left without paying, and they would have said to him, "Thank you, Guy, come back soon!" He couldn't go into the bar of the Hotel Lafontaine without being offered a drink, by the management or any one of the other drinkers.

Sometimes he saw the boys he'd known when he played Pee Wee and Bantam. A lot of them worked at Maclarens or Singer; they would be workmen all their lives. They came to talk to him, looked at him with warmth and envy, listened to him, congratulated him. They all knew he was rich. The signing bonus the Canadiens had given him, $55,000, had been in all the papers. This was almost five times the salary of a skilled worker, almost ten times the salary of a labourer. And he would get his salary, too: $25,000 a year. He would travel, he would be on television, fame and women would be his.

Though these workmen, old friends, were desperate to buy him a drink and show him their affection, Lafleur couldn't accept, nor did he dare offer. He didn't want to be ostentatious about his money. Everyone knew and said that he was rich; he alone acted as though he still didn't know. He was even thinking, he told Chouine, of trading his Riviera for a smaller car because it "guzzled too much gas." Chouine knew Guy wanted to show him that he hadn't changed, that he had the same worries as everyone else, and that he, too, had to watch his money. Chouine had smiled. He now had a girlfriend, a teacher, and he was going to marry her. Soon he would be leaving Thurso. He and Guy would see each other only occasionally. Guy *had* changed, like everyone, but more than everyone else. His mind and spirit were elsewhere. He had already moved on.

Everything was going extremely well for Guy; he had only one problem. Since he was terrified of appearing to be a snob, he played the extrovert, turning his shyness into friendliness. If someone called his name in the street, Guy would stop, cross the street if necessary, ask about his health, his work, his family. Doing this also made him feel trapped, but in a kind, comfortable way.

He had gone to meet Scotty Bowman in Montreal, and had found Bowman cold and distant. But when his father asked him about Bowman when he came back, Guy said, "He's very polite. He knows what he's doing."

"I knew you'd tell me that."

"In that case, why did you ask me?"

"Just to see if you had changed."

Réjean Lafleur knew his son almost never spoke ill of anyone. When he had a criticism to make to someone, he spoke directly to the person, bluntly and without kid gloves, as timid people often do when they've made up their minds to speak out. But unless there was a crisis, it was always difficult to know what Guy thought about other people. He accepted people as they were.

The Canadiens organization had given Elise Béliveau,

the cheerful and elegant wife of the beloved Jean Béliveau, the task of helping the newcomers find and furnish their apartments. Guy, trusting her judgment, was willing to take whatever apartment she suggested, provided it had a good view and was on the south shore.

She found him an apartment in Longueuil, on the fourteenth floor of the brand new Iberville Towers, near the Jacques-Cartier Bridge. The river view was very attractive: Île Sainte-Hélène with its apocalyptic remains of Expo 67, La Ronde with its lights, its ferris wheel, its fireworks, and in the background the city with its steel-and-glass buildings, its mountain and its sunsets. He hadn't chosen to live there for the landscape, but because it was close to Highway 138, and the road leading back to Quebec City.

Whenever he had a chance, he jumped into his Buick Riviera and made for Limoilou to see his friends. For him, Limoilou was his real life, his only life—Limoilou, the Cendrillon, the Doyon brothers, his teammates Brière and Richard, the forbidden Eve . . .

Because the Iberville Towers apartment wouldn't be ready until mid-September, Elise and Jean Béliveau had kindly invited Guy to live at their place, in Boucherville. So he found himself that morning in the house of the man who had been the idol of his childhood, and who still intimidated him as much as ever. At five in the morning he was wide awake, in spite of the absolute silence, the clean and comfortable bed, the fresh air that rose from the river. He was thinking about the training camp and this new team of battle-hardened players in which he would have to find his place. He was also worrying, even more, about the medical exam he would have to take the following week.

For several days he was sure that he'd noticed his heart had an irregular way of beating. It seemed loud, much too loud. When he was in bed or a quiet room, he could hear it all the time. It was always getting louder. Boom! Boom! Boom! He had come to believe he might have something wrong with him, an illness or anomaly that the Canadiens' doctors would be sure to discover. And they would declare that he couldn't be allowed to play professional hockey.

He got up quietly, so as not to disturb Jean and Elise, sleeping upstairs. He got dressed and walked on tiptoe into the huge living room. Through the windows he saw the river, above it the red clouds of daybreak. He looked at the statuettes, the plaques, the trophies—an Art Ross, a Hart, a Conn Smythe—the expensively framed photos of Béliveau in full flight in the uniform of the Senior As, of the Montreal Canadiens, photos of him with Elise and the children in front of the Eiffel Tower, or in London or New York . . . On a coffee table there were some souvenir photos taken the summer before on the occasion of Béliveau's fortieth birthday. Elise had organized a party with friends and relatives, some Canadiens players and some people Guy didn't know, people from the real world, at ease and sure of themselves.

He contemplated the serene and opulent order that reigned in the household of his idol. He thought about his career—classy, successful, unmarred by mistakes or lapses in judgment. And he thought about his own, still virginal, an emptiness to be filled. What would it be like? What sort of player would he become in twenty years? It seemed as though others had decided for him, burdened him with all sorts of responsibilities and tasks. For two years the journalists had been describing him as a second Jean Béliveau. But would he one day have the calm assurance and serene strength of the man who was sleeping upstairs? And his heart was still beating. Too loud. Boom! Boom! Boom!

Lafleur had been put under tremendous pressure. A few days earlier, they had still been talking of giving him sweater number 4, Béliveau's number, and also that of two of the greatest players in hockey history, Newsy Lalonde (who had just died at eighty-three) and Aurèle Joliat, who at seventy still went skating every winter on Ottawa's Rideau Canal. Three legendary men whose equal he was supposed to be.

The journalists presented Lafleur as the legitimate heir of this prestigious dynasty, the guardian of the glory and soul of the Montreal Canadiens, the one who alone could assure the continuity, perpetuate the tradition, lead the club out of the darkness into which it would sink without truly great stars. In fact, the Montreal Canadiens had almost always had their electrifying superstar—Howie Morenz, Maurice Richard, Jean Béliveau—men whose talent and aura dominated the team. Would Guy Lafleur be the next? In the papers, whole pages were filled with hopeful predictions—he would be a saviour, he would fill the Forum, he would stamp the decade of the seventies as Morenz had stamped the thirties, as Richard the forties and fifties and Béliveau the sixties. For a nineteen-year-old young man, this burden was terribly heavy. Sometimes it gave him wings, but often it weighed him to the ground.

Jean Béliveau, known as a man who gave good advice, who twenty years ago had himself arrived in Montreal from Quebec preceded by fame and expectations, counselled Lafleur to take a different number.

"Don't try to be a second Jean Béliveau. Be the first Guy Lafleur. Take a number and make it your own."

It wouldn't necessarily be a lesser burden. But at least, if things didn't work out, he wouldn't disappoint.

He went for a walk along the river. When he came home it smelled so good inside the house that something inside him collapsed. Timid and happy, he sat in the big kitchen and had breakfast with the man he admired most in the world. Four eggs, bacon, cup after cup of coffee.

Jean Béliveau always talked to Guy about very serious matters, not directly about hockey, but about the way he should conduct his career, about the fact that his first years would probably be the most difficult, about the patience he would have to develop, about how he would always have to show respect for the team.

With Guy Lafleur, Jean Béliveau was very paternal.

"If you ever need to talk, come see me and I will try to help you."

And after having told him about some of the high points of his career, Béliveau added, "You'll see how quickly it all happens."

• • •

On September 11, Guy Lafleur went for his medical exam.

The doctors were astonished by his heart. But despite his fears, they showed no sign of being worried. They were absolutely astounded. Guy Lafleur had the ideal athlete's heart. At rest it beat less than forty times a minute, the same as the celebrated heart of Eddie Merckx, the champion Belgian cyclist, who was then considered by sports doctors to be a medical marvel. Also like Merckx, Guy Lafleur had unusual recuperative powers; that is, after a violent and prolonged effort, his cardiac rhythm returned to normal very quickly. His musculature was well developed, he was flexible, amazingly strong, his reflexes were quick and sure. He was one of the most perfect hockey machines ever seen in the Canadiens' clinic. After his examination, as though a spell had been lifted, Guy Lafleur stopped hearing irregular sounds from his heart.

That day he went to sit alone in the players' room, a closed and sacred place that common mortals were never allowed to enter. It was a sort of grotto hollowed out of the enormous mass of the Forum. On the walls were pictures of the heroes who had preceded him: Dickie Moore, Bernie Geoffrion, Jacques Plante, Aurèle Joliat, Newsy Lalonde, Maurice Richard . . . They were all there, these demi-gods who were watching him and seemed, for his benefit, to be declaiming "Flanders Fields," John McCrae's great war poem that Dick Irvin, the Canadiens' head coach from 1940 to 1955, had posted—in both languages —above this gallery of photos: "To you from failing hands we throw/The torch; be yours to hold it high!"

He was willing to carry the torch. He wanted to, with all his heart. But the battery of publicity surrounding him was beginning to weigh him down. Jean Béliveau had left, but there were still many star players, both defencemen and forwards. What need had the Canadiens of a saviour? What could Montreal want of him?

A week later, September 18, 1971, he played his first game in a Canadiens uniform, number 10, his Pee Wee number. It was a pre-season match against the Boston Bruins. He wasn't given much ice time, but he managed to get two assists. And the journalists, who had been following him closely since the beginning of training camp, praised him in their articles: he skated extraordinarily well, he knew how to be aggressive, he had a unique ability to anticipate the play, his shot was hard and accurate; in sum, he was all that had been promised.

He was flattered but worried—grateful for the attention but uncomfortable under the magnifying glass. He began to understand that he was expected not only to score goals, but to score them brilliantly. The Montreal public wanted a show, they wanted magic! That was what he was supposed to deliver.

He had as yet done nothing more than attend training camp and already everyone was talking about him. Even the intellectuals and the artists. *Maclean's* magazine put his picture on the cover with the headline, in big red letters: "A star was needed." Why a star? Guy asked himself. The variety-show artists could declare that he was a star and possessed of a magnetic charisma, but such claims had nothing to do with making him a better hockey player.

Victor-Lévy Beaulieu, a young pipe-smoking writer with a big beard, long hair, jeans and plaid shirt, had come to interview him. He had talked to him about hockey, but also about things he knew nothing about—politics, rock and roll, labour unions, feminism, the trial of the territorists who had kidnapped Pierre Laporte, the sociological role of stars, what he thought of this and that. How was he supposed to deal with all this? Were Robert Bourassa, René Lévesque, Robert Charlebois asked to play hockey or run a four-minute mile? Why should he, Guy Lafleur, have all the answers, know about everything, be able to do everything?

On September 20, 1971, two days after the game against Boston, Guy Lafleur turned twenty. "Twenty on the twentieth, it's your lucky year," said his friends who had come from Quebec to celebrate with him. They had brought a huge cake with twenty candles that they gave to him in a restaurant on Sainte-Catherine. This time Guy stayed sober. He was even one of the first to leave. He was serious, but also happy and excited.

His first season with the Canadiens was respectable but not outstanding. Expectations had been so high, however, that everyone was more or less disappointed. If any other rookie had scored twenty-nine goals and thirty-five assists in his first NHL season, everyone would have shouted his praises. In fact he was the fifth-highest scorer on his team and the twenty-eighth in the league. But Guy Lafleur was expected to be more than good, he was expected to do what had never been done before.

His rivals, drafted by less prestigious NHL clubs who were infinitely more generous with money and ice time, had finished with better point totals. Marcel Dionne, who was playing with the Detroit Red Wings, got seventy-seven points and Richard Martin, of the Buffalo Sabres, seventy-four. In certain circles people were already starting to whisper that perhaps Sam Pollock had made a mistake, that he might have been better to set his heart on Perreault, Martin or Dionne.

Claude Ruel was indignant. "When Lafleur scored 130 goals with the Remparts, everyone said it was because he wasn't playing with good players. Now it's Perreault and Dionne who aren't playing with good players, but every time they score a goal you praise them to the skies. You're forgetting that Lafleur is playing with the world's best. I tell you, he is a great player. You will see that I'm right. It's just a matter of time."

What Ruel didn't dare say openly was that Lafleur didn't get as much ice time as Dionne and company. The Canadiens had several excellent centres and right-wingers, veterans like Cournoyer, Henri Richard, Lemaire, Mahavolich, and even Larose and Houle. There could be no question of leaving these men on the bench. They had proved themselves and earned their ice time by the sweat of their brows. Guy Lafleur had not.

Because of this, the people of Quebec City hated Bowman, Pollock and all of Montreal. To this city they had given their best, and it didn't even know how to recognize the true value of what it had received. He was being left on the bench, like some unimportant rookie from an American college.

The Québecois felt they had been swindled, as did Guy's

fans from Thurso. But a lot of them still came to see him play at the Forum, on Saturday nights, and they would go to say hello to him after the game.

One fine evening, while they were waiting for Guy to emerge from the players' room, they spotted Scotty Bowman. Someone, a lawyer well known in the Thurso area, spoke out loudly: "That one should have stayed in St Louis. No one would have missed him." Scotty Bowman turned towards them. He had clearly understood. Born and raised in Montreal, a star with the Junior Canadiens before being badly injured during a game, Bowman spoke fluent French. But he didn't reply. He just gave them an icy look, while grinding his jaws, pushing his chin forward several times, in a characteristic gesture. Then he shrugged his shoulders and walked away. During the following weeks, as though to thumb his nose at his detractors, he gave Lafleur even less ice time. Lafleur couldn't talk to him about it. Such things weren't done. In signing with the Canadiens he had taken a vow of complete and blind obedience.

Bowman had decided that Guy Lafleur was a born centre. He put him on a line with Pete Mahovlich and Yvan Cournoyer. During practices they created a sensation. Bowman had triumphed. But Lafleur found the responsibility of playing centre—starting plays by passing the puck to Mahovlich and Cournoyer—difficult to bear.

Saturday, October 10, during his first regular season game in a Canadiens uniform, he seemed frozen. But two weeks later, October 23, in Los Angeles, while he was going in behind Pete Mahovlich, Mahovlich left the puck for him and Lafleur, with a powerful slapshot, put the puck past Gary Edwards, the Kings' goalie. Everything had happened so quickly that he was even more surprised than the goalie he had just fooled. He showed no reaction, not a smile or a wave or a bow to the crowd, the way players usually do when they've scored a goal and want to celebrate. But big Pete Mahovlich came back to him and punched him affectionately. Then he grabbed Lafleur's arm and, laughing, turned him towards the crowd.

There were other goals, other well placed passes,

intelligent and original plays. But Lafleur found that he wasn't really comfortable playing centre. Rather than changing his position, Bowman put him with Réjean Houle and Marc Tardif, on a less important line that spent less time on the ice.

In December came the ultimate humiliation: Lafleur was loudly booed by the fans at the Montreal Forum, the best informed hockey fans in the world. He had missed some good passes and inopportunely broken up some plays that he hadn't understood. So the public was disappointed, and they began to say that he was perhaps not, after all, a great player like Jean Béliveau.

There began to be a certain amount of malicious talk about favouritism. Supposedly, the Canadiens organization was so eager to have its traditional francophone star to satisfy its fans that it was ready to impose Lafleur no matter what the cost. An American journalist wrote that if Lafleur had been called John Smith, he would probably already have been sent to the Canadiens' farm team.

Of course Lafleur was aware of this talk. He became sullen and spoke to no one, not even his teammates. He was always the first to arrive for practice, then he worked with all his strength. But he stayed alone, in his own world. That was when two very different players decided to befriend him.

First there was Pierre Bouchard. He knew what it was to warm the bench and only get on the ice for a few minutes a game. He had been drafted by the Canadiens organization in 1965, when he was seventeen, and had been left to cool his heels for five years with the Junior Canadiens before being invited to join the big team. And since then, his ice time had been parsimoniously measured out.

Pierre was a good companion, warm-hearted, easygoing, generous, spiritual, who liked laughing and making others laugh, and was known for his tremendous sense of humour. Even when he was most depressed, he had the courage to laugh at his own expense. He taught Lafleur to express his feelings, to show his discontent, to laugh at himself, to see the good side of things. Most of all he helped him remember that there was more to life than hockey.

He taught him to play cards. Lafleur didn't really like playing cards, but enjoyed the company of the other players. The friendship Pierre Bouchard brought him was comforting. Bouchard introduced him to his friends and family. His father had a restaurant on de Maisonneuve where they got into the habit of getting together after games. Pierre Bouchard had great respect for Lafleur.

"You have talent, a lot more than I do. You'll break out of this situation. Ruel is right, it's just a matter of time."

The other player who moved towards Lafleur was Pete Mahovlich, one of the club's best scorers, twenty-five years old, left-wing, six feet five inches tall, two hundred and fifteen pounds, imposing and intrusive, a big talker, sometimes a bore, excessive in everything but enormously generous. He had decided to take young Lafleur under his wing. Often he replied to journalists in Lafleur's place, presenting himself as his mentor. Lafleur, who hadn't yet mastered English, and who, even in French, sometimes found it difficult to express himself, let himself get involved in Mahovlich's games. Sometimes he felt uncomfortably trapped in this friendship, but he submitted to Mahovlich's slaps on the back and sarcastic remarks. After every game and practice session Mahovlich would, in front of everyone in the dressing room, give his critique of Lafleur's performance. Lafleur never knew how to react or what to say. Pete Mahovlich always talked louder than anyone else. And he often finished his commentaries by demanding that Guy agree.

"Well, young man, is what I just told you true or isn't it?"

"Yes, Pete, it's true. You're right."

"Your passes are too soft."

"Yes, Pete."

"You have to give them a bit of zip, right?"

"Right, Pete. Okay."

In his heart, Guy was absolutely certain that one day he

would put Pete in his place and get him to shut his mouth. That, too, was just a matter of time. But gradually he began to like him. Mahovlich was the only player who had ignored everything the journalists had written about Lafleur "the Saviour." He didn't feel it necessary to flatter him, nor, like the others, to close his eyes to all his mistakes. Lafleur began to respect Pete for his candour.

Guy was having trouble understanding Scotty Bowman. The man was absolutely imperturbable and impenetrable: "the Iceman." He gave his orders, wanted them to be carried out without question, explained himself to no one, never praised, seldom reproached, never consulted. Guy Lafleur, used to working in close collaboration with men like Madden and Filion who trusted him, consulted him and listened to him, was perplexed and totally bewildered by Bowman.

But Sam Pollock and Claude Ruel were not losing their confidence in Lafleur. They had noticed that every time something bad happened to Lafleur, he eventually reacted in a spectacular way. For example, on December 17, a few days after he had been so cruelly booed at the Forum, he scored three goals, his first hat trick, against the Vancouver Canucks.

And Guy had found his best partner. More than Houle or Tardif or Mahovlich or Cournoyer, it was Jacques Lemaire. He didn't know how to explain the bond between them, but it was something like music, a perfect and total harmony. Sometimes it seemed as though the two of them were alone on the ice against the enemy, who they eluded, one after the other, passing the puck back and forth with incredible accuracy. Not only did Lafleur always know where Lemaire was, he even knew where he would be, when he would shoot. He could always guess and anticipate his play. He discovered a pleasure in playing he had never known with anyone else. It became so exciting that when Bowman sent them onto the ice together (along with Houle or Cournoyer or Tardif, it didn't really matter) Lafleur had a completely new fear: he was afraid that the magic wouldn't happen.

But every time, they found it again. It was as though they had always played together.

Off the ice they never talked about the powerful feeling that existed between them, out of superstition and the fear that words would destroy it.

But Bowman was constantly juggling his lines. How could he not have noticed that they worked infinitely better when they were together? During the Christmas holidays, Guy had realized that, apart from his friendship with Pierre Bouchard and the idyllic moments with Lemaire, he wasn't really enjoying playing for the Canadiens. He was bored to death, spending long lonely hours in his apartment watching the river flow and the sun set behind Mount Royal.

In February, on a free Saturday evening (the Canadiens had played an afternoon game against the Chicago Black Hawks) he attended the International Pee Wee Tournament in Quebec. As soon as it was announced that he was in the crowd, everyone in the Colisée rose to their feet and gave him a huge ovation. So, the people of Quebec had not forgotten him. They still loved him. They still trusted in him.

Watching the little Pee Wees move clumsily on the ice, he thought nostalgically about the good times he had known, a century ago, in minor hockey. Then he'd had nothing to worry about and there was ice as far as he could see, ice given to him and not measured out. That evening, sitting beside Paul Dumont, he understood that he was now forever cut off from his childhood. He had become a grown-up. And he realized that things would no longer take care of themselves, the way they used to. He would have to take himself in hand, make decisions, assert himself, do battle. He could no longer count on anyone but himself. Until now, everything had been given. Now he would have to take. To learn how to take.

After the game he went to eat with Paul Dumont, Maurice Filion and a few others at the Aquarium, a well-known restaurant in Old Quebec. They talked late

into the night about the big subject in the world of hockey at
the time, the giant draft that had just taken place (on
February 12, 1972) at the Royal Coach Inn in Anaheim,
close to Los Angeles. The World Hockey Association,
founded by the visionary eccentric Gary Davidson, had
drafted more than a thousand players, including Valeri
Kharlamov, the Russian, and the veteran Gordie Howe, the
greatest scorer of all time, who had decided to make a
comeback. The World Hockey Association had decided to
compete with the NHL. The geography and economy of
North American hockey was about to be re-made.

Dumont was furious. According to him, this "madness"
would kill hockey. First of all junior hockey: the WHA was
going to draft eighteen-year-olds, so the junior leagues
would soon lose their best players. The NHL, in order to
compete, would also have to draft the younger players.
Consequently the quality of its hockey would also
deteriorate.

"Maurice Richard is right," said Dumont. "He understood what was happening right away. In his day you saw
the hundred and fifty best players in the world, the best of
the best. Today, with expansion and that stupid WHA,
you're talking about the best two or three thousand players.
Hockey will never be the same."

But that evening, there was another subject of conversation at the Aquarium. A Toronto lawyer, Alan Eagleson,
had suggested to the directors of the WHA clubs that they
might be able to draft Guy Lafleur, if they wanted to put
together a good club in Quebec. He pointed out that
Lafleur had been under twenty years old at the time he had
signed with the Canadiens and that, therefore, his contract
was probably not valid. Pure speculation, of course, but
with enormous consequences. The NHL owners, already
far from sympathetic to the WHA, were outraged. Not only
were these fanatics draining the life-blood from junior
hockey, they were also trying to take players from the
NHL.

Lafleur was also shocked. At the first opportunity he
announced to the journalists that he had no intention of

going back on his decision, and that he found Alan Eagleson's allegations hurtful and annoying.

"I don't see how that ignoramus I've never met in my life can think I'm the type to go back on my word!"

However, he also added that when his two-year contract with the Canadiens was over and he had duly fulfilled his engagements there, he would be happy to play in Quebec, provided that the right offer was forthcoming. Lafleur's statement did not go unheard. Some Quebec businessmen had established a corporation with the objective of obtaining a WHA franchise. They had even found a name for the new club, the Nordiques, and some players, all Québecois, had been approached. Maurice Richard himself would be part of the new organization, along with the former premier of Quebec, Jean Lesage. The old dream of a truly Québecois club might finally be realized. But a star was needed. And they had decided to try for Guy Lafleur.

In the meantime, he would have to play out his contract with Montreal. Lafleur wasn't always happy there, but at least he could see light at the end of the tunnel. In a year and a half he could be back in Quebec. In his heart he had already said yes to the new Québecois club, and everyone knew it.

Reading the papers on May 17, 1972, put Sam Pollock in a very bad mood. A report was given of the press conference held the day before at the Chateau Frontenac in Quebec to announce the formation of the Quebec Nordiques of the WHA. The presence of many journalists and numerous personalities from the world of sport was noted, and in the front row of most of the pictures accompanying the articles was Guy Lafleur, the Montreal Canadiens' number 10. In all of the photos he was wearing a broad, relaxed smile that Sam Pollock had never seen before. Obviously, the boy was perfectly happy and functional when he was in Quebec, and unhappy and awkward in Montreal.

The Canadiens had just been defeated by the Boston Bruins in the Stanley Cup final. Montreal was disappointed, both in Guy Lafleur and Scotty Bowman, two men

Sam Pollock had imposed on the organization. Against the truly great players who had lined up for the Bruins, led by Bobby Orr and Phil Esposito, poor little Lafleur had not really held his own. Lafleur, thought Pollock, had everything that Boston's heroes had, and more. Except desire. In Montreal he didn't really have the desire to win and be the best. All year long he'd acted like an unhappy exile. Now, in all the newspaper pictures from May 17, he was glowing, he had the look and the smile of a conqueror, a champion. Sam Pollock believed it was because Lafleur was in Quebec. And because the Nordiques organization had made Lafleur happy by their offers.

But that had nothing to do with Lafleur's state. Guy Lafleur was smiling because, for the first time in his life, he was in love. Sam Pollock couldn't have known it. Lafleur himself was still unaware.

• • •

When he first got to Montreal, Guy phoned Limoilou almost every day. Sometimes he spoke to Madame Baribeau, other times he called the Cendrillon and would talk to the waitresses, the clients, the chef, the dishwasher, Lorenzo or Jean-Yves Doyon. "When are you coming?" he would ask. "Tell me what you're doing."

Whenever Doyon had the time, he would make a trip to Montreal. And when Lafleur had time off, he'd jump into his Riviera and get together with the gang in Limoilou. Madame Baribeau had told him he would always have a room at her house. He would bring her flowers, perfume, sometimes a bottle of wine.

But the Canadiens weren't too happy about these excursions. Even Jean Béliveau thought he should tell Guy, "You can't play in Montreal if your heart is in Quebec." Deigning, for once, to break his silence, Scotty Bowman made Guy come to his office, looked him in the eye and said exactly four words: "Get yourself together, Guy."

Sam Pollock was also worried. He knew Lafleur always drove very fast. He also knew that he'd had an accident on Highway 20 near Saint-Apollinaire. It had happened on a Monday morning, while he was driving Madame Baribeau back to Quebec, where he was planning to spend the day. Realizing at the last second that the left lane he was driving in was blocked due to construction, he had braked suddenly, then executed a perfectly controlled skid. But the car behind him had run into the Riviera. Nothing serious.

"You were lucky," Béliveau told him. "We can't afford the luxury of losing you, Guy. Sam Pollock wishes you'd stop going to Quebec, or at least go less often."

Lafleur hated Montreal. He was suffocating there. He didn't feel at home, either in the streets or on the ice. He spent evenings all alone at his apartment listening to Barbra Streisand or Mireille Mathieu, writing poems and being bored. He lit candles and then watched them melt down in the darkness.

Just as in Quebec he had first made friends with the personnel at the Colisée and the Cendrillon, in Montreal his first friends were the maintenance staff of the Forum and the superintendent at Iberville Towers, a Monsieur Riverin, a big, good-natured man who often invited Guy to have a coffee or share a meal with him and his wife. The Riverins could see that Guy was totally bored. They would say to him, "Go out! What are you waiting for? There's a city full of girls and they're just waiting for you!" But he didn't know where to go. Riverin lent him a passkey that gave him access to the swimming pool and the gym, and when he had the choice Lafleur preferred to work out there rather than at the Forum.

One day, Riverin came to tell him that a girl from Quebec had just moved into the building, on the eleventh floor, a good-looking girl, alone, about twenty years old, very classy, seemingly unattached.

"If I were you," he told Lafleur, "I'd go get a better look. Her name is Lise Barré."

"Lise Barré? What does she do?"

"She's an air hostess."

"Then I know her. She's Roger Barré's daughter."

"Another reason to go see her. If you already know her, the ice is broken."

But things weren't so simple. Lise Barré was the daughter of a rich man. Everyone in Quebec knew her father, a big businessman, a shareholder of the new Nordiques and a General Motors dealer. One day, when he was playing for the Remparts, Guy had gone to see the cars on display at Barré Automobiles. The owner himself had come to shake his hand and talk with him. Roger Barré was an affable and cheerful man who put everyone at ease. While they were examining the Corvettes, a girl had appeared on the mezzanine, just above them. Roger Barré had made the introductions: "Guy, this is my daughter, Lise Barré."

Lafleur had looked up. From where he was standing he had an excellent opportunity to admire her legs. A little embarrassed, he gave her a big smile. But she had been very stand-offish. In any case, that was how he remembered their meeting. While all the salesmen and secretaries had been excited by the presence of Guy Lafleur, already a well-known star in Quebec, she had hardly looked at him. Lafleur had found her snobby and stuck-up, and didn't have any great desire to go see her. He didn't want to get the same treatment again.

"You know," Riverin said, "three-quarters of the time people play the snob because they are shy."

"Not necessarily. My father is shy, but no one would ever call him a snob. And the same goes for me."

"You should at least go see her, Guy. You have nothing to lose just going to say hello. Tell her that if she ever needs anything, she can count on you. If, for example, she wants to go to Quebec you'd be glad to drive her."

After a few days, Lafleur resolved to pay her a visit. She welcomed him politely and offered him a drink. They talked about Quebec, about cars, about hockey, about Roger Barré. They quickly became good friends and got into the habit of going swimming together. But despite what Riverin had thought, Lise did have someone in her life, a man she saw occasionally and about whom Lafleur knew little. Lise was both curious and talkative, but she didn't much like talking about herself. Unlike Guy, she was very happy to have left Quebec. She wanted to live in Montreal, in Paris, in New York, to travel to all the countries in the world. That was why she had become an air hostess. She liked big cities and living in hotels. And in fact she was often away.

One Saturday evening in spring, after a game at the Forum in which he had played very well, Lafleur rang her doorbell. No answer. Her flight must be late. He used the passkey Riverin had given him and went inside. He opened himself one of those little bottles of cognac they give on airplanes, and sat down in an armchair to leaf through some magazines while listening to music. When she came home a few hours later, Lise Barré found him asleep. In effect, she had just penetrated a territory that Guy Lafleur had appropriated for himself, the way, a few hours before each game, he would take possession of the rink. Without her knowing it, he had slipped into her life.

They talked about everything and about nothing. At three in the morning, Lafleur said goodnight and went to his own apartment to sleep, without even kissing her on the cheek. In the months that followed they were almost always together: in the swimming pool, at the movies, in restaurants, sometimes in Quebec. He thought about her constantly, and she about him, but they never kissed or talked about love. They were crazy about one another, even though they pretended not to be in love. Their lives had been transformed. No longer did Lafleur feel like an exile; instead, he had the shining smile and the air of a conquering hero that had so worried Sam Pollock on May 17.

One day, a short time after she had finally broken up with her boyfriend, they had an argument. Lafleur was in her apartment. She was on all fours, cleaning the floor after dropping an egg. He had said to her that she was a bit overweight and that if she wanted to go out with him, she'd better slim down. Lise, angry not because he'd accused her of being fat but because he claimed she wanted to go out with him, showed him the door.

The next day she went on a diet.

Meanwhile, Lafleur had found a real girlfriend, another air hostess. Lise's heart was broken, but she acted as though nothing was happening. They were almost always together, but didn't dare admit to each other that they were on the edge of something big, something frightening. The other air hostess, Colette, was one of those women who are fascinated by athletes, and she didn't hide the fact that she was determined to marry a hockey player. Lafleur went to bed with her sometimes, while thinking and talking about Lise.

"I don't understand you," Colette said to him. "How come you don't go to bed with her?"

"I don't know. Maybe I respect her too much."

"Charming! And so you don't respect me?"

"It's not the same with you, and you know it. We go to bed together. You like it and so do I. But that's as far as it goes, for you as well as for me. With Lise there's something else."

"What?"

"I don't know."

"Maybe you should find out."

"I think so."

During the summer, Lise Barré invited Guy Lafleur to her parents' house several times. They lived in a luxurious house in Sillery. It was a veritable chateau with an immense front window through which, from the street, you could see the monumental spiral staircase that took up the centre of the big living room. All around were magnificent lawns, hedges, flower gardens, and behind the house a swimming pool. That was what Guy found the most attractive.

At the beginning he had been intimidated. Madame Barré, a small and gentle woman, hardly ever spoke. Roger Barré, a forceful and intelligent man, impressed Lafleur. He was a hard worker, a leader, a persuasive man capable of taking risks and making important deals. He had succeeded and he was proud of it. Always full of ideas and plans, he had the soul and the charm of an adventurer. Lafleur admired the strength and exuberant success of this man, and also his formidable energy, his unshakeable confidence and his warmth. When Roger Barré spoke, everyone listened and agreed. There seemed to be an extraordinary understanding between him and his daughter, great affection and mutual admiration.

To Roger Barré, Guy Lafleur was doubly interesting. First, he was an excellent prospect for his daughter. Second, he had been approached by the Nordiques organization, of which Barré was a shareholder.

When he left Quebec in the middle of August, Lafleur had a new car, a Cadillac Eldorado from Barré Automobiles. He had become very close to Roger Barré. They had enjoyed some good nights of drinking together, talking about everything under the sun—about women, cars, hockey. But Lafleur's relationship with Lise had not progressed; they were still like brother and sister. Their friendship, six months old, was still absolutely chaste.

In the fall, Lise had her apartment redecorated. Guy invited her to stay at his place while the work was being done. He had a small guest room for her, with a single bed, a dresser, the spectacular view of the river and city. When her apartment was ready, two weeks later, she stayed on at Guy's, still as brother and sister. She kept house, made the meals, helped Guy reply to his fan mail. The girls wrote him love letters; the boys wrote to ask his advice.

Like her father, Lise had an innate ability to organize and plan. It took her only a few days to put order into Guy's life, from his correspondence to his cupboards.

Meanwhile, Guy continued to lead his bigamous existence. He had a woman in his house who he respected. She was his accomplice, his friend, his sister. And he had a mistress who never came to his house.

Lise was jealous of Colette. Although they both worked for Air Canada, she had met her only two or three times. She wanted to see her again, not to talk to her but just to see what sort of person she was and how she looked. Thinking about this, Lise finally realized she was in love.

A little before Christmas, the Canadiens organized a big celebration for the players, a chic dinner dance in a big downtown hotel. Lafleur invited Colette to go with him.

Lise, deeply hurt, said nothing. But as soon as he had gone out, she went downstairs to see their friends, the building superintendents.

"Give this key back to Guy Lafleur, please."

"What's happening?"

"Nothing. Exactly nothing is happening."

Riverin, who regularly asked Guy about his progress with Lise, was surprised. Lafleur often talked to him about Lise, told him that he wanted her but was afraid the bond that already existed between them would be destroyed.

"What do you mean, destroy what's between you?" Riverin would say. "If you make love, nothing will be broken. On the contrary. Making love brings men and women closer. That's what it's for!"

Even Madame Riverin had jumped in.

"You should be careful. It's good to treat a woman with respect, but when you're in love, maybe you can be *too* respectful!"

That evening, seeing Lise give back Guy's keys, they knew Guy had exceeded those limits and that things would not be easy to repair. Lise did not seem crushed. She wasn't crying. She was simply very angry.

"For months I live with him, I make his meals, I do his laundry, I answer his mail, but when the lord and master has somewhere important to go, he asks another woman to go with him."

"You should have said something."

"I have nothing to say. He's twenty-one years old. Which is old enough, it seems to me, to know what he's doing."

"But he loves you, too."

"What do you mean, 'too'? Who told you I love him?"

"If you're hurt, it's because you love him."

"I'm not hurt, I'm frustrated."

"Anyway, it's obvious he loves you. He lives with you."

"Because it's convenient, that's all. He lives with me, but he sleeps with someone else. That's his right. But as for me, I don't want that. Give him back his key. I've moved all my things back to the eleventh floor. When he gets home he won't find a single trace of me in his apartment. Not even my

perfume—I aired the place out. I don't want anything to do
with him any more."

In spite of everything, she stayed amazingly calm. She
was enormously hurt, even though she denied it. But she
had thought things over and rationally decided to close the
book on Guy Lafleur, knowing that in the end she'd forget
and feel better. She left for her parents' home in Quebec
that same evening.

Meanwhile, at the Canadiens' banquet, Guy was feeling
glum. As he was leaving he had realized that Lise was upset.
And he was worried. After the dinner he said to Colette:

"I won't come back to your place. I have to go home to
Longueuil."

Then, after having hesitated for a few seconds, he took a
deep breath and added, "I think it's over for us. I'm in love
with someone else."

"I knew it."

"How?"

"Guy, you've talked to me about her a million times. I
know her two brands of perfume, I know the books she
reads, that she likes skiing, that she's a champion rider. I
also know she's a year and four months older than you and
that she's perfectly bilingual . . ."

Colette did not make a scene. On the contrary, when
Lafleur parked in front of her place she gave him a chaste
kiss on the cheek and wished him good luck in the future.
"From the bottom of my heart."

Half an hour after midnight, Lafleur realized that what
he had vaguely feared had come to pass. Lise was no longer
there.

He telephoned her place. No answer. He went
downstairs, knocked at her door, went inside. No one.

He woke up the superintendents, bursting into their
apartment.

"What happened?"

"What happened is that she left. Your relationship with
her doesn't make any sense, my boy."

"Where?"

"She didn't tell us."

He telephoned Lise's parents' house. Roger Barré answered.

"Listen, young man, do you have any idea what time it is?"

"I want to talk to Lise."

"Lise is in bed. Everyone is in bed. In our house, at one in the morning, people sleep."

"Not Lise. I want to talk to her."

Roger Barré knew his daughter wasn't asleep, that she was sad and bewildered. She had confided in him. She had always been closer to her father than her mother.

"Hang on, I'll go see. But I'm warning you, Guy Lafleur, you'd better behave with my daughter or you'll answer to me. Understand?"

Lise came to speak to Guy. She was very cold.

"Lise, why did you leave?"

"Guess."

"I couldn't have known you would want to go to that party."

"Oh great! But you managed to guess that Colette would like to."

"She asked me. It's not the same thing."

"I didn't know it was necessary to draw you a picture and make a special request to get something from you."

"I would rather have gone with you, Lise, I swear it."

"In that case, why didn't you ask me?"

"I don't know. I didn't dare."

"Poor you."

He was humiliated. She, still chilly and firm, talked down to him, bitter and ironic. He babbled apologies.

"You don't have to apologize, Guy. You're a free man. You can do what you want."

"But I'm not a free man."

"Did Colette ask you to marry her?"

"I want to see you."

"Is that all right with her?"

Less than an hour and a half later, the Barré doorbell rang. At the wheel of his new Cadillac Eldorado, Guy Lafleur had covered the 150 miles between his place and

Sillery at an average speed of 100 miles per hour, sometimes going as fast as 140 miles an hour.

Lise wasn't asleep. When she saw him, she burst into tears.

"What do you want?"

"Do you have any cognac?"

They talked all night, laughing and crying.

"I can't live without you."

"I don't want to be your servant."

"Then be my wife."

"That might be the same thing."

They went back to Longueuil the next afternoon. At seventy-five miles an hour.

"This isn't the time to have an accident," Lise said. "We have other things to do."

Lise Barré had just re-entered the life of Guy Lafleur. She knew exactly where they were going. From now on, she would be doing the driving.

• • •

Historians consider September 2, 1972, the most important date in the history of hockey. That day, after years of discussions, negotiations and hesitations on both sides, a team from the USSR was finally going to play against the best of the NHL.

For fifteen years, the Soviets had regularly beaten junior and amateur hockey teams from Canada and the United States. But the North American professionals would say, "That's easy. They send their best players against our young ones. You can bet it would be a different story if they had to play the NHL's best."

The morning of September 2, watching the Russians practise at the Montreal Forum, no one could have guessed what was about to happen. The Russians seemed completely lost, slow and disorganized, exactly the way they had been described by the Canadian writers who had gone to see them play in Moscow a month before. As for the Canadian players, they had just given, on the same ice, a dazzling demonstration of their ability: speed, accurate and hard shots, sophisticated fakes and passing patterns.

The journalists, massed along the boards near the players' gate, joked to each other. Back from Moscow, they had all written that the Canadian team would demolish the Russians. One of them had even promised to eat his own newspaper if the Russians won a single match in this best of four series. Their worst weakness, everyone said, was their goalie, Vladislav Tretiak, clumsy and awkward, pitiful. That evening the crowd that filled the Forum had no doubt they would witness a massacre.

A few minutes before the game, Jacques Plante, the famous former Canadiens goalie, went to see Tretiak in the Soviet dressing room. He knew that Tretiak admired him, and taking pity on the Soviet goaltender, Plante spoke to him about the players he would have to watch most closely: Mahovlich, Henderson and especially Phil Esposito, whose shot was always dangerous, even from far out, and Yvan Cournoyer, the speedy skater who could shoot equally well from both sides.

The crowd gave the Soviet team a polite but cool welcome. When the Canadian team came onto the ice, there was thunderous applause. Thirty seconds after the game began, Phil Esposito scored on Tretiak. Six minutes later it was Paul Henderson's turn to score. Canada 2, USSR 0. The fans started to laugh and make sarcastic jokes about the Russians. The Forum organist played them a funeral march. But the Russians gathered themselves, and gradually won almost total control of the puck while soundly defeating Canada's elite players, 7 to 3.

This Soviet victory sent shockwaves through the Canadian hockey world. The Russians knew how to play hockey! As well or better than the Canadians and Americans. Above all, they had an amazing ability to play as a team. They played a game of extraordinary precision, and showed an incredible ability to adapt. In less than ten minutes they had figured out the North American style of play and worked out a strategy to counter it. Everyone was astonished. It was understood, on the ice and in the stands, that hockey would never be the same.

The defeat was equally humiliating for the Canadian

press, who had almost unanimously predicted a one-sided victory over the Soviets. In fact, no one in North America had taken the Soviet team seriously; it was unimaginable that there could be a place in the world where hockey was played better than in North America. But it seemed that the Russians had remarkable puck control. The Canadians shot harder, but the Russians' defence system was fool-proof. The biggest revelation was that the Soviets had a goalie of pure genius. The journalists couldn't believe Tretiak was the same man they had seen at work a month earlier in Moscow.

The fans had also been defeated, their confidence shaken. In Vancouver, where the last match of what was by then being called the series of the century was played, the Canadian team was loudly booed, even though they had given their best.

"We're trying hard," said Phil Esposito. "Let's face facts. They've got a good team."

The series of the century had raised so much interest throughout Canada that many schools gave their students time off so that they could follow the four final matches played two weeks later in Moscow and transmitted live over Canadian television.

Happily for the NHL team, the Russians became over-confident after their victories in Canada. Thanks to a very physical style of play that stretched the rules to their limits, and a lot of luck (Paul Henderson scored the winning goal with just thirty-four seconds to go in the last game) the Canadian team was the winner in Russia.

But the myth of North American invincibility had been broken forever. Great new players had been discovered, along with a pure and effective conception of the game of hockey.

Guy Lafleur was not a member of the Canadian all-star team, but he had greedily devoured the series on television. He was especially fascinated by the famous Soviet troika, three players—Kharlamov, Petrov and Mikhailov—who had worked together in a harmonious trinity that took complete possession of the ice.

He wished that some day he, too, could be part of such a trio. But with whom? When? He didn't even know if he wanted to keep playing in Montreal, or if the Canadiens still wanted him.

• • •

In 1971, Sam Pollock had used diplomacy, charm and ingenuity in order to get Guy Lafleur, the most sought-after rookie in the NHL. Now, two years later, Lafleur was in danger of slipping away. There were some who thought Pollock should just let him go, that he could easily find someone better. But the cunning Pollock knew he had captured a worthy prize. In the spring of 1973, a few weeks before the termination of the contract he had signed with Lafleur, he decided to use his influence to make sure that Lafleur would be in the organization for a very long time to come.

As usual, during the playoffs, the Canadiens' players were put up at La Sapinière in the Laurentians. Rustic but chic, La Sapinière was situated in a beautiful landscape, away from the temptations of downtown Montreal and far from the sweet and soothing pleasures of home.

The program was simple. In the morning, after a big breakfast, everyone got into a luxurious bus that took them to the Forum for their daily practice session. After an hour and a half of work and sweat, it was back to La Sapinière. The afternoon had compulsory relaxation, including walks in the fresh air or a little television. Of course it was forbidden to go skiing, Pollock didn't want any broken bones. If there was a game in the evening, then everyone took a nap, ate late in the afternoon (the recommended dish being steak) and then went back down to the Forum.

Lafleur loved the Laurentians, the smell of pines, the fresh air, the austere landscape. It all reminded him of his childhood. At that time of the year, the beginning of April, the weather was mild and the land spectacularly beautiful. He felt at home there, much more than in Montreal. In the afternoon, instead of sleeping, he would walk for hours, always alone. He was thinking about Lise . . . and, a little, about hockey.

His second season with the Canadiens had just ended. It had been a little less productive than the first: twenty-eight goals, one fewer than in 1971–72; and twenty-seven assists, eight fewer. A very respectable total, but hardly what was required to support the immense reputation he had brought with him two years earlier when he had arrived in Montreal. People had now stopped talking about him in inflated, heroic terms. To many people, it seemed evident that Guy Lafleur would be a good player, nothing more. He would have an honourable career, with some high points, but he would never be a player like Jean Béliveau or Gordie Howe, let alone Maurice Richard. Marcel Dionne, Gilbert Perreault and Richard Martin, young men of his age who had come into the NHL at the same time, already had a higher profile. And there were other players who had become bigger stars than Lafleur, players like Bobby Clarke, Darryl Sittler and Bobby Orr, who was becoming more and more famous.

But Sam Pollock had his own view on these matters. He was convinced Lafleur would be a great player and that everything possible should be done to keep him in Montreal. But first he had to be cured of his past, that is, he had to acclimatize himself and feel at home with the Canadiens. This meant that he had to forget the Remparts once and for all.

"There are no problems that time can't solve," the Fox told himself.

He decided to offer Lafleur a ten-year contract, which would practically force him to learn to love Montreal. First with his head; his heart would follow. That was the gamble Pollock was considering. He knew the Nordiques were also in the hunt, and that they had made various proposals to Lafleur. So he would have to be shrewd.

On April 4, 1973, at the Forum, the Canadiens were meeting the Buffalo Sabres in the quarter-finals. During the morning skate, Lafleur saw his agent, Gerry Patterson, waving at him.

"I want to see you right after practice. It's very important."

"I can't. We have to go back to La Sapinière."

"I arranged things with Sam Pollock. You can spend today in town. I reserved you a hotel room so you can rest before tonight's game."

Everything arranged with Pollock! Lafleur told himself that he'd better be careful. And, no matter what, he'd better not approve or sign anything too quickly.

After the practice, Patterson came to see him in the dressing room and, whispering nervously, conspiratorially, drew him aside.

"Congratulations, my boy. You're a millionaire. Sam Pollock has made us an offer: a million dollars over ten years. Guaranteed."

Patterson was bursting with excitement, but not Lafleur. A million over ten years wasn't much better than what the Nordiques had offered him in February: $90,000 a year for three years plus a $50,000 signing bonus.

"But Pollock's contract can be renegotiated after three years and after six years. Guy, think about it seriously. A million guaranteed, that's a lot of money."

"The Nordiques' contract also would have been renegotiable after three years. And you agreed that we should turn it down."

A few weeks earlier, Patterson had turned back the first offer of Marius Fortier, the managing director of the Nordiques, telling him that Guy Lafleur found his offer "insulting." Less promising players than he had been offered more than twice as much by obscure World Hockey Association clubs. The Los Angeles Sharks had held out a truly golden bridge to Marc Tardif, whose point production had been clearly inferior to Lafleur's. Same thing for Réjean Houle, who had scored only thirteen goals in the regular season and who the Nordiques had offered a lot more than he would have been paid by any NHL club.

Lafleur had the idea that people in Quebec thought they could get him for nothing, just because he liked to live there and wasn't happy with Bowman and the Canadiens.

"I don't think they're very clever," he said. "The way they're going I could end up hating Quebec."

A few days later the Nordiques returned with a contract worth almost half a million over three years: a $60,000 signing bonus, $125,000 the first year followed by $135,000 and $145,000 for the following years. But they offered no guarantee, so that if Lafleur were injured or played poorly, he might get less than $100,000 a year. Again Patterson had refused, this time warning Fortier that Lafleur no longer found the process amusing and that if they didn't want to lose him, they should make a serious proposition. Fortier seemed to have got the message: he promised to come up quickly with something new.

That was where things stood when Sam Pollock, on April 4, arrived with his million-dollar contract, a contract officially prepared and typed out. Patterson pulled it from his briefcase and set it before Lafleur.

"If you sign, you'll be a millionaire."

"You want me to sign today!"

"Sam Pollock has given us twenty-four hours. He said take it or leave it. Tomorrow morning it will be too late."

"Listen, Gerry. I'm getting married in three months. I can't sign without talking to my wife."

That very morning, at La Sapinière, he had taken a phone call from Roger Barré, his future father-in-law: the Nordiques organization was readying a new proposal that he would get that evening, or at latest the next morning.

"You can't chase two rabbits at the same time," Patterson said. "Guy, you have to decide. If you don't sign, Pollock will think that you don't trust him."

Lafleur was unable to reach Lise, who must have been somewhere in the sky between Boston and Montreal. He called Roger Barré's office in Quebec, then tried to reach him at his house, at Maurice Filion's, at Marius Fortier's. Lafleur concluded that he msut be on his way to Montreal with the new offer. He left a message at the Queen Elizabeth Hotel, where Roger Barré stayed when he came to Montreal. But at six-thirty, an hour before the game, there was still no news. Gerry Patterson and Sam Pollock became more and more insistent.

Out of arguments, convinced that the Nordique offer couldn't be much better than the two they'd already presented, Guy Lafleur signed.

He played half-heartedly, convinced that he had stupidly committed an irreparable error. Once again he had been too passive. His signature could just as well have waited a day. There was something fishy about the way they had pushed him so hard. He began to suspect Patterson and Pollock of having connived against him.

After the game he met Roger Barré. Barré gave him the Nordiques' offer: a million dollars over five years. Exactly twice the Canadiens' offer.

He broke into tears. Not only because he had just thrown away an incredible amount of money, but because he was humiliated. He had been taken. He had behaved like an idiot. He was angry at Patterson, but he was even angrier at himself for not knowing how to say no and for letting himself be manipulated once again.

"I should have told you not to trust him," Roger Barré said. "But it seemed to me you would figure it out yourself, Guy. Gerry Patterson is Jean Béliveau's adviser. You must know that! And Béliveau is the vice-president of the Montreal Canadiens. Marius Fortier told me that every time the Nordiques made you an offer, Patterson seemed very pleased and said he had never hoped to get so much."

"He was double-dealing."

"It could be that he was making sure the Nordiques would make you offers you wouldn't want to accept. Anyway, it's obvious he wasn't on our side."

"Nor mine, if I understand correctly."

They called lawyers, hoping that the contract signed under pressure could be annulled. But this would have meant undertaking a complex and endless legal battle. And no one would sympathize with an NHL player who declared war against his own organization.

"There's just one thing left for you, Guy. You'll have to learn to like Montreal. Perhaps one day you'll even thank Patterson. At least here you'll be playing with winners. You

What neither Ruel, nor Bowman, nor the journalists, let alone the public, could have possibly known—though Pollock had begun to divine the problem—was that Guy Lafleur wanted to be forgotten for a while. A deep transformation was taking place inside him. For the first time since he had left Quebec, he was beginning to feel at home in Montreal. He loved Lise and he adored their little place in Verchères. In addition, his slow and progressive slide into obscurity had more or less relieved him of the unbearable pressure he had felt since he had joined the Montreal Canadiens. Finally, the journalists had stopped writing about his every action, trying to make him into a messiah, and comparing him to Béliveau, Orr, Geoffrion, Richard, Hull and the rest. Finally, they had left him in peace! And he was in love! Who could ask for more?

Then, imperceptibly at first, and then more and more sharply as the summer of 1974 wore on, he began to feel again, for the first time in a long time, the need to play hockey, the pure and violent desire for the physical pleasure that it offered.

That fall a different Guy Lafleur went to training camp. The true man had emerged, the real "Blond Demon."

• • •

Athletes are compulsive and inveterate gamblers, naturally fetishistic and superstitious. When something has gone well for them, they do everything they can to recreate the circumstances. They are all always looking for the winning formula, the ideal model, the magic words that will put an end to chance and assure them of victory and the ineffable paradise of applause.

So, hoping to be able to match one night's prowess, they take exactly the same route to get to the next game, arrange once again to pass on the way a woman in black or in red or a drunken youth, they wear the same sweater until they lose, recite the same prayers at the same time, eat the same food before the match, make the same—sometimes tortuous—ritual gesture, wear medallions or lucky undershirts, always lace up the left skate before the right, always tuck in the bottom of their sweater to the right side of their shorts, would pay for the privilege of playing. Ruel was convinced that Lafleur had been and still was a truly great player. So?

Ruel advised Bowman to stop assigning Frank Mahovlich as Lafleur's roommate on road trips. The ageing Frank (he was thirteen years older than Lafleur) had scored no fewer than thirty-eight goals the preceding season, but he was still the king of defeatism. Lafleur's roommate became the likeable Steve Shutt, then the dynamic Henri Richard, then the very determined and opinionated Jacques Lemaire. But none of them had a positive effect on Guy Lafleur.

It should be said that the team wasn't playing very well that year. Not only had Houle and Tardif left, slamming the door behind them, but the indispensable Ken Dryden (with whom Pollock had tried to be too clever by refusing to renegotiate his contract) had returned to law school in Toronto.

Towards the end of the season, Lafleur was buried in a slump: two goals in twenty-two games. The fans and the media didn't seem to care; they appeared to be losing interest in him. Even worse, Lafleur himself seemed to accept his situation. He always came to practice on time, was obedient and polite. He did his duty. When Bowman made him ride the bench, that was just fine. If he called on Lafleur to play, Guy leapt onto the ice. After the game he hung up his skates, took his shower and went home. Although he seemed indifferent to what was happening on the ice, he was relaxed and happy the moment he left the Forum. Happy in life, unhappy in hockey.

One day Sam Pollock said to the sports writers: "From now on we consider Guy Lafleur to be an ordinary player. If he has some good moments, so much the better. But we aren't expecting anything from him."

The next day, Pollock's remarks were in all the papers. Everyone expected Lafleur would be upset when he came to practice. Not at all. He arrived looking fresh and happy, as though nothing had gone wrong. His play was neither more nor less intense than usual.

always get dressed standing up and without talking or go out before the game and shoot the puck into the empty enemy net. And the longer they play and the more successes they have, the more rigid and complex their ritualistic ceremonies become. They are like the medieval knights who wore their ladies' colours when they jousted, believing they gave them strength and luck.

Lafleur was not especially superstitious, although like everyone else in his world he believed in lucky and unlucky signs.

The second day of the 1974 training camp, Guy played with such pleasure and intensity that his teammates and the watching journalists applauded and cheered him. That day he had forgotten his helmet in the locker room. It was fifteen years since he had last played bareheaded, except for one game in March 1972, against the Pittsburgh Penguins. At the time, it hadn't brought him any luck. Some of the journalists had written that if young Lafleur had wanted to be noticed, he would do better to come out of his shell, to skate, to gather in some of the passes that his generous teammates were directing to him, and to score some goals.

But that day at training camp he was absolutely dazzling. Right there and then he decided he would never wear a faceguard or helmet again. As though by magic he had rediscovered the pleasure of playing. Lafleur himself knew and admitted it probably had nothing to do with the helmet. But the helmet would be banished as a negative fetish for him, a bearer of unhappiness.

Thus, at the beginning of the 1974–75 regular season, the public saw a new Guy Lafleur. He who had been so colourless and unremarkable a few months earlier was now everywhere on the ice, so visible and mobile that it seemed Scotty Bowman must have assigned him the entire rink. He initiated plays and executed them with such style and flash that the fans screamed with joy. Suddenly he was an athlete unlike any other, and was staking his claim to be considered one of the truly great players.

The marketing specialists and image makers couldn't

have dreamed of anything better. Lafleur's abandonment of his helmet was both symbolic and effective. In uncovering himself, both literally and figuratively, Guy Lafleur had given himself a new look, his blond hair streaming behind him as he skated, at the same time as he was displaying unexpected resources of energy and inventiveness. It was almost as though he'd had an innate knowledge of how to launch the marketing of his image!

In a few hours he had entirely conquered first the demanding fans at the Montreal Forum, then all of Quebec. By mid-November, barely a month after the season's beginning, he was being talked about in every hockey city on the continent, the next hockey superstar.

At one time, all the attention and the cameras trained on him had been more than he could bear; now they stimulated him and gave him energy. Not only was he playing well and with fantastic energy, but his enthusiasm spilled over to the practices, so much so that even the cynical sports writers of the Montreal dailies got into the habit of coming early to the Forum in order to watch Guy Lafleur train.

In fact, every day that the Canadiens were at home, number 10 went to the Forum a couple of hours before the team practice, jumped onto the ice and gave an amazing demonstration of his skills. And when the other players came, all eyes would still be on Lafleur. Even in a nondescript practice jersey, he was immediately recognizable. The most uneducated watcher could pick out Lafleur, even in the midst of a dense scramble for the puck. Not just because he was bareheaded, but because of his formidable skating ability, and his absolutely unique way of moving about the rink, as though he were hardly touching the ice, as though with skill, grace and ease he were riding the surface of this frozen light, as though the light itself were carrying him.

From time to time the writers would set down their coffee, take out their pens and notebooks and search for new words with which to praise Lafleur. Some compared him to

Mercury, messenger of the Roman gods, the swiftest and most agile of all.

That year Guy Lafleur discovered something important: talent by itself, no matter how extraordinary, is not enough. Nor is the most rigorous discipline. Not even the two together. He discovered that there was another equally important ingredient, something that didn't depend only on himself, but was connected to mystery and grace, divine goodness or luck, pure and simple.

He had always been vaguely religious, but had stopped going to mass in the days when he played for the Quebec Remparts. He had even permitted himself a few white lies to the very religious Madame Baribeau, who he allowed to believe that he went to the Saint Francis of Assisi Church when really he was going to meet his friends at the recreation centre or the Cendrillon. He no longer practised his religion, therefore, but he had kept a very strong religious sense, one that was both deep and primitive. He still prayed, especially when he was sad or confused.

During the 1974–75 season, while in top form and near the peak of his glory, he had none of his usual reasons for prayer. But he got into the habit of saying some prayers before each game: a Lord's Prayer, a Hail Mary, a Glory Be to the Father, a few invocations, a few good thoughts for Brother Léo and his grandfather Damien, who had recently died. He had the absolute conviction that he was dependent on a superior power that might abandon him at any moment, just as it had been able to lend him strength. And he prayed that it would remain with him.

It seemed to him that everything he had learned during the past fifteen years—the advice, the lessons and the admonitions of Ti-Paul Meloche, Brother Léo Jacques, Jean-Marc Lalonde, Martin Madden, Maurice Filion, Jean Béliveau, Roger Barré, Madame Baribeau—was now finally beginning to come together and take on a coherent meaning.

He found it amazingly easy to submit himself to a severe regimen from which he never deviated. He went to bed early, ate well, drank little, smoked less and less. Just as he had appeared inattentive and hesitant the previous year, now he was infused with passion, a mystic who only lived through and for hockey.

In November, when the Canadiens were in Los Angeles to play the Kings, the weather was brilliantly sunny, hot, smog-free. While his teammates relaxed around the pool or at the Venice beaches, Lafleur shut himself up in his air-conditioned room or went all alone to exercise at the Los Angeles Forum. He claimed that the sun and heat softened his muscles.

"So what," said Steve Shutt. "We could beat the Kings with our hands tied behind our backs."

But Lafleur was incorruptible. In the same way, on January 7, 1975, in Detroit, he refused to go to a WHA game between the Quebec Nordiques and the Michigan Stags. Instead he stayed alone in his room at the Pontchartrin Hotel, just a few steps from the arena where he could have seen his good friends Réjean Houle, Maurice Filion, Martin Madden . . . He knew it would be upsetting to see the people from Quebec and that it would make it difficult for him to concentrate on the next evening's match against the Red Wings.

When someone asked him why he hadn't tried to discipline himself this way when everything was going so badly before, he replied that he wouldn't have been able to. He had been feeling too bad then, bore a grudge against the whole world and believed he could never be happy until he started to play well. What had happened was the exact opposite. He had started to play well because he was happy. He therefore made himself a rule to be in a good mood every time he had a game to play. Like Voltaire deciding to be happy because it's good for the health!

Madame Baribeau had done much to inculcate Lafleur with this positive attitude. She had always been in favour of cheerfulness. She would often say, "We mustn't let our old age grab hold of our youth." When, during his first season with the Remparts, Lafleur had problems, she kept telling him, "Don't be so gloomy, it will only make things worse. Go out, have fun. Things will go better, believe me."

Guy Lafleur

1975

Guy Lafleur and sister
Suzanne
1952

Guy Lafleur, playing Junior B
hockey for the Canadian Tire
and Repair team
1966

●

Guy Lafleur and Lise Barré
on their wedding day
1973

The wedding party: (*left to right*) Serge Savard,
Claude Larose, Jacques Laperrière, Jean Béliveau,
Guy Lafleur, Lise Lafleur, Pierre Bouchard,
Guy Lapointe, Jacques Lemaire, Marc Tardif;
(*kneeling*) Yvan Cournoyer, Henri Richard,
Réjean Houle

1973

Guy Lafleur with hockey legends
Jean Béliveau (*left*) and
Maurice Richard (*right*)
1974

Guy Lafleur, on the ice for
the Montreal Canadiens
1977

Guy Lafleur with his friend,
racing car driver
Gilles Villeneuve
1979

Guy Lafleur with his son,

Martin

1981

The Lafleur family: (*left to right*)
Suzanne, Lise, Réjean, Pierrette,
Guy, Lucie, Gisèle

1984

Guy Lafleur at a celebration at the
Forum marking his retirement from the Montreal
Canadiens: (*left to right*) Pierrette Lafleur, Réjean
Lafleur, Guy Lafleur, Lise Lafleur, Eva Baribeau,
Martin Lafleur (*front*)

1985

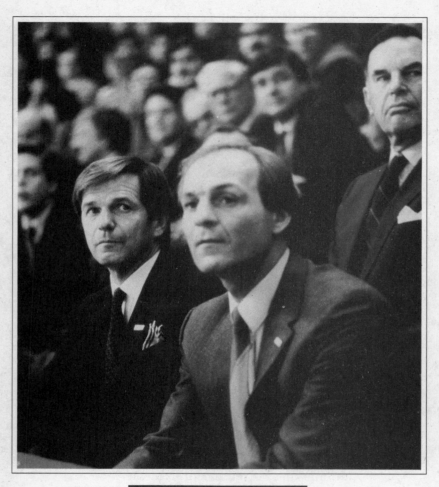

Guy Lafleur with Ronald
Corey, president of
the Montreal Canadiens
1985

(*left to right*) Wayne Gretzky,
Yves Tremblay, Guy Lafleur
1989

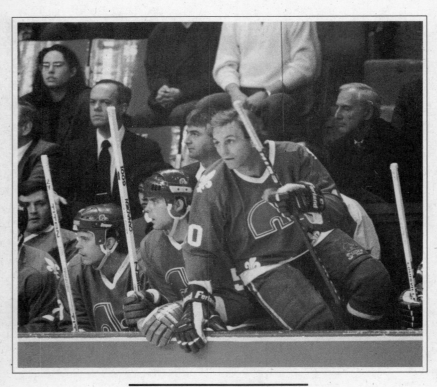

Guy Lafleur in uniform
with the Quebec Nordiques
1989

arguments. Guy liked open spaces, and wanted to knock down almost all the walls to make huge rooms. Lise wanted to keep the original floorplan; she was fond of small, intimate rooms. He didn't want curtains on the windows; she did. He wanted the house to be surrounded by trees; she didn't.

Even before training camp began, Scotty Bowman and Sam Pollock realized that, more than ever, Guy's mind was elsewhere. As it turned out, his third season with the Canadiens was the worst of all, the least productive: twenty-one goals, thirty-five assists. Pollock had seen it coming and had done his best to help Lafleur. Right at the beginning of the season he had asked Claude Ruel to work with him.

"Use whatever method you want. Prod him or pamper him, whatever it takes to wake him up and get him going."

Ruel had tried everything: he bawled him out, he preached to him, he listened to Lafleur's problems, he arranged special practices for him, he threatened him. Nothing worked. Lafleur was not even sad or depressed. He seemed to have simply turned off. Ruel was terribly upset. He was supposed to be a man who knew everything about hockey players, but Lafleur was too much for him. What could have happened to Lafleur? Where was the great hockey player he had once been?

The departure of Houle and Tardif from the team didn't explain anything. Lafleur had liked them, yes, and he had sometimes seemed to enjoy playing with them or seeing them socially, but they hadn't been his closest friends. Moreover, the contact between Lemaire and Lafleur seemed to have been broken, the magic gone. What could the explanation be? The deal he had missed with the Nordiques? It must have been disappointing, but not enough to ruin his game. Ruel had seen Guy Lafleur at his best. Then he had played with such intensity, such passion, that it was clear his play had nothing to do with money. The really great players never played for the money; in fact, they can still grow. Going to Quebec would have been a step backwards. Stay here and fight."

Two and a half months later, on June 17, 1973, Guy Lafleur and Lise Barré were married. It was a day marked by high winds and driving rain. The wedding celebration was lavish, and took place at the Lac Beauport Inn. There was champagne, caviar, an enormous Stanley Cup sculpted out of ice and filled with lobsters. In attendance were most of the Canadiens players, who had just won the Stanley Cup by beating the Sabres, the Flyers and the Black Hawks. Bowman and Pollock were also there, along with the owners of the Quebec Nordiques, Filion, Dumont, Madden. Jean-Yves Doyon, Chouine, Ti-Paul Meloche were all there. And so was Gerry Patterson. Roger Barré, who had met Patterson several times before, went up to him and said, "Gerry, I hope you've made a good decision for Guy, because he's just committed himself for a long time."

Patterson replied, "Me? But I assure you, Monsieur Barré, I had absolutely nothing to do with it. Guy was the one who decided to marry your daughter."

Roger Barré laughed. As did his daughter and his son-in-law.

During the summer, the young couple moved temporarily to the Île-des-Soeurs. Guy was hoping to find a place a little outside the city to build a house. His father-in-law gave him the inspiration. Roger Barré had a house in Saint-Antoine-de-Tilly, a half-hour drive from Quebec. It was its own little kingdom, a place where he was lord and master, that he could fix up to his own taste and use as a refuge from the worries of business.

Lafleur dreamed of a traditional, steep-roofed Québecois farmhouse, a wooded grove, an orchard, everything a little run-down so he could spend some time fixing it up. Lise, who loved riding, wanted there to be a small stable.

They found something in Verchères, just beside Pierre Bouchard's place, a tiny farmstead of a dozen acres with an old house that needed serious work. For the next year, that was their main activity, and the most fertile source of

In the same way, during the summer Roger Barré had often told him that he should "get his head around" liking Montreal.

"You can't spend the next ten years of your life in a city that you hate."

"But I can't do anything about it. These sorts of feelings can't just be decided."

"But of course they can," Roger Barré would say. "You have to make an effort, otherwise it's clear that you'll never get anywhere."

He was determined to fall in love with Montreal, and he had finally succeeded. On evenings off he went to restaurants and movies with Lise. On their way back to Verchères they would sometimes make a detour by the mountain, and would stop for a moment to look down at the city, stretched out at their feet in its bed of twinkling lights. They would go back home and talk long into the night. Often, when Lise woke up, Guy had already gone out. He would have left her a note on the refrigerator or in the soap dish or sugar bowl, a poem, a few tender words.

One October evening she told him she was pregnant. A few months earlier, in the depths of his slump, this news would have terrified him. But that day his first thought was that nothing more wonderful could have happened to him. Lise had become pregnant at the moment when everything in his life seemed in perfect harmony.

But things were not really going well for the Montreal Canadiens. Everyone was dazzled by the performance of the new Guy Lafleur, and delighted both at the return of Ken Dryden and the departure of Frank Mahovlich. But team morale was low. Although Jacques Lemaire was having a good year (thirty-six goals, fifty-six assists) he didn't feel completely himself. And the team captain, Henri Richard, was on the eve of his retirement and at loggerheads with the coach, Scotty Bowman.

But Lafleur, as though he were deliberately attempting to be contrary, was flying. Bowman had finally understood that he played better on right wing, and put him on a line with Pete Mahovlich at centre and Steve Shutt on left wing.

In his fourth season with the Canadiens, Lafleur scored two and a half times as many goals (fifty-three) as in the preceding season, and almost twice the number of assists. In eleven playoff games he scored twelve goals and got seven assists. Only Jean Béliveau had done better. In 1956 when Béliveau, too, was in his fourth season with the Canadiens, he had got twelve goals and seven assists, the same as Lafleur, but in one game fewer. And Maurice Richard, in his second season, had had a similar success: twelve goals and five assists in only nine games.

Nevertheless, in April the Montreal Canadiens were eliminated by the Buffalo Sabres, and the Sabres were then crushed by the brawling Philadelphia Flyers, who thus carried off the Stanley Cup for the second year in a row.

The Philadelphia Flyers had established a true reign of terror in the NHL. They were coached by Fred Shero, a kind of aesthete of violence for whom hockey was not quite war, but more than just a game. He claimed that life was nothing more than the insignificant and boring limbo between hockey games. His players and the Philadelphia fans became fanatics. At the Spectrum, home of the Philadelphia Flyers (nicknamed the Broad Street Bullies), the crowd wore SS helmets and waved Nazi banners and swastikas. For Flyers fans, Enemy Number One was and always had been, since the beginning of hockey, the Montreal Canadiens.

The Flyers' players included Dave "The Hammer" Schultz and Bob Kelly, two bloodthirsty brutes who, along with a few other labourers, cleared the path for the team's scorers: Bobby Clarke, Bill Barber, Reggie Leach. They had been cruelly disappointed when the Sabres eliminated the Canadiens in the semi-final, because they had wanted to be the ones to demolish them. So long as the Broad Street Bullies had not yet themselves vanquished the Canadiens, their glory would not be complete.

The clever Shero had invented a threatrical effect designed to terrify the enemy. In every other Amercian NHL city, the American national anthem was sung before games; in Philadelphia, Kate Smith sang "God Bless

America." While she sang, the Spectrum lights were turned out, except for blinding spotlights that were turned on the enemy team. Exposed on all sides and surrounded by threatening shadows, the visitors invariably lost their nerve.

Fearing a rise in violence, the Canadiens advised Lafleur to start wearing his helmet again. He would hear none of it, saying that it would only get in his way and slow him down. But by this time new materials were available to make padding and helmets much lighter and more effective. Nevertheless Lafleur, out of pride or superstition, continued to wear his old shoulderpads, his soft leather skates that offered no more protection than moccasins, shinpads so short that his ankles were left exposed.

Lafleur had become the man to beat in the NHL. Every coach assigned him a checker to cover him like a shadow. Gerry Korab of the Buffalo Sabres, Dave Schultz of the Philadelphia Flyers, John Wensink from the Boston Bruins—all the biggest and roughest players of the league were brought out to face him. Despite his incomparable speed and ability to avoid checks, he was often checked to a standstill.

Bowman had no choice; Lafleur would have to adapt himself. Since Fred Shero had completely changed the rules of the game, everyone was going back to hockey as a rough and primitive sport. Following the Flyers' success, several other clubs had already armed themselves with some strong and aggressive players. The new teams were made up of a few good players escorted by bodyguards, goons who made space for them and opened the path to the opponent's net by knocking down anyone in their way. The Canadiens, who were not equipped to carry on this sort of war, prided themselves on playing civilized hockey, highly sophisticated and aesthetic, the somewhat colourless hockey of the Béliveau era. Now they had to make fundamental changes in their strategy and style of play.

Bowman had understood that in Guy Lafleur he had a true winner, a high scorer, but especially a great star capable of generating intensity and excitement. With

Pollock and the other Canadiens strategists, he decided to build his club around Lafleur. He would give Lafleur his own goons to protect him and create open ice around him. Of course Lafleur was capable of taking care of himself, but his great talent was for putting the puck in the net, and doing it brilliantly enough to rouse the spectators. Aside from his powerful and accurate shot, he had something indefinable, a charisma, an aura, a precious asset that the very religious Sam Pollock called his "gift from God."

Thus the Canadiens moved to a very offence-oriented game, the style of the seventies, and made themselves bigger and more aggressive than ever. Lafleur was surrounded by tough and fearless players. And with him, on a line that would be the toast of Montreal, were Steve Shutt and Pete Mahovlich.

Lafleur himself was trying things no one else had ever dared: going into the most difficult places, into the corners that players had always avoided because they knew they would be trapped. But Lafleur seemed to enjoy throwing himself into the jaws of the lion. Shutt and Mahovlich passed him the puck just the same, knowing he would somehow escape. Lafleur was never so inventive and brilliant as when he was in the heart of the action, in the midst of the enemy zone. He was never satisfied to do things the easy way. After a few weeks together, the three players, had developed such an original style of play that they completely bewitched and confused the opposing players, and had a wonderful time doing it.

Lafleur was now firmly established in his position on the right wing. He was also established in his fame. But it was a conservative fame, perhaps too much so. Of course the difficulties he'd had along the way, his hesitations, his timidity, had made the hero human and more likeable. But he was too perfect. He didn't yet have a mythic quality; he had never made a serious or foolish mistake. He had yet to stumble.

● ● ●

At this time there was another immensely popular star in

Quebec, a French singer with the air of being very distant and contrived. Her name was Mireille Mathieu. She was about the same age as Guy and had come from a socio-economic background comparable to his own. Born in a small town in France, she was the daughter of a large and poor working-class family that espoused traditional values.

During the seventies Mireille Mathieu crossed the Atlantic two or three times a year. She alone could fill Wilfrid Pelletier Hall, the largest in the Place-des-Arts, for three weeks running. She would tour the province of Quebec, from Chicoutimi to Rouyn, Rimouski and Sherbrooke. Her songs were heard almost continuously on the FM airwaves. Her manager, Johnny Stark, was a Don Juan of the masses and had a genius for promoting stars. For Mireille Mathieu, he'd had the idea of associating her with the French sports stars and politicians. He'd thus created, in *Paris Match* style, a sort of Olympian meeting ground for everyone who was popular, whether it be through rugby, car racing, singing, film or politics.

With the help of the show business manipulators and financiers of Quebec, Stark brought together Mireille Mathieu and Guy Lafleur, trying to flatter and attract the Quebec audience while also making inroads among the anglophones. Lafleur was now a North American star, and could bring Mireille Mathieu to the English-Canadian and American masses.

The two stars clicked. And Lise Barré also liked the timid and polite singer who, unlike many French people, was not overbearing or boring. On the contrary, Mireille was warm, attentive and curious. The Lafleurs began to spend time with the strange Mathieu-Stark twosome. The public has always found such friendships fascinating. People applauded the sight of their top hockey player being paired with France's top singer.

Mireille presented Guy, who collected watches, with a magnificent watch with his likeness inscribed on the case. It was hard to understand what Guy found so interesting about these small animated machines: their regularity? their automatic functioning? the synchronized precision of their movement?

"No, it's not that. What I like is being able to see and hear the passing of time. I keep my watches in a drawer. When I open the drawer I can feel seconds, minutes, hours marching by. And I tell myself that everything passes—things, people, even nature—and that you can never go backwards, or stop, or prevent time from carrying us away. I like to think about that, even if it's a bit frightening."

He would say, "My wife is pregnant. If it's a girl we'll call her Mireille; it it's a boy we'll call him Mathieu." He played the game like a pro. The friendship that bound him to Mireille was above suspicion. It confirmed his status as a great player, as a (soon-to-be) father, a loving and faithful husband, a son of the people who by his ardour and intelligence had climbed to the top, meanwhile remaining simple and honest. Even Brother Léo Jacques, who a few years before had written a praise-filled book about Guy Lafleur, would have been proud of his hero.

But the Quebec intelligentsia found the alliance shocking. The artists had been complaining bitterly about the French hegemony over Quebec show business. And critics considered Mireille Mathieu to be a mediocre cultural product of France. People were talking about intellectual alienation and cultural dumping. Meanwhile, the ordinary people were perfectly satisfied. They saw in the liaison a visible and official confirmation of the stature of their heroes. The connection was good for Guy, good for Mireille, good for hockey and good for show business.

Sam Pollock was relieved. For at least five years he had worked to provide the Montreal Canadiens with a francophone star, a true "Canayen" son of the people, like Jean Béliveau or, even better because he had been more passionately inspired, Maurice Richard. Pollock had chosen Guy Lafleur not only because he was an excellent hockey player, but also and especially because he had the mark of a superstar. And the Canadiens without a francophone superstar were no more than a superb machine, a Rolls-Royce without an engine.

"A hockey team is managed like any other business," the foxy Pollock would say when he was feeling philosophical. "But it is obviously a lot more emotional than other businesses. And then there are the superstars. They are the ones people come to see. Just as they go to movies to see the famous actors. The Montreal Canadiens team has itself had star status for a good half-century. But we still need individual stars, superstars. To attract big crowds, to win, to make the other players better, to make The Legend live on. And the superstar has to be a francophone. A great anglophone star could never be imposed on Montreal. There have been and will continue to be some very good English-Canadian or American players. But the truly great star that separates the Montreal Canadiens from the rest of the NHL must be a product of Quebec. The Canadiens' soul is Québecois and francophone."

Pollock was in charge of a legend, and he knew better than anyone how to provide the sacred cows that populate this legend. He knew how they had to be treated, how to break them in, how to make them eat out of his hand, all the while having great respect for them.

"The outstanding players have an irrepressible need to be stars, to be the best in every game they play, even when their team is losing. And they have that wonderful ability to leave their problems behind the moment they get onto the ice. When they play, their mind is never elsewhere. They do what they do with their whole beings. That might seem easy, but it requires moral fibre and extraordinary powers of concentration. True stars think only of shining; they want all the ice and they want all the attention."

In the eyes of common mortals, superstars become saviours, a kind of omniscient and all-powerful demiurge. Editors, journalists, gossip-columnists got into the habit of consulting Lafleur on anything and everything: fashion, the weather, politics. Everything he said was oracular, everything he did exemplary, everything he touched consecrated. He was admired, he was praised, his every word was followed. Of course he loved it. When he walked into a downtown restaurant or disco, people ran up to greet him, a place was made for him, drinks were offered. Sometimes he came out with a few naive, even shocking statements, but always with such candour that no one ever held what he said against him.

"Hockey is the most important thing in my life. It even comes before my family, my wife, my son."

Shocking but frank. Feminists weren't so appreciative of this sort of remark and they said publicly how unfortunate it was that Guy Lafleur hadn't used his immense fame to modify hockey players' macho image. But Lafleur gave the logical reply that he hadn't worked like a madman for fifteen years with the goal of being a model husband or an exemplary father, but to be a great hockey player.

In any case, his wife didn't take issue with Lafleur's declarations. She also thought that her husband's career should come first. She had made a sort of tacit agreement with him. He would play hockey; she would take care of the rest. Thus it was she who kept the family afloat.

In June 1975 she gave birth to a child they called Martin, her idea, rather than Mathieu, as Lafleur had said in front of the Radio-Canada cameras. Martin was a name that could be said as easily in English as in French.

Guy Lafleur now lived in a world entirely different from the one he had come from. He was living the good life and enjoying it, but he was sometimes nostalgic for the simple and uncomplicated existence of his parents. Lise came from a very different kind of milieu, not at all working-class or proletarian, less blindly accepting of Catholicism, and much more oriented than the Lafleur family towards American culture and values.

For years, Roger Barré's family had spent a good part of each summer in the United States, in Florida or on the New England coast. They also travelled there for the Christmas holidays. Roger Barré loved the American way of life, jazz, Frank Sinatra, the Big Bands. He liked the way Americans' minds worked, their business acumen, their style of family life. He would often play the game Monopoly with his

children. It was through this game that he introduced Lise
and his son, Pierre, to the world of business. He liked to
speak English, as did Lise. Unlike Guy, who felt a bit ill at
ease and a bit lost amidst luxury and wealth, Lise knew how
to appreciate money without embarrassment, in the
American way. Between her and the little world of Thurso
in which Guy was still deeply rooted, there was a wall of
incomprehension. Despite Roger Barré's warmth and
friendliness, the distance between the two families never
stopped growing. They didn't see the world or life in the
same way, and although there was friendliness and respect,
it was from a distance.

Guy had entered a world of money, contacts and
privilege, a truly marvellous place. It was exciting, but
occasionally, when he thought about his parents and
Thurso, he was torn by nostalgia. He sensed that he'd given
up a lot of himself in order to live in this new world, and it
made him feel like an exile. He was all alone in Lise's
universe, the world of the rich.

• • •

The ascension of a superstar is never entirely smooth. The
ice and the glory that is given to one is lost to another.
Already, Lafleur had offended the team's best players,
revered veterans who, because of him, were less visible than
they had been. After every game the journalists rushed into
the dressing room, aiming their cameras at Lafleur,
pressing him with questions. Sometimes it was extremely
embarrassing for his neighbours. While they silently
changed, in the shadows, Lafleur was carefully anointed
with the sacred light, praised and quoted.

In the dressing room Guy had been assigned the place
formerly occupied by the great Jean Béliveau. Near him, on
one side, were the two goalies, on the other Pete Mahovlich
and Yvan Cournoyer. Like Lafleur, Cournoyer, also known
as "the Roadrunner," played right wing. He was faster and
more agile than anyone, and after the departure of Henri
"the Pocket Rocket" Richard in 1975, he had been elected
captain of the team. Cournoyer had certainly been one of
the most stylish, the best, the most spectacular and most

likeable players of his era. He had scored fantastic and unforgettable goals. In one game he had got loose with the puck and, finding himself alone in front of the opposing goalie, had done something never before attempted: a left-hander, he had switched his stick to the right side and let go an amazingly hard and accurate shot. It was an unstoppable and incomparable shot, a true stroke of genius.

At the beginning of 1976, Yvan Cournoyer was the third-leading goal-scorer (behind Maurice Richard and Jean Béliveau) and the third in assists (behind Béliveau and Henri Richard) in the history of the Montreal Canadiens. He was thus assured of an eternal position among the leading scorers, and of his place in the legend beside Béliveau, the Richard brothers, Geoffrion, Howie Morenz and Aurèle Joliat. But the way things were going, he would sooner or later be overtaken by those young wolves now in favour with Bowman and the fans: Guy Lafleur, Steve Shutt, even Jacques Lemaire and Larry Robinson. The best years of the Roadrunner were already behind him. He was thirty-two, the age when an athlete slows down and begins his decline, whether he wants to or not. The reflexes deteriorate, the muscles weaken, stamina decreases. Guy Lafleur, who was beside Cournoyer in the dressing room, was approaching the peak of his powers. More and more often, Bowman used Lafleur in place of Cournoyer on right wing. In the dressing room the pack of journalists almost always made for Lafleur rather than the venerable captain.

A good loser, Cournoyer moved his things to the other end of the room, saying that he felt cramped, trapped as he was between the goalies with their massive equipment, Guy Lafleur with his court of journalists and fans, and Pete Mahovlich, who never stopped talking and often smelled of stinky feet and liniment. Of course people concluded that Cournoyer had distanced himself out of spite, and that he was bitter and frustrated. Perhaps beside Lafleur he had felt a certain helplessness, but the allegations of the press hurt him deeply. For the first time Lafleur reprimanded the journalists.

"How can you know what someone is thinking or feeling? Yvan Cournoyer has always been good to me. When I first came, he helped me. He still has four or five good years ahead of him. It's almost certain he won't continue to be the team's high scorer, but you must know he doesn't need you to tell him that."

Like everyone else, Lafleur felt a pang in his heart as he watched the once-great Cournoyer sinking slowly into the shadows. But that was the order of things. It was nothing to feel bad about.

"One day it will be my turn," he thought. "Someone faster and stronger than me will come onto the scene, and I will have to yield my place. I'll get less ice time. That is the way things happen. Every record is made to be broken. I just hope that when it happens, I'll behave as well as Cournoyer has with me."

But that time was still far in the future. The summit and the best were yet to come. That's what everyone was telling him.

On May 16, 1976, the Canadiens won the Stanley Cup at the Philadelphia Spectrum. Their victory was hailed as the end of an era. Fred Shero, Dave "the Hammer" Schultz, Bob Kelly and the Broad Street Bullies had been defeated by the "Cannibals of Sainte-Catherine," Rick Chartraw, Pierre Bouchard, Larry Robinson and company. Scotty Bowman had proved the Canadiens really were the strongest and the smartest. Unlike Shero, Bowman didn't insist on a rigid system. He used every system, quickly adapting to anything his opponent tried. His team was talented, quick and intelligent, versatile and the best skaters in the league. The players were fearless and could play in any system. The Montreal Canadiens had beaten the Flyers at their own game.

For Bowman, it was a personal victory over Shero. He had ordered his men not to let themselves be intimidated by Shero's theatre of the macabre, and to skate around while Kate Smith sang "God Bless America." Usually, of course, all the players listened closely to the anthem, their heads lowered, their helmets in one hand and their sticks in the other. But that evening the Canadiens put their helmets back on and, getting away from the blinding spotlights, starting skating in circles while the Spectrum fans booed. Having done that, they'd practically won already. Shero and his men were disconcerted. Bowman's players had seized the initiative before the game had even started.

During that final, Pierre Bouchard played magnificently. He scored twice, which was twice his regular season production of one goal. Guy Lafleur scored the winning goal, his seventh of the playoffs. Throughout the series he had played well and with great spirit. But some careful observers noted that he sometimes seemed to let up. He was always the best, always unpredictable, incredibly quick with his fakes, and his shot was still formidable and accurate—nevertheless, something wasn't right.

Lafleur had gone through some bad periods during the season. In the fall he had gone ten games without scoring a single goal. No one understood what was happening to him. Especially since, during these periods of drought, Lafleur became even more timid and secretive than usual. The journalists would imagine all sorts of possibilities and draw their own conclusions. During the series against the Flyers, certain sports columnists insinuated that Lafleur was afraid of Fred Shero's goons; others suggested that the pressure that had been put on him during the season was starting to weigh him down, and that he was frustrated to see that many players not as good as he were making more money.

In fact, these explanations had nothing to do with the truth. No one could know what was worrying Guy Lafleur. It was a secret shared by only a few members of the organization and the police, who had asked him to be absolutely discreet.

A few days before the series, the Quebec Provincial Police had arrested a young man they knew well. He had been involved in the famous Brinks robbery that had brought its clever and daring perpetrators a tidy $2.8 million. Wanting to reduce his sentence, the bandit had revealed various secrets. There was a rumour, he said, that certain of his former colleagues intended to kidnap Guy Lafleur and demand a ransom from the Montreal Canadiens. A million at least, and in small bills.

The police informed Jean Béliveau, the Canadiens' vice-president of public affairs, who took the matter extremely seriously. Two policemen hired by the Montreal Canadiens went to the Lafleur residence in Verchères and a plan of defence was quickly established. Lise and Martin were put in the Hotel Bonaventure. Lafleur stayed at the house with the two policemen. One of them was armed, the other wasn't. Lafleur had a .308 carbine and a .375 Magnum, but he didn't like the prospect of having to shoot at people, even if they were dangerous criminals. In another way he found the whole business amusing. It was flattering and increased his stature. A group of criminals, not small-time thieves but large-scale operators, clever and ingenious enough to have pulled off what some people considered the robbery of the century, now proposed to kidnap him. And in their opinion he was worth a lot.

"I can't help having, somewhere inside me, a certain sympathy for those guys," Lafleur joked to the policemen who were guarding him. "They think I'm worth ten times more than the Canadiens do."

He had never been able to accept the way his last contract had been forced upon him. He was one of the best players in the NHL, but at least twenty others were much better paid. He had just scored fifty-six goals during the 1975–76 season, a team record, and he had also got sixty assists, for the impressive total of 116 points. But even among the Canadiens players, where he was the uncontested star, many had salaries much higher than his, including Jim Roberts, who was getting old and had accumulated only twenty-one points during the season. Marcel Dionne, who'd had the good sense to play in the United States, was making more than $300,000 a year, more than three times what Lafleur was paid. Sometimes Guy had the impression he'd been duped, and that bothered him.

These thieves who wanted to kidnap him knew what

things and people were worth; they were treating him with more respect than the Bronfman family, owners of the Canadiens.

It had been decided that everything should be kept quiet. Not a word to the press or even the other Montreal players. It was hoped that the bandits, not suspecting they'd been informed on by one of their own, would try to carry out their plan. The police thus hoped to make a good haul.

But after a few days Lafleur began to feel ill at ease in his role as bait. First he was worried about his wife and son, and then he began to feel very disturbed by the whole business. He couldn't stop thinking about what had happened a few years earlier, after the FLQ had kidnapped the government minister, Pierre Laporte. Of course the circumstances had been entirely different. But you could never know. This kind of thing could always turn sour. The pressure on him was tremendous. They were right in the middle of the playoffs. He slept badly, lost his appetite, couldn't concentrate.

It was known that between his home and the Forum there were three places the bandits could strike: two red lights (one at Varennes, the other at Boucherville), and the access road to the Jacques-Cartier Bridge. When Lafleur entered or left the city, the police followed him in an unmarked car. But they weren't supposed to interfere. If the criminals succeeded, they would be tracked. Lafleur always wore a transmitter.

The morning of May 16, three bandits were arrested in Ottawa for a bank robbery. The informer immediately told the police that they were the ones who had been planning to kidnap Guy Lafleur. Contacted at his hotel in Philadelphia, Guy was told that the danger was over. He was relieved but exhausted.

That evening, after bringing the Montreal Canadiens their twentieth Stanley Cup, Guy was unable to celebrate. In the dressing room, where the champagne was flowing freely, the absence of Lafleur—hero of the day and of the year—was suddenly noticed. Pete Mahovlich, Jim Roberts, the trainer Eddy Palchak and a few journalists, including Claude Larochelle of the Quebec newspaper *Le Soleil*, set out to look for him. They finally found him at the far end of the Spectrum. He had shut himself into a small, poorly lit room, and was sitting on a stool, a Coke in his hand, clearly unhappy to see them.

The overly exuberant Pete Mahovlich shook him like a rag doll trying to get him to be happy. But Guy had only one desire: to be alone, not to have to speak or even to listen to anything from anyone, to be left in peace for once.

For years it had never, never stopped. The whole world was always running after him. He was always having to explain himself and give his opinion on every subject, whether things were going well or badly. He felt empty, and at the same time, brimming with tears. He would have liked to have been left in peace to cry alone. He didn't have the strength to respond to Mahovlich and to tell them all to go away. Fortunately Larochelle and Palchak, more sensitive than Pete Mahovlich, understood his feelings and tried to talk to him gently, the way you talk to a sick person, so sweetly and softly that he almost burst into tears.

When they got back to the dressing room most of the players had already left to party elsewhere. Larochelle and Lafleur went to find a restaurant. Lafleur liked Larochelle, a journalist who had been following him since the happier times with the Remparts. He was a serious person, not a sycophant or flatterer, but a knowledgeable professional who loved hockey and was candid both with the players and his readers. He could also talk about things other than cars and women. And best of all, he came from Quebec.

Quebec! Suddenly his life there seemed light-years away. Hidden away with Larochelle in a small Philadelphia restaurant, he realized that he was no longer part of Limoilou. Eagerly, he pumped his friend about the Colisée, Dumont, Filion, Doyon, every little detail of life in Quebec City. But for the first time, he felt as though he had really emigrated. He had left the city of Quebec, forever.

He told himself, while quietly savouring the excellent wine that Larochelle had chosen, that once more, but on a bigger scale, he had succeeded in the impossible task of seducing and winning an audience, a city, a country. This time it wasn't just the small and almost familial spectators at the Colisée, but the best hockey fans in the world, those of Montreal, of the rest of Quebec, and even hockey fans all over North America. This time he had accomplished something big, something truly immense. He was the champion. He was at the top, the absolute peak. He began to think that, in the end, Gerry Patterson had been right in pushing him to sign with the Canadiens rather than the Nordiques.

As his fatigue and tension dissolved with the wine, everything began to seem simple and cosy once more. Tomorrow he would rejoin Lise and Martin, and it would be summer.

For various reasons, he and Lise had decided to move from Verchères. The plans they'd had to develop the land around the restored farmhouse had turned out to be totally unrealistic: a track for horses, a stable, an indoor swimming pool—all this would have cost at least a million dollars. In addition, it was far from the airport. When the Canadiens played on the road and came home after the game, Lafleur had to drive for almost an hour to get home. Most of the players lived in Montreal's West End, and it was on that side of the city, in Baie d'Urfé, that the Lafleurs were looking.

Baie d'Urfé is a very pretty and well-to-do suburb, entirely new. Most of the houses are enormous, the properties large and the population relatively young and mostly anglophone. Lafleur found a house to his taste, a mixture of Swiss and Quebec architecture, in stone and wood, with five bedrooms, three floors, two fireplaces, a huge lawn with mature trees, rock gardens and a swimming pool. The house was new, it was just being built, and in fact it was the plans that had appealed to Lafleur. Just as he used to have a passion for road maps, he now developed one for house plans. Maps and plans—plans for trips and plans for houses—would become his main reading and the material for his day-dreams.

In his Verchères house, he spent hours looking at the plans for his house in Baie d'Urfé. Several times a week he would go to see how construction was progressing and have long discussions with the workers. He, who had never been interested in manual labour, now enjoyed carting cement, bricks, lumber. He watched the house being born just as he had watched the birth of his son, Martin. He felt that it truly belonged to him, not just because he was going to pay for it, but because he had contributed time and labour to its making. According to Lafleur, money alone could not give someone the right to own property. To really own things, you had to give something of yourself, the way his father had for his small house on Rue Bourget, in Thurso, where he had raised his five children. To truly be at home somewhere required not only money, but also work, attention, love.

Alas, a superstar has other things to do. Other duties beckoned Lafleur. His new agent, Jerry Petrie, had renegotiated Lafleur's contract with the Canadiens and had founded Guy Lafleur Enterprises, Ltd., a company that was charged with the responsibility of planning the star's career.

During the preceding season, Lafleur had accepted advertising contracts worth more than $60,000. These would allow him to live without using more than a small amount of his hockey salary, which was prudently re-invested in a trust administered by the Canadiens hockey club.

Guy Lafleur's name and face were everywhere, all the time. Bernard Brisset, a journalist, calculated that in Montreal newspapers alone there had been at least six hundred articles on Lafleur during the 1975–76 season. And it wasn't going to slow down. On the contrary. Lafleur was required to make innumerable appearances during that summer at various social clubs, sports organizations, breweries needing publicity, service stations, hotels, golf tournaments and so on. He granted innumerable interviews for radio, newspapers and television. He received innumerable titles and trophies at various celebrations and galas. Each appearance required a little thank-you speech to a public that grew ever more avid. But public speaking was difficult for him, it was stressful, and when he was finished he felt emptied. His fame had caught him and he couldn't escape. He didn't know how he would ever get away from it, or even if he should or wanted to. He was finding out that fame was demanding, but also exciting.

• • •

A Toronto lawyer, Alan Eagleson, the same man who in 1973, at the time of the formation of the WHA, had let it be understood that Guy Lafleur's contract with the Canadiens might not be valid and that the future Nordiques organization might be able to draft him, had just had the brilliant and lucrative idea of organizing an international super-tournament for the Canada Cup. All the big hockey countries—Canada, the United States, Finland, Czechoslovakia, the USSR, Sweden and others—would play in September 1976 on different Canadian rinks. The Canadian team was made up of the best Canadian NHL and WHA players, including, of course, on the first line, Guy Lafleur.

At the training camp Lafleur was very pleased to meet again with his old friend and rival from Remparts days, Gilbert Perreault. Perreault had become the best player on the Buffalo Sabres and one the league's top scorers. Cheerful and straightforward, he never took himself too seriously.

But in general, Lafleur was discouraged by the extremely tense atmosphere that prevailed. The team was made up of superstars with overgrown egos who were offended that they weren't getting enough passes, although they made as few as possible, because all they wanted was to score goals and embellish their own point totals. Among others, there was Phil Esposito, the loudmouth, who claimed to have the right to more ice than anyone else because he held this or that record, and who put himself forward as the indispensable leader under the pretext that he had saved the honour of his country in 1972, during the Canada–Russia series.

There was one person on the team who totally fascinated Lafleur. He was Bobby Orr, a self-effacing man who talked quietly, sometimes stammering a little, chewing his words,

like Lafleur. Certain people thought he was the greatest
player of all time. His knees had been injured so often that it
was amazing he could even stand up on his skates.

When Team Canada was on the road, Lafleur and Orr
shared a room. Usually, Lafleur didn't like to talk about
hockey, but with Bobby Orr, things were different. For
hours they would tell, down to the last detail, about their
successful attacks and rushes. How this or that defenceman
or goalie could be faked out or made to lose his
concentration. How great the feeling was when they were
suddenly sure that they were bound to score a goal in the
next few seconds, and how everything, starting at that
moment, in the moving and kaleidoscopic geometry of the
play, began magically to take shape around them, giving
them the intoxicating feeling that the forces of chance were
under their control.

They spoke the same language. In Bobby Orr, Lafleur
found a man as fanatical about hockey as himself, and for
the same reasons. He had never been able to express himself
so clearly with his teammates. Lemaire, a hockey
theoretician, much too cerebral, was always planning out
plays on paper, like football players; he wanted to codify
everything into an organized system. As for Steve Shutt, he
never took anything seriously; he wouldn't mind if people
thought that he had become a great player almost by
accident, because he had followed in the wake of
Lafleur.

Lafleur never knew, and never had known, even as a boy,
what he would do when he leapt onto the ice. Of course,
some patterns occurred more often than others. Thus, at
least a thousand times he had come into the enemy zone on
the right side, first skating along the boards, then moving
away as much as possible after crossing the blue line, in
order to improve the angle of his shot. Then he'd shoot from
far out, a bullet that sometimes reached the speed of eighty
miles an hour. Often he would go into the corners, both his
corner and the left-wing side. He liked the free-for-alls.
Sometimes, when the players made a sort of swarm buzzing
around the puck, he would get so excited that he would
break out laughing in the midst of the action.

He never had a defined plan. He just tried to do everything, without strategy, without even thinking about holding his position. And when he realized that he was taking on certain habits or ways, he broke them. Unlike Lemaire, for example, he forced himself never to do the same thing twice. On that subject Lafleur and Orr understood each other perfectly. You had to be "unforeseeable, man, unpredictable," always improvising.

"In the end," Lafleur said, "you almost have to get to the point where you're surprising yourself."

Like Lafleur, Orr always went to the arena long before the rest of the team. During this tournament they would go to the various arenas even earlier, three or four hours before the game, pursuing their conversation, quietly getting their sticks ready, Bobby Orr anointing and bandaging his scarred knees. They skated a little, talking about women and cars, they faked out the invisible man, shot into the empty nets.

Lafleur had never been at his best in this kind of international encounter. In 1972, when the Canadian professionals had played the Soviets for the first time, he had not yet proved himself in the NHL and was not a member of the all-star team. On December 31, 1975, he had played in a game against the Red Army team, and had given a poor performance. He wasn't able to concentrate and he wandered all over the ice like a lost soul, unable to understand the plays, getting rid of the puck as soon as he got it.

The journalists wrote that he seemed to be afraid of checking the foreigners, but the puck was what he truly feared, because it symbolized such heavy responsibilities. He was so anxious to do well that he was terrified to do anything. His teammates had quickly understood, and stopped passing the puck to him. Bowman hardly let him on the ice.

Now, in the Canada Cup tournament of September 1976, the Canadian champions would face teams from various countries, but the game everyone was most excited about was against the USSR. The Swedes, the Czechs and the others, though often as strong as the Russians, aroused infinitely less interest. The Canadians' only true adversary, the only one that could pose a serious challenge and arouse the fans, was and probably always would be the Soviet team.

On August 24 and 25, Canada played the United States at the Colisée. Guy Lafleur hadn't skated on this rink since 1971, when the Remparts had won the Memorial Cup. The crowd gave him a huge ovation when he skated out with Bobby Orr and Gilbert Perreault. Orr and Perreault understood what was happening, and they stepped back for a moment, leaving Lafleur alone in the centre of the rink. He turned in circles, smiled, lifted his arms to the joyous crowd. His dearest friends and his true fans were there: Madame Baribeau, Jean-Yves Doyon, Paul Dumont, Roger Barré, Maurice Filion . . . They were cheering for him, they loved him. It was sweet and good, but it was hard to bear. Once more they wanted him to be the best. With the Remparts, that was always possible. But this evening, it would be more difficult, because he was with the best players in the world.

Canada beat the Americans easily, but Lafleur didn't contribute much to the victory. He played well enough, but unproductively. It was the same story at the Forum, a few days later, when Canada defeated Czechoslovakia, and the same against the Russians at Maple Leaf Gardens in Toronto.

Bobby Orr, the uncontested hero of this series, delighted the spectators, his teammates, opponents. This Canada Cup series turned out to be his swan song; right after the final game he announced his retirement. Lafleur had become his confidant and had been aware of Orr's plan. He knew Bobby Orr was very sad to be leaving hockey, but that he had sworn to exit gracefully, putting all of his strength and genius into his final games. When he was on the ice with him, Lafleur wasn't thinking about hockey, but about Bobby Orr and what he was going through. Not for anything in the world would he have wanted to outshine him. A champion always feels a twinge when he sees someone else perform some incredible feat. But in September 1976, when Bobby Orr skated the length of the ice and put the puck in the Swedish, or the Russian, or the American net, Guy Lafleur exulted and cheered.

The departure of Bobby Orr was one of the most moving and spectacular in the entire history of the NHL. For Guy Lafleur, who was then very close to him, it provided an unforgettable lesson. He learned that he, too, would sooner or later have to think of leaving. He especially understood that each person must model his career, just as an artist shapes his oeuvre. He had seen so many players retire bitter and desperate, without new ambitions or plans. Bobby Orr's exit was a masterpiece. His career had culminated in a dazzling finale; he was leaving satisfied and happy. Guy Lafleur swore to do the same.

It seemed obvious that big Pete Mahovlich, in so many ways Orr's opposite, would not know how to arrange a graceful exit. He was going downhill and drinking heavily. His skating had deteriorated. He was letting good passes get by him, missing golden opportunities. His shot had grown soft and inaccurate. This year his point production would be cut in half. But Scotty Bowman still let him centre the first line between Lafleur on right wing and Steve Shutt on left. This trio remained the most productive on the club and even in the league, but it was no longer really because of Mahovlich. Pierre Bouchard had nicknamed the Shutt–Mahovlich–Lafleur line the "Donut Line" because there was a hole in the middle.

In January 1977, Bowman saw the light. He put Lemaire with Lafleur and Shutt. The most powerful and spectacular line of modern times had finally been put together. For three years it would totally dominate the NHL, and bring three more Stanley Cups to the Montreal Canadiens.

• • •

On March 24, 1977, the Forum was gripped by almost unbearable suspense. All eyes were glued to Guy Lafleur who, that evening, was in a position to break a seventeen-year-old record. The record was held by Bronco

Horvath of the Boston Bruins who, in 1960, had scored at least one point in each of twenty-two games in a row.

The Canadiens were totally dominating the game against the St Louis Blues. By the third period, Lafleur had already wasted several good chances to score. He was nervous and suffering from the flu. Bowman had given him masses of ice, and all his teammates seemed to have decided to try to set him up, but it wasn't working. Finally, in the middle of the third period, Réjean Houle and Doug Risebrough succeeded in piercing the St Louis defence and getting the puck to Lafleur, who beat the goalie on a backhand. The crowd erupted with such joy that the game had to be stopped for the celebration.

Although he'd gone to sit down on the players' bench, Lafleur had to come back on the ice, towel around his neck, to salute the crowd. Then Sam Pollock came to congratulate him. He had even prepared a short speech, which he recited to Lafleur in a shaky voice, in front of all the players. He told Lafleur that breaking the record was the feat of a very great athlete, one who played with his whole heart, and that his exploit reflected well on the entire team. Lafleur had now got at least a goal or an assist for twenty-three games. The streak continued for 14 games more, so that in 37 consecutive games he scored 26 goals and got 52 assists for a total of 76 points. Bronco Horvath sent him a telegram of congratulations, then returned to his obscurity. When the great stars reach their zenith, they shine so brightly that, one by one, the others disappear.

In the great, mythic legend of the Canadiens, only two players remained: Guy Lafleur and Maurice Richard. That year, all the Canadian and American sports writers produced knowing analyses and stirring editorials on the question of who was the greater, the nobler, the stronger. Most decided the two were incomparable and equal.

Meanwhile, in other NHL clubs, various excellent players of Lafleur's generation were also making their marks and establishing enviable records. Out of modesty, but also because he knew Lemaire was right when he said

that only the team and team records really mattered,
Lafleur pretended to be uninterested in his own point totals
and those of his rivals. From time to time, though, he would
call his father in Thurso. His father had continued to collect
everything written about Guy, and was putting together his
gigantic archive. Guy asked him:

"Papa, is it true that Dionne is catching up to me?"

Réjean Lafleur, a bit worried, consulted his statistics and
reassured his son.

"No way. He's lost ground the past two weeks. It would
take a miracle for him to catch up before the end of the
season."

"And Leach? And Clark?"

No player's popularity approached Lafleur's. Even in
the United States, where they had been slower to take to
him because he didn't talk much to American journalists,
he had become an enormous star. And he assumed the
responsibilities of a star and profited abundantly from the
privileges. Nor did he hesitate to speak his mind.

One day, Scotty Bowman had punished Rick Chartraw
for missing an optional practice. When the journalists asked
the players why Chartraw had been benched, Lafleur told
the truth and gave his opinion. He thought Bowman had
acted improperly.

"It was an optional practice. I'm not saying Rick was
right not to go. On the contrary, as you know, since you saw
me go, I think you should always attend practices, optional
or not. But Bowman has no reason to punish Chartraw
because, in principle, he gave us our choice."

NHL players did not often publicly repudiate their
coaches. Only Henri Richard had dared argue openly with
Toe Blake, or question the competence of Al MacNeil. In
the well-protected sanctuary of the dressing room, the
players might sometimes complain about Bowman, call
him unrepeatable names, but saying anything against him
to journalists was out of the question. The coach held
absolute and incontestable authority.

The Chartraw affair created a stir in the press. In fact, it
was one of the first confrontations between Lafleur and

Bowman, one of the first of Lafleur's blows against the established order and the venerable institution of the Montreal Canadiens. There would be more, many more. Lafleur would not be silent. He began to speak his mind with amazing frankness.

To a Los Angeles journalist who asked him who he thought was the best goalie in the NHL, he gave the name of Rogatien Vachon. Vachon was then thirty-two, not young for a goaltender, and his last season had been mediocre. Also, Lafleur's answer had been hurtful to the two Canadiens goalies, Ken Dryden and Michel "Bunny" Larocque, who had both had excellent seasons and would almost certainly win the Vézina trophy. Bowman informed Lafleur that he had lacked both delicacy and discernment.

"I was speaking for myself," replied Lafleur. "The goalie who makes my life the most difficult is Rogatien Vachon. Bunny and Dryden might have better averages, but don't forget they don't have me to deal with. They've never had to play against the best club in the NHL."

Rogatien Vachon, asked by the same journalist who was the best player in the league, had answered "Guy Lafleur." Like everyone else. Like Dryden and Larocque. Like singer Robert Charlebois who, during a show at the Olympic Stadium, had called out to the crowd:

"Do you like Guy Lafleur?"

The crowd had roared. Charlebois had added:

"I like him, too. In the winter, he replaces the sun."

The 1977 playoffs might have been colourless and boring. Fortunately, a few other things got mixed in with the hockey—politics, nationalism, racism, a maelstrom of passions and emotions and, most of all, Guy Lafleur.

● ● ●

At the end of the 1976–77 season, the Canadiens were stronger than they had ever been. Too strong. They had only lost 8 games out of 80, winning 60 (14 shut-outs) and tying 12. That season almost all the NHL players' awards went to Montreal players—Dryden, Larocque, Robinson, Shutt and, more than any other, Lafleur. All in all, Lafleur's achievements were rewarded by more than $25,000 in prizes and bonuses. After a continent-wide competition, readers of *Sports* magazine elected Lafleur "best athlete of 1987," and the magazine gave him a Thunderbird. He also won the Hart trophy as the most valuable player to his club, the Art Ross trophy as top scorer (with 136 points from 56 goals and 80 assists), and the Conn Smythe trophy for being the best player during the playoffs.

Both in the media and among ordinary hockey fans, there was more and more talk about the fact that the Canadiens were too powerful. The precarious balance that had existed for the past ten years in the NHL now seemed to be in danger of being destroyed. Since the result was almost always predictable, the only real interest in games involving the Canadiens was the electrifying play of Guy Lafleur.

When he played, Lafleur aroused and galvanized the spectators. Like Babe Ruth, Howie Morenz or Rocket Richard, he always managed to amaze, even when his plays backfired. Other NHL players had or would have bigger point totals—Phil Esposito, Richard Martin, Marcel Dionne, Steve Shutt—but Lafleur was the one who dazzled. When he scored, it was a work of art, drawing cries of appreciation from the crowd.

Despite their domination of the league, the Montreal Canadiens of that era were easy to like. Half the players were Québecois. Together they were doing something exceptional and the whole province was behind them, loved them as though they were part of the family. They spoke English on the ice, even Lemaire and Lafleur, but they were defending Quebec's honour against the American brutes, the Protestants and the English.

In September 1976, in Toronto, before the first Canada Cup match against the Soviet team, the announcer, Claude Mouton, was booed when he introduced the players in French after doing so in English. And when the francophone players came onto the ice they, too, were booed. Lafleur was shaken and hurt. "What's happening? What did we ever do to them?" He didn't understand that, just like everything else, hockey, sports, the Olympics were sometimes a matter of politics. The rise of Quebec nationalism that would culminate, two months later, in the election of the Parti Québecois, was aggravating Torontonians. For them, the enemy to beat that night wasn't the Soviets but the Québecois. And the Québecois were identified with the Montreal Canadiens. The NHL strategists were pleased. This meant that within the NHL were rivalries deep enough to arouse the fans, which would mean large crowds at the games and high television ratings. Rivalry and passion meant money.

On March 12, 1977, Mario Tremblay, who was nicknamed "the Bionic Blueberry," publicly declared himself for Quebec sovereignty. And when he buried his fist in Pete Mahovlich's face, everyone concluded, even though in reality it had nothing to do with it, that he was settling his political scores. Sam Pollock had succeeded beyond his wildest dreams: he had positioned the Canadiens perfectly in the dynamic of conflicting nationalisms, and his team was doing a beautiful job of riding the crest of Quebec politics.

But even though this was a time when everything was being questioned, no one had any desire to tamper with the Montreal Canadiens—even though everything having to do with the word "Canadian" was considered a disgrace. For example, no one dared to think that they might start to call the team the "Québecois," even though they were the strongest, most cherished, most prestigious, most deeply Québecois institution that existed.

The white H surrounded by the red C in the Canadiens' logo is there as a reminder that the French Canadians are the real "Habitants" of Quebec. In 1976 the word "habitant" had a very negative connotation in French Canada; it was a synonym for being rustic, rural and backwards. Thus the Canadiens, "the Habs," were projecting all across North America, and even in Europe and the USSR, an image and values that the people of Quebec now rejected and from which they were violently dissociating themselves. They didn't like what "Canadien" meant, and they no longer wanted to be looked upon as "habitants." Nevertheless, they approved of, supported and loved their Montreal Canadiens, their Habs.

The program of the Parti Québecois, which had come to power a few months before, included Quebec's separation from the rest of Canada. Quebec was seeing itself with new eyes; with pride and sincerity it was affirming itself in the face of the North American giant.

Lafleur had never hidden the lack of sympathy he felt for PQ policies and ideology. He had moved to the West Island, to Baie d'Urfé, which was a very anglophone district. And he said openly that he intended to send his son to an English school.

"I needed to speak English to play hockey in Montreal. To succeed in any area you have to speak English. I am Québecois, but I live in North America."

He was a continentalist and an opportunist. When anyone asked him, he always said he was against separatism. But at this time almost all the leading personalities in Quebec were in favour of independence. The intellectuals, the labour movement, the students —everyone supported the PQ. Not Lafleur. He, the most loved of all, the man more admired than any other Québecois, their herald and their prophet, was totally dissociating himself from their collective project. And his fame was not the least affected. Every right, every favour was his. During those passionate years, there was no one else who enjoyed an equivalent unconditional support, both from the Establishment and from the ordinary people. He floated above everything and everyone, more or less aware of the immense freedom that was his. If he had wanted Quebec's independence, everyone would have done anything to make it happen for him. The political parties courted him, especially the PQ, but he always reminded them of his anti-sovereignty stance and said that politics didn't interest him. Hockey was what he loved. Hockey was his life.

"For me it's more important than my wife and my son."

If almost anyone else had made such a statement, people would have turned away. But no one turned away from

Lafleur. He filled the Forum, the Spectrum, the Garden and the Coliseum. Everyone followed the 1977 playoffs, even though the outcome was a foregone conclusion. A certain amount of spice was provided by various spectacular incidents, in which Guy Lafleur was closely involved.

The Philadelphia Flyers, who hadn't really recovered from their shattering defeat of the previous year, were quickly crushed by the Canadiens, who then flattened the St Louis Blues in four straight games. Bowman had barely used Lafleur against the Blues. This infuriated the spectators who'd come to the Forum expressly to see him, but Bowman had decided to be careful with Lafleur. He knew there were Blues players who would have liked to injure Lafleur, and he wanted to keep him intact for the meeting with the Big Bad Boston Bruins, an opponent he thought would be more difficult to beat.

The Bruins were coached by the flamboyant Don Cherry. They had a good team, not as sophisticated as Montreal, but tough, intense and very motivated. It would be an interesting battle between Scotty "the Iceman" Bowman, emotionless and impassive, and Don Cherry, provocative, anti-Establishment, a volcano in a perpetual state of eruption.

Cherry had some skilled hockey players, but his team also included several goons, assault tanks who had terrorized the NHL all season long. In addition, the Bruins had a particularly detestable player called Don Marcotte, whose assignment was to cover Guy Lafleur. This he did better than anyone. The same height, the same weight, with the same skating ability as Lafleur, Marcotte shadowed him. He had watched him long and carefully, viewing and re-viewing everything available. In the end he was able to imitate him, guess what he was going to do, anticipate even his most subtle moves. Marcotte was setting out to possess Lafleur.

During the first two games the Canadiens played against the Bruins, at the Forum, Lafleur was almost shut down by Marcotte. Finally, he became so agitated that he shot a bullet right at Mike Millbury, who was in his way. A violent altercation followed. The Bruins' goalie, Gerry Cheevers, accused Lafleur of deliberately trying to hit Millbury in the face. Lafleur replied that Cheevers should try to learn to be a better goalie rather than lecturing others.

The next morning, Montreal's *La Presse* and Quebec's *Le Soleil* published an extraordinary photo of the confrontation, a magnificent composition worthy of a master artist. Gerry Cheevers, his mask pushed back on his head, was jabbing his finger towards Lafleur; Lafleur was staring back haughtily. Another Boston player had got between Lafleur and Cheevers, and behind him, by his height and position dominating the entire tableau, Larry Robinson stood ready to intervene. The force and intense expressiveness of the looks these four men were exchanging gave the scene a beautiful and powerful dynamic. In the background, behind the main characters, could be seen a few transfixed onlookers.

The Bruins were furious. The game was practically lost. They felt they had been unfairly brutalized. But they weren't at home. And, furthermore, they were in a poor position to complain about another team's tactics. They left Montreal threatening revenge. They knew the Canadiens would soon be on their territory, on the small Boston Garden rink, surrounded by their fans. Then they could make them pay dearly for their arrogance.

Two days later, on the evening of May 11, the night before the third game of the series, the Canadiens checked into to the Sheraton Hotel in Boston. Guy Lafleur and the Canadiens team and organization were worried, even the biggest and toughest players, like Bouchard, Chartraw and Robinson. They knew they'd have to defend Lafleur against the Boston goon squad, and that an all-out battle could easily develop, with its attendant blood, broken teeth and bones.

At this time Lafleur's roommate was Jacques Lemaire. When he woke up on the morning of the 12th he was alone in their room at the Sheraton. He dressed quickly and went down to find Lafleur in the hotel restaurant. Lafleur was upset, hardly replying when Lemaire spoke. He seemed vacant and distracted.

Jacques Lemaire almost never read the sports pages. According to him, it just made things difficult for the players and ruined their concentration. Unlike Lafleur, he almost always refused to talk to journalists and he hated having his picture taken. Of course he knew the Bruins had sworn vengeance, but leaving Montreal he had told himself that the whole thing was just another invention of the sports writers, who were always giving in to blatant sensational-ism. But when Pierre Bouchard came to join them at their table and showed them the Boston morning papers, Lemaire realized that things had got serious.

In big black letters on page one of every paper, John Wensink, the Bruins' dirtiest player, was quoted as saying that when Guy Lafleur stepped on the ice of the Boston Garden, he would tear his head from his shoulders.

Lafleur admitted to Bouchard and Lemaire that he'd read the papers. He said they didn't bother him and that he wasn't afraid. But it was easy to see that Lafleur wasn't himself. All he could do was play with his food; he didn't have the heart to eat.

But Lemaire and Bouchard realized that when Lafleur said he wasn't afraid, he wasn't necessarily lying. They knew Lafleur well enough to know he never lied, except sometimes to himself. Sometimes he would hide things from himself, or let himself believe certain things. So he always refused to admit he was afraid because he knew that would make things worse. But that morning, no matter how much he denied it, fear was in his voice, the way he moved, the way he looked.

Lemaire said, "Look, Guy, you know we're with you. What's written in the newspapers isn't what makes things dangerous. Every day, in the NHL, there's guys who'd like to have your head."

"I know, Coco. Don't worry about me."

He didn't want to talk. He went out for a walk. In the middle of the afternoon, after a short nap, he came down to the hotel lobby. When he spotted Pierre Meilleur and Eddy

Palchak, he rushed up to them and convinced them to go to the Garden. Three hours before the game! He wanted to take the offensive against his fear, to neutralize and destroy it. He couldn't wait for the game to start.

That evening the Canadiens went to the Garden in a state of extreme tension. The arena was charged with excitement. Wensink's threat had roused the crowd, and they were eager for blood. When Lafleur leapt to the ice he was greeted with a huge roar. But Don Cherry made the crowd wait. He didn't send Wensink into the fray immediately, because hockey is also show business. A good coach, at least in Don Cherry's mind, is also a stage director. He also calculated that having to wait would make Lafleur and his protectors, already anxious and upset, unable to play effectively. But he didn't know Guy Lafleur. As soon as Guy had laced on his skates, his fear had dissipated, along with the knot in his belly. He was filled with energy. Never had he skated so well. He avoided every bodycheck, shook off Marcotte, took passes easily.

That night he played one of the great games of his career. After four minutes of play he scored on Cheevers. By the end of the game he had two goals and two assists. The Canadiens won 4 to 2, Lafleur participating in every goal. The crowd wanted blood; they got thrills instead. Boston fans had no reason to cheer Lafleur, but it seemed that for having the courage to confront the Bruins' toughest players and, at the same time, give a brilliant performance, he had conquered Boston.

Don Cherry, the Bruins' coach, gave Lafleur his due and recognized him as an extraordinary player. However, Lafleur, who would not be silenced by modesty, said proudly, "I've shut them up for a long time." He'd had his revenge.

If Wensink had not told anyone about his unsavoury plan, he might have found it easier to execute. If kindness was what could always disarm Guy Lafleur, provocation had the opposite effect. In challenging Lafleur openly, Wensink had given him the strength and the courage to confront him, to be ready for war. *Si vis pacem, para bellum.* If you want peace, prepare for war. That was what Lafleur had done.

But there was another adage that hockey players liked and often quoted: "He who lives by the sword, will die by the sword." In other words, you beat your opponent by playing his game. It's on his own ground that you truly defeat your enemy. Lafleur had humiliated the Bruins on their own ice. His victory over Wensink was incontestable.

"For me, pressure is a challenge," Lafleur confided. "It's like the bar for a high jumper. It's part of my job."

That night in Boston, Guy Lafleur had demonstrated something more than courage. He believed that he was the best. In a way he felt almost invulnerable, and it seemed that he was. Except at the beginning of his NHL career, when he wasn't sure of himself, he had never been afraid to attack. In 1977, no matter which rink he was playing on, Guy Lafleur knew no fear he was incapable of confronting.

Sometimes he told himself that sooner or later he'd meet his Waterloo. He was thinking of a serious injury that could cut short his career. But things would not happen in the way he expected, though in the end the result would be the same.

● ● ●

The Lafleurs were very fond of the French Riviera, especially Saint-Tropez—the sea, the good restaurants with flower-filled terraces, the ultra-chic discos where you could see rock stars and Arab sheiks, the outrageously expensive boutiques, the yachts, the unbelievably luxurious cars and hotels, all the elegant, refined and wealthy people, the "beautiful people," who they had now joined. Guy wasn't yet twenty-six; Lise had just turned twenty-seven that spring. The world and the future belonged to them.

They were also very fond of the Shutts, Steve and Ninon, who had come to meet them after having spent a few days in Scandinavia. Like Lise, Ninon was a compulsive organizer. Together, the two women decided on everything, which suited the men perfectly.

While drinking champagne on the night of their reunion,
Lafleur had told his friends what he planned to do on his
vacation. It seemed to be very simple. His plan was to do
nothing, absolutely nothing, for the whole month of July.
Lise said to him:

"Flower, you know you'll never be able to. You're
incapable of doing nothing. In two days you'll crack."

"He's already cracked," laughed Steve Shutt. "Already
cracked up."

A few weeks before, on the evening of their Stanley Cup
victory, Guy Lafleur had, in fact, cracked. At the moment
that he least expected it. He had come out of the shower
wrapped in a yellow towel, crossed the dressing room, sat
down in his corner and then, suddenly, while looking at his
equipment, his old skates with the leather all wrinkled, his
sweat-soaked socks and jersey, he had burst into tears,
without knowing why. Larry Robinson, Réjean Houle and
Steve Shutt had come up and surrounded him. He was
trembling like a leaf and said he didn't have any feeling in
his legs.

"Do you want us to get the masseur?" Houle asked.

"You've been constantly on the go for nine months,"
Robinson said. "You're tired, that's all."

"You need a break," said Steve Shutt. "Guy, for your
own sake, give yourself a break."

The three of them were so kind, so brotherly, that they
made him cry even more. He was happy and despairing at
the same time.

"You have to stop," Houle kept saying to him. "The
journalists are waiting for you on the other side of the door.
You have no choice. They won't leave until you talk to
them."

"Drink some champagne, it'll do you good."

He had dressed, chug-a-lugged a half-bottle of Dom
Perignon, then gone out to meet the journalists who asked
him the same old questions for the thousandth time. But
tonight he had some new answers to give them.

"You want to know what I'm going to do with my
summer? Nothing, absolutely nothing. I won't put on my

skates even once, I promise you. No jogging, no softball, no bicycling, not a millisecond of training. I need a change of scene. Never again the craziness of my first years with the Canadiens when I spent my summers wearing myself out training and started every season already exhausted. You can write it down, it's official: this summer, Guy Lafleur is doing nothing."

In fact, he needed to take a break. For several weeks, well before the playoffs, he had been having unpredictable and uncontrollable emotional swings. During the playoffs he had had terrible outbursts of anger against his checkers, especially the Detroit Red Wings' Paul Woods, who stuck to him like a scab. Twice he'd hit him, trying to injure him, which was not his kind of game. If something went wrong at practice, he would break his stick against the boards. One time, after Pierre Bouchard, good old Pierre, his friend, had checked him a bit too hard, he had reacted violently.

"Who are you working for? Are you trying to injure me too? Haven't you figured out that you're here to protect me?"

He'd left the ice, then slammed the dressing room door so hard that the sound had echoed through the whole Forum. Then he had smashed his stick across the table.

For a long time he'd known he'd have to pull back, not only from hockey, which was relatively easy and in any case inevitable, but also and especially from everything connected with hockey. The task of being a star was becoming more and more of a burden. The first few weeks of his summer of idleness were filled with various duties.

Thursday, May 26, he filmed a commercial in Duvernay, a new and beautiful suburb for the well-to-do. The next day he lunched with the publishers of *Reader's Digest*, who took him on a tour of their offices, introduced him to their secretaries, their writers, their printers, their advertisers, everyone. The following day, Saturday the 28th, he went to a large banquet in Thurso, where he was generously praised and congratulated. The morning of the 29th, he took a plane to New York where he received his Thunderbird from *Sports* magazine. Two days later he was

in Las Vegas to receive the 1977 Hockey Award. He liked
Las Vegas, all its lights, its magnificent, sexy young women,
the limousines, the good life. Lise and his parents were with
him and it was a party, champagne and all. The following
day he was received in San Francisco by the owners of
Shasta, the soft drink company for which he was the Quebec
spokesman.

Meanwhile Jerry Petrie, his agent, had been approached
by researchers on behalf of Johnny Carson and Merv
Griffin. Both men wanted Guy on their talk shows, but
Petrie had to refuse. There was no time. Lafleur had to dash
back to Montreal for the annual NHL dinner, where he was
awarded more prizes, made polite and thankful speeches
and signed hundreds of autographs, always followed by a
mob of journalists and photographers.

Then, in spite of the fact that he had always hated golf,
there were two tournaments he was obliged to play in, one
for the Quebec junior major league, and another for Scouts
Canada. Next, two filmmakers from Marseille, Mario
Bévali and Louis Aznarian, who were putting together a
film about his friend Mireille Mathieu, wanted to meet
Lafleur to hear him talk about her and also to persuade him
to be in their film. Then he visited some schools, a centre for
delinquents, a home for the aged, eight radio stations and
three television studios. That was how he spent the first
three weeks of his summer vacation. He saw even less of his
wife and son than during the regular season.

Sometimes Lise would remind him of the promise he had
made to the journalists that he would do nothing all
summer. And Guy would reply angrily:

"I know. But I'm busy. What do you want me to
do?"

"Learn to say no once in a while. It won't cost you
anything, Guy. Just say that you're busy elsewhere."

"But these people love me. It's thanks to them that I've
got where I am. I owe them something, a little visit, three or
four hours of my time."

"You owe nothing to anyone. It's they who should be
thanking you."

"You couldn't understand."

"What I understand is that the only person in the world to whom you say no is me. We never see each other. You see everyone except your wife and your son."

It was true. On the rare occasions when he did see his father, Martin was so excited that he would shake. "Daddy!" His father would take him in his arms, talk to him, fuss over him a bit, give him the teddy bear or the truck he had bought him while he was away, then put him down. He was tired. It never stopped.

Lise loved Guy deeply. She had no doubt he was the man of her life. Even when she was angry at him because he had again agreed to go to a meeting or a dinner and he was calling to say he'd be home late, at the sound of his voice, she melted. And when he came back even later than he'd said, her anger dissipated as soon as she saw him. She liked the way he moved, his build, the quiet strength of his gestures, the way his mind worked. She was less happy, though, about her life as the wife of a hockey player.

She was well aware that hockey was a man's world, exclusive and closed, in which women had absolutely no role to play, no say, no authority of any kind. This was even truer for the loving and legitimate spouses than for the exciting and easy groupies. She discovered that in marrying a hockey player she'd had to embrace a religion that was both excessive and totalitarian. When an offer was made for the players' wives to accompany the team on a road trip, they were almost always kept to one side, sometimes even put up at a different hotel from the one where their husbands were staying. The players weren't to be upset or excited. If a wife disturbed her husband in some way, the club was capable of bringing her into line. The organization reached everywhere, even into the players' beds.

At the Forum, as in many other NHL arenas, there was a room for the players' wives, with a bar, a television set, armchairs, a few women's magazines and sports magazines, plants, soothing and edifying pictures on the wall. The women gathered there before the games to gossip, compare their outfits, talk about their children and their husbands.

There were rivalries and jealousy. Different cliques were established. Lise Lafleur belonged to none of them. She found it all a bit silly, degrading and often very depressing.

"No man would accept a situation like this," she said to her husband. "Try to imagine things the other way around. Imagine a women's team on tour with their husbands dragging along behind them, always waiting for them, waiting for them to finish their games or their meetings or their drunks. You would get together before the game in the room for players' husbands, to compare your ties and talk about your cars, your children's report cards and your golf handicaps. With nothing else to do but twiddle your thumbs while waiting for the game. Your wife would always be surrounded by groupies, dozens of handsome, elegant boys, unattached, always making eyes at her and offering themselves. And of course your wives would find them charming, and give them autographs. Can you imagine what that would be like? How do you think the husbands would like it?"

"What do you want to me to say, Lise? That's how it is. That's hockey."

Some evenings, instead of going to the game, Lise left the Forum and went to a movie. She wasn't really a hockey wife like the others. To begin with, she had never been a groupie at heart. And she wasn't sure she liked hockey. She was in love with Guy, his beautiful eyes, his talent, his success. But the world of hockey was something else. When they had married, he wanted her to quit her job as air hostess. Now she was thinking of going back to work. As soon as Martin was old enough for nursery school, she would find something to do. Meanwhile, she would bear her difficulties patiently. After all, it wasn't so terrible. And anyway, for once, during this month of July 1977, they were on a real holiday. No coaches, no practice, no telephone. Guy had even made Jerry Petrie swear that he wouldn't try to contact him, even if NASA called to offer him the moon.

So for a month they lived the good life, and explored the

joys of idleness. They got up late, spent the day wandering on the beaches and the small lively streets of Saint-Tropez. At the cocktail hour they would meet Steve and Ninon at the villa, dress for the evening, always very chic. Lafleur liked fine clothes. They went to the best restaurants, the most sophisticated discos. They came back late, the men a bit drunk. They were all happy and content.

After two weeks, Lise was amazed to discover that her husband was bored. He was rested, relaxed; he was kind and considerate of her; he always laughed whole-heartedly at Steve when he joked and fooled around. But he was missing something: the warm presence of his fans. The first few days, he had been relieved to be surrounded by emptiness. But after two weeks, he felt like a king in exile.

One day, on the Croisette in Cannes, a Québecois couple came up to greet them. They were from Lac-Saint-Jean, polite and friendly. Lafleur was delighted. He lost no time in drawing them into a conversation. "Where have you been? What are you doing? Where are you going?" If it hadn't been for Lise's obvious indifference, he would have invited them for dinner. He had to admit that he was madly in love with the attention people paid to him. Because of Lise and Martin, he felt guilty about it, but life as a star didn't displease him. He met interesting people, other stars, but the main thing was that he was always surrounded, always listened to. He was always holding court, like a king.

"How can you ask a guy to hate that?"

When they got back to Quebec, it was also back to the round of golf tournaments, good works and interviews. Lafleur had bought himself a Ferrari to go with the Thunderbird he'd been given by *Sports* magazine and the Toronado he'd had for a year. To Lafleur, the black Ferrari (there were only thirty in the Montreal area) was the best and most visible symbol of success. He had gone to Thurso to show it to his parents. He had taken them for a ride, one at a time, because the Ferrari could seat only one passenger. His father hadn't been at all appreciative.

"Let me tell you one thing, my boy. A man who buys a machine like this is looking to kill himself. Don't ask me to be happy for you. I don't like your machine."

Guy had laughed. But he couldn't forget his father's words. Sometimes he told himself that Lise was right, that he should stop for a while to take stock of his situation. But everything was going too quickly.

In August he had an experience that made him think about and reconsider his privileged status as a successful star. He had accompanied Jean Béliveau to a camp for disabled children at Saint-Alphonse-de-Rodriguez. At first a bit worried, ill at ease and awkward, he began talking with two small boys, about ten and twelve years old. They knew the names of plants, clouds, insects, birds, rocks, hockey players and many other things. The scope of their interests, their curiosity, their good nature had shaken him. He was truly touched, almost shattered. These children who would never skate, probably never travel—at least not as much as he—who would spend their lives in their wheelchairs, had extraordinary courage and strength.

Lafleur had participated in other good works of this nature: Yvon Deschamps' OXFAM–Quebec, the campaign against Friedreich's ataxia led by Claude Saint-Jean. But nothing had ever touched him as closely as this victory over despair that he had witnessed at the camp in Saint-Alphonse-de-Rodriguez. These children possessed a true and profound happiness, something that he, one of the most pampered people in all of Quebec—strong, rich, admired, adulated, in perfect health, talented—didn't truly have. How was this possible?

He realized that at his very centre he was haunted by some sort of sadness that he couldn't overcome. He was not satisfied. And the worst thing was that he had no idea what he might want that he didn't already have.

He had read somewhere in a magazine that this was the disease of his generation. The Rolling Stones, the spoiled children of the London bourgeoisie, had written the lyrics of the baby-boomer anthem, "I Can't Get No Satisfaction." The baby-boomers had been given everything—schools, arenas, teachers, platforms, jobs. In addition he, Guy Lafleur, had been given ice, all the ice he wanted, glory, all the glory he had sought, and more money and love than he knew what to do with. And it still wasn't enough! He was still hungry and thirsty. But for what?

Jean Béliveau had also been moved. But Lafleur was certain that Béliveau didn't have that gnawing feeling of desperation. Béliveau was a mature man of good will, sure of his own worth, who believed in certain principles, in a solid, established order. He had remained Lafleur's true idol, no longer just as a hockey player but as an example of a man who knew how to live. Most of all, there were things about which Béliveau was certain. Not Lafleur. Not enough. Lafleur was a successful young man, dissatisfied and unsure, a true member of his generation.

Apart from those calm weeks in Provence, he had spent the whole summer on the run. A hundred times he had broken the promise he had made to the journalists, except on one count, physical conditioning. And he wasn't embarrassed to say that he had not trained over the summer. He considered that his development as an athlete was now completed. He denied himself nothing, eating a lot, never hesitating to have a drink when an agreeable occasion presented itself, sometimes smoking a pack of cigarettes a day.

He had arrived at the point where conditioning and training were essentially psychological. That was what he believed. Training consisted of mastering fear and nervousness, of eliminating his inhibitions.

At that time there was a book that sports theorists were all talking about, *The Handbook of Inner Sports*. This book explored the American theory of flow. It said that the body of a talented athlete knew how to act, how to move, how to carry the puck, how to hit and how to dodge. Thus what the athlete should do was to have complete confidence in himself, stop telling himself what to do and let himself be carried by the flow, by his own inner energy. That was delicate and difficult and demanded enormous concentration and detachment. It was a theory that paralleled the literary technique of stream-of-consciousness, used by some of the most explosive of modern writers. They wrote without plan, in a sort of unleashed automatism, allowing ideas to come forth and organize themselves more or less at random. Its basis was very zen, and it demanded receptivity to the potent inner forces of the self.

Lafleur knew little about these theories, which had evolved from beatnik and hippie ideologies, but like everyone else he was surrounded and influenced by the fashionable ideas of his time. Moreover, he knew that his own body "knew." He had no moral certainty, but he had a sure and intuitive grasp of certain things: how to train, what foods to eat, how to trust in the intelligence of his body.

Jean Bonneau, the physical efficiency adviser who had tested the players before the Canada Cup a year earlier, had been amazed by Lafleur's physique and conditioning. "It's a gift from God," he said. "Guy Lafleur chose his parents well, heredity has favoured him."

In January 1978, the Spartak team from Moscow came to the Forum, where the Canadiens beat them 5 to 2. Lafleur scored two goals. This time, the Russians were finally impressed. Victori Tikhonov, coach of the Soviet national team, told the magazine *Sport in the USSR* that Guy Lafleur had all the attributes of the ideal attacker. Everyone agreed with him, but the fact that Tikhonov, the great Russian theoretician, would say so was an event.

Lafleur was also the darling of the hockey research group at the University of Laval. These researchers included Gaston Marcotte and Charles Thiffault, who had met Lafleur during the sixties at the Modern Hockey School. Since that time, he had continued to impress them.

When all around him was in motion—the puck, his opponents, his teammates, himself—everything shifting at varying speeds and following infinitely complex traject-ories, Lafleur was capable of instantly perceiving the geometric parameters of the space in which he was operating. He constantly carried out a kind of analytic geometry, like a radar scanner sweeping the rink from one end to the other. From the available possibilities he would select the best, then do the right thing at the right time. He could "read" the play incredibly quickly; he had a constantly renewed perception of everything that was happening on the rink. As Tikhonov said, he had a strategic appreciation of the game. And he was endowed with that magic faculty, the sixth sense that athletes call anticipation, that allows them to keep one step ahead of everyone else by knowing just what they are going to do.

Jacques Lemaire admired his right-winger's knowledge and artfulness. But he regretted that he couldn't get together with Lafleur to plan their plays. Lafleur practised what Steve Shutt called "organized confusion"; he believed in improvising. Lemaire, who believed in being orderly and rational, was horrified by anything that was uncontrollable or unpredictable.

Lemaire had a great admiration for the famous Russian troika of Petrov, Kharlamov and Mikhailov. Victor Tikhonov, when he had told *Sports in the USSR* that Guy Lafleur was the greatest offensive player in the world, had also insisted that nothing in North America could equal the efficiency of his great line. It was a perfectly functioning machine, precise and unique, a creative masterpiece of sports high-technology. Because of Lafleur's idiosyncratic method of playing, it was impossible for the Canadiens to put together a line equal to the Soviets'.

For now, it wasn't a serious problem. Lemaire, Shutt and Lafleur were each scoring fifty goals a year. But the whole team depended on Lafleur; without him, it would collapse. According to Lemaire, a truly good hockey team could not be built around just one player, no matter how good. Ideally, it should be like the Soviets'—a well-balanced machine in which each player had a specific role. The star should be the team, not the player.

In 1978, in Montreal and throughout the NHL, the brightest star was Guy Lafleur. Despite his excesses of the summer and the fact that he hadn't trained at all, he hadn't gained weight, and he was as quick and strong as he had ever been. But now he faced a new challenge: he had to prove he could maintain his level of play.

In the history of the NHL there have been players who have established remarkable records. For example, Reggie Leach of the Philadelphia Flyers scored 61 goals in the 1975–76 season. But then he had fallen below the 50-goal mark. A true champion must have lasting power, without ever stumbling.

At Christmas, the Islanders' Bryan Trottier was the league's leading scorer, with 51 points, including 21 goals. Lafleur and the Toronto Maple Leafs' Darryl Sittler also had 21 goals but had only 22 assists, whereas Trottier had 30. Nevertheless, in February, Lafleur sprinted into the lead. He finished the season with 60 goals—14 more than Trottier, 7 more than Mike Bossy—and 72 assists. That season, the Shutt–Lemaire–Lafleur trio amassed 145 goals and 315 points, one less than the previous year. It had become predictable, almost boring. The Montreal Canadiens won the Stanley Cup for the third consecutive year.

Once again it was Lafleur who broke the back of the Bruins by scoring the winning goal of the second game. The score was tied in overtime at two goals each. Lafleur let go a bullet from the blue line. Gerry Cheevers didn't even see it, but the noise of the crowd told him he had been beaten. He didn't bother turning around to look at the puck in the net. Head lowered, he went to the dressing room. The Bruins never recovered from that defeat.

The night of the final win, Lafleur was injured. Just the same, he and Bob Gainey skated around the rink, holding the cup high in the air. Lafleur's sweater was stained with blood, but in spite of the twenty-six-stitch cut on his face he was radiant. This time there were no tears. The warrior had hardened in battle. Pressure? Now he liked it so much that he could no longer do without it.

A few days later the Stanley Cup parade took place in the streets of Montreal. As always, the players went to finish their celebrations at the Henri Richard Tavern. With the help of Pierre Plouffe, Lafleur got his hands on Claude Mouton's car keys. He got duplicates made at a small hardware store on Rue Bleury and, the same evening, he

and a few accomplices went into the Forum garage, opened
the trunk of Mouton's car and spirited away the Stanley
Cup.

An hour and a half later, the venerated object was in the
kitchen of Guy Lafleur's parents in Thurso. Guy poured in
a magnum of champagne and got his mother, father and
sisters to drink from it. Soon all of Thurso knew that Guy
Lafleur had come to his father's home with the most
prestigious trophy in the world. People came from all over
town to see, to touch, to photograph and be photographed
beside it. People started to talk about organizing a parade
through Thurso, but there wasn't time. Guy had done the
whole thing to make his father happy, and he had
succeeded.

Together, they crossed Rue Jacques-Cartier to go to the
Knights of Columbus Hall, Guy brandishing the cup in the
air.

• • •

During the winter of 1978, Guy had signed remunerative
advertising deals with Yoplait and General Motors, and
then with Koho, the Finnish hockey stick manufacturer.
Guy Lafleur Enterprises, with its office next to that of the
NHL in the Sun Life building, made more than $100,000
that year. Lafleur had become a one-man corporation.
When advertising people wanted an athlete for a
commercial, they thought of him first. Steve Shutt might
have scored as many goals, but no one ever asked him to
represent a product or a cause. In Quebec, Lafleur had a
virtual monopoly on product promotion, just as Darryl
Sittler did in English Canada.

In the spring, right after the playoffs, Lafleur began
working on a radio show in order to amass the thirty credits
the artists' union required to authorize him to appear in
televised commercials. For six weeks he co-hosted "Le
Monde des Champions" on CKVL, a Montreal station
whose programming was almost all based on open-line
shows. At the beginning he didn't feel very comfortable in
front of the microphone. His voice was dull, unmodulated,
his speech slow and hesitant. But the lines were always busy.

People were finally getting their chance to talk directly to their idol and hear his opinions. He spoke out on everything: on Bowman, on the Canadiens, on women, on fashion, on God, politics, his plans, his regrets, his parents. And his frankness sometimes got him into trouble.

In March 1978, the Toronto *Globe and Mail* had disclosed the salaries of the NHL's best-paid players. Lafleur was in fifteenth place. Gilbert Perreault, who was playing for the Buffalo Sabres, made almost twice as much: $325,000. So did Marcel Dionne and Richard Martin. It was humiliating and maddening for Lafleur, who had good reason to consider himself the best player in the league. When a listener asked him about it, he made a very astonishing declaration. Was it out of spite, like the fox in the fable who, since he couldn't reach the grapes at the top of a vine-covered wall, decreed that they were green? In any case, Lafleur claimed that no price tag could be put on the privilege of playing for Montreal, and that he would only go elsewhere if someone put a gun to his head.

It was a way of telling Perreault, Martin, Dionne, Guèvremont and the rest that he didn't envy them their fates, and that he even felt a little bit sorry for them, belonging to lacklustre organizations and playing for fans who didn't understand the sport. But it also gave the Canadiens organization, with whom he would soon be renegotiating his contract, some powerful arguments.

"Not very clever," his father-in-law, Roger Barré, laughed.

But Lafleur had spoken his mind.

"I want the Canadiens to pay me what I'm worth. What I think or say shouldn't be important. I'm paid to play hockey, not for my ideas. I don't sell my ideas and opinions, I give them."

Just the same, during the NHL meetings in June, Lafleur spoke at length about the escalation of violence in hockey, both amateur and professional. But when, following his diatribe, it was suggested that wearing a helmet be compulsory, Lafleur strongly opposed the suggestion, saying that the more players were armed, armoured and

protected, the more violent they would be. In fact, the real
truth of the matter was that he associated wearing a helmet
with failure. Just as Samson had to keep his hair intact, and
saw it as the source of his strength and his enemies' fear, so
Lafleur displayed his flowing blond hair, which had
become his banner and his fetish.

In the spring he also signed a contract with Bauer, the
sporting goods company whose skates he had started to use
a few years before. In mid-April Bauer was trying out a new
skate that had a dazzling white blade. The first time
Lafleur wore them for a morning practice at the Forum,
everyone was impressed. Except for Bowman.

"But you're not going to wear those skates for tonight's
games, are you?"

"Of course I am."

"I don't like it. I have a bad premonition. At the
beginning of the year I wouldn't have said anything. But
now that we're in the playoffs, Guy, I'd prefer you not wear
those skates."

"That's your problem, Scotty. I have a contract with
Bauer."

Ten minutes later, Lafleur's face was cut. Nothing
serious, but he had to go to the hospital to get the wound
stitched up. As he left the rink Scotty asked him, with his
sarcastic little smile:

"Are you still planning to wear those skates for tonight's
game?"

Scotty, like all hockey men, was deeply superstitious. He
was terrified of anything new. He had never coached an
important game while wearing something new on his back.
Lafleur could understand that. He had his own tics and
manias. For example, he liked his friend Pierre Meilleur,
the team trainer, to slap him on the back as he went out of
the dressing room to play. And he always went on the ice
just before Larry Robinson. When he came off, he liked to
have the trusted Larry behind him. For several years they
followed this ritual, never missing even once.

Lafleur went to the Royal Victoria Hospital with his
journalist friend, Claude Larochelle, who was then writing

a book about him. On the way to and from the hospital he talked to Larochelle about Scotty Bowman, a man he found both execrable and likeable. Execrable because he never let go an opportunity to exercise his authority and he never allowed himself to be questioned.

"I could even believe he's happy when things go badly because then he can shout at us and give us orders."

Bowman was a cold and distant man, unfailingly severe. He had forbidden himself all bonds of friendship with his players. Off the ice, he almost never spoke to them. If, by chance, he ran into them on the street or in a hotel corridor, he nodded at them drily as though to say, "Okay, I saw you, now leave me alone." No smile, not a word.

"In spite of all that, I like the man," Lafleur told Larochelle. "I don't know why, but I really do like him. He's a great hockey man. And he makes no concessions. With him, things are never complicated. You know where you're going. Perhaps you have no desire to go there, but at least you know. Scotty is frank and honest. But he doesn't want anyone to know it, because he's afraid people will realize he's a good-hearted man. That would just complicate his life. But the players know it. When he's not there, they say they hate him, but deep down everyone admires him. He's a strong and generous man."

That evening Lafleur played wearing his old Bauer skates. The Detroit Red Wings were easily defeated. As for the new skates with the shining blades, he never put them on again. He became more and more conservative about his "sacred" hockey outfit. Rather than get new skates, he would ask Eddy Palchak, who was in charge of equipment, to replace the blades five, six or even seven times, until the boots were in tatters. In the same way, he wore his shinpads and shoulderpads to the absolute limit.

He was just as conservative about his street clothes, but not in the same way. Just as he liked the old and broken-in on the ice, he liked to wear new clothes outside the rink. Everyone agreed he was the most elegant hockey player of all. His tastes were very classic. He liked wearing ties, three-piece suits, and almost never wore the jeans that were the uniform of the era.

He was approached by *Penthouse* magazine, which was preparing an article on the ten best-dressed Canadians, one from each province. In spite of his agent's insistence, because it would be good "exposure," Lafleur refused. It was a matter of his image. He had just agreed to represent Yoplait. He also knew that he was a role model for young people. He considered that an appearance in *Penthouse*, although he himself sometimes looked through it, could only soil or confuse his image.

Petrie had gone into business with designers to create T-shirts, shirts and sweaters sporting a stylized flower, Guy's symbol. He sponsored a line of leather clothes made by Crown Waterproof of Ville Saint-Laurent. Two lines of men's toilet products—the "blue line" and the "red line," as in hockey—had also been created. The products included lotion, cologne, soap and a deodorant, "Number 10"—"a clean lemon fragrance" said the advertisement, a "mixture of exotic woods with a hint of musk for the mature man." There was a big campaign on radio and television. There were also plans to market women's fragrances under the brand name "Guy."

In July, at the invitation of Koho, Guy and Lise travelled to Helsinki. Afterwards they went on to the Soviet Union for a trip that included guided tours of Leningrad and Moscow. They went to the Red Square, the Kremlin, ate caviar and drank champagne, had long walks along the Moskva River during the warm, clear evenings when the twilight lingered until almost midnight. They found the Soviet Union sad and austere. Lise was particularly horrified and exasperated by the slow service, the pitiful state of facilities like elevators and telephones, the discomfort and unhealthy dirtiness of public places, people's paranoiac fearfulness.

One day, in line for a visit to Lenin's tomb, Lise got into a conversation with a young man who was jabbering to her in English. He was intelligent, curious and cultivated. She offered him some chewing gum. An armed guard

intervened and violently demanded that the young man
hand over what he'd received. Lise made a scene and left the
line while letting the guard know, by making signs that
couldn't be mistaken, that he was ridiculous and an
imbecile. Nothing in the world made her angrier than
seeing individual freedoms threatened. The next day they
went back to Helsinki, their vision of the communist world
unchanged.

The Koho firm had a stick made especially for Guy
Lafleur. It had the perfect weight, the ideal flexibility, the
most suitable curvature. It had a soul. It was a magic wand
that had extraordinary responsiveness and made it possible
to really feel the puck.

If Yvan Cournoyer was the biggest user of skates (up to
seven pairs a year), Lafleur was the grand champion of
hockey sticks. He used more than forty dozen a season.
Some were autographed for his fans. He also broke several
dozen in fits of anger. Before each game he himself wrapped
the tape around three or four new sticks, then tested their
weight and flexibility.

The Quebec manufacturers complained bitterly about
him. Manufacturers like Victoriaville, Sherwood and Les
Bâtons canadiens, of which his teammates Savard,
Cournoyer and Lapointe were shareholders, claimed to
make sticks that were as good as Koho's. Why encourage
the Finnish manufacturers when most NHL players, the
best players in the world, were happy with sticks made right
here at home? Lafleur had an answer for that. The answer
of an elite hockey player for whom performance was the
most important thing.

"I have nothing against Quebec products. On the contrary. But I advertise the products I believe in and which
serve me well. And I think I know a good hockey stick."

Lafleur had truly become a cultural monument, an icon.
He was the centre of the world. Everyone watched him and
paid attention to him. But just as the actors blinded by the
footlights are unable to see those who applaud them, so
Lafleur found it difficult to understand the society that
adulated him. He couldn't really get interested in anything

beyond himself. Things he had nothing to do with had little importance in his eyes. The outside world was vague and shapeless. He didn't read the newspapers, except the parts that had to do with sports.

Joe Clark, the future prime minister of Canada, came to a game at the Forum and was eager to meet Lafleur and have his picture taken with him. As always, Lafleur was gracious in agreeing. But after the photo session he asked the photographer, "Who was that?"

• • •

In August 1978, a few days after the Lafleurs returned from Finland, the Bronfman family's Carena-Bancorp (Canadian Arena Banking Corporation) sold the Montreal Canadiens to Molson Breweries in a $40-million transaction. Sam Pollock resigned as manager of the team, in order to exercise his talents elsewhere in the Bronfman empire.

These front office developments had grave repercussions on the ice. Naturally, coach Scotty Bowman expected to be named general manager. But Pollock was firmly opposed to this. In his eyes, the job of a general manager was to put together a winning team. He should be able to purchase players, trade them, sell them, always think in the long term, be able to spot great talent in a wild young player, be equally skilled at using veterans, be able to negotiate profitable trades, and so on. On the ice, Bowman was a genius, but Pollock did not think he would be competent as a general manager. Pollock's replacement would be one of his own close friends, Irving Grundman. Grundman was a bowling alley owner, not a hockey man, and his appointment was poorly received by the players, and by Scotty Bowman.

"I won't be working for you long," Bowman told Grundman.

Bowman agreed to pilot the Canadiens for the duration of his contract, one more season. But the feelings emanating from the front office were ominous. The players felt it. The team spirit that had distinguished the Canadiens now began to evaporate. Scotty Bowman was still firm and severe, but he was more distant than ever, almost indifferent. He was waiting for it to be over, resigned to his fate.

Guy Lafleur had ideas of his own. Lafleur had just begun to realize how much money was involved in professional sport. While he had been in Helsinki the summer before, European hockey financiers had offered him a veritable fortune to play there. And though he had no desire to go to Europe to play, the offer had set him thinking. After training camp, he began saying that he wanted to be better paid, and that, if necessary, he was ready to go on strike.

On October 25, 1978, the Canadiens played the Maple Leafs in Toronto. The previous evening, Lafleur had delivered an ultimatum to Grundman. If his salary were not raised, he would go on strike. A mob of journalists was waiting for him at the Toronto airport. He told them that his contract, signed under pressure, was ridiculous, that Sam Pollock had tricked him. For three years in a row, he had been the NHL's leading scorer, and players like Dionne, Perreault and Esposito, who had slowed down in recent years, were each getting at least $100,000 a year more than he was. He also told them that his agent, Jerry Petrie, had prepared an offer, and that if Grundman didn't sign, he wouldn't play that evening.

"How much do you think you're worth?" a reporter asked him.

"About 2 percent of the amount that Molson just paid for the Canadiens, which would be $800,000 a year. But I don't want to exaggerate. I would accept less . . . a bit less."

That day he didn't practise with the team. He stayed in his hotel room at the Sutton Place, in downtown Toronto. He was nervous and tense. He felt jittery, threatened, cold. He wanted to fight, but at the same time he was afraid, and he was sorry that he'd ever got into this fight. He wrapped himself up in a blanket and tried to watch a movie on television. But he couldn't understand anything. Everything suddenly seemed confused and incoherent.

The journalists had stayed away from the Canadiens' practice. They wandered about the lobby and bar of the

Sutton Place. From time to time one of them would gather up the courage to phone Lafleur to find out what was happening. Nothing.

At 5:25 Lise called Guy to tell him to go as quickly as possible to Maple Leaf Gardens. Grundman was there with Langvary, his executive assistant. Jerry Petrie, who had left from Dorval on a four o'clock flight, would join them as soon as he arrived. Lafleur, followed by the journalists, went to the Gardens.

Grundman reviewed Petrie's proposal and refused to sign it, calling it insane. But he was ready to negotiate. He gave Lafleur his word of honour that he would do everything in his power to reach an agreement with him. Guy found himself in a difficult position. He had said that he wouldn't play if Grundman didn't sign. And the journalists were there, waiting for him, on the other side of the door. If he played, it would be giving in. If he didn't play, he risked poisoning his relationship with the organization. He had spoken too quickly.

Half an hour before the match, Petrie met the journalists and told them that he and Grundman were on the verge of an agreement.

"Has he signed your proposal?"

"The negotiations are going well," Petrie replied.

"But he hasn't signed yet. Right?"

"Not yet. He has to think it over."

"Is Lafleur playing?"

"That's for him to decide."

"Can we talk to him?"

"Of course. But first you have to find him. I think he's in the players' room."

The journalists were puzzled. Usually Lafleur sought them out, even when he had nothing important to say. Now, for the first time, he was trying to get away from the press. The writers gathered in front of the players' room and waited. Would he play or wouldn't he?

When the players came out for the warm-up, Lafleur was there, in uniform, long-faced and evasive. No one dared ask him anything. It was evident that, in front of Grundman, he had folded.

A few days later the business was settled. Guy Lafleur was to be paid $325,000 a year, about $4,000 a game. He had at last become the best-paid player in the history of the Montreal Canadiens.

It was then that Guy began spending a lot of time at bars and discos. His favourite hang-outs were Thursday's, Gatsby and 1234, an old Rue Crescent funeral parlour refurbished as a very chic and expensive discotheque. The atmosphere of these places made him feel good. He liked to lose himself in the sound of the heavy disco music; its rhythm, like a beating heart, calmed him down. It was impossible to talk. Just drink, smoke, look at the girls, be seen.

One day a girl, the most beautiful in the place, asked him to dance. Lafleur had had a bit to drink. In a macho tone he replied:

"If I wanted to dance with you, baby, I would have asked you."

The girl went back to sit down, visibly offended. Later, as she was leaving 1234, she walked by Lafleur, leaned towards him and shouted in his ear:

"You're a real drip."

No doubt hoping his wife would approve of this, Lafleur told her what had happened. Lise, unshakeable, replied:

"That girl was right. You are a drip."

Lise laughed, but in her heart she was sad to see her husband spending his time at bars and discos. Every day he seemed more distant. They used to talk to each other for hours, about their problems, their moods, their feelings, good or bad. Now he no longer made the time. And when she wanted to get close to him, he got nervous and impatient. At the slightest reproach—"You never see your son," "You forgot our anniversary," "Where were you?"—he exploded, saying there was enough pressure on him already and he didn't need her to make it worse.

In spite of everything—the sale of the team, Pollock's

departure, Bowman's disappointment, Lafleur's battle with the front office—the 1978–79 season turned out well. For the fourth consecutive year, the Canadiens won the Stanley Cup. The final game took place on May 21, 1979, when they defeated the New York Rangers, ending their hopes of drinking from the cup for the first time in forty years.

However, knowledgeable observers had seen that Montreal was no longer invincible. Some of the best players were retiring. There had been management changes. The sacred flame was being poorly tended. But, most important of all, new powers had emerged in the NHL, and the Canadiens were vulnerable. It was not yet obvious, or even visible, but something had gone wrong with the once perfect Blue, White and Red machine.

Certain informed observers began to say that Sam Pollock had been absolutely right: the key to success in hockey, as in any business, is stability. At the beginning of the seventies, the club had been in a state of flux. Pollock had asked Béliveau, who wanted to retire, to stay on for two more years in order to assure continuity, to give the organization a chance to find a good coach, to give the new players a chance to establish themselves.

From 1971 to 1979, Bowman had unified the team, given it balance and direction. Everyone was operating on the same wavelength. Then, following the sale of the team and the departures, first of Pollock and then of Bowman, things began to fall apart. In the two years from fall 1979 to fall 1981, the team had three different coaches: Bernie Geoffrion, Claude Ruel and Bob Berry. And to make matters worse, three key players left the team. Jacques Lemaire, Yvan Cournoyer and Ken Dryden all retired, all of them intelligent and talented players with twenty-five Stanley Cup rings among them. Sam Pollock's prized stability was shattered.

The loss of the extraordinary Ken Dryden in the net meant a rethinking of the team's approach to the game. With a reliable goalie and a solid defence, it was possible to take risks, carry off spectacular rushes, live dangerously.

They would now have to be more cautious and emphasize defence, which meant scoring fewer goals and consequently putting on a less attractive show.

Lemaire's departure also left an enormous hole. For seven years he had been Lafleur's alter ego on the ice. Lemaire was a scientific player who knew about the game, a thoughtful and methodical man, the very opposite of the impassioned and instinctive Lafleur. They had complemented each other perfectly. Lemaire was not only a valuable player who knew how to set up plays and let his teammates score goals, he was also someone who could truly appreciate Guy Lafleur's amazing artistry. When Lafleur scored a particularly good goal, he would often turn to Lemaire and skate towards him. Guy would miss Lemaire's look, his smile, his encouragement.

When the players left for the summer, they knew that an an era of greatness had come to an end, and that when they came back, they would find themselves in a totally new world.

● ● ●

Jean Cocteau once called glory an "*éclairage artificiel*," an "artificial light." Those who have known it—artists, athletes, politicians, heroes and creators of all kinds—often love it so much that they can't do without it. They quickly become its consenting slaves, eager and docile.

Just as heliotropes turn towards the sun, Guy Lafleur, without knowing it, was always seeking the artificial light. In its glow he felt properly displayed, comfortable and warm. He spent more and more time in the Rue Crescent bars and discos, the most expensive and fashionable that the city had to offer. He drank good scotch, good wine, champagne.

Late afternoon would sometimes find him at Thursday's. Though he always sat alone, in an out-of-the-way spot, he would soon be surrounded by people wanting to talk to him, shake his hand, see the famous star up close, have a drink with him. He liked the way they flattered him.

Some evenings he would buy all the flower-seller's roses and give them away to the women in the restaurant. He bought champagne for everyone. He liked to project the image of a good-hearted man, generous but aloof.

"You like to show off," Lise told him. "You like to be noticed."

"The people encouraged and supported me. Now I should give back some of what I received."

"And you honestly think that you have to show your gratitude by being seen in bars and getting drunk with perfect strangers?"

"I need to let off steam. You don't know how it is."

"I know very well that you need to let off steam. I'm not talking about that. What I'm saying to you is that you could sometimes do it with your wife and son."

Lise was a skilled dialectician. She was better than Guy at arguing a point. Moreover, she had both reason and common sense on her side. Every time he got into one of these discussions with her, he was disarmed and reduced to silence.

No matter how skilfully she argued, however, he continued to believe that he also was right. Since the age of ten he had led the life of a monk, done without all sorts of things, working hard, always under enormous pressure, always on the firing-line. He had had no adolescence, no youth. At thirteen years of age he had already been a professional. All his life he had travelled the straight and narrow, never allowing himself the slightest detour. Jacques Richard, the bad-boy of the Quebec Remparts, used to tell him that it wouldn't hurt anyone if he sometimes went to bed with a groupie, had a drink or smoked a joint. But Lafleur had never slept with a groupie, never touched a joint, never had a drink the day before, or even two days before, an important game.

Now he had begun to think that perhaps there was something to what Jacques Richard had said. Of course, Richard had not become a superstar, but he had lived the good life. And in the end, wasn't that what counted? Wasn't living well the first and foremost reason for being on this earth?

Lafleur began to think that he had now earned the right,

at twenty-eight years of age, an accomplished star, to enjoy some good times, to relax for a bit. He tried to explain to Lise that to have all this money and fame and not enjoy it, that was the torment of Tantalus!

"What do you mean 'enjoy it'?" Lise asked.

"I mean that a guy in a job like mine is sometimes faced with temptations that a normal person couldn't always resist."

"I would have hoped, Flower, that you were stronger than that. You disappoint me."

There were hordes of groupies around, and many of the Canadiens players could not resist. The girls were young, beautiful, free, patient. The most desired player was Lafleur, the Blond Comet, the Blond Demon, Flower. He had remained timid and reserved with the girls, but there are few barriers a determined groupie is unable to cross.

It didn't take long for people to start talking. Malicious rumours began to spread, first among Lafleur's crowd, then to the media. Guy Lafleur was drinking, taking drugs, picking up women, consorting with thieves and criminals, deceiving his wife.

Claude Larochelle, a journalist and friend who had just published a book about Guy called *Le démon blond* (*The Blond Demon*), was stupefied to discover that the athlete he had portrayed, the athlete with irreproachable morals and impeccable standards, had suddenly changed. Larochelle began to hear, from all sorts of people, stories in which he could no longer recognize his friend, the hero of his book.

Lafleur was now fascinated with the world of the night, a world of artificial light. He liked meeting new people, who had other ways of seeing things, other ways of living than the ones he had always known.

At the same time that he was having these encounters and making these discoveries, he realized that everything that had motivated, sustained and driven him up to now was slipping away. He was no longer in motion, no longer growing, no longer climbing. The arrow, when it has reached its goal, remains fixed in the target. That was how Guy Lafleur felt in the summer of 1979. He was at the end of his voyage, he had arrived, and now he was immobilized.

He was certain that he could do no more, go no further. His life was in the process of violent change. It was exciting and worrisome at the same time. He often came home late, then later and later. Sometimes it was already light when Lise heard his car arriving, and then she would turn over in her bed and finally fall asleep. The next day she sulked. She wouldn't answer Guy when he spoke. He was disturbed. He was afraid. Sometimes he was sure that he was ruining his career and his life with Lise.

When he became the spokesman for General Motors, the company asked him to sell his Ferrari, and he had been pleased to do so. That car, too beautiful and too powerful, had started to scare him. He had begun to drive more and more quickly. One night he had gone from Quebec to Montreal, bridge to bridge, a distance of 230 kilometres, in less than an hour. That was too much. It was crazy. Nevertheless, a few months later he bought a big Harley-Davidson. And sometimes, while he was driving at 150 kilometres per hour on the suburban highways, he thought about what his father had said the day he'd made him take a drive in his new Ferrari: that a man who buys himself such high-powered vehicles is unconsciously looking for a way to destroy himself. Then he would grow afraid and drive home slowly, sad and bewildered. For a few days he would be kind and thoughtful with Lise, then boredom would take hold once more, and he would begin again to haunt the bars at night.

Sometimes he met friends, like Guy Cloutier or Claude Quenneville, and he would confide in them. But most of the men of his age and in his circle had the same sorts of problems he did. And they behaved as he did. They were trying to forget themselves. Many succeeded easily enough. Not Guy Lafleur.

On the morning of September 4, 1979, the *Montreal Star*'s headline story, written by Red Fisher, was that Bernie

Geoffrion had been named coach of the Montreal Canadiens. "Boom Boom" Geoffrion was forty-nine years old. He was one of the most engaging and spectacular personalities in the annals of hockey, one of the "Twelve Apostles" who had succeeded in the unequalled feat of winning five Stanley Cups in a row. He had married the daughter of Howie Morenz, the first of the great stars of the Canadiens dynasty. Geoffrion was a warm and humorous man, a cheerful character and a master of public relations, but he was also in dangerously fragile health.

Twelve years earlier, when he had coached the Rangers for three months, he had had to quit because of stomach ulcers. Three years later he helped get the Atlanta Flames off the ground, got them into the quarter-finals in the playoffs, then fell sick again. Wouldn't the same thing happen with the Canadiens? The players were delighted to work under a legend of the game. But much as they enjoyed it, they found it unsettling.

Fortunately, good old Claude Ruel was there. He himself had coached the Canadiens from 1968 to 1970. Ruel had the skill, but not the manner. He didn't know how to talk to journalists, how to establish his authority over the players, or how to resist the unreasonable demands of the public. He had resigned, claiming that he couldn't take the pressure of the media and the fans. Geoffrion, on the other hand, loved talking to the fans. He had even flirted with show business, trying out a career as a crooner. He loved the spotlight. People liked to say that between them, Ruel and "Boom Boom" had all the qualities of a terrific coach.

Lafleur was reassured. He adored Geoffrion and he also liked Ruel, who, when he had first arrived in Montreal, had been very encouraging to him.

But the feeling of euphoria wouldn't last long.

• • •

At the beginning of the eighties a Canadian writer, W.P. Kinsella, wrote a very amusing story that recounted the picaresque history of a pathetic hockey team from a small and poor Indian village in the depths of Alberta. The players were poorly equipped, badly coached and out of condition, but they had great team spirit. They also had an extraordinary mascot, a fiercely partisan dog with magical powers. It was a big collie with a white collar that barked joyously every time his team got the puck, but growled and howled whenever the enemy took it away, or one of his own players made a mistake. It was a brave, intelligent and passionate dog that rebelled against all injustice and incompetence. The boys had named it Guy Lafleur. Kinsella's story was entitled "The Truth."

At the beginning of the eighties, Guy Lafleur (the hockey player) had in fact begun to bark out various truths. Some were insightful, others hurtful, but they were always necessary. They were realities that would have a profound effect on the Canadiens organization, and on the way the Québecois saw and understood hockey.

The first time that he barked loudly, he was on board an airplane heading out west. Lafleur loved to travel. He loved the trip itself, the sense of being in motion, the road. Airplanes made him especially euphoric. When the Canadiens set out to play the western divisions of the league, he was usually in an excellent mood. He had adopted the habit of sitting at the back of the plane beside a window on the left side.

Unless there was an important game that evening, he would gladly have a drink (or three or more) with the journalists who also sat at the back. Then he would begin to fool around. His favourite game was borrowing the steward's vest and serving people drinks and food. He would also confide to whomever was listening. He had discovered the infinite pleasure of freely saying what he thought. His statements, often biting and incisive, delighted the writers, who recorded them and used them for the next day's headlines.

Few people in a society can get away with saying whatever they want to whomever they want. And among those who can, few dare. Lafleur dared. Of course he would make mistakes, say stupid or inept things, but he never denied himself the pleasure of speaking when he had something to say. And once he had said something, he never took it back. He could apologize, be sorry he had gone too far, be upset that he had hurt someone, but he never blamed journalists for misquoting him or misrepresenting his ideas, or exaggerating his anger or indignation.

There was another Quebec star known for his sometimes ill-considered candour, Robert Charlebois. Lafleur and Charlebois were alike in many ways. They were born rebels, compulsive speakers of the truth. They had also both been said to lack judgment and discretion.

Charlebois was famous for having spoken his mind freely to two of Canada's political leaders. It was at the time of the Superfrancofête, in the summer of 1974, just after the memorable show on the Plains of Abraham, *Le Loup, le Renard, le Lion* (*The Wolf, the Fox, the Lion*), in which Charlebois had participated along with Felix Léclerc and Gilles Vigneault. Pierre Elliott Trudeau and Robert Bourassa had come to their box to congratulate the three Quebec singing stars. Charlebois said to Trudeau:

"Pierre Elliott, you're really a good prime minister."

Then, nodding at Bourassa he added: "I can't say the same for him."

Trudeau had the presence of mind to say, "But you know, I wouldn't mind having his majority in the House."

Everyone in the box was uncomfortable, except for Charlebois. He had said what he had to say. And as an untouchable and incontestable superstar, he spoke as an oracle. He was truth incarnate. That was how Guy Lafleur saw himself at the beginning of the eighties. He *was* the truth.

When the newspaper *La Presse* had the idea of getting Charlebois and Lafleur together to interview each other, the first question the hockey player asked the singer was about the famous scandal Charlebois had caused while performing in Paris a few years earlier. Charlebois had thrown his guitar and his drums into the crowd and accused the French of being completely without passion. Lafleur wanted to know what he had felt and thought right at the moment, and why he had acted and spoken as he did.

Charlebois replied that he had nothing against the audience itself, but that at the time he was struggling against the show business mafia, "which is like the one that exists in sport, you should know what I'm talking about. It's an Establishment, and Establishments make me sick."

Of course Guy Lafleur knew what Charlebois meant. Was not he, also, battling against a system, against the Establishment, against the government of hockey?

Guy began to realize that if his first three years with the Canadiens had been lacklustre, it was because he had been sacrificed to the system. The club had been in the process of transforming itself, and to make sure the young players didn't make too many mistakes, the organization had emphasized a cautious and defensive style of play. Forwards were often asked to return to the defensive zone in order to keep away from the other team's attackers. But Guy Lafleur preferred attack and evasion over defence. His great talent had always been, by outguessing the other players or simply by his own audacious strategies, to penetrate the enemy zone and make for the net. Just the same, he had been obliged to follow the directives from above and renounce his raids against the enemy. He had especially been obliged to content himself with limited playing time. But he had been young then, and willing to believe that things would change, as soon as he proved himself. In 1979 the situation was completely different. Lafleur was an established athlete. He felt that he had a right to his share of ice and a right to speak his mind.

Unlike Scotty Bowman, "Boom Boom" Geoffrion had no precise plan. He was coaching the team with Ruel. Lafleur quickly understood that the Ruel–"Boom Boom" tandem couldn't work, and he was the first to say so.

In November, aboard the airplane taking the Canadiens west, he confided to Bernard Brisset of *La Presse* that the club lacked leadership and that the players were no longer sure who to follow. Ruel or Geoffrion? Who was the boss?

Guy had already made his choice: Geoffrion. And he castigated Ruel, telling Brisset that, in his opinion, Ruel should keep quiet and hand the reins of the team over to Geoffrion alone. Of course Lafleur preferred the offensive playing style of Geoffrion, a born attacker, to the Ruel style. Ruel preached prudence and advised Geoffrion to get his forwards to attack less zealously.

Geoffrion was of the old school. He was always thinking of the attack. He loved to make devastating incursions and raids into enemy territory. For him, hockey was also show business. You had to win, of course, but it was also necessary to put on a good show, to get the fans excited, to create events for the media. The trouble came when he tried to pay attention both to his own instincts and to the advice of the cautious Ruel. Ruel had never won the respect of the players, but he had an incomparable store of experience, and at the Forum he had great moral authority.

The players didn't know whose side they were supposed to be on. There was a schism at the heart of the team. In Lafleur's eyes, the hybrid coaching situation had made the team fall apart.

"If we're not united, we can't win," he told Brisset.

Brisset's article, published the next day, had an explosive effect in Montreal. Ruel was deeply hurt, especially since he had taken Guy under his wing, supported and encouraged him at the beginning of his professional career. He had spent hundreds of hours watching him, advising him, talking with him. Those who knew believed it was Ruel who had got Lafleur back on track after his first disappointing years. And it was Ruel, too, who had insisted during the 1971 draft that Lafleur be chosen rather than Dionne.

Of course Lafleur was sorry to have hurt Ruel, but he couldn't retract his words, for the good and simple reason that they were the truth. He thought he was in the right to speak as he did. It was for the good of the team. That magnificent machine of genius, once so well maintained by Sam "the Fox" Pollock, was now coming apart. It had lost its harmony, its balance, its vigour, its soul.

Lafleur wanted Ruel to take care of the training and conditioning of players, but to keep away from the coaching of the team. The new division of labour that he proposed might have been brought into effect, but "Boom Boom" fell ill and had to quit. A little before Easter, Ruel was once more at the controls. For Lafleur, and for all the offensive players who liked to attack, Ruel's accession was bad news.

The team was doing badly. But Ruel and the front office administrators were not the only ones to take the blame. A few weeks later, in January 1980, the team was on its second trip west. Having just beaten the pathetic and short-lived Denver Rockies, they were now flying to Los Angeles to play the Kings. Exactly above the Grand Canyon, Guy Lafleur, ensconced as always in his seat at the back of the plane, expressed himself on the subject of the pitiful performances of his teammates, castigating the lazy ones, "the players who laugh at everyone and who are content to score thirty goals a year and refuse to play if they have a little headache." Another explosion the next day in the Quebec media. Once again, Guy Lafleur had triumphed in his role of official critic and taught the writers a thing or two.

Serge Savard had succeeded Yvan Cournoyer as captain of the Canadiens. But, in fact, it was Guy Lafleur who was leading the team. It was he who provoked changes, raised questions. And it was his declarations above all that the press wanted to hear.

In his time, Jean Béliveau had also exercised great authority, but in a completely different way. When Henri Richard spoke out in the dressing room against coach Al MacNeil during the 1970 playoffs, calling him incompetent to coach the Canadiens, Béliveau got up, and walking by Richard on his way to the showers, he put his hand on Henri's shoulder—fraternally, firmly. Richard, who had been about to explode, fell silent. Everyone fell silent. Bertrand Raymond, the journalist who was then in the Montreal dressing room, notebook in hand, wasn't able to get one more word out of the Pocket Rocket. Like all the players of his generation, Jean Béliveau believed that nothing that happened in the locker room should be made public. He believed that the spirit and honour of the team should be protected behind closed doors.

Lafleur, on the other hand, had made himself the apostle of transparency, of *glasnost*. He wanted everything to be known, everything to be publicly debated. At the time, Quebec's intellectuals, artists and advertisers were all talking about the importance of expressing themselves. "We are six million people, we have to speak to each other," everyone was saying. And that, without thesis or theory, was what Lafleur was doing. He was expressing himself. He had the floor. He, formerly so timid and slow to speak, would, during the next years, become the Great Divulger, the Great Truth-sayer, the Great Asker of Questions. It is no exaggeration to say that he had an enormous influence on the sporting press.

In spite of the fact that he criticized the other players harshly, he had a powerful influence on them. He was still the most talented among them. He never did anything like anyone else. To the players who wore jeans, ate at McDonald's and drank beer, Lafleur had "class." His clothes came from the great couturiers. He ate fancy dishes, drank champagne and fine wines. His pen was a Mont-Blanc, his shoes were Guccis, his suitcases made by Louis Vuitton. Many of the players, especially the English ones, were cautious with their money. Dryden, like Lafleur from a working-class family, always double-checked his restaurant bills. Bob Gainey wore his clothes until they were threadbare. The Québecois, on the other hand, had the reputation of being spendthrifts, and Lafleur was incontestably the most prodigal. He always wanted to pick up the cheque. On the road, he would take a party of his teammates out to a good restaurant or a new discotheque where he knew the owners. It was delicious and expensive. And often, he paid for everything. One evening, when he was enjoying his melancholy mood at a bar called the Privé, he called to the waiter:

"Twenty bottles of champagne, please. Put two of them at my table, and distribute the rest."

It was almost two thousand dollars' worth of champagne, and Lafleur paid with pleasure. To bankrupt himself? To show off his wealth? Out of despair? So people would like him? The players were naturally impressed by these acts of generosity. They were fascinated by him. The power he held over them was similar to that which Roger Barré, the king of elegant and spectacular gestures, had over Lafleur himself. When his teammate Pierre Larouche got married, Guy organized a gigantic and costly wedding celebration at his own home at Baie d'Urfé. During the party, the rugs were burned and all sorts of things were broken, but Guy was happy. For Guy, being able to pay was a symbol of success and authority.

But his power really came from the public. The people sided with Lafleur just as they sided with Charlebois when he confronted the music multinationals, when he assailed the rich, rebuked the poor, told the politicians what he was thinking and presented himself as an "ordinary guy." Lafleur could play the big man and make grand gestures that, from anyone else, would have seemed arrogant or insignificant, but from him took on legendary dimensions.

For example, in Calgary, in January 1980, a nine-year-old boy, Corey Gurnsey, was stabbed on his way home from school by a crazy man. He was taken to hospital and, miraculously, he lived. But his Montreal Canadiens sweater, number 10, with Guy Lafleur's name on it, had been thrown out because it was torn and bloodstained. A reporter who was investigating the story contacted the public relations man at the Forum, Claude Mouton. Mouton informed Lafleur, who called the boy and promised he would score a goal for him that very evening and send him the puck.

That night the Canadiens were playing at the Forum against the Toronto Maple Leafs. Four minutes and twelve seconds into the first period, Guy Lafleur scored. Then he was seen to do something unusual, which puzzled hundreds of thousands of people. He pushed the goaltender aside, went into the net and retrieved the puck, which he brought over to Claude Mouton, behind the Canadiens' bench. A player does that when he has scored a hat trick, broken a record or reached an important milestone. But what importance could Guy Lafleur have attached to this particular puck? The next day, all of Canada knew the answer. Pictures of Guy Lafleur getting the puck from behind the Leafs' goalie, and of little Corey, smiling, were in all the newspapers.

Once again the famous number 10 had scored an extraordinary goal. It went beyond hockey. It was a masterpiece of show business, sport and legend, all rolled into one. Guy Lafleur was demonstrating the fact that he had become more than a personality; he was an author, a true creator of events. He was a symbol, too. He was the prototype of the boy who has risen to success and who defends the rights of the poor against the powerful and the rich, who cries out against injustice and incompetence.

Pierre Larouche, an extremely talented but erratic player, was now playing centre between Lafleur and Shutt. Larouche proved to be good at setting up plays, quick and inventive. During the regular season he, like Lafleur, scored 50 goals. Shutt got 47. Between the three of them they scored almost half of the team's 328 total regular season goals. Things seemed to be going well. But the team had become very vulnerable. During the era of Bowman and Pollock, they had had everything in duplicate and triplicate. A left-handed forward, weighing 185 pounds, was injured? No problem, there were several others in reserve, same weight, same style, same speed. Then the club had had depth. Not now.

Once again the team was in transition. In less than a year the Canadiens had lost much more than some great players, more than an extraordinary coach and an unequalled general manager, they had lost something that couldn't be measured or defined—faith, spirit, the real desire to win.

On April 27, 1980, the Minnesota North Stars eliminated the Canadiens in the quarter-finals. For the first time in five years the Stanley Cup would not be theirs. Guy Lafleur had not played; a few days earlier he had been accidentally injured by Pat Boutette of the Hartford Whalers during the third game of the playoffs. At the conclusion of the game against the North Stars, two outstanding NHL players announced their retirement: Gordie Howe and Bobby Hull. It would also be said that the game of April 27, 1980, marked the end of the truly great Guy Lafleur. Afterwards, he would never be the same.

That defeat, in which he had not been able to participate, troubled Lafleur deeply. No matter how he told himself that it would make a change, pose a new challenge, that always winning had become tiresome, in his eyes the loss had come at the wrong moment. The club had been in a position to break the record of the 1950s Canadiens, who between 1956 and 1960 had won five cups in a row. Twelve men, known as "the Twelve Apostles," had played throughout that whole period. They were a legend within the legend, both of the Montreal Canadiens and in the history of hockey and modern sport, like the New York Yankees of the same decade. They were sainted, free now to rest on their laurels at the very summit of the Hall of Fame.

Lafleur would have loved to belong to a team like that. To accomplish individual successes was exciting and exhilarating, but to perform great feats as part of a team was even better. Now they were back where they had started. It was still possible, but they would have to act very quickly to rebuild a team strong enough to win the next five Stanley Cups. Everything considered, it seemed very unlikely. For the first time in his career, Guy Lafleur could see a goal that he might not be able to achieve. For the first time in his life, he doubted himself.

At the same time, he was having very serious problems in his personal life.

•　•　•

From time to time, like every sports writer concerned about maintaining good relations with the players and the Canadiens organization, Claude Quenneville went to a practice at the Forum or the Ville Saint-Laurent arena. One fine day, right at the beginning of the 1980–81 training camp, he had hardly taken his seat behind the players' bench at the Forum when Lafleur approached him.

"I have to talk to you, Claude. Wait for me, will you?"

Lafleur was well known as the first to arrive at practice and the first to leave. He held the speed record for showering, changing, putting away his equipment and getting out the door. He was so fast that one night someone had to run after him, but wasn't able to catch him in time to come out and wave to the spectators after having been chosen one of the game's three stars. Thus Quenneville did not have to wait long. Ten minutes after practice, they were driving towards Rue Sherbrooke when Lafleur, turning to Quenneville, announced that he had left Lise.

"I hope for your sake that you're joking."

"It's no joke, Claude. I swear it. I have left Lise."

For a long moment, Quenneville stayed silent. He knew things weren't always smooth between Lise and Guy, and that they fought more and more often. But he couldn't imagine how his friend could live without his wife. He had known them from the beginning of their relationship, and he had often met Lise since. He had seen how important she was to Guy. She was nothing like the typical hockey player's wife—timid, attentive and obedient. On the contrary, she was very independent, opinionated, determined about everything. Lafleur never made a decision without consulting her. He even went so far as to joke that she was his real coach. It was a way of complaining a little about the absolute authority she had over him, but also a way of saying that she was central to his life, that more often than not she was right, that she was strong.

Quenneville was very fond of Lise Lafleur. He found her intelligent and articulate. Lise, after having at first lumped him with her husband's undesirable friends, found out that he was serious and responsible. In the past two years he had stopped drinking, stopped smoking, started jogging and swimming. He was the most sensible of Guy's friends, and also, perhaps, the closest to Lise. She liked his thoughtfulness, his humour, his unpretentious culture.

"It's very serious," Lafleur told him. "I left the house yesterday evening."

"And Lise?"

"I think she's going to go to her father's place in Florida."

"Martin?"

"Martin is with her."

"And you?"

"Me? I've rented an apartment here."

He had just parked the Cadillac in front of the Ritz, on Rue Sherbrooke. One liveried valet opened the door for them while another parked the car. They went to the restaurant right away and, at Lafleur's request, were given a table away from the other patrons, behind a barricade of plants.

"So that's what I have to say, Claude. I've left Lise and right now I don't want to be alone. That's all."

Then he started to say that he was worried about his son and that he couldn't live without seeing him.

"Are you worried about Lise, too?"

"I don't know."

It was only halfway through the meal and the bottle of Chablis that he confessed to Quenneville that he was having an affair, and that it was both painful and wonderful.

"Do I know her?"

"Of course! Everyone knows her."

"What does she do?"

"She sings."

"Well, then, I know who she is. Are you in love with her?"

"I don't know. Perhaps. But I hope not."

He had met her at the beginning of the summer in a restaurant, Le Toit Rouge, during a launch party for a disco album. She was rich, cultivated, independent. She had brought something new into his life, opening a whole new world to him, the world of show business. He was fascinated by her assurance, her elegance, her way of saying and feeling things. She knew everyone. She liked to have a good time. She liked to talk, and made Guy talk about his feelings and emotions. Guy had always liked women who knew how to make him talk. With Lise, he felt he had said everything too often. He had no more secrets; she had no more mystery. With another woman, he was rediscovering the pleasure of speaking his innermost thoughts.

She got into the habit of coming to meet him at the Forum—very discreetly, at first, but that kind of thing doesn't stay quiet for long. By the end of training camp, most of the players had realized what was going on. At the end of September, she followed the team to New York to watch a pre-season game with the Rangers. That night, Lafleur was dazzling. After scoring a goal, he looked for her in the crowd at Madison Square Garden, but he couldn't find her. Then he started thinking of Lise and Martin. In spite of the applause and the happiness of making a fine scoring play, he wanted to smash his stick against the boards. Why did it all have to be so horribly complicated and tortured? He knew lots of other men who had all sorts of affairs, for a night or a week or a lifetime, and they managed things easily. Why not him?

Lise had indeed gone with Martin to Florida. And of course she had told her father everything. She wanted him to be angry at Guy, but Roger Barré told her:

"I feel very badly, Lise, when I think about what's happening to you. But don't ask me to hate him. I am very fond of him."

In fact, the transformation his son-in-law had undergone during the past year was not entirely incomprehensible to Roger Barré. He himself had a very epicurean idea of life. He liked to eat well and drink well; he liked money, beautiful women, power, every kind of pleasure. He was not a cautious, sedate man, but he was extremely engaging and always interesting. Lise had always criticized Guy for not being like her father, for not having his flamboyant air of authority, his strength of character.

Ten days passed and still Guy had not tried to reach his family. He was enjoying his freedom, awkwardly, excessively, always a little worried. It was like the feeling of finding yourself at the steering wheel of a new and very powerful car that you don't yet know how to handle.

He would have liked his liaison with the singer to have stayed a secret, but neither of them could appear in public without being recognized. Every time they went out, they were noticed, first in hockey and show business circles, then gradually by the public.

One evening at the Kyoto, a Japanese restaurant, they ran into some friends of Lise's. A few days later they were having dinner at the Bradley House, in Hudson, a wealthy Montreal suburb.

"Don't turn around," she said.

"Who's there?"

"The charming wives of three or four of your colleagues just walked in the door."

"And you think that I should hide?"

"I don't think anything, Guy. Do as you like."

He got up. He went over to greet the four wives. He knew that the next day the whole Canadiens organization would know that he had been at the Bradley House, having dinner with a famous singer. He was flattered, and incensed.

"Any ordinary man could go to bed with his next-door neighbour and no one would know. But I can never do anything without the whole world knowing."

"That's because you want the whole world to know. That's the life you have chosen to live. You are a public man. You have to assume your responsibilities."

The next morning he telephoned Florida. Roger Barré answered. Lafleur didn't know what to say. He was ashamed.

"Are you well?"

"I'm well. And you?"

"Okay. What's the weather like in Florida?"

"Listen, Guy, I have two things to tell you. First, that you would walk out on my daughter hurts me deeply, as you know. But it's not my problem, it's your life. I'm in no position to give you a lecture on that. In a way, I can understand what you're doing. But that you would let ten days go by without even inquiring about your son, that I cannot take. You are almost thirty years old! If you can't fulfil your responsibilities . . ."

"I'd like to speak to Lise."

"What do you take Lise for? Can you believe even for a second that she wants to talk to you?"

"I just want to say a couple of words to her."

"My daughter doesn't want to speak to you."

"You haven't even asked her!"

"She told us that if you called, she didn't want to speak to you. I can't do anything about it. If you think I make her decisions, you don't know my daughter, Guy Lafleur. Even if I wanted to, I wouldn't be able to change her mind."

"May I speak to Martin?"

Martin had turned four in June. He laughed over the telephone. His father cried. He had never felt so alone, so confused in all his life. To try to make himself feel better, he went out drinking; he moved from bar to bar; he called his singer. But in the morning, when he was alone again in his suite in the Ritz, it was hell.

When she came back from Florida, Lise called Claude Quenneville to find out how Guy was doing. She was tanned and feeling well rested. Quenneville knew she had the moral strength to survive this test. He was more worried about Guy. Lise was also worried.

"What does he do?"

"I can't tell you. I haven't seen him for five days. The team is on the road."

"Do you think she's with him?"

"I'd be very surprised. You know better than me there's no place for women on these trips."

They went to see *Les Plouffe*, Gilles Carle's latest film. Then they played backgammon into the night. Lise started talking about Guy.

"He never wanted to go to the movies with me, or to the grocery store, or shopping. He never wanted to go anywhere. He was always saying that people were after him, that they wouldn't let him breathe."

"It's true that he doesn't know how to maintain his

privacy. He tries to be too nice to everyone. When he goes out, he's never left alone. There's always a crowd around him."

"But deep down he likes it. He goes to bars and restaurants. When he's not with me, he chases after people. When he is with me, he doesn't feel right. He never feels right with me. That's what's breaking my heart."

"He doesn't feel right with anyone any more. Even when he's alone with himself. He's going through a bad time. But if you wait a bit, things will work out, you'll see."

"We used to spend hours, whole nights, talking. He listened to me, he wrote to me, even when he was in the house. When I woke up in the morning, if he had already left I would often find a letter on the refrigerator. Sometimes, when he was on the road, he would send me a telegram just to tell me that he was thinking of me. But for the last year we haven't been talking. He never writes to me any more. He never calls me, even when he's on the road. If he does, we almost always end up fighting."

What could Quenneville say to her? He was hardly in a position to throw stones at his friend. Until his sudden reform, he himself had lived wildly. Lise's position was honest and clear. She believed that she and Guy had an agreement. He had cheated. He was guilty. For her, everything was finished, there would be no forgiving. In her eyes, the rules of love and business were the same.

On his side, Guy had realized that his affair, though exciting, was going nowhere. He talked to his mistress all the time about his wife and son. She said to him:

"It's obvious that you love your wife. What are you doing with me? You must see that you're making all three of us unhappy."

She was criticizing him in the same way that Lise had so often done. For not making up his mind, for letting things happen or not happen on their own, for leaving it to others to sort things out. Now it was his mistress who was pushing him to make a decision, who was making him understand what he wanted, telling him that he should go back home.

One night he was at Chez Gatsby with his friend Brian Travers, Sam Pollock's chauffeur. Travers thought the whole story was completely twisted. If only Lafleur had been able to get some pleasure from his affair. But it was tortured, complicated, painful. Lafleur was always talking about his problems.

"You know something," Brian said to him. "From the way you talk, it sounds like you had a lot more fun when you were with your wife. Usually, a man has a mistress because he enjoys it. With you, it must be the drama."

Lafleur admitted that he was trying to find a way to go back home. Travers dug into his pocket and pulled out a quarter.

"If you really want to go back, you'll have to start by putting this in the machine."

"But if I call her from here, she'll hear the music. She'll know that I'm still in a disco."

"Listen, Guy. There's no point trying to convince your wife that you've totally changed in a month. And anyway, maybe she'll soften up when she realizes that you're all alone in a discotheque, thinking of her."

His heart beating fast, Guy got up and telephoned Baie d'Urfé. No answer. "Where is she? What's she doing?" Every quarter of an hour he called back. At midnight there was still no answer. "She must be at her mother's. Or her sister's. Her friend Michèle's." Brian laughed at the way Lafleur was worrying.

Guy wasn't able to get in touch with his wife until the next day, Sunday afternoon. She was icy. And he, without being completely impassioned, spoke from his heart. He wanted to begin all over, everything forgotten. But Lise could not accept that.

"Women who claim everything is forgotten are liars. I never forget anything and you should know that."

She finally agreed to meet him on neutral ground, at the Latini, a downtown Italian restaurant they often went to.

"The experience I've just been through has proved to me

that I need you to live. When you're not there, nothing works. I'm completely disorganized . . ."

"Oh, I see. And you want to come back and live with me because you can't take care of yourself. You've made a mistake."

"It wasn't a mistake, it was an experience."

"Well, I think it was a mistake. You've hurt me. You've deceived me. And after all that you have the nerve to come and complain that you found it hard."

"I'm just telling you that I can't live without you."

He begged her forgiveness, promised never to do it again. But she remained cold and distant. She said that she was prepared to separate. She would keep Martin, of course. Guy could see his son when he wished.

"In fact, how would that be different for you? You hardly ever see him anyway. The only thing that counts is your career."

That evening he was told a few home truths. Calmly, Lise enumerated the ways in which he had hurt her, pointed out the errors he had committed.

"There's something you have to understand, Guy Lafleur. My heart is broken, but I don't need you in order to live. I can get along without you, emotionally and financially. The sorrows of love are always cured, in time."

He drove her back to Baie d'Urfé. After he got to the house they stayed for a long time in the parked car, talking. He wanted to embrace her. She pushed him away, gently, firmly. It was a strange and exhilarating sensation, as though he were courting a young girl, parked in front of her parents' house, and she didn't want him to come in.

Going back to the city he felt euphoric. Never had anyone been so honest with him, so truthful and perceptive. Usually it was he who told others how things were, who criticized Ruel for not being a good coach, Geoffrion for listening to Ruel, his teammates for their uninspired play. No, for once, someone was talking to him about himself, was giving him back an image of himself that certainly was not flattering, but seemed accurate. And he was convinced that in order to have looked at him in such a penetrating way, Lise must love him deeply. No one had ever had such a clear and true vision of him. No one had ever talked the way she had. With Lise, there was never weakness, no wrong turns. She had even said that she loved him. But she remained the mistress of her emotions and feelings. As he did on the ice.

The next day he sent her flowers; he called her, wanting to discuss immediately how he could come back home. He was more in love than ever with Lise. But she insisted on thinking things over. In the meantime, he had broken with his mistress, who had her own observations to make.

"You were never really with me."

He protested. But in his heart he knew it was true. He had been seduced, not by love, but by novelty and the desire for change. Now he was once more alone, and he had only one goal: going home.

Roger Barré, when he came back from Florida, had a very serious meeting with his son-in-law.

"I'm not here to tell you what to do. But if you go back to live with my daughter, you have to know what you're doing. A marriage is first and foremost about love. But it is also a business relationship, a bargain, a deal. You can't just change your mind whenever you want."

"I won't change my mind."

"My daughter has the right to demand certain guarantees on paper, a new marriage contract. Think it over carefully before you make any promises."

"I'll give her any guarantee she wants. When I got married, I was twenty-one years old, and I knew, more or less, what I was doing. Today, I am almost thirty. I know exactly what I'm getting into."

"For your sake, I hope so."

After signing a new contract with Lise Barré, Guy returned cautiously to the hearth. From now on, she would be holding the big end of the stick.

"The next time, it's all over. I hope you know it."

"There won't be a next time. I love you."

"And I love you."

She would become more and more important in his life
and career. But she couldn't help being mistrustful. She was
well aware that her man had been badly shaken. After a few
days of their new life together, she realized that he had not
entirely returned to her. Part of him was still somewhere
else.

• • •

On March 24, 1981, Guy Lafleur went to Thursday's late in
the afternoon with the idea of sitting alone in a corner and
drowning his boredom. He knew that sooner or later
someone would come to amuse him, or join him in his
melancholy. The people who came to this place liked to
show off their money and connections. But they were never
too pushy.

That was the best thing about snobs, Lafleur thought,
they left you alone. The style at Thursday's was to be
indifferent and pretend not to notice when you saw Guy
Lafleur at the next table, as though you had just left a
meeting with the Aga Khan, Mick Jagger or Indira
Gandhi. Somewhere else, in an east-end bar where real
people went, everyone would have made for him, asked for
autographs, asked his opinion on various matters, been
oppressively familiar with him. Now he didn't want that
any more. He wanted to be left in peace. And this evening
he had decided to get a bit drunk before going home, to give
a bit of colour to the grey sameness of his life.

It was five months since he had started living with Lise
again. But things weren't working.

"You're only half back," she said.

She was right. He hadn't entirely returned. And
moreover, the little of him that had come back was hardly
ever there. After the excitement of the first days of their
reunion, he had started going out again, coming home later
and later. Lise was convinced he would leave again. She
had already mourned the death of their love.

"What are you looking for?" she asked him.

He didn't know. He was looking for himself. He wouldn't
have known how to describe what he wanted. Women, of
course, were at the top of the list of his objects of desire. But

he didn't dare approach them. Once bitten, twice shy. From now on he would content himself with looking at them, wanting them.

Sitting upstairs at Thursday's, near the window, he tried to think about his life, to weigh the good and the bad as objectively as possible. But it was beyond him. It was as though he were in a void, weightless. On television he had seen a documentary about space travel, in which technicians grappling with an extremely complex problem were interviewed. The problem was knowing how to weigh objects in a state of weightlessness, in the void. He had the same problem. In the emptiness of his life he was trying to weigh the good and the bad, but he was getting nowhere; he didn't understand anything any more.

He was thinking seriously about going home when, about seven o'clock, Robert Picard arrived. Picard was a defenceman the Canadiens had acquired just a few days before. Six foot two, over two hundred pounds, twenty-three years old, Picard was the kind of player who was coming into favour with the organization because, more than ever, Claude Ruel was emphasizing a defensive style of play.

During that winter, Lafleur himself had several times observed that the organization should get some large players. As always, he attacked poor Ruel through the media. He said aloud what many were thinking, that the team was divided into clans and cliques, that many players were very unhappy and that the absence of leadership was hurting the team. The club was poorly suited to the new style of hockey being played in the NHL. The other good clubs possessed bigger and stronger players who had no trouble barging through the frail Canadiens defence.

The Canadiens could boast all they liked about having the most skilled and knowledgeable hockey players in the world, but they were still regularly crushed by teams made up of talentless goons. The only big, aggressive offensive player the Canadiens had was Chris Nilan, like Guy a right-winger. Nilan liked to use his body, and made headlong rushes, hoping to flatten the enemy into the boards as much as to put the puck in the net. The team needed three or four of these aggressive players. The Canadiens were scoring less and less, and were losing more and more frequently. Grundman, getting Lafleur's message, had started to equip his team with solid defensive players, like Picard. His role would be to bar the route to the net.

Picard had played in Washington for three years and spent a few months with the Toronto Maple Leafs. He wasn't unhappy to be back in Montreal, with the Canadiens, but he had good memories of Washington. He told Lafleur about the advantages of life in Washington, the winters that were more like a Canadian spring . . .

At that time Lafleur was experiencing serious problems. His tenth season with the Canadiens (1980–81) was drawing to a close. As usual, he had managed some spectacular moments. Three weeks earlier, in Winnipeg, he had broken the 1000-point mark during his 720th NHL game. This put him into a very select circle of very great players. His legendary status was now assured, and it was obvious to everyone that he would one day be in the Hall of Fame, even if he never scored another goal.

But this year he had scored only twenty-seven times, half last year's total. Steve Shutt, with whom Lafleur had enjoyed his great successes, had himself scored his lowest point total in six years, and their centre, Pierre Larouche, had scored only twenty-five goals, compared to fifty the year before. It was a worrisome collapse. The Canadiens were still the most prestigious club in the NHL, still a giant, but the giant was tired, uncertain, unhappy.

According to Lafleur, the cause of the problem was Ruel's defensive style. Offensive players like himself were being given a lot less playing time. And the small amount of ice time they had was ruined by the opposing goons, who neutralized them by checking them.

"What we need are two or three big attackers. Grundman just has to find them. It's easy to say our opponents are goons who can't play proper hockey, subtle and refined like us, but that doesn't stop them from winning. And if I understand the game correctly, the idea is to win. What we need is to think like winners."

Poor Ruel had to react to Lafleur's attacks—his declarations, recriminations and sharply-worded advice. And the fans, in turn, saw this as an opportunity to express their own opinions, to approve or disapprove of each of Ruel's decisions. The direction of the Canadiens had become a matter of national debate: to play offensively or defensively? To use this or that player? Who to trade for whom? Ruel, his every move watched and argued over, no longer knew which way to turn, and so the team was constantly changing its style and its strategy. In February, the reporters began talking about "the Year of the Chameleon."

In addition to publicly exposing the dilemma facing the team, Lafleur offered his own opinions. He reminded everyone that the Canadiens' tradition, the one that had succeeded in establishing the famous and sacred dynasty, was based on the offensive game. Toe Blake, a great player and the coach of the Richards, Geoffrion and Béliveau (ten Stanley Cups among them), had always said that offence was the best defence. If you want peace, prepare for war.

Lafleur criticized Ruel for having broken with this noble tradition and having opted instead for a more cautious style of play. As soon as the Canadiens had a one- or two-goal lead, the offensive players were taken off and retreated fearfully into their own zone to protect the lead. Formerly, they would have gone on scoring; they wanted not only to win but to crush the opposition.

In the present circumstances it had become difficult for Lafleur to score. Certain other players, however, had the opportunity to shine. This was the origin of all sorts of tensions and conflicts. For example, Bob Gainey, a defensive forward, now had the right to a lot of ice time. Gainey was perfectly suited to Ruel's vision of a cautious team, able to protect a lead.

"For you, it's different," Lafleur told Robert Picard.

"You're a defenceman. There's a future here for players like you."

Picard listened to Lafleur's grievances. He more or less agreed that the Canadiens were going nowhere.

When, a little drunk, they had exhausted the subject of their noble profession, they began to talk about cars, money and women. They said to each other the things two men say when they're in a bar on their sixth or tenth drink: that women are all the same, all willing to make a scene about anything and, as the group Offenbach sang, all "hanging on to the blues."

Lafleur told Picard about his problems with Revenue Canada who, in December, had come to investigate his past income tax returns. That worried him, not directly but because of what Lise said.

"When your wife starts to worry about money, it's not fun any more. I don't really care about money. I do all that for my wife. Women spend their lives plucking feathers to make a nice soft nest. It smothers me. I'd like to live in the woods. That's where I feel good. In the woods, there are no problems. But in the cities, it's always the women who decide how things should be and tell us what to do, when to do it and with whom."

The night was getting late, and slowly, quietly, Guy was being overtaken by remorse. He thought about his wife, alone at home, who no longer waited up for him, who no longer expected anything from him. When he got home, she wouldn't speak to him. She didn't try to understand him.

"If you call to say you'll be late, you get an earful. If you don't call, you get it the next day. One way or the other, you have to pay. Every time you have a bit of fun, you have to pay. You don't have the right to go out for a drink. A woman is incapable of understanding that sometimes a man needs to let off steam. You always have to be there, by her side, a docile little dog, a poodle. But as for me, I'd rather be a wolf. Like I told you, Picard, I'd like to live in the woods."

But Thursday's bar, on a spring evening, was not at all

like the depths of the woods. There was plexiglass, mirrors, disturbing perfumes, enticing women, champagne, intoxicating music.

Suddenly, Lafleur grew tender. He told Picard that he loved his wife, that he couldn't exist without her, that she was intelligent and loving. He talked about his son. And then he said that she was stopping him from living, making a martyr out of him.

"Me, I've been married twice. For seven years with my wife and eleven with the Canadiens."

They'd had several aperitifs, wine with their meal and followed it with liqueurs. They were passably drunk when, towards midnight, they left Thursday's to go to Privé, a nearby bar, just to top things off. They watched the girls dancing with little enthusiasm. About two o'clock in the morning, tired and disgusted, they decided to end the evening. Picard, who lived downtown, was going to walk home.

"Flower, give me your keys."

"What do you mean, give you my keys?"

"You can't drive, Flower, you're too drunk. Pick up your car tomorrow."

"What are talking about? I can drive my car."

"If you get arrested, you could lose your licence. Imagine the scandal. You already have enough problems like that, don't you? Give your keys to the guy in the parking lot."

"Okay."

But the parking lot attendant had left long ago. Picard and Lafleur then decided that, having gone this far, they might as well have another drink at Saga's, a discotheque whose back door opened onto the lot where Lafleur's Cadillac was parked.

Guy Cloutier, who was Nathalie and René Simard's manager, was there with a musician and a sound man. A native of Lac-Saint-Jean, Cloutier had once played hockey with the Alma Aiglons of the Saguenay Junior A league. Now one of the pillars of the Québecois star system, the fertile creator of numerous personalities and events,

Cloutier had become a manager in the style of Colonel Tom Parker or Johnny Stark. Always cheerful, Cloutier had retained his distinctive accent and his sense of humour. He knew Lafleur well. Dozens of times they'd gone out on the town, eating and drinking. They both drove Harley-Davidsons and they often rode together. When Lafleur had had a bit to drink, he would drive without a helmet, taking incredible chances.

That evening, Cloutier immediately saw that the Blond Demon was completely drunk. Lafleur had sat down at his table, ordered champagne and tried to play a game of backgammon with one of Cloutier's musician friends. After losing two or three games he angrily pushed the board away. When he tried to stand up to leave, he knocked over the table, the game, the glasses, his keys. Cloutier picked them up.

"Give me my keys."

"You're in no state to drive, Guy. I'll keep your keys for you. I'll have your car sent to you tomorrow morning."

Lafleur didn't laugh. He shoved Cloutier, grabbed his keys and left. Cloutier followed, trying to reason with him. Lafleur sat on the hood of his car and told Cloutier to mind his own business. Cloutier knew he would not be able to persuade Lafleur. He went to get Picard, who was on the dance floor. When they came back, Guy had already driven away.

Guy started driving towards Baie d'Urfé. The Turcot interchange, with its tangle of ramps and connecting roads, kept him alert. Then he started driving along Highway 20's straightaway. A few minutes later, near Ville LaSalle, at the top of Rue Notre Dame, he fell asleep at the wheel. His car smashed into a road sign, mowed down six vertical posts in the metal barrier separating the highway from the service road and came to a halt in the wire fencing. The horizontal support rail had gone through the windshield, through the circle of the steering wheel, and buried itself in the back of the driver's seat, grazing Lafleur's right ear on its way. If he'd been awake and sitting straight he would have got it right in the face or throat and been killed instantly.

Just before the accident began, Guy had passed a small car driven by a policeman on his way home from work. The policeman saw the Cadillac leave the road right in front of him and smash into the fence. He parked behind. He found Guy Lafleur sitting on the railing. He was crying and his limbs were trembling.

Having made sure that Lafleur wasn't seriously hurt, the policeman made him get into his car, telling him it would be best if he left the scene before the Quebec Provincial Police arrived. He took Lafleur to the hospital in Lachine and Guy asked to be driven to the Montreal General Hospital.

The policeman telephoned Lise. She wasn't surprised. For a long time she'd told herself that, sooner or later, this was bound to happen. She went to the hospital. Her husband, his head bandaged, was resting in a small room beside an operating room. At first she thought he was badly hurt. The doctor told her that they would not be able to operate until the alcohol level in his blood came down. It was almost noon the next day when they were at last able to operate on his ear.

That night, Brian Travers was in Quebec City. At four in the morning the telephone rang. Irving Grundman told him about Guy's accident. Grundman, in fact, considered Brian, part of the Canadiens organization's "unofficial opposition," an unsuitable companion for Lafleur.

Travers got into his car and drove to Montreal before dawn, straight to the General Hospital. There was already a bodyguard in front of Guy's room, a hulking brute. No entry. Brian pulled some strings. He would take care of everything—of Guy, of Lise, of the press . . .

The next day Grundman summoned Picard to his office and demanded an explanation. Picard, still new to the Canadiens, was horribly ashamed. He told Grundman the whole story, that Lafleur had spent a good part of the afternoon and the whole evening drinking, and that at the time of the accident he was drunk.

Irving Grundman might not have been a great hockey man, but he had a good heart. He was shaken and pained, not only because Lafleur had had an accident, but also because the man was unhappy enough to spend hours getting drunk in bars. He went to the hospital to reassure Lafleur.

"This could be the beginning of a new life for you. I'm convinced this experience will make you think about things. I hope you'll be able to profit from it."

He asked the journalists to leave Lafleur alone, but the reporters, of course, wanted to know every detail. Guy Lafleur, advocate of openness and hard truths, the darling of the media, was in a poor position to reproach them for their understandable curiosity. Impressive photos of the wrecked Cadillac appeared on page one of each of the four Montreal dailies. Each of the accompanying stories called his survival a miracle. Each article also claimed that Guy Lafleur was not drunk, drugged or driving too fast; he had only been tired.

In a strange twist, the press were now covering up for the man who had made a policy of never hiding anything. No one dared attack the idol. And they acted in good conscience, saying to themselves that to expose Lafleur would not only have overwhelmed the Canadiens' best player but also blackened the name of the team.

Brian Travers convinced the policeman who had aided Lafleur to speak anonymously to the tabloid *Allô Police* about the incident. They published a glowing article, affirming and repeating that the Blond Demon had not been drunk, had not even smelled of alcohol, that he had just been tired. There had been no test for alcohol level because he alone had been involved in the accident and had not been seriously hurt.

Lafleur's teammates and friends were not surprised by the accident. They all knew that he lived dangerously and loved to drive fast. The organization had been relieved when General Motors forced him to sell his Ferrari. But they had panicked when he bought his Harley-Davidson a few weeks later. Grundman himself had intervened and asked him to get rid of it.

Lafleur spent four days in hospital. Some of his friends came to see him, and Guy laughed and joked about the adventure he'd had, his spectacular brush with death. But as soon as he was alone again, the idea terrified him. He was afraid. Of course he felt it was his fault. But he also thought that he was jinxed. His accident was only the latest and most serious of numerous setbacks he'd had that season:

October 2: Injury to his right knee during a pre-season game.

October 25: Ankle injury during skating practice.

November 14: A Vancouver journalist wrote that he had serious domestic problems, that he was living dissolutely, and that his injury of October 25 was his own fault because it had happened not at the Forum rink, but falling down the stairs of a disco.

November 17: Tonsillitis.

November 26: Another attack of tonsillitis.

December 15: Revenue Canada audited his books.

December 30: Injury to his right eye.

January 10: Injury to his left ankle.

January 31: Groin injury.

February 3: Injury to his left eye.

March 17: Injury to his left thigh.

He had already missed twenty-nine regular season games. And then, on April 14, a few days after the Canadiens had been eliminated in the quarter-finals by the Edmonton Oilers, Lafleur was injured during a game at the world championships in Stockholm.

A few days later, still in the Swedish capital, he met Vladislav Tretiak at a press conference. He had played against Tretiak, the famous Soviet goalie, several times. The conference was at a big hotel, and the international sporting press was there. Seeing Lafleur, Tretiak came up to him and said (through his interpreter) that his car accident had been reported in the Soviet newspapers.

"You should be careful, Guy. Drink coffee instead of whisky, it's less dangerous."

Lafleur, embarrassed, did not know how to respond. But he resented the fact that Tretiak had humiliated him in public. Tretiak's own reputation was beyond reproach. He was a superior athlete, had just been named best goalie of the championship and had received a trophy for being the best player in Europe and the USSR.

The Soviet press had been overjoyed when Lafleur, asked why he thought the Russian team was so powerful, had replied, "Because they are patriots." Nothing could have induced Lafleur to try life in the Communist world, but just the same, the Soviet players had something that he envied, a kind of wisdom, purity, frugality. It was hard to describe, but he would have liked to share their passion. Compared to them, he felt as though he no longer believed in anything more important than himself.

Once he'd recovered from the numerous injuries to his ankles and his face, he still had to contend with the less obvious wounds to his self-esteem, his ego, his image. He had fallen into a state of hopeless and bitter confusion.

A twenty-year-old Edmonton player, Wayne Gretzky, was the leading NHL scorer that season, and he monopolized the attention of the media and the public. Bit by bit, the light was receding from Guy Lafleur. During the preceding season he'd scored only 70 points. Gretzky had 164 (55 goals, 109 assists), a new record. It was far beyond the highest totals of the Blond Demon who, during his best NHL season (1976–1977), had scored only 136 points.

The reporters were writing: "The last decade belonged to Guy Lafleur, the next will be Wayne Gretzky's." Soon Lafleur would be thirty years old. Everyone said his reflexes had slowed by a tenth of a second. It was almost imperceptible to the naked eye, but, in the game of hockey, it was enough to make all the difference.

A little bitter, a touch jealous, Lafleur let it be known that the exploits of the young Gretzky would have been more difficult to achieve had he played with a winning club. His statements got under the skin of the "Wonder Boy" who replied:

"Guy Lafleur should keep track of what happens in the playoffs. He'll see what a winning club is."

When the time came, the Oilers defeated the Canadiens before being eliminated by the New York Islanders for the second year in a row. It was not the final victory of the

Islanders that hurt the Canadiens, but the rise of the young Oilers, who had taught them a lesson. Needing a new argument to downplay his rival's records, Lafleur now announced that Gretzky moved about the ice freely because he was protected by the Oilers' bullies, Dave Hunter and Lee Fogolin, whereas he, Guy Lafleur, was constantly being stopped by checkers.

Over the summer, when reporters met him on the golf course and questioned him about the gap between his and Gretzky's performances, he kept putting the blame on Ruel and Grundman.

"Things will change, if the team is managed more consistently."

To this, Grundman lashed back: "Guy Lafleur has no discipline. He'd like the club to be built around him, but that is no longer possible."

Lafleur replied: "If he's not happy with me, let him trade me."

Lafleur had entered his period of decline. But he didn't want to know it.

• • •

Before the beginning of the 1981–82 season, Canada, the United States and half a dozen European countries were to play for the second Canada Cup. Scotty Bowman, the coach of the Buffalo Sabres, had been chosen to coach the Canadian team. When he announced that Lafleur and Gretzky would be part of his first offensive line, the whole world was excited. Finally the two superstars—one thirty years old, the other twenty; one close to the end of his career and the other just beginning—would play together. The anticipation surrounding this match-up was even greater than for the Canada–USSR encounter. It was a huge event. Gretzky and Lafleur. Which one would carry the puck and set up plays for the other? Who would stay forward, waiting for the pass?

It was soon discovered that the Blond Demon and the Wonder Boy played together in perfect harmony, and that both of them enjoyed the experience. Lafleur had silenced his resentment. An exhibition match was played in Edmonton, Gretzky's territory. Lafleur was applauded as he had rarely been over the past year. "Guy! Guy! Guy!" chanted the crowd every time he got the puck. Gretzky and Lafleur, without ever looking at each other, exchanged perfect passes, never a mistake, never an error. They were perfectly synchronized.

One day, to get back downtown after a practice, Lafleur and Claude Larochelle of *Le Soleil* took the rapid-transit train. Larochelle was looking through the day's papers. Lafleur happened to see an article by Soviet hockey expert Anatoli Tarasov in the *Edmonton Journal*. Tarasov had some very harsh things to say about Lafleur. Guy, at thirty years old, had overindulged himself, wrote Tarasov. He was no more than a shadow of what he had been. Tarasov said that he'd seen Lafleur play in Stockholm in the spring and that he had found him sluggish and slow.

"Who's Tarasov? Who does he think he is?"

Guy threw the newspaper down, picked it up again, reread the article, visibly shaken. He was willing to acknowledge that he was slower, but he was rusty because he was no longer getting enough ice time. Tarasov didn't know what was going on. When the Russians had a good player, they let him play. Not here. Tarasov couldn't understand. But he had ruined Lafleur's good mood.

After the elimination of the Czechs, the Swedes and the Americans, the long-awaited game between Canada and the USSR took place at the Montreal Forum. Though the Canadian team had the home ice advantage, the Soviets soon led by three goals. During the first period, Vladislav Tretiak shone, but for the rest of the game he had an easy time of it. The Canadian players seemed incapable of organizing an attack and fired no more than a few weak shots. What had happened to their fierce determination to win? Tretiak had never seen players like Lafleur so lacking in intensity, so indifferent. He had been told that even during their worst defeats, players like Gretzky, Lafleur and Perreault never gave up. During the third period the

Canadian players were just wandering around the Forum ice, waiting for the match to be over. They had stopped playing. The final score was 8 to 1.

Lafleur didn't know what was slowing down Gretzky and Perreault, but for himself, he understood, too late, that Tarasov's article had been intended to upset him. It had worked. He had been wounded—in his self-esteem, his muscles, his reflexes—to the point that he had forgotten the great lesson of Ti-Paul Meloche: that, first and foremost, the game of hockey is played between the ears. In lacking vigilance, he had proved Tarasov right.

The Russian coach had aimed at Lafleur rather than Gretzky because he sensed Lafleur's vulnerability. Guy had defended himself poorly. When he read that stupid article, he should have wanted, with all his strength, to prove Tarasov wrong. He should have come on to the ice determined to make him regret his words, raring to go. That was the way he used to react, against John Wensink and the Big Bad Bruins or against Philadelphia's Broad Street Bullies. Instead, he had rebelled against what Tarasov had written. And he had been beaten; the battle had been lost in his head.

It's always important to understand why and how one has been defeated, but it is not necessarily reassuring. Lafleur felt his age; he was no longer innocent or invulnerable. And perhaps, he said to himself, if he was mentally slower, to the point of letting himself be influenced by the remarks of a Soviet coach, he might also be slower on the ice.

Bob Berry was the Canadiens' new coach. Claude Ruel, unable to take the pressure from the public, had handed his resignation to Grundman and resumed his position as the man in charge of player training. Only in Montreal was a coach so closely watched, argued with and challenged. In New York, Los Angeles or Toronto, people had other things to worry about. Their sense of pride rested elsewhere. Hockey was enjoyed as one diversion among many. But the soul of Montreal was to be found not at the stock exchange, but in the Forum. It had been too burdensome, too stressful for Ruel. He was relieved to cede his place to Bob Berry.

Berry, a native of Montreal, had demonstrated his coaching talent with the Los Angeles Kings. His record was more than honourable: 107 wins, 94 losses, 39 ties, in three years. Berry, a fearless coach, favoured order and discipline. He knew the Montreal public expected a lot from him, and that at his first mistake the finger would be pointed at him, just as it had been at Ruel and "Boom Boom." What would be his attitude towards his players? Geoffrion had dressed them down, and public opinion had skinned him alive. Ruel had tried to be kind and understanding, but both the press and the public had sent him out to pasture.

At the first meeting of the new season Berry talked to his men about motivation, cooperation, discipline and punctuality. A few days later, September 20, 1981, right at the beginning of training camp, Lafleur failed to show up for morning practice at the Forum and did not arrive until afternoon. Bob Berry immediately summoned him to his office.

"What happened this morning?"

"It's my birthday. I'm thirty today."

"So?"

"I celebrated last night."

"So?"

"I drank a bit too much. I went to bed at five this morning."

"The night before a practice?"

Bob Berry fined him two hundred dollars and sent him home. To the reporters he said that, despite everything, he appreciated the fact that Lafleur had told the truth.

"He could have made up a story, that his wife or his son was sick or that he had had an accident. He told me the truth. I appreciate it. I think we should get along well."

As for Lafleur, he said that he approved of Berry's firmness.

This period of mutual understanding, alas, did not last long.

In November, Guy Lafleur got another eye injury and
missed several games. People began to say that his reflexes
had slowed, that he could no longer avoid being hit, that it
took him longer and longer to recover. Guy, to defend
himself, claimed once more that it all resulted from the fact
that he wasn't playing enough. If only he could play instead
of getting rusty riding the bench, his reflexes would come
back.

Grundman replied, using statistics to back himself up,
that during the fifty-one games in which he had played the
preceding season, Lafleur had been the most utilized
player. "But we can't give him ice time when he's hurt, or
when he's in hospital because he's driven into a fence at two
in the morning."

Everyone was in a bad mood. Pierre Larouche, who
played on the same line as Lafleur, also let his unhappiness
be known. He had signed a very modest contract when he
was traded from Pittsburgh to Montreal in December 1977,
and he wanted it to be renegotiated, hoping for a significant
raise. Now, not only was he being denied his request, he was
also being denied playing time. It was openly said that he
was unsuited to the defensive style of play the Canadiens
were promoting.

Lafleur thought otherwise. He claimed and confided to
his journalist friends that Larouche was being given less ice
because he complained publicly; it was typical of the
organization. By reining Larouche in, they made him look
unproductive. That justified knocking down his price and
also silenced his complaints.

The fact that Berry would play this game upset Lafleur
even more. He did not hesitate to say, during a televised
interview, that Berry was no more than a puppet
manipulated by Grundman. He reminded viewers that
during the months preceding the renegotiation of his own
contract with the Canadiens, in 1973, he had been kept
from a central role on the team and had, therefore, played
badly and scored little. "It's normal. A player who plays
little plays badly. Everyone knows it." He had been de-
valued on the players' market. According to Lafleur, it was

all intentional, planned, disgusting and unacceptable.

Guy Lafleur's opinions carried a lot of weight with the public. In Quebec, rebels are well liked, and Lafleur was courageously battling authority. He was confronting the English, the Establishment, the rich and the owners. He had the hero's role. He knew, instinctively, that in the eyes of the public he would always be immune. Grundman was well aware of this. He avoided the reporters as much as possible and, when he was cornered, would only say that Lafleur's allegations were paranoiac and far-fetched, and that no club would fail to use a productive player. But he was in no position to win an argument against Lafleur. In December, a few days before Christmas, the whole Canadiens team was booed at the Forum. The angry recriminations of Lafleur and Larouche continued, louder than ever.

One day, in the bus that was taking the team to the Saint-Laurent arena, Larouche and Grundman had a violent argument in which several other players participated. Someone called Grundman a "damned Jew." Grundman, hurt and discouraged, did not reply; he did not even want to know who had voiced the insult. The bus fell suddenly silent. How could the team be tearing itself apart this way? How could they hope to compete for the Stanley Cup when they were so divided?

Guy Lafleur, who for six years had carried the team, began to ask himself if he might not be superfluous in what they called the "new system," and if it was still worthwhile to fight for more playing time.

In the old days, with Lemaire, he never asked himself this kind of question. He had just played, as a child plays. As soon as the other team entered the Canadiens' offensive zone, Lemaire turned back and chased after them. Lafleur stayed forward and waited ahead of the play, ready to take off as soon as he had the puck. Lemaire would look for him, pass to him; Lafleur would get away and score. Or Shutt would take care of things. That was the classic scenario to which the three men, over four years, had brought an infinite number of variations.

But since Lemaire's departure, no one made plays like

that any more. Even worse, the management of the Canadiens practically forbade this kind of play, even though it had always worked so well. The flamboyant attacks, improvisation, this jazz on ice was no longer wanted. Lafleur was supposed to play sensibly and follow well-orchestrated scores. In this system, Lafleur no longer had his old place. He wasn't sure he wanted to play this way.

One December evening, while he was watching television, he heard Bertrand Raymond of *Le Journal de Montréal* say that the Canadiens might be wise to trade him.

"Guy Lafleur doesn't have his old role with the Canadiens any more. But he could be very useful to another team. In return, the Canadiens would get three or four young players they could train to suit their system. As for myself, I find it obscene that a talent like Lafleur's is going unused. If Lafleur stays with Montreal, he is wasting his time."

Lafleur's first reaction was revulsion. But after thinking it over and talking with Lise, he decided that Bertrand Raymond's idea was not so bad. He might enjoy playing with one of the league's young clubs, like the Vancouver Canucks or the Los Angeles Kings. He would get to play a lot. He would get to know another city, find new friends. For a few days he toyed with the idea. Los Angeles was especially appealing to Guy and Lise. It wasn't necessarily hockey heaven, but there they would live the beautiful life, the good life, with palm trees, ocean sunsets and American dollars.

But then, in mid-winter, the Canadiens started playing better. Berry's system, with four lines and twelve forwards who each got their bit of ice time, started to yield results. By this time Guy, however, had slid into a deep lethargy. Berry's success with the new system seemed to imply that he could do without a player like Lafleur. Moreover, he forced Lafleur to retreat as soon as the other team got the puck. There was no question of his staying forward and waiting for a pass. As a result, Lafleur's production dropped and he was only the fortieth leading scorer in the league, he who for years had been all alone at the top.

Despite the team's improvement, there was a harsh setback to come: on March 22, 1982, the Canadiens suffered the supreme insult. They were defeated in the playoffs by the Nordiques. The Nordiques were coached by Michel "the Tiger" Bergeron, a small aggressive man who was both arrogant and provocative. This defeat, which showed the Nordiques to be the more talented team with better players and a better team spirit, shattered the Canadiens organization.

The defeat was both humiliating and highly symbolic. From the beginning, the Canadiens had considered Quebec their private hunting ground, but now the Nordiques had broken the stranglehold. Henceforth, hockey in Quebec would never be the same. From now on there would be a contest other than for the Stanley Cup, one infinitely more important and exciting: the battle for supremacy in Quebec. Between Montreal and Quebec City, war had been declared. In this power struggle, Guy Lafleur had an important role to play. But not the one that had been predicted for him.

• • •

On May 8, 1982, Guy and Lise Lafleur were at the Château Frontenac. Guy was in the bathroom shaving when Lise called to him from the living room: "Guy, Gilles is dead!"

Lafleur had several friends called Gilles, but he instantly knew she meant Gilles Villeneuve. He came out of the bathroom and stood in front of the radio.

"Gilles dead. I knew it! I knew it!"

They had met at Mont Tremblant, during the Formula Atlantic race in 1976. At that time, Villeneuve had just begun to make his mark on the international racing circuit. The following day, all the newspapers had published magnificent photos of the two athletes leaning over powerful racing cars. They looked like close friends. Lafleur, wearing a fireproof suit and a driver's helmet, was

shown receiving advice from Villeneuve. Then a Formula
Atlantic car sped over the course with the Canadiens'
number 10 at the wheel. Connoisseurs of car racing said
that Lafleur was extremely talented and that he could
easily have been a race driver.

A few months later, at the gala festivities for the Medaille
d'or, Gilles Villeneuve and Guy Lafleur were named
together as the athletes of the year for 1975, the jury having
been unable to decide which of the two should be placed
ahead of the other. At that time they had exchanged a few
pleasantries. But at Mont Tremblant, a strong understanding had sprung up between the two, as though they had
always known each other, always talked to each other, like
compatriots meeting by chance in a faraway country. They
understood each other right away, laughed at the same
things at the same time.

Their passion for cars and speed drew them together, but
there was something else. They were then without doubt the
most adulated personalities in Quebec. Lafleur had once
again brought the Montreal Canadiens the Stanley Cup.
Villeneuve had just signed on with Ferrari—the company
that is to racing what the Canadiens are to hockey—and was
leaving with his family to live in Italy.

Lafleur and Villeneuve both lived under the enormous
pressure that goes with being a superstar. They were of the
same race, the same calibre—grand champions. While
common mortals felt obliged to talk to them about sports
and question them endlessly on their fantastic feats and the
state of their psyches, Lafleur and Villeneuve expected
nothing from each other and had nothing to say to each
other. It was marvellously restful.

Lafleur had rubbed shoulders with many athletes in his
life. With all of them, he had felt there were things in
common. With some, naturally, things clicked better than
with others. Racing car drivers—like hockey players,
downhill or slalom skiers, boxers—are beings in a state of
high tension. Their antennae are always alert, their claws
always extended. Cyclists, marathon runners or deep-sea
divers are, on the other hand, masters of calm and

relaxation. The first kind of athlete is explosive, while the second accumulates his energy and lets it burn long and slow, like charcoal.

What is common to all elite athletes is enormous discipline and an unusual strength of character. All great athletes are masters of meditation, of contemplation, of the descent into the depths of the self. They are like samurai, mystics who know how to reach deeply into themselves and draw out the strength or the madness they need to achieve their successes. In fact, it is as though they all quench their thirst at the same source, as though the same power runs through all of them. Perhaps that's why they so easily recognize and resemble one another, even when they practise very different disciplines.

Gilles Villeneuve had the same kind of intensity and tension as Lafleur. Like Lafleur, although he seemed calm and cold, he was the explosive type. He was quite short, and weighed about fifty pounds less than Lafleur, but he was driven by an inexhaustible energy. And, again like Guy, he was always very serious. Even when he laughed, the seriousness could be heard in his laughter.

After that day at Mont Tremblant, Guy and Gilles had seen each other several times, in Montreal or on the Côte d'Azur, and each time the deep attachment they had to each other was instantly re-established.

"I knew he'd end up killing himself."

Guy Lafleur did not believe in fate. In his eyes, death was an error committed. Each person was responsible for, if not guilty of, his own death. Sooner or later each person made his inevitable error, his last mistake. He found the same reasoning attributed to the test pilots in Tom Wolfe's book, *The Right Stuff*. When a pilot took the controls of an experimental aircraft and died trying to break the sound barrier, his mourning friends would not talk about bad luck or mechanical failure. They just said, "Poor Bob! He didn't have the 'right stuff.' "

Guy believed that his friend Gilles Villeneuve had died because of a lack of concentration and judgment, "because he must have been frustrated in his life."

Lafleur turned on the television. He saw the accident replayed again and again. The dislocated body of his friend ejected from his racing car, a projectile hurtling through space, flying over the track and crashing . . . in slow motion . . . into the fence of the Zolder track in Belgium. Everyone running up and standing around him, in shock. Guy thought and spoke about his own death, of the accident he had had a few months before.

"People said I had an accident because I was drunk. But that's meaningless."

"The real question is, why were you drunk? Because at that moment in your life you wanted to die. Despite everything that you had. Why weren't you satisfied? Why weren't you happy?"

"You know what my father said when I came to Thurso with my Ferrari? That I was a man who was looking for my death."

"He wasn't wrong. Do you remember how you used to be in those days? With your Ferrari, then your big Harley. Your father was right. You were looking for your death."

"Like Gilles with his Formula One."

"The difference is that he found it."

"You're right. He was faster than me."

In that era there may have been a fascination with the idea of pointless death. Once people died defending their country, their values, their ideas. But the greatest heroes of Lafleur's generation—Janis Joplin, Jimi Hendrix, Jim Morrison—had died very young and more or less by their own mistakes, like Jimmy Dean had before. And their deaths had increased their stature and made them transcendent figures to the generation that was fascinated by death's absurdity.

Lafleur knew the intoxication of speed. Speed, the true conquest of space and time, had been the great challenge of the century, a challenge that could only be met by the affluent, the powerful and the brave. Speed had been the domain of the rich and the young. Time is money, and so is speed. And both kill. Lafleur was afraid: afraid of speed, afraid of himself, afraid of death.

Less than three weeks later, on May 29, 1982, Roger Barré, Guy's beloved father-in-law, died after a long and harrowing illness. Roger Barré had loved life, and certainly had not wanted to die. It would not be said, as with Villeneuve, that he had desired and sought his own death. This time, it was necessary to believe in fate. Lafleur was deeply grieved. He had lost a friend, a supporter, an adviser, a model, one of the truly important men in his life.

The summer was a sad one. Lafleur spent whole days doing nothing, thinking dark thoughts, drinking.

Every summer, the Canadiens' softball team would tour Quebec playing local amateur teams. One August evening, at Saint-Georges-de-Beauce, Guy Lafleur showed up for a game in a fairly tipsy state. During the afternoon he had attended the opening of a bar and had had a lot to drink. Claude Mouton realized what was happening and advised him to slow down a bit. The spectators also noticed. He played badly, swung wildly, laughed loudly, argued with the umpire.

As always he was surrounded by reporters and was generous with his thoughts. He got talking about the huge gap between what he was paid and the salaries of the other top NHL players. He was then making a little less than $400,000 a year. He said he was determined to get more, and even threatened publicly to go right to Morgan McCammon, the president of the Molson Breweries. He claimed that Mike Bossy and Wayne Gretzky were both getting more than he was. Also, many players who were less useful and less productive had salaries comparable to his own.

"Agreed, I score fewer goals," he admitted, "but that's because, for three years, I've been slowed down by the organization. When Bowman was around, I played up to thirty-five minutes a game. Today, I'm lucky to be on for fifteen. Ask yourself why I score less."

The next morning, Quebec learned through the newspapers and radio that Guy Lafleur intended to renegotiate his contract in the fall, and that he alone would do the negotiating. Jerry Petrie, his agent and friend for a decade, was now looking after the business interests of the number-one Montreal Expo player, Gary Carter; Lafleur didn't think he would have time to look out properly for him as well.

Lafleur formed a common front with Larry Robinson, who also wanted his contract renegotiated. All sorts of rumours made the rounds. One day it was said that they would be sold or traded to another NHL club. The next day, that wealthy financiers had come from Japan to see them and that probably they would be playing in Sapporo next winter. Robinson and Lafleur neither confirmed nor denied these rumours. They just smiled. Lafleur let it be known that he would be glad to leave, saying that he was tired of being eaten up by the Quebec taxation system.

It was, in truth, out of respect for the memory of his father-in-law that he had decided to make this stand. During their last conversation, Roger Barré had strongly advised him to renegotiate his contract with the Canadiens.

"It's not a question of money," he said. "It's a matter of principle and dignity. Otherwise, you're being taken. And someone else is getting rich thanks to your work. Have a little more respect for yourself."

August 12 saw the launch of a book by Johnny Rougeau. Rougeau was a well-known boxer who made no secret of his sympathies for separatism and the Parti Québecois. At the launch, some reporters asked René Lévesque what he thought of the Lafleur–Robinson affair, then in the headlines. Without naming names, the Quebec premier made some acid remarks.

"I find it a bit much," he said, "that for a few thousand dollars more, professional athletes will desert the public that has, in some way, made them. I find that a bit hard to take."

He went on to call professional athletes "the most spoiled of all our spoiled children." He added that he found the whole affair—during a time of recession and government cutbacks—somewhat scandalous. His own salary, as Quebec premier, was at that time $84,296 a year, roughly one-fifth of Guy Lafleur's.

Guy had always made it clear that he had little sympathy for the separatist movement. He was a continentalist and considered himself, first and foremost, a North American. He reacted sharply to René Lévesque's lecture.

"Everyone says that French Canadians have undersold themselves for too long. I don't see how a man like René Lévesque can disapprove of the actions of one man who doesn't want to be exploited. . . . With Maurice Richard, Geoffrion and the others, the Canadiens organization made a colossal fortune. Everyone knows that. Everyone is angry because Maurice Richard, the legend, is not a rich man today, as he should be. He didn't benefit from the wealth that he created for others. As for myself, I don't want to be a puppet, I don't want to be manipulated and exploited like the others. I want to be independent. It seems to me that Monsieur Lévesque should be able to understand that."

On September 12, a laconic press release carried the information that Grundman, Lafleur and Robinson had resolved their differences. There were just a few clauses left to straighten out.

Lafleur now had every reason to be happy and look forward to the new season. He was the best-paid hockey player in Quebec, with almost $475,000 a year. Along with Gretzky, Bossy, Dionne and Denis Potvin, Lafleur had one of the top five salaries in the NHL. Of course none of the NHL players could keep up with the salaries of the Expos' players. Gary Carter got more than $1.5 million; Steve Rogers received $750,000; in all, nine Expo players were paid more than Lafleur. But hockey couldn't compete with baseball salaries because baseball teams played 162 games a year in stadiums with more than 50,000 seats and had, in addition, huge television revenues.

That fall, tennis player Jimmy Connors made a triumphant return to his sport. "Jimbo" Connors, born in 1952, was an extraordinary showman. In 1974, at the age of twenty-one, he had proved himself tennis's top player by winning the doubles championship at Wimbledon (partnered by Ilie Nastase) as well as both the Wimbledon and U.S. Open singles championships. Nine years later, it was said that he was "all washed up"; Bjorn Borg, the rising star, would finish him off easily. Obviously, they did not know Jimmy Connors.

In 1982, Connors crushed all his opponents at Wimbledon and at Flushing Meadows. He worked with iron determination, training wisely, rediscovering his former energy and the desire to win, climbing the slope a bit at a time. At thirty he once more experienced the glory he had known almost ten years before. "When you're willing to fight, you're never quite dead," he said.

Connors' spectacular comeback made a deep impression on Guy, and he decided that he too would fight, train, make a comeback. He had no false illusions. He knew that at thirty-one years of age and, moreover, playing within the defensive system adopted by the Canadiens, it was very unlikely he could once more become the NHL's leading scorer. That was no longer his position and he had to face it.

The previous winter he had agreed to make a commercial for Eveready Energizer batteries. The commercial was shot on the ice at the Forum. Guy's son, Martin, wearing Gretzky's number 99, skated past and faked out his father. The narration made reference to the ideas of durability, of energy, of overtaking. For Lafleur, the comparison was a humiliating one. Number 99 was indeed taking the place of number 10, just as the Energizer battery took the place of its competitors. He had to admit that he had been surpassed by better players: Gretzky, Bossy, Stastny. But he remained persuaded that he still had some good years left in him.

The embarrassing drunk at the Saint-Georges-de-Beauce softball game, the deaths of Gilles Villeneuve and Roger Barré, the spectacular comeback of Jimmy Connors—it all prompted Guy to take himself in hand. He began drinking Perrier, and it made headlines in all the newspapers for a week. He settled down to serious training and a strict diet; he had finished the previous season at 195 pounds, a good 15 pounds over his normal weight.

All Quebec followed the transformation of Guy Lafleur,

as though his project was a collective one, a sort of "work in progress" in which the whole population was participating. Solicited by the press, the specialists and doctors gave their opinions. According to Dr Jean-Paul Bédard, for example, it would take eight to ten months before Lafleur's body regained its former equilibrium. "After that, he'll be on fire." It was also said that he had surely gained in maturity what he had lost in speed, and that by getting back to his proper weight, he would be even more dangerous than before. Everywhere people were talking about the new Guy Lafleur.

He arrived at training camp weighing 183 pounds. He kept working hard. On October 10 he brought the Forum crowd to its feet. He was skating as he had in the old days, making moves never before seen, electrifying escapes; he was all over the ice.

In December 1981, Pierre Larouche was sent to Hartford. After what had happened between him and Grundman, it would have been hard for him to stay in Montreal. He was not, like Lafleur, an untouchable monument. Young Doug Wickenheiser was assigned to replace him as the centre between Lafleur and Shutt. "Wick" was a big, solid and energetic player, with excellent powers of anticipation. Many people believed that this new trio would function well but, alas, Lafleur was injured again and was out of action for a few weeks. This injury and absence would provide the basis for one of the craziest episodes in Guy Lafleur's life.

• • •

The whole business had started ten months earlier, in November 1982, on the ice of the Montreal Forum. Lafleur had just doubled back into his defensive zone and was getting ready to face the invaders when he felt a heavy blow against his right skate. In the heat of action you don't really feel the pain, so Lafleur kept playing until Berry called him off the ice, about a minute and a half later. On the bench, he felt sharp, shooting pains in his right foot. But as soon as Berry sent him back on the ice, the pain went away. It wasn't until after the game, taking off his skate, that he realized his foot was swollen, bruised and very painful. The club trainer sent him to the hospital, where an X-ray showed that he had broken the little toe of his right foot. The doctor recommended three weeks of rest. Guy Lafleur could now boast the most famous little right toe of the century!

One of Guy's friends was Georges Guilbeault, head of the Sherbrooke Jets, and manager of sales and marketing for the Sherwood company, a large hockey stick manufacturer located in the Eastern Townships. Guilbeault suggested that Lafleur join him on a deer-hunting expedition. Guy had wanted to go hunting for a long time but was normally unable to, since the hunting season and the hockey season coincide.

On November 27 he got up at 2:30 in the morning and drove to the Eastern Townships where he met Guilbeault and Léo Drolet, the owner of Sherwood. A few hours later he shot (with a .306 Tika carbine) a handsome Virginia stag. A professional photographer took a fine picture of Guy Lafleur proudly posing beside his victim.

The expedition was for both pleasure and business. Lafleur had dropped Koho sticks and was now the official representative for Sherwood. From this touching photograph fifteen thousand posters would be made, with the name "Sherwood" in big, three-inch-high letters. The posters would be distributed across Ontario and Quebec, at all sporting goods stores, sports centres, pubs and so on.

Two days later, on November 29, Lafleur appeared with his trophy in the Sherbrooke newspaper, La Tribune. That day he drove back to Baie d'Urfé with his deer stretched out on the roof of the car lent to him by Léo Drolet. His neighbour couldn't hide his amazement.

"I thought the hunting season was over!"

"Not in Maine."

The next day, sports open-line shows were inundated with calls from scandalized listeners. People wondered, perplexed and puzzled, how it was that Guy Lafleur, their cherished Guy, could go hunting with a broken toe when he was unable to play hockey. He replied that walking was easy for him, that a few days ago he had even gone hunting for partridge with his friend Claude Quenneville in the forest near Thurso. But by skating, he risked aggravating his injury; when a skater pushes to accelerate, the force passes through the toes.

But the damage had been done; the public was aroused and considered itself the injured party. If Lafleur still had the sacred fire, they said, he would have denied himself the pleasure of hunting.

"Be realistic," he said, not without humour. "If I'm seen in the discos on Rue Crescent, you argue with me. And if I go into the woods, the same thing!"

By the time Guy had returned to action, the Canadiens had slumped into lethargy. The year 1983 had begun badly. The Canadiens' power play was hardly ever able to score. Their defence was loose and easily penetrated. The plays were scrambled. Bob Berry, like Ruel two years before, was confused and constantly changing the club's style of play. Lafleur's centres—first Wickenheiser, then Ryan Walter—turned out to be unsuitable; they were too nervous and too slow. Young Guy Carbonneau was tried. During Lafleur's absence he had shown himself to be a promising player, but he lacked experience.

Lafleur missed Lemaire more and more. He dreamed of having a centre like him again. But it was a difficult position for any player to fill. Even Lemaire had cracked in the end. The centre for a player like Guy Lafleur had to be a foil. He would toil in the shadows, always working hard but seldom visible. Lafleur demanded a high level of play that put a lot of pressure on his linemate. If the centre did his job well, Lafleur received the praise. If he did it poorly, he got booed.

Lemaire had not been immune to these pressures. Usually he managed to get control of the puck and draw the checkers to himself so that Lafleur could get free. Then he would pass him the puck and the Blond Demon would score. But one evening, none of Lemaire's plays worked; all the passes he attempted for Lafleur were intercepted. In vain, Lafleur waited for the puck. Someone in the crowd yelled to Lemaire that he was a good-for-nothing. Lemaire, crazy with rage, went over to the boards and, finding the man who'd insulted him, held out his stick and shouted:

"Do you want to play instead of me? You think what I'm supposed to do is so easy?"

In mid-January, despite all the changes and the fact that he had missed eleven games, Lafleur was the team's leading scorer. It should be said that the club wasn't scoring very much, and that playing time was being divided among a lot of players. In fact, there was a new rule allowing teams to dress eighteen players, so that Berry always had at his disposal four offensive trios, which he used in rotation. In his peak years, Lafleur had always played on two lines, so that he was often on the ice. But nowadays Berry sent his lines out for short periods, changing frequently.

On February 8, 1983, Lafleur allowed himself another of his explosive statements. He told reporters that the Canadiens had no reserves. According to him, the Nova Scotia Voyageurs, the Canadiens' farm club, had no good players. Lafleur's statement caused an outcry; the Voyageurs were insulted.

But once again Guy was saying out loud what many people were thinking. The Canadiens had, in fact, exhausted their reserves and lost their depth.

"If this isn't remedied right away, it will be a long time before the Stanley Cup comes back to Montreal."

This was an arrow aimed at Grundman. A good managing director should make long-term plans. Grundman had let the club grow older without thinking of future replacements. It was obvious that the old guard would soon be gone. Shutt, Robinson, Gainey and Lafleur, the strong men of the team, were all almost thirty years old or older. No one seemed to be worried about what would happen after their departure.

Lafleur hoped to leave the Canadiens feeling that he had participated in the construction of something worthwhile and lasting. Now it was increasingly obvious that he would leave nothing behind him. The continuity had been broken. The dynasty would end with him. And suddenly, right in the middle of the season, Lafleur lost all motivation. The Edmonton fans and sports writers who had applauded him so warmly when he came to play with Gretzky and Perreault for the Canada Cup found him, at mid-season, diminished and listless. Everyone talked about his decline.

"Lafleur, who used to be the best passer anyone had ever seen, now gets rid of the puck as soon as he has it. He skates aimlessly, he makes bad passes, he is unable to pick up the passes he's given."

In February 1983, at an exhibition staged by sporting goods manufacturers, the main attractions were Gretzky, Bossy and Stastny. Since Lafleur's accident and the rising number of rumours that he was not living the way athletes should, the advertising executives had grown cool. According to them, his image had been tarnished. Nevertheless, the public found him as attractive as ever.

The great majority of athletes only hold the public's attention when they produce. A hockey player has to make good passes, outstanding checks, dazzling goals. As soon as they pass their peak and stop scoring, they are forgotten and replaced. But not Lafleur. His fall and the slump in which he was foundering was as spectacular and exciting, and followed just as closely, as his rise had been. His moods, his mistakes, his various griefs were reported in great detail. Long studies analysed his biorhythms. Astrologists made their pronouncements. Psychiatrists, doctors and hand-writing experts also had their say. Former greats and the star players from other teams, including Gretzky, Marcel Dionne, Maurice Richard, Mike Bossy, were consulted and gave their opinions and advice. Everyone had something to say.

Guy Lafleur had become a national curiosity, and the public was offered all sorts of explanations and theories for his rise and fall. They spoke of his "muscle memory." It was said that Guy's muscles were experienced and could function automatically, that all he needed was to be put in a motivating context, and he would start scoring again. The people of Quebec were the scientists; Guy Lafleur was the model and guinea pig. But all this put enormous pressure on him, and once more he felt trapped in a vicious circle.

"I'm worried because I'm playing badly. And the longer I play badly, the more I worry. Somehow I have to clear my head."

Guy had no more idea than anyone else what direction to go in, what strategy to adopt. He tried one thing after another: sarcasm, rebellion, submission. One day he decided he would no longer read newspapers, talk to reporters or listen to advice from anyone; he would be positive and obedient. If the system wouldn't change, Guy Lafleur would. He would do everything Bob Berry asked him to do. With a smile. Berry asked him to be part of a defensive line with Bob Gainey and Keith Acton. It was absurd. It infuriated those who wanted to see their Blond Demon scoring goals again. But Lafleur did what Berry asked.

On February 22, the deafening and savage chant was heard once again at the Forum: "Guy! Guy! Guy!" The crowd was screaming at the top of their lungs because they thought they'd got their idol back. He scored two magnificent goals. The next day, everyone was talking about the return of Guy Lafleur. But a month later, a few days before the end of the 1982–83 season, the affair of the deer and the little toe come back to haunt him.

Lafleur had to admit publicly that he had killed the animal not in Maine, as he had explained, but in Saint-Evariste-de-Forsyth, in the Beauce, on property belonging to Réal Bureau. Bureau's land was a fenced-in domain of 188 acres that he maintained for hunting; it held a hundred Virginia stags in captivity, a few moose, some wild does and caribou, as well as innumerable rabbits, partridge and pheasants.

It was terribly embarrassing. On the one hand, Guy Lafleur, the man who always told the truth, had lied; on the other, he seemed to be an armchair hunter. Killing a stag in captivity is not exactly hero's work. One cartoonist showed him aiming his rifle at a stag that was being led on a leash. And that wasn't the end of it.

Civil servants from the Ministry of Recreation, Fish and Game were informed that the animal had been killed out of season and that Lafleur had been hunting without a permit. That was why, on the morning of September 8, 1983, Guy Lafleur and his companions—Georges Guilbeault and René Bureau—found themselves in the small town of Megantic in the local courthouse.

Three charges had been laid against Guy Lafleur: hunting large game out of season, hunting without a permit and having killed large game in his possession. Guilbeault and Bureau had been accused of incitement to crime, as had Léo Drolet, who was unable to appear due to the fact that he was in hospital.

"Family name, first name, age and profession."

"Lafleur, Guy, thirty-one years, hockey player and hunter."

The small crowd jammed into the cramped room where Judge Laurent Dubé from the Sherbrooke sessional court had come to render justice burst out laughing.

For a few hours, Megantic was the capital of Quebec. The three men pleaded not guilty. Witnesses filed in front of the judge: a man who had gutted the stag Lafleur had killed, two gamekeepers, a photographer . . .

At the end of the afternoon, Judge Dubé handed down his judgment. Lafleur, Drolet and Guilbeault were innocent. As for Bureau, his trial was re-scheduled for a later date. (He would also be declared innocent.) The affair was closed, but people went on talking about it for a long time. For almost a year it had been the subject of hundreds of newspaper articles and was discussed endlessly over the radio. For the first time in his twelve years in Montreal, the public had something for which to reproach Guy Lafleur.

• • •

On October 25, 1983, Guy Lafleur scored the 498th goal of his career and thus became one of the ten best scorers of all time, along with Maurice Richard, Jean Béliveau, Phil Esposito, Gordie Howe, Marcel Dionne, Jean Ratelle and company.

The game had been hard-fought and was drawing to

what would have been an honourable finish for both sides, a scoreless tie. Suddenly the crowd began to chant, "Guy! Guy! Guy!" again and again. Less than a minute and a half was left when Berry finally sent Lafleur onto the ice. The crowd immediately fell silent.

He didn't go straight towards the puck; the puck came to him. You might have said that Lafleur was hidden, or playing as the invisible man. In a fraction of a second, everyone had practically forgotten he was on the ice. He had placed himself so as not to be seen by the opposing team but only his teammates, who quickly passed him the puck. From then on it was pure magic, pure ecstasy, just like the good old days of 1976 and 1977 when he scored a good fifty goals a year. Everything was done with a kind of voluptuous slowness. The spectators were hypnotized. Even the opposing defenceman was in a deep sleep when Lafleur arrived in front of him. He didn't see anything. The puck slid peacefully beneath him. Lafleur brushed by him, taking his time, then picked up the puck again on the other side and found himself alone in front of the goaltender. Seeing Lafleur approach, the goalie fell to the ice. The poor man probably thought that there were two or three Guy Lafleurs who were attacking at the same time—to the left, to the right, down the centre—three Guy Lafleurs passing the puck back and forth to one another, right in front of him. What was he supposed to do, one against three?

One of the Guy Lafleurs, working slowly, gathered up the puck on his backhand, taking the pass from another Guy Lafleur, then shot it over the goalie's shoulder. The net waved gently, like a flag swollen by a puff of wind. The red light went on and the crowd, on its feet, galvanized by the electricity of the moment, once again began to shout: "Guy! Guy! Guy!" All that in less than sixty seconds. Without a hitch. It was so beautifully done, so perfect. The crowd, eyes swollen with tears, still breathless, burst into laughter. It was a pure masterpiece!

Carried along by his own momentum, Lafleur swept round the net, his arms held high to celebrate his victory. On television, millions could see his shining face, his smile.

His teammates threw themselves on top of him, punching him, pulling his head, knocking him in the chest, grabbing his ears, crushing his nose against their pads. The fine, barbarous, virile ritual. "Guy! Guy! Guy!" the delirious crowd continued. He was back. The Magician. The Force. Guy Lafleur was back.

But a few days later, Bob Berry didn't hesitate to leave Lafleur riding the bench during the last minutes of play when the Canadiens were losing the game by only one goal. The reason? To punish him. Because he'd let Willi Plett, the North Star player he was supposed to be covering, get away. And Plett had then scored the winning goal: 4 to 3 for the North Stars. Berry held Lafleur responsible for the Canadiens' defeat. He should have turned back, but he hadn't. In other words, Guy Lafleur, a forward, was punished for not having played well defensively.

This wasn't the first time Berry had done this to him. He had made the same move, under similar circumstances, during the previous playoff series. It had been in Buffalo, in the quarter-finals, with a minute to go. The Sabres were leading 4 to 3. In such circumstances a coach, as Berry did, takes out his goalie and sends his six best scorers onto the ice. But that evening Berry decided to leave Guy Lafleur on the bench. The minute went by. The Canadiens didn't score and found themselves virtually eliminated from the playoffs, in the first round, for the fourth consecutive year. If such a thing had happened at the Forum, the people would doubtless have lynched Bob Berry. The next day, in the sporting press and on the radio open-line shows, everyone said how incredibly stupid Berry was. A month later Berry was gone. And so was Grundman, who, bitter and disappointed, went back to managing his bowling alleys.

When Serge Savard was named managing director, he immediately rehired Bob Berry as head coach and gave him Jacques Lemaire and Jacques Laperrière as assistants. Lemaire was responsible for the training and conditioning of the forwards; Laperrière, a brilliant theoretician and practitioner of the defensive game, worked with the defencemen.

During the summer, whenever he was asked his opinion on the coaching staff, Lafleur said he was happy with these appointments. For a while he believed, once again, that things had been righted, and that once more the team would be a happy and cohesive unit, that everyone would have a chance to get ice time. But Berry went back to his old ways and once again left Lafleur on the bench at a critical moment when he might have helped his team. It was provocation, pure and simple. Lafleur felt like getting up and going to the dressing room. But the crowd started to yell—"Guy! Guy! Guy!"—so loudly that the players on the ice could hardly keep track of what was going on. Lafleur gave a shadow of a smile. After the game, when the journalists approached him, he, with an Olympian calm, let them know he had nothing to say. The crowd had spoken and their message was clear.

That evening Bob Berry realized that he could not freely take charge of the Montreal Canadiens in front of the Montreal public. In Buffalo, yes. But at the Forum, it was the people who led, and the people were madly in love with Guy Lafleur. Lafleur had, in effect, made the people the real team coach. Lafleur kept his fans up-to-date with the club's problems, the conflicts and dramas being played out within it, the struggles that were being carried on. And it seemed obvious that the public, grateful for the trust Lafleur had placed in them, would from now on be his whole-hearted supporters.

Nevertheless, the new managing director, Serge Savard, had no choice but to defend his coach and give him his unconditional support. He came out with a famous and controversial statement that journalists spent days examining:

"No one player is more important than the sport he is playing."

This was not just a stance or a profession of faith; it was a clear message. Savard was saying that he had no intention of sacrificing the well-being of the team for the happiness of Guy Lafleur.

"Either we build a team of nineteen players around Guy, or we have a team of twenty players, of which Guy Lafleur is one."

Often, young NHL clubs chose to build a team in the first way, with one player at the centre. They didn't really have a choice. If they were lucky enough to acquire an outstanding player, they would try to organize their team and their future around him, according to his strengths and weaknesses. He was given passers, protectors, all the playing time he wanted. It was often very effective, but it was also a very vulnerable practice. If the one pillar fell, everything else crumbled.

Savard refused to take this chance; he was infinitely more ambitious. He didn't necessarily want to win the next Stanley Cup, but first and foremost to rebuild a team, a solid and invincible team that he would construct in his own way. That was the goal towards which he was working. He had quickly understood that there was no place in this plan for an ageing player like Guy Lafleur. He and Lemaire, who had been away from Montreal for two years, had been astounded at the feeble performance of the Blond Demon. Lemaire especially was of the opinion that it would be illusory to hope Lafleur could once more be a great hockey player.

Just the same, Savard tried to find him a centre. He got someone very good, Bobby Smith. Smith was an attractive and intelligent player, a skilful playmaker, a twenty-eight-year-old gentle giant, six feet four inches tall and weighing 210 pounds. He joined the team in October.

"This time," Savard murmured, "Lafleur won't have any excuses."

In fact, Savard was delivering an ultimatum. For two years Lafleur had been complaining, among other things, about not having a good centre. Almost a dozen had been tried but none had satisfied Lafleur. Mondou, Larouche, Acton, Wickenheiser, Walter, Carbonneau—every one of them had come up short. In giving him Bobby Smith, a player for whom he had paid dearly, Savard hoped he was buying Lafleur's silence. But what Lafleur wanted was not only a good partner, but ice time, and Savard and Lemaire were determined to give him no more than anyone else.

When he tilted his head back, took a puff from his fat cigar, looked down at the reporters and declared that no one player was more important than the sport he played, Savard believed himself to be stating an undeniable and unarguable truth. But in fact, it was just a pious platitude. In the heart of Quebec fans, Guy Lafleur was infinitely more important than the sport he played. Guy Lafleur *was* hockey.

Once more Lafleur and the Canadiens organization were confronting each other. Or, rather, the organization was confronting the public. Lafleur no longer had either the need or the desire to talk. Others did it for him. He wrapped himself in an arrogant silence. It was the Cold War of the winter of 1984. Lafleur spent long afternoons at the Ritz drinking cognac or scotch. In the evenings he was to be seen in the chic and expensive discos on Rue Crescent. He came to practices and games at the very last minute, whistled while he changed, infinitely calm, relaxed, perfectly indifferent.

Sometimes, in a formidable burst of energy, he shook off his lethargy and played great hockey. One evening he beat the Quebec Nordiques almost singlehandedly. Two weeks later, in February, he pulled off a spectacular hat trick. Then he fell back into a sort of torpor. Berry sat him on the bench more and more often, for longer and longer. He considered Lafleur to be a poor defensive player. And when the puck was to be dropped in Canadiens territory he replaced Lafleur with Mark Hunter.

Gradually, despite the unremitting, contemptuous treatment meted out to their idol, the chants of "Guy! Guy! Guy!" became less pressing. There were just a few eccentrics here and there in the crowd who sometimes shouted out a loud "Guy Lafleur!" that echoed lugubriously from one end of the Forum to the other, without being picked up by the rest of the crowd.

Lafleur sat on the bench, impassive, absent. He looked at

his feet. He waited for the game to be over. Sometimes he felt as though he was sliding quietly into darkness, that he was disappearing without anyone noticing. No one would even ask, "Where did Guy Lafleur go?" He would become a Forum ghost, a has-been. He saw clearly that he was finishing his career in the style of Pete Mahovolich, not Bobby Orr. It only hurt a little; he could hardly bring himself to care.

In the back of his mind Guy harboured the notion of one day being given a public relations post with the Canadiens or Molson, but he knew that he would sooner or later have to make certain compromises and change his attitude. In recent years his image had suffered. He still sometimes saw the very honourable Jean Béliveau with his impeccable reputation—never a slip or a mistake in thirty-three years with the Canadiens, either as star player or vice-president of public affairs. But Guy Lafleur's image had changed considerably in the last twelve years. The taciturn and self-effacing boy he had once been, the well-behaved and serene champion of his great years, had given way to the delinquent hero, to the rebel, to the broken man.

But maybe, in the end, that was why people loved him so much, for his mistakes as much as for his triumphs, for his dark side, his unpredictable moments.

Of course, the big bosses of the Molson Breweries and the Canadiens did not see things that way. They probably would not want, as their representative, a man who caused chaos everywhere, who drove into highway barriers at two in the morning, who left his wife and called his bosses incompetent. Too bad for them.

Anyway, if the Canadiens or Molson ever did close their door to him, he had other possibilities. He could always get together with Pierre Barré, his brother-in-law, who had taken over his father's business. They would open a garage for luxury automobiles: Lamborghini, Ferrari, DeLorean. Nothing in the world was more fascinating than these sophisticated machines and the people who bought and drove them.

He concocted other plans with his friends from the

Sherwood company, Guilbeault and Drolet. But the dream that most appealed to him was to drop everything, to buy himself a plot of land or a bit of forest and to build himself a house. He thought of Roger Barré's country home, and Léo Drolet's place in the Eastern Townships.

Even on the bench he would sometimes be soothed by this dream: a stone house surrounded by trees, a nearby stream that would babble during the summer, paths through the forest. He would do everything himself. He would have a tractor. Lise would have horses. They would be happy.

One day, when the club was leaving for a road trip in the west, Lafleur came to the airport fifteen minutes late, without excuse, not even pretending that he had hurried a bit or that he regretted having made the team wait. When they arrived in Winnipeg, Serge Savard summoned him to his room, offered him a cigar and a drink, and tried to talk honestly with him. But Lafleur warily refused the cigar and the scotch.

"What do you want?" Savard asked him.

"You know what. I just want to play hockey."

"Then why don't you?"

"I've always found it hard to play sitting down."

Savard, upset, didn't want to get into this pointless discussion. Lafleur, he thought, was not being straightforward. The year before he had had more ice time than any other player.

"Just the same, it's less than I used to have."

"But that has nothing to do with anything, Guy. Times have changed. The team has changed. Hockey has changed."

"It's you who want to change everything. If you give me ice, I'll score goals."

"You've had it . . ."

"Not enough."

"I honestly think you are refusing to face reality. And I think you should stop holding the whole world responsible for your problems. You want the team to be built around you. I am telling you that is no longer possible. And it never will be possible. Your problem is that you're thinking of yourself instead of the team."

"And who are you thinking of?"

"To tell you the truth, I'm wasting my time thinking about Guy Lafleur and the problems he is giving us."

"If I'm no longer what you need, you can always trade me."

"It would be so much simpler, Guy, if you would be part of the team."

"And if I would ride the bench until my career is over? To tell you the truth, Serge, that doesn't really interest me."

"What interests you?"

"Keep going. Sooner or later you'll figure it out."

• • •

In the spring of 1984, three weeks before the beginning of the playoffs, Jacques Lemaire replaced Bob Berry as head coach, a position he had refused a year earlier because he hated the pressure that went along with the job. Lemaire liked to be the man in the shadows, an *éminence grise*. He found it absurd that a hockey coach should have to deal with journalists and bow down to all the moods and reactions of the public. He felt the Canadiens' coach was practically powerless. The internal affairs of the team should be of no concern to reporters. Their insatiable curiosity, their untimely commentaries were, according to him, a kind of interference for which there was no excuse. He dreamed of a pure hockey, without commentary or criticism, an almost abstract art of hockey. But he realized that it was an impossible dream and, since Savard insisted, he had finally accepted the coaching position.

Lafleur was then at the end of his least productive season in ten years. It seemed to Lemaire that Lafleur had changed considerably since the era when, with himself and Shutt, he had triumphed. Something in the way he looked had hardened or died. He was no longer the innocent he used to be. With Lemaire, he was now mocking and sarcastic, a little cynical, as though the whole thing was not to be taken seriously, as if a companion in arms could not really become a boss. "He isn't the same man," Lemaire thought.

Lemaire was surprised and sorry to see him in this state. At the same time, he had always known that things would end this way with Guy. With such talent and faith in himself, Lafleur was in some way more vulnerable than other players. He didn't recognize his own limits. When he began to score less, he was unable to see it as his own fault. He looked outside himself for the cause of his lethargy. A grave error, according to Lemaire.

Lafleur still skated as powerfully as ever. During practices, when one of his shots bounced off the boards, the puck's boom filled the arena. He seemed just as strong, as flexible, as quick. But he didn't score any more. He seldom was able to get free of his checker, something he formerly managed with masterly ease. But the worst thing was that, even when he had the chance, he no longer took a shot. All this puzzled Lemaire.

"It's as though he has lost the desire to win," Lemaire said.

Might it be possible that a man, at certain moments in his life, might want failure or defeat? Lafleur seemed to be seeking it out. A head coach cannot let himself use a player who does not want to win. Lemaire, knowing full well that the press and the public would hold him accountable, used Lafleur very little during the spring of 1984.

One thing particularly worried Lemaire. People were saying and writing that Lemaire was getting his revenge. When Lafleur had come to the Canadiens in 1971, Lemaire had gradually become a playmaker, a passer, a plumber. For three years he had scored more points than Lafleur, getting fewer goals but making many more assists. Then, beginning in 1974, when Lafleur really got rolling and began his run of six great years, Lemaire's point totals began to decline. Never again was his total equal to Lafleur's.

Now he had become Lafleur's superior, his coach, his boss. It might be true that he had been jealous of Lafleur. He carefully examined his conscience. Perhaps he was committing a grave injustice in not playing Lafleur. But letting him play just because he was afraid of the reaction of the fans would be wrong. It might make the whole team suffer. What should he do?

He had on hand a great player who was no longer suited to the style of play currently in practice. It would have been easier if Lafleur was obviously and visibly bad, out of condition, inept. Or, ideally, Lafleur himself would decide to leave. But Lafleur persisted in demonstrating during practices that he was still the best, so that Lemaire was tempted to use him during games. When he did, Lafleur played poorly.

"Why is he still here?" Lemaire wondered. "When I was his age, when I'd had enough, I left."

Lemaire, in fact, had been thirty-three when he had hung up his skates to accept a coaching position in Switzerland in June 1979. He had stayed there two years, to learn as much as to teach. He wanted to get to know European hockey, its techniques, its principles. Of course the Swiss were not as strong as the Soviets, but they used the same theoretical models, the rigorously planned team play, and they had perfected some remarkable techniques of training players.

Thus he had come back with a new conception of hockey, a hockey in which there was less room for instinct, for individual initiative . . . in other words, for a player like Lafleur.

Now he was no longer sure. Now it was he, Lemaire, who was asking himself if he had done the right thing to retire in 1979. Had it been the right time? Had he left because he was fed up with playing in the crushing shadow of Guy Lafleur, with being his foil, his servant? Was he unconsciously exacting his revenge now, as some journalists claimed?

Lemaire tried to have a straight, man-to-man conversation with Lafleur. But he realized he had lost the trust of his former teammate. He had the vague impression that it was because Lafleur felt he had no right to be his boss. But in fact, Lafleur was at odds with authority in general. He would have liked a real boss, bigger, older, more experienced than himself, a mentor. But there was no one in his life, on or off the ice, who could tell him anything any more. No one had the advice he needed. He had no more role models; he had gone beyond them all. Even Béliveau, the man he had admired so much and for whom he still had deep feelings, could not help him.

Bowman had been a real boss, able to dominate his players. Roger Barré had been a great teacher, a man who really understood what was important in life. But Lemaire and Savard—for years he had rubbed shoulders with them on the ice. He had gone drinking with them hundreds of times. He had seen them make the same mistakes that he made, over and over again. How could they now be coaching, correcting, motivating him? How could they unilaterally decide that he, Guy Lafleur, was no longer suitable for the Montreal Canadiens?

During a meeting in Los Angeles, Lemaire reminded his players that there was a rule against drinking in the hotel where the team was staying. A few minutes later, he noticed Lafleur sitting in the hotel bar, a beer in his hand.

"Guy, are you doing this on purpose?"

"Of course I'm doing it on purpose, Coco. The rule is stupid. You yourself, Jacques Lemaire, always said so, in the old days, every time we made a road trip. How many times did we hide from Bowman, you and me and all the others, to have a drink? I've decided not to hide any more. Because it's stupid. I am thirty-two years old. I'm big enough to know what I'm doing. Be serious, Coco, be cool. Come and sit down, I'll buy you a drink."

He really hoped Lemaire would accept. They would have had a drink together and talked, the way they used to. They would have talked again. Lemaire, who knew how to listen so well, would have helped him understand what was happening in his life.

"I can't do that, Guy."

"Why not?"

"You know very well."

"Just because you've become the boss doesn't make the rule less stupid, Jacques. You've changed."

"Naturally I've changed. I'm no longer a hockey player, I'm head coach of the team. I have another kind of responsibility. Why can't you understand that?"

In the old days, when the team was on the road, Lafleur and Lemaire almost always sat together at the back of the plane. Lemaire would bring the milk, Lafleur the Tia Maria, and they would make "Nestlé's Quik Specials." They would talk about their plans, their children. Lemaire liked to give advice on the education of children. He'd read books on the subject. And on boats as well. He wanted to buy a sailboat. He took sailing lessons. He could talk about winds, the marine currents of the St Lawrence, the stars. He could be passionate, even if he was always reflective, serious and reasoned. Perhaps too much so. He never fooled around too much. He never drank too much. He always weighed his words. In front of reporters he kept silent, his lips permanently sealed. If they persisted in talking about him, he was ill at ease. Nothing irritated him more than seeing his face in the newspapers.

That was doubtless the only thing that he and Guy disagreed about. Guy liked journalists; he knew how to get along with them, what to say to them, how to get them to say what he wanted. Through them he won the approval and support of the public. When Lemaire was made coach he realized that Lafleur had gained enormous power through the media, and that it would be hard to assert his own authority.

As for Lafleur, he felt no particular conflict of authority with Lemaire. For eight years he had played with him in extraordinary harmony. And without doubt, in his heart, he still sought Lemaire's approval. Lemaire, the brilliant hockey theoretician, still knew better than anyone how to appreciate a good play, how to make it happen, how to carry it to a conclusion.

A few days before the 1984 playoffs, a Sorecom poll surprised many by revealing that the Montreal Canadiens still had deep roots throughout Quebec. Almost a third of the two thousand people questioned considered Guy Lafleur the most popular athlete in Quebec, far in front of Michel Goulet and Peter Stastny, who between them got only 16 percent. Everywhere in Quebec, except in Quebec

City and the small, outlying villages of Bas-du-fleuve and Côte-Nord, the Canadiens still had more support than the Nordiques.

Over time, however, the Nordiques had proved themselves to be a better team than the Canadiens. They were more dynamic, more effective and, although less experienced, infinitely more determined. But they lacked the almost religious cult of the Canadiens. Making his team a cult object for the Québecois became Michel Bergeron's self-appointed task.

The rivalry between the two teams was one of the most fascinating phenomena of the 1980s. It was a case of primal, barbarous passions and pure racism. Swastikas were brought to the Quebec Colisée, and the Canadiens were accused of being the lackeys of the Rue Saint-Jacques Jews. The Nordiques had become a fetish, the team representing the hopes of the hard-line separatists. Bergeron, the ordinary guy from Trois-Rivières, was the perfect symbol of the Québecois go-getter who dug in and fought. Then, one night, something happened at the Colisée that had never been believed possible: Quebec began booing its own darling, Guy Lafleur, the "traitor to his country."

The Canadiens' francophone players were considered cowardly sell-outs. Taking up the old dream, the dream of Maurice Richard, the fans wanted Guy Lafleur, Mario Tremblay, Guy Carbonneau and the few other Montreal Canadiens francophones to come over to the side of the Nordiques. If it had happened, it would have meant the confrontation of the century.

Montrealers, more cosmopolitan, aggressively challenged the ideas of the Nordiques' supporters and, more than ever, supported their own players. What was being contested on the rinks of Quebec and Montreal was infinitely more than a hockey game. It was a battle of ideologies.

In mid-April, during an important match against the Nordiques, Jacques Lemaire left Lafleur on the bench longer than usual. Lafleur, confident, waited for the protests of the crowd. They came: "Guy! Guy! Guy!"

Lemaire didn't budge. From time to time, Lafleur looked at Lemaire from the corner of his eye. He seemed determined to let them shout themselves hoarse. "They won't make me change my mind," he was saying to himself. The crowd quickly understood and was quiet. Lemaire allowed himself a small, satisfied smile. He had won. From now on the fans would leave him to his work. Later in the game, when the Canadiens already had a comfortable lead, he gave Lafleur a bit of ice.

The next morning, the players were brought together for the video analysis of the game. Lemaire was a fanatic for videotapes, as were many coaches at the time. But while other coaches, like Bob Berry, made the players watch the game in order to see their mistakes, Lemaire preferred to draw their attention to their good moments and to the mistakes of the other team. It was a more positive approach, and the players who had previously been horrified by the videos because they were used to remind them of their blunders, were now eager to attend Lemaire's showings of the tapes.

On the day following the game, when the players came to the studio, Lemaire called Guy over and said, very calmly: "Guy, you go practise with the reserves."

Lafleur didn't say a word. He turned aside and went to skate while the team watched the tapes from the night before. In fact, it suited him, because the night before he had not really done much. But he wondered if Lemaire was doing this to humiliate him, or to allow him to work back into shape from the injury he'd received the week before. Or, he said to himself, perhaps Lemaire wanted to let him know he had no good moments to show him, only mistakes. And as that was not the purpose of the exercise . . .

He could have asked him. But he couldn't talk to Lemaire now. He no longer knew how. Contact had been irreparably broken off.

A week later, after eliminating the Nordiques, the Canadiens faced the New York Islanders, winners of the Stanley Cup for the last four years, in the semi-finals. Lafleur hadn't scored in twenty-five games, and he had not, since he was eight years old, more than a quarter of a century ago, gone so long without putting the puck in the enemy net.

The day of the third game against the Islanders he had a real conversation with Lemaire, at the moment when he least expected it. It was at Uniondale, the Islanders' arena. As usual, Lafleur had come before the others, had found himself a place in the stands and, plunged into dark thoughts, was looking into the emptiness and smoking a du Maurier. Suddenly he realized he was not alone. Someone was leaning against the boards, his back to Guy, and looking at the ice, like him. It was Lemaire.

"Is that you, Coco?"

Lemaire didn't turn around.

"Guy, how's it going?"

Lemaire's voice was warm, but Lafleur said nothing. Then Lemaire came up to sit near him, two or three rows down. And asked him again very softly:

"Guy, how's it going?"

"Not so well, Coco, to tell you the truth."

"Do you see a solution?"

"I already asked you for more ice."

"That's not the only problem. Guy, I've been watching you for months. You don't shoot. You don't take shots on goal. I don't understand what's going on. What are you waiting for? An empty net?"

"I don't know, Coco. I don't know what's going on. Something always happens when I'm about to shoot. The puck bounces. Or there's another stick. Or someone in my legs. There's always something."

"But there was always something, Guy. You have to shoot anyway."

"Listen, Coco. Get real. For two years you've been telling me to play a defensive game. Now you come and tell me to shoot."

"You know what I mean, Guy. Get back into the game, one way or the other. That's all I'm asking. You're never part of the play any more."

Guy fell silent, uncomfortable. Lemaire was right. He

wasn't part of the play any more. On the ice he felt like an outsider. The game would be happening all around him and he couldn't get into it. It was always ahead of him or behind him. Sometimes he could still get the puck and carry it along the boards, but when he got into the enemy zone, where he used to be so good, so fast, so dangerous, he no longer knew what to do. Unable to control the puck, he would either get rid of it right away or lose it.

Lemaire, too, was silent. The two of them looked at the ice. Then Lemaire got up to go back to the dressing room.

"You have to get back into the game, Guy. There's no other solution."

"Give me playing time, Coco. I can't be in the game if I'm only on the ice for thirty seconds. It takes me longer than that."

"In the old days, you stayed involved in the game even when you were on the bench. It's not a question of time, Guy. It's a question of what's going on in your head."

That evening, no doubt softened by the conversation they'd had, Lemaire gave Lafleur a bit more ice than usual. Lafleur made a good effort but nothing worked for him. The Islanders eliminated the Canadiens, beating them at their own game. As soon as they had a two-goal lead, they went into a defensive mode and concentrated on protecting their own zone.

Lafleur went back to the dressing room feeling dead inside. He got undressed, took his shower without talking to anyone, then, on his way back to his locker, stopped in front of the mirror, unable to take his eyes away from the sight of his reflection, his naked body. For a long time he looked at himself. The other players brushed past him. He looked old. He was losing his hair. He had really tried to get into the game but it had been closed, barred to him. Lemaire was right. It wasn't a question of playing time. He had to stop blaming everyone. Even the journalists were no longer receptive to his verbal shock tactics. They were just old refrains. He had criticized his last four coaches — Geoffrion, Ruel, Berry, Lemaire — and the managing directors of the team. He had said that Berry lacked imagination, that

Keith Acton was without talent and hogged the puck, that Savard didn't keep his word. He had to find something else, look elsewhere for the solutions to his problems.

Perhaps even the players were tired of his recriminations. He had begun to notice that some of the guys didn't listen to him any more, just nodded mechanically. Gainey, for example. Mario Tremblay. Sometimes even Larry Robinson. And what might the young players be thinking about him? One day Ryan Walter had confided that he had been intimidated when he started playing with him, because he had been his idol. Was he still?

He thought about what Béliveau had said about his role with the team: "You could help the younger players, motivate them. Stop thinking everyone is against you." Béliveau had talked to him about the role of the veterans on a team. He said that veterans were very useful, especially when the team was experiencing difficulties. It was up to them to initiate the young players, to be a calming influence. And the journalists! They were always after him to say what they wanted to hear.

Standing in front of his misted mirror he thought about something Chouine had often told him, that he always let himself be influenced and manipulated. Was it still happening? Did he sometimes talk to journalists just to make them happy?

He could no longer see his reflection. He looked at the mist. His image had blurred; he had become invisible. A ghost. Even the fans were starting to forget him. Not once during the Islanders series had there been the cry: "Guy! Guy! Guy!"

That was the worst blow. The fans had abandoned him. Why?

He was cold. He went to get dressed, then left to catch up with the others. They went to a discotheque where the music was so loud they couldn't talk. He tried hard to get drunk, but it didn't work. Still, deep inside there was a small flame that might soon light up his life again. That very evening, when he called home after the game, Lise had told him she was sure she was pregnant.

The Canadiens had been eliminated, but the Stanley Cup finals were still of great interest to Montreal. The Islanders, with their four consecutive championships from 1980 to 1983, were in a position to equal the most prestigious record in all of hockey history, that of five consecutive Stanley Cups won by the Montreal Canadiens, from 1956 to 1960.

Fortunately, the Edmonton Oilers defeated the Islanders. Honour had been saved. The Canadiens had been defeated, but they had fought valiantly. In a few months Lemaire had established himself and gained the respect both of his players and of the public. He was now Quebec's hockey strongman.

On May 17, for the second year in a row, the Lafleurs did not go to the Canadiens' annual dinner.

That summer the Lafleurs saw almost no one. Together they watched the Los Angeles Olympics. Guy was on his best behaviour. He played for the Canadiens' softball team, participated in a few charitable golf tournaments, sometimes beat his friend Quenneville at tennis, and every two or three days ran the eight-mile circuit he had made for himself at Baie d'Urfé. Sometimes Lise and Martin would follow him on their bicycles. Lise was pregnant, and the rest of the world no longer mattered.

● ● ●

On Thursday, October 18, 1984, an amazing thing happened at the Montreal Forum. It was the third period and the Canadiens had a comfortable 4 to 1 lead over the Los Angeles Kings. The outcome of the game was obvious to everyone; the seats of the Forum had begun to empty. But suddenly, without anyone knowing why, without anyone having expected or prepared for it, just as sometimes clouds suddenly come from nowhere to cover blue sky, it was heard—softly at first, then in a crescendo that rose to an explosion, the stirring chant: "Guy! Guy! Guy!"

Everyone looked around, surprised, at the Canadiens' bench. Some players on the ice stopped and looked for an explanation. An assassination attempt against Lafleur? Or had Lafleur attacked Lemaire? Why this "Guy! Guy! Guy!" Lafleur himself, sitting on the bench, was astonished. Why was he being called for this way?

A poll published a few days earlier had cruelly underlined his fall from public grace. To the question "Who is your favourite professional or amateur athlete?" 11 percent of those surveyed had replied Gaëtan Boucher; 8 percent Sylvie Bernier; 8 percent Gretzky; 6 percent Gary Carter, the Montreal Expos' star. Only 2 percent named Guy Lafleur.

The sole possible explanation for the shouts of the spectators was boredom. This game had been woefully dull. The Canadiens were winning, but there was no dazzle, no magic. Nothing was happening. This was bureaucratic hockey, mechanical and banal.

Since the beginning of the season the club had been doing well. Lemaire had succeeded in raising the team's morale and giving it an overall direction. People were even talking about a return to glory for the Canadiens. Lemaire knew how to give his club an original style. Or, rather, several original styles. In fact he had put together four very individual and specialized offensive lines. For four years the Canadiens had played a game that was very straightforward; they were very predictable and thus vulnerable. With the four lines Lemaire now had, they became dangerously versatile, capable of adapting themselves in no time to any situation, able to counter any plan the opposing team might try. The Canadiens were good and they were winning. But, alas, they now lacked all charisma.

So that evening the crowd was emitting a long groan, a cry of mourning. It realized that it was being bored to death and the good times, of which Lafleur had been the genius and master, were ending. The shouts were a way of rejecting the style of Jacques Lemaire. It was horrible for him. He had renewed the team but now he was being told that he had been on the wrong track, that something more was wanted. Once again the spectators were saying that Lafleur was the one who was right—Lafleur, and an idea of hockey totally different from Lemaire's. Winning was not good enough. It had to be done with style. Better to lose with a flourish than to win like a robot. Style, razzle-dazzle, beauty—that was Lafleur's terrain. Without him—they felt it, they knew it—everything would slide into deathly boredom.

At the Forum that evening, it began to be clear that a great passion was almost over, and the crowd didn't want to let go of the man it had loved so deeply. Tradition and continuity would be broken. For the first time since the Second World War, the most prestigious and sacred dynasty in hockey would be interrupted: Richard, Béliveau, Lafleur . . . and after him? No one. Before, there had been not only superstars but stars of a lesser brightness, stars like Geoffrion, Harvey, Henri Richard, Dickie Moore, Tremblay, Cournoyer and so many others, great players who had come from the people, given by them to the *Tricolore*. Now the great days were over, and with them the love and passion of the past.

Never, for more than two generations, had the Canadiens' players borne so little resemblance to Montreal-ers. In 1971, when Lafleur arrived in Montreal, almost two-thirds of the Canadiens' players were francophones. In 1984, there were only six Québecois on the team, along with six Americans, one Swede, one Czech, one native Indian and a good dozen anglophone Canadians from Ontario and the west. The only possible francophone stars in sight were Guy Carbonneau, and perhaps Stephane Richer and Claude Lemieux who, although they had been acquired by the organization, were still playing in the junior league. But not one of these players had either the charisma or the broad appeal of Lafleur, Béliveau or Richard. "Guy! Guy! Guy!" was a heart-rending cry of anguish, of mourning.

A week later, on October 25, playing against the Buffalo Sabres, Lafleur scored his 518th regular season goal, to set a new team point-scoring record. It was his second goal in thirty-nine games, a nothing of a goal that he scored almost accidentally and without pleasure, because he had waited for it too long and stopped believing in it. Nevertheless, the crowd rose to its feet and gave him a long ovation. He waved. But he found these outbursts excessive and ridiculous. Around him, there were fifteen players who struggled body and soul—Gainey, Walter, DeBlois, Hunter, Smith, among others—who scored better goals than he did but were never favoured with this kind of attention from the spectators.

And then suddenly, as if in a few days all the media had been infected with the same virus, Lafleur fell into disfavour. He had, at the beginning of November, complained once again about not being used sufficiently by Lemaire. The next day the journalists wrote: "By his inflammatory declarations, Lafleur does himself more harm than good." "Lafleur has just played the offended virgin once too often." "Lemaire can no longer be blamed." "The Montreal Canadiens are more important than Lafleur. It might be time that he realizes this." Even Maurice Richard wrote, in his *Dimanche-Matin* column: "Lafleur should stop talking and score goals."

The wind had shifted. Rather than see Lafleur decline, people now seemed to want him to disappear. A mini-poll taken by the *Journal de Montréal* revealed that 70 percent of the population wished he would be traded to another NHL team.

And evening after evening, the torture went on. Three or four times a game Lafleur leapt onto the ice, wandered about for a bit in a game he seemed not to understand, then meekly returned to the bench, his head lowered.

On Friday, November 23, he met with Serge Savard on the second floor of the Forum, the same place where twelve years earlier he would sometimes come to see Sam Pollock or Claude Ruel. It was the same little office, the same armchairs. Only the décor had changed. Pollock had left with his Canadian landscapes and in their place Savard had hung paintings and photographs of hockey players. Sitting down in front of him, Lafleur had the impression that the whole team and organization were watching him.

Serge Savard had an extraordinary sense of politics; he wasn't called "the Senator" for nothing. He knew how to dissimulate, manipulate, impose. He also knew how to be direct, frank and tough. Thus, the week before, he had got rid of Steve Shutt, with whom he had played and lived for almost ten years. He had told him quite simply that there was no longer a place for him on the team, and that he should go elsewhere if someone else wanted him.

"The team isn't right for players like you any more."

Shutt had been deeply humiliated. He had gone to the Los Angeles Kings, without even seeing his teammates again, with no farewell. He had been one of the best players in the NHL for nine years and regularly figured among the top scorers, but he had always been in the shadow of Guy Lafleur, always number two. And he had learned to live with it, even though it sometimes worried him. He was intelligent, and had enough of a sense of humour never to complain about his fate.

Even luck seemed to be against him. About a year earlier, on December 12, 1983, playing against the New Jersey Devils, Shutt had scored his four-hundredth career goal. But the same evening, after a twelve-game drought, Lafleur had scored his five-hundredth. Of course Shutt's achievement had passed almost unnoticed. As always, he was in Lafleur's shadow.

Savard could not behave with Lafleur as he had with Shutt. To a reporter who'd asked him following the *Journal de Montréal* poll whether he would agree to trade Lafleur, Savard had given a categorical no. "You don't trade the columns of the temple."

Lafleur had heard this the same evening, on television, and had thought, "He doesn't trade the columns of the temple, but he does everything he can to knock them down." He wanted to meet Savard for an explanation.

"I know you've decided to get rid of all the players you once played with."

"Where did you get that idea?"

"I know it. You've said so. I have witnesses."

"Who?"

"At first I didn't believe it. But last week when I found out you'd traded Shutt, I realized I was next on your list. You know very well that I'm right."

"I don't know anything at all. It's not me who wants to trade you, Guy, it's you who wants to leave. I've made it clear to the press that there's no question of trading you."

"There are other ways of getting rid of a player. You'd like me to make this easy for you by disappearing."

"Let's admit that, in the circumstances, that might suit me. It's true. But that's not what I wanted. That's not the way I would have liked you to end your career. If you were still a good player, don't you think the organization would do everything possible to keep you?"

"If I had ice time, I would be a good player."

Savard took a moment to relight his cigar and take a few puffs, looking in the air over Lafleur's head, the old habit that gave whoever was talking to him the painful impression of being unimportant. This discussion was starting to exasperate him. After a long silence, he added, "Tomorrow night we play the Red Wings at the Forum. I'm going to ask Lemaire to play you. But he's the one who has to decide. He's the one in charge of who plays and who doesn't. Not me."

Then Lafleur did something he immediately regretted. He thanked Savard, as though he'd just received an undeserved favour. It wasn't a champion's attitude. Savard read it perfectly. He gave him a small, malicious smile, got up and said, "Tomorrow night we'll see what you're made of."

The next morning Lafleur arrived at the Forum almost two hours early for practice. He worked hard, calling out encouragement to his teammates. He had decided to spend the afternoon at the Forum, the way he used to. At about three o'clock he went to see Lemaire, to whom Savard had indeed spoken. Lemaire confirmed that he would be playing him, and that, among other things, he would use him for killing penalties. Then he added, without thinking, some words that hurt Lafleur deeply.

"Prove to me that you're still capable."

Leaving Lemaire, Lafleur thought, "What's that supposed to mean? 'Prove to me that you're still capable.'

posed to mean? 'Prove to me that you're still capable.' How can someone like Lemaire doubt that I'm still capable?"

That was what hurt the most, that his former companions, those who had hundreds of times seen him take the puck and fake out the defencemen and goalies of the NHL, now doubted him. It was true that he had been unproductive over the past few months, but Ruel himself said he was still one of the best skaters and hardest shooters in the whole NHL. At the Verdun arena he had again broken the glass with a shot from more than fifty feet.

But if he wanted to play well against the Red Wings, he shouldn't be thinking about all that. He had enough experience to know how to rid himself of the black thoughts that were assailing him. At about six o'clock he went to sit high in the seats of the Forum. It was empty and peaceful. Occasionally he heard, from afar, the noise of horns and sirens. He looked at the ice, trying, the way he had years ago, to imagine the plays, the rushes.

He had telephoned Lise and talked with her about his conversation with Lemaire, telling her only the positive parts. Lise didn't really believe Lemaire. She had often told Guy, "That one will get you in the end." When Lemaire was leaving for Switzerland to study European hockey, and it seemed that he would come back even more rational, more coldly and implacably wedded to technique than before, Lise had said, "When Lemaire comes back, he'll get rid of you."

The day of his wedding, his father-in-law, Roger Barré, had told him, "Me, I don't like that guy's face. Don't trust him."

But Lafleur had decided to forget all that.

"He told me that he'd let me play. When someone tells me something, it's as good as cash in the bank."

"Let me know how it goes."

Eight months pregnant, Lise preferred to watch the game on television rather than at the Forum. Before the end of the first period she realized that Savard and Lemaire had set a trap for her husband. She found that inconceivably cruel. It seemed obvious that they wanted to break him.

During the first two periods, Lafleur got on the ice for only seven or eight minutes. He had hoped for at least twice as much. Just the same, he found a way to waste a golden opportunity in front of an almost empty net. He had a moment of hesitation, and when he finally shot, it went ever the net. Lemaire called him back and left him on the bench until the end of the period.

Then Lafleur turned to Monsieur Charest, the security guard on duty behind the players' bench, and asked him to go get Serge Savard, who would be, as always, in the Canadiens' box along with Ronald Corey. After five minutes, Charest came back saying he hadn't found Savard. He was obviously lying. It was at that moment, between the second and third periods, between the door to the skating rink and the dressing room door, that Guy Lafleur decided to leave. He knew his decision was irrevocable. Whatever might happen, he would not change his mind.

During the third period, Lemaire let Guy on the ice twice. But he was too distracted, too filled with emotion, to be able to do anything. After the game he quickly changed and left the dressing room to telephone Lise. He ran into Claude Mouton, who instantly realized that something was wrong. Guy wanted to tell him about his decision but when he tried he burst into tears. Claude Mouton gently took him aside, to get him away from curious onlookers.

"I'm not going to Boston," Lafleur finally said to him.

"How's that?"

"I'm quitting."

Claude Mouton, himself on the verge of tears, did not know what to say. He was there, standing in front of Lafleur, gripping his shoulder. He saw no solution. He was devastated by the idea that such a brilliant career could end this way.

"Think about it, Guy. Think carefully before you decide."

"It's all thought out."

Lafleur telephoned his wife.

"What did I tell you?"

"Do you think I did the right thing?"

"It was the only thing to do. Come home. I'm waiting for you."

Going back to the dressing room he ran into Savard and Corey standing in the corridor. Savard must have known that Lafleur had asked for him between periods. Passing close to them, Lafleur said, "It's finished, Savard. You've got what you wanted."

He hadn't taken three steps when Savard called him back.

"What's to be said to the press if you don't come to Boston?"

"You haven't understood, Serge. I'm not going anywhere with you any more."

"What do you mean?"

"You know very well. You've got what you wanted. I'm leaving."

"You didn't answer my question. What is the press to be told?"

"You'll tell them what you want, the way you always do. It's not my problem."

A few minutes later, Savard went up to Lafleur in the dressing room.

"Listen, Guy, when Monsieur Charest came to tell me you were asking for me, I didn't think it was so urgent. I thought you wanted to see me after the game."

"Don't take me for an idiot. You always come round after the game, anyway. I don't need to send for you for that."

"Come see me in my office Monday morning. For the Boston game, we'll tell the reporters you have the flu."

"I don't have the flu."

"We'll say you have a groin pull."

"I didn't hurt myself."

"All I'm asking you, Guy, is to think things over until Monday before you talk to anyone. Okay?"

"Okay."

Lafleur picked up his bag and put it in his car. He was

driving Larry Robinson and Chris Nilan to the airport. Nilan adored Lafleur. One night, two or three years earlier, both injured and unable to accompany the club on a road trip, they had gone to practise together at the Verdun arena, all alone for an hour and a half.

At the beginning, Nilan had been nervous and terribly intimidated by Lafleur. A native of Boston, Nilan had once hated Lafleur with a passion when, year after year, Lafleur almost single-handedly eliminated Boston from the Stanley Cup playoffs. Even Don Cherry, their coach, said that if he had only a wedding ring and no Stanley Cup ring, it was because of Guy Lafleur. But when Nilan came to Montreal to play with the Canadiens, he had immediately been, like everyone else, charmed by Lafleur's kindness. And strangely enough, Nilan, who was afraid of nothing and liked to fight and argue with everyone, had become very shy about his famous teammate. He seldom spoke to him. During practices he avoided bodychecking him, and he always gave him perfect passes.

That evening at Verdun was one of Nilan's great memories; he and Lafleur became friends. After their practice they went to have a drink together. Nilan also felt ill at ease in Lemaire's system. An aggressive, offensive player, he liked to plunge, head down, into the opposing defence. In his fifth season with the Canadiens he had already accumulated more than a thousand minutes in penalties and seemed well on his way to beating Maurice Richard's penalty record. He was, like Lafleur, a man who operated by instinct.

Usually, when the team left for Boston, Nilan was very excited. But that evening, sitting in the back seat of Lafleur's Jaguar, he stayed quiet. Lafleur had told Nilan and Robinson everything. For a moment, no one in the car spoke. Then, as soon as they reached the highway, Robinson said, "Don't do it, man. Things will work out."

"You know they won't."

Guy drove slowly, as though he wanted to savour one last moment of the warm friendship he had with Nilan and

Robinson. At the airport he got out of the car to shake their hands. Nilan said nothing. Robinson's eyes were filled with tears. He hugged his old companion.

"Don't do it. Wait a bit longer."

"I've already waited too long. I've had enough."

"What are you planning to do?"

"I don't really know yet. But I'm sure of one thing: people will hear about it."

• • •

Guy, Lise and Martin spent the next day, Sunday, at Thurso. Guy and Lise had agreed not to talk to his parents about his plans. He just told them that he had pulled a groin muscle and was resting for a few days. He didn't want to upset them for nothing. They were already worried enough about the various rumours that were circulating about him. Moreover, despite the fact that Guy earned more than half a million dollars a year, more than his father had made in his whole life, his father was always afraid that Guy would suddenly find himself broke. He often talked to Guy about Joe Louis, Jake LaMotta and Jesse Owens, great athletes who had died penniless. He firmly believed that the golden legend of the idolized athlete always had a tragic ending. He often asked his son if he had made good investments. This amused Guy enormously, and he sometimes asked back, "And you, Papa?"

"For me it doesn't matter, my boy. You mustn't worry about me. I have nothing to lose."

Sometimes Guy thought it must be nice to have nothing to lose. What freedom! What peace! For so long, it seemed, he'd had everything to lose—money, fame, love.

Suzanne, his older sister, had also come to visit her parents that day, and reminded Guy that he'd promised them a box for a Montreal game. Guy Lafleur realized then that those he loved would never again see him on the Forum ice. His father, his mother, his sisters, all his friends, so proud of him, so happy for him, would no longer have this pleasure. And that idea hurt him so much that he couldn't follow the conversation. He was stifling in the small Thurso parlour. He got up, saying he needed to buy cigarettes, and went to walk through the village. He made a tour of the new development of pretty bungalows now being erected in the fields where he had spent the summers of his childhood. No more frog pond, no more frothing stream. Even the big flat rock they used to use as their headquarters when they played Cowboys and Indians had disappeared, dynamited, swallowed up like all the rest.

He crossed the railway track and found himself back in the field behind the arena, where about fifty cars were parked. Occasionally he could hear noise coming from the building. The door with its perpetual padlock and the old wall made of grey boards with his long-ago secret entrance had now been rebuilt. The roof, too, was freshly painted. Everything had changed.

But in Thurso, there was still hockey on Sunday afternoons. He was tempted to go inside. He would have liked to see if they still had the same boards with the same advertisements that he and Ti-Paul had repainted so many times: Hotel Lafontaine, Valiquette Sports, Singer, McLarens. But they would have thrown themselves at him. They would have asked him, "What are you doing here, Guy? You're not in Boston?" And he would have had to explain himself. He would not have known what to say.

He crossed the parking lot, and then Rue Guy-Lafleur, walked around the playing field and went back towards Rue Principale, almost deserted. An old man came up to him.

"Hello Guy! You're not in Boston?"

Taken by surprise he replied, "No, they gave me time off. I've got the flu."

"They did the right thing," said the old man, laughing. "That way you won't give it to the others."

Guy began to think that the others might be relieved that he was gone. What would they have said on board the plane to Boston when they saw he wasn't there? What could Lemaire and Savard have told them? He realized that even if he gave them his resignation tomorrow, the pressure would remain for a long time. They would ask themselves why he had left, analyse everything.

At the end of the afternoon Guy, with Lise and Martin, drove back to Baie d'Urfé. The sky was grey and there was a fine drizzle. While Lise made dinner, Guy kept her company in the kitchen. They talked about what he would say to Savard the next morning.

He wanted only one thing: to slam the door in Savard's face. Even if Savard made him promises, even if he said that from now on he could have all the ice he asked for. He didn't want it any more. He no longer believed him. Lise saw things totally differently. She said he should demand a position in the organization.

"It's your right. As much as Jean Béliveau. You gave them five Stanley Cups. They made a fortune with you."

"They also made a fortune with Rocket Richard, and look how they treated him."

"Okay, they're bastards. But there's no reason to let yourself be taken. You can still reach an agreement with them."

He knew she was right. Pregnant women are always right. They are strong and reassuring; they know how to see and understand reality. But that didn't stop him from having this crazy desire to slam the door in Savard's face.

Since his Pee Wee days he had understood that hockey is not only played on the ice. It is also, as Ti-Paul Meloche would say, played between your ears. There are power struggles, Cold Wars, games, and influence-peddling. What had happened to make his allies, his old companions in arms, turn so quickly against him and become enemies?

"Maybe they're right. Maybe I'm no good any more," he repeated to himself. "Maybe I am slower and weaker."

But Lise was still convinced that he could be the best and the strongest. And he would prove it decisively, in front of everyone, in the newspapers, in the minds and hearts of the public.

"People like you and you know it," she would say. "That's your strength. Savard and Corey know it very well. You can be a bigger threat to their authority by going than

by staying. They're going to bend over backwards to make
sure you don't leave angry. You're the one in the position
of strength. Don't you think you should take advantage
of it?"

But Guy was angry and his pride was wounded. He saw
what they had done that night as a mark of contempt that
would be almost impossible to erase. He didn't see how he
would be able to come to an agreement with them.

"I'll slam the door in their faces, as hard as I can. With a
smile." He had constructed a scenario that he continued to
refine long after Lise went to bed. He would go into the
Canadiens' office and tell them what he was thinking. His
remarks would be brief, precise, stinging—all delivered
with a little smile that would add a nice spice to the
whole operation.

"I just want you to know one thing: it's not right to
discourage a man the way you did. You were too cowardly
to tell me to my face that you wanted me to leave. But you
can never boast to yourselves that you got rid of me. I'm the
one who's walking out on you."

He supposed that Ronald Corey would try to be aloof, the
super-cool guy who didn't know what was going on.

"He'll tell me that I'll always have a place with the
Canadiens, that everything can still be worked out, that
there is no problem. I can't let myself be taken in. Not by
Savard, who will try to make a fool of me, or by Corey, who
will want to soothe me."

He went to bed confident that he'd mastered his role. But
the next morning, on the way to the Forum, he was no
longer sure of anything or anyone, except for Lise and his
family. It seemed, strangely, that the worse things went with
his career, the better they went with Lise.

In the spring of 1976, when he had won all the NHL
awards and reached new peaks of achievement, he had said
publicly that his career came first, before his family, his wife
and even his son, Martin, who was then less than a year old.
His statements had been repeated in all the newspapers, on
the radio, everywhere. Some people had been shocked;
feminists and moralists of all types said that Guy Lafleur

was an egotistical and chauvinistic man. But Lafleur had responded, "At least I say what I think." He was happy that he had always said what he'd thought, that he'd never hidden anything from anyone. Except perhaps from himself.

That morning, if someone had asked him what counted most in his life, his answer would have been the exact opposite to the one he had given at the height of his glory. He would have said that what came first for him now was his family, his wife and his eight-year-old son, Martin, and especially this new child who was on the way. His career was over. In one hour, when he walked out of the Forum for the last time in his life, it would be finished. They would make the trips Lise had always dreamed about. He would finally build that house that he'd planned so carefully for so long.

But then what would he do? Moving, buying a new car, digging a garden, skiing, having a baby—all that was well enough, but then what? What was he going to do from now on? Twiddle his thumbs? Watch television? Get drunk in peace? Would he be like Elvis Presley who, fat and soft, had told a journalist that his plan was to look out the window and wait until it was over?

Lise was doubtless right. Rather than slam the door, he should perhaps demand a position in the organization. Lise always knew how to understand and analyse situations. That reassured Guy, it warmed his heart, because she was his ally, she understood everything, she would make everything work. He knew it.

Lise had never liked Jacques Lemaire, even during the years of glory when he had played with Guy and, along with Steve Shutt, had made up the Canadiens' most formidable line, scoring 150 goals a season among them.

As for Ronald Corey, Guy had never really connected with him. It wasn't that he hated him. He felt something worse, a sort of contempt. First of all, because he wasn't really a hockey man. Like all great athletes, Lafleur was aware that he belonged to an elite, and he dissociated himself from mere mortals. But in addition, he found

Ronald Corey a shrewd and cunning man, calculating and elusive, all sugar and honey, impossible for him to trust.

From the first time he met him, when Guy was playing for the Quebec Remparts and Corey had come to see him to offer his services as business agent, Lafleur had not wanted to associate his career with Corey's. He said to his friend, Jean-Yves Doyon, "I don't like that guy's smile."

He knew now that this natural antipathy was mutual. One evening, a few years before, in a restaurant in Montreal, Ronald Corey, then a vice-president at Carling O'Keefe, was expounding on the stupidities committed by Guy Lafleur. Unfortunately for him, Lise Lafleur and some friends were at a nearby table. She got up "charitably" to warn poor Corey that she was Guy Lafleur's wife and that perhaps he had better stop talking.

Corey changed direction with amazing speed. A few minutes later he had a bottle of Dom Perignon sent to Lise Lafleur's table. She instantly sent it back to Corey. "And tell monsieur he knows where he can put it."

But all things considered, Corey had behaved correctly with Lafleur, unlike Savard and Lemaire. Guy had truly loved and trusted his former teammates. The three of them had played, drunk and travelled together, and now they had dropped him; Guy felt betrayed. And this morning, when he saw them, he was going to tell them what he was thinking, and make them understand that he was more than capable of living without them.

He bought the daily papers. Only the *Gazette* mentioned his resignation. No doubt Chris Nilan or Larry Robinson had told Red Fisher, the sports columnist. The francophone reporters would be annoyed at not getting the scoop. Right now they must be chasing all over the city after him. But it was too late. Like so many other things, this business was out of his hands now. It was a shame.

It bothered him that he was still losing his hair. He stretched his neck to look at himself in the rearview mirror and saw his drawn features, his pale colouring.

Slowly he drove up Atwater, crossed Dorchester, then was faced with the imposing mass of the Montreal Forum.

For a second he saw himself on the ice, in the light, at the height of his glory, with the swelling sound of the crowd chanting his name: "Guy! Guy! Guy!" And he raised his arms to mark his victory, and to gather in the tribute.

Nevertheless, somewhere deep down inside himself, he felt that sooner or later there would be something else. He knew that when he walked into the Forum he would be at home again. One last time. He would find the words and the ways to say what was on his mind. And afterwards he would finally be free. Afterwards he would start his life again.

As he climbed the small stairway he shook a bit. Seeing him arrive, the secretary and the receptionist interrupted their conversations.

The door of Savard's office was wide open. When he saw Lafleur, Savard stood and extended his hand. Lafleur grasped it. This was not in any of the scenarios he had constructed during the night.

He understood then that something had just escaped him. He was no longer master of the situation.

• • •

Guy found himself standing in front of Savard, ill at ease, all his anger suddenly revived. He knew he would not be slamming the door in anyone's face. Ronald Corey dropped in, as if by chance, affable and smiling, of course. He greeted Lafleur in a manner that said it was all for the best in the best of all possible worlds. Lafleur sat down again and said, "You can stay here, Ronald. I'd like you to hear what I have to say."

Then he launched into a long and awkward recital of the conflict he'd experienced with the organization over the course of the past year. He said he would have preferred to have known earlier that he was no longer wanted. Politely, Corey protested that they had always acted towards him in good faith. Lafleur replied by reminding them that Lemaire had often promised him ice time, then had not kept his promises. Savard and Corey listened to him, a little embarrassed. Then Corey said, "I'll be back in a moment, I have an important call to make."

Less than two minutes later he was back, with a large smile. He put his hand on Lafleur's arm and said:

"Guy, everything is arranged. You have a job for life with the Canadiens, $75,000 a year with indexation. You'll do marketing and public relations."

Lafleur knew Corey had called Molson, his bosses. It seemed to him that $75,000 a year wasn't much. As a hockey player, he earned that in two months. But Corey explained that the indexed salary was the equivalent of $1.2 million over ten years. The organization guaranteed a raise of 10 percent a year, so that in the last year of his contract, in 1994, he would be getting more than $175,000. There would be tempting fringe benefits: a new car, a membership in the area's most chic golf clubs, a generous expense account, great freedom and very long vacations.

But that wasn't the only thing to be considered. What Corey was offering him was a function, a reason to exist. He remembered what Lise had told him:

"It's all very fine to slam the door in the boss's face, but what do you do after? It's not normal for a man of thirty-three to do nothing, Guy. You know having nothing to do drives you crazy. What will become of you if you have nothing to do?"

As though in a dream, Lafleur listened as Corey proclaimed the advantages of the lifetime job he was offering.

"Of course you'll be paid for your option year. And to begin with, you'll take some time off. You'll come back after the holidays, after your wife has had the baby. You'll get an office. You'll work with us. You'll help us get the team going again."

Lafleur was thrown. He felt sure they were buying his silence. They did not want him to say publicly that he had been badly treated by the Canadiens. Maurice Richard's recriminations had damaged the organization.

While Lafleur thought, Savard puffed on his cigar and Corey cleared his throat.

"If you agree," Savard finally said, "we'll organize a press conference for this afternoon. You'll announce that you are retiring. Next, Ronald Corey will announce that you've joined the Canadiens organization. Okay?"

There was a long silence. Then Lafleur said in a flat voice, "Okay."

As soon as Guy had spoken, Corey left the office. No doubt he wanted to let the bosses know that everything was arranged. Savard spoke to his secretary and told her to call a meeting of the Canadiens' senior management.

"When?"

"Right away."

No one seemed to be worrying about Lafleur any more. He crossed the small hall with its walls covered with photos and paintings of players. He glanced at his own portrait, and wanted to rip it off the wall. He was angry at himself. He knew he had just put himself into a box. But he continued walking and left the building at the Rue Lambert-Closse exit.

He had eaten practically nothing since the previous evening. He wasn't hungry, but he knew he wouldn't be able to face the press on an empty stomach. This might be the last press conference he would ever give. It would be hard, terribly moving. He had to eat.

He wondered if he should call Lise and talk to her about the offer that the Canadiens had made him, and tell her that he had accepted. Too quickly, perhaps. Without thinking, without bargaining. Wouldn't she tell him that he had folded, once again? That he had let himself be had? That he should have imposed his own conditions?

Then he noticed Brian Travers coming towards him. It was obvious that Travers already knew about his resignation and the arrangement that Corey had proposed to him. Brian Travers always knew everything that happened within the organization. It was even said that he sometimes knew things before they happened.

"Are you going to eat, Guy?"

"Yes."

"May I come with you?"

Brian Travers was the kind of friend you like to have around when times are troubled. If he liked you, there was

nothing he would not do to lend a hand. You could trust
Brian Travers to fight your enemies and then move heaven
and earth until everything was back in your favour. A close
friend to Roger Barré, Travers had gone up to Quebec and
he had helped, advised and consoled the family after Barré's
death. Then he had stayed in close contact with Pierre,
Lise's brother, and had convinced him to leave school and
take over his father's business. He had arranged for Pierre to
get big contracts with Maislin, the trucking and transport
company for which he worked. In the same way, when Guy
had his accident, Brian Travers had come running. He had
reassured Lise and helped keep the press away. It was even
said that it was Travers who had convinced the policeman
who witnessed the accident that Lafleur wasn't drunk, and
that it would be charitable of him to go tell that to the *Allô
Police* reporters. When Brian liked you, you had a powerful
ally. And Brian liked Guy Lafleur.

They walked without speaking along Rue Sainte-
Catherine and up to the Restaurant de Paris, where they
were given a table off to the side.

"What are you going to eat?"

"Whatever."

"You have to eat something that's not too heavy. Bring
him calves' liver with mashed potatoes. Two orders. The
liver medium-rare."

"What are you drinking?"

"Whatever."

"You have to drink something. It will relax you. A
Pouilly-Fumé."

Then Brian tried to explain to his friend Guy Lafleur that
what was happening could be marvellous.

"You'll see, things will go well. There won't be any
problem."

"At least I'll finally have all that pressure off my back.
It's over."

"It's not over, Guy. Things are just beginning. And if you
ever get bored in the Canadiens' front office, you can just
leave. You're not married to the Canadiens."

● ● ●

The press conference at which Guy Lafleur officially announced his retirement took place in the Forum restaurant called, ironically, the Mise au Jeu, or "the Face-Off." It was November 26, 1984. At the conference, everyone said exactly the opposite of what they meant. It was "double-speak," to borrow from George Orwell's famous novel, *1984*.

Orwell's hero, crushed by an all-powerful totalitarian machine, ends by submitting joyfully to the supreme authority represented by the omnipotent and omniscient Big Brother. At the very end, completely subjugated and defeated, he declares with conviction that he finally loves the system, loves Big Brother. In the same way, Guy Lafleur announced that day that he loved the Canadiens organization.

A lectern had been placed in front of the barnboard wall of the restaurant, and just in front, an impressive bouquet of microphones. Starting in the middle of the afternoon, a crowd of journalists and curiosity-seekers had gathered at the edges of the restaurant. Everyone was absolutely sure that something historic was about to happen. Just before four o'clock, the administration of the Canadiens made their entrance, Savard and Corey on either side of Guy Lafleur. Everyone was visibly nervous and tense. Almost at the same time, the team's players, who had scarcely finished their practice, arrived, still sweating, many of them still wearing their uniforms. All the Forum personnel were there —the secretaries, the support staff, the guards.

For a moment nothing could be heard but the clicking of cameras. Then Claude Mouton introduced Lafleur, who moved in front of the microphones and cameras. He started by explaining that for a long time he had felt lethargic and could no longer play productively. Almost immediately his voice broke. But he managed to choke back his tears.

He explained that he was retiring because he no longer had the desire to play. These were more or less the same words Rocket Richard had used to announce his retirement in September 1960. Then Lafleur said he was convinced that he was leaving at the right time. The team was going well, in his eyes, and its success seemed assured. He told how two days before, while getting ready for the game against the Red Wings, he had asked himself what he was doing, and he had finally realized that he should quit. During the weekend he had talked things over with his wife. She agreed with him that it was time for him to retire.

Next he talked about his parents, his son Martin, of the other child his wife was expecting, about Madame Baribeau, his hard-working, understanding coaches. He thanked the Molson Breweries. Then, after Ronald Corey announced that he would be taken into the fold of the organization, Lafleur added that he was happy not to have been traded to another club, like Steve Shutt, and that in becoming part of this venerable institution he was finally realizing a long-held dream.

Not a hint of reproach to the organization. Nothing about the well-known conflict that had so long opposed him to Lemaire and Savard. Guy Lafleur had decided to play the game, the *other* game. For the first time in his career he was hiding the truth.

Next he said that he greatly regretted not having broken Maurice Richard's record of 544 career goals. However, in 961 games he had scored 518 goals and obtained 728 assists, for a total of 1246 points, a team record.

Finally, he said how difficult it was leaving players like Larry Robinson, Bob Gainey, Mario Tremblay, Bobby Smith and the others, all those who had for thirteen seasons supported him as he established himself as one of the great players in the NHL.

"I consider myself lucky to have played with these men. They were of great help to me."

The reporters, deeply moved, did not know what to say. They who had always been so demanding now stood back and watched, knowing very well that Guy was not telling the whole truth, that for once he was looking out for himself and not giving the real reasons for his departure. For the first time, Guy Lafleur, the perfectly transparent man, was hiding something. And no one was holding it against him. For the first time, the journalists didn't insist. They, too, kept quiet about the truth. They closed their eyes and respectfully kept their distance. In the next day's papers they faithfully reported the soothing words Lafleur had spoken.

Thus, on November 26, 1984, at the end of his hockey-playing career, Guy Lafleur solemnly swore fidelity to an organization that, deep down, he despised. Following the example of George Orwell's hero, he proclaimed aloud that he loved and respected Big Brother. Better yet, he said it had always treated him well. On that day, Guy Lafleur loved the Montreal Canadiens.

THIRD INTERMISSION

●

THE REASONS FOR Guy Lafleur's departure remained a topic of interest for a long time. Reporters approached everyone—trainers and managers, teammates, the public, parents and friends—to try to understand the gospel according to Guy Lafleur.

Some people, implacable moralists, asserted that Guy Lafleur had lived loosely and that he was now paying the price. Others, more defeatist, saw his decline as an example of the tragic nature of a man's life, of the fact that, after thirty, a man is no longer as handsome, as fast, as strong. Guy Lafleur, the superb athletic machine, the nation's proud creation, had fallen to pieces; at thirty-three there's nothing left but to sit and wait for the end. The majority opinion, however, held that Lemaire, Savard and Corey were responsible for the fall and departure of Guy Lafleur. In this scenario, Guy was regarded as an exemplary hero who stood up to power and the Establishment.

Guy Lafleur had rebelled against the government of hockey. Because of that, the people of Quebec had a special love and admiration for him. It was the uncompromising revolt of Guy Lafleur that made him, like Maurice Richard, a rebel hero to all.

Jean Béliveau had fit the hockey Establishment's pattern perfectly. He had played centre and had remained a man of the centre, never compromised, never bending. Perhaps for that reason he never rose to the heights of the truly popular

367

hero. A real hero should oppose and rebel, should fight against threats and dangers, even if he ultimately fails.

Serge Savard, as a manager, a boss, could be neither a hero, a symbol nor a myth. Especially not in French Canada, where the managers and the bosses are so often believed responsible for keeping their workers in their place, limiting social mobility. Certainly he was respected. He had power and authority, but only as a mortal has such things, nothing more. He had succeeded, but without poetry, without real risk, without having invested himself, body and soul, in a great adventure, without having given himself to the public.

The day following Lafleur's resignation, the federal member of Parliament from Yorkville–Lambton, Lorne Nystrom, offered him this tribute in the House of Commons:

"It may be that everywhere else in the world the ascendance of Flower Power began and ended in the sixties, Mr Speaker, but in Montreal it began in 1971 and ended yesterday when Guy Lafleur retired.

"This is the end of a great era, Mr Speaker. I am certain that the House and the entire population of Canada will join me in wishing him good luck in the future and thanking him for the unforgettable moments he has given us."

The House stood and gave a long round of applause to a great Canadian, Guy Lafleur.

Of course the news of his leaving was known throughout North America almost immediately. Even before the press conference everyone in the world of hockey knew everything.

The Nordiques were in the midst of a practice when reporters came to ask the players what they thought. Richard Sévigny, a goalie who had worked with the Canadiens for the four previous years, severely castigated Serge Savard and Jacques Lemaire, whose iron rule he had experienced.

In Boston, the Bruins were also practising when they were told the news. Their goalie, Gerry Cheevers, who had several times been deprived of the Stanley Cup by Guy

Lafleur, talked about him with a touching admiration. He admitted that he didn't understand what could have happened in Montreal, but he affirmed that a hockey organization that couldn't satisfy such a great player must be held to blame.

Marcel Dionne, the long-time beloved enemy of Guy Lafleur, was reached at his home in Los Angeles by reporters who interviewed him carefully. Dionne was the same age as Lafleur. He had started his professional career at the same time. He had always, like Guy, been a leading scorer, and he continued to score at a very good rate. He was astounded by the news of Lafleur's retirement, but, unlike Sévigny and Cheevers, he didn't accuse the Canadiens organization of having broken Lafleur's career.

According to Dionne, the problem stemmed from the fact that Lafleur was trying to be more than a hockey player. He played on the ice and with the media at the same time. He was chasing two rabbits at once. It was stressful and it created too much pressure. Dionne reminded the reporters that in Montreal, more than anywhere, the public monopolizes their hockey stars. The public—too demanding, too pressing— was thus in a certain way responsible for the defeat and departure of the great player it had loved above all others.

Sam Pollock, who after leaving the management of the Canadiens had become an administrator in the Bronfman empire and continued to follow amateur hockey, was surprised and disappointed by Lafleur's departure.

"The whole business is absurd.

"When he arrived with the Canadiens in 1971, we were in the midst of a transition. Over a few years the club's personality was completely changed. It was a sort of cocoon in which Lafleur's great talent was able to develop. There was a perfect harmony between him and his milieu, a kind of osmosis that worked perfectly for years.

"Then there were new changes, a new team personality began to be built, one to which Guy Lafleur was poorly suited. I don't know what went wrong. But it seems certain that, as a result, everyone lost. The context wasn't the same.

Hockey had changed. Because of the WHA, and because of the Russians. Guy also changed. That's how life is."

Paul Dumont was surprised and hurt when he learned of Lafleur's departure.

"There's something in this story that I still don't understand. Nothing is less like Guy Lafleur than a resignation. Before, difficult circumstances seemed to stimulate him. I knew that. I knew Guy always came through the worst difficulties stronger than ever. When, in 1981, I saw that he had begun to slow down, I told myself he was just going through a bad phase, that he would make a great comeback, as he always had. But the bad phase dragged on, for a year, then two, almost three. And I started to follow him as closely as I had when he was scoring so much. It became intriguing and mysterious. How could it happen that a great player, still in full possession of his powers, could become so lacklustre and unproductive?

"At first, the way it was being explained in the newspapers—that he was fighting with Ruel, then Lemaire and Savard—seemed completely ridiculous. I had seen them play together for so long, and so well, with Shutt, too, that I found it difficult to believe these men couldn't get along. There had to be something else, I said to myself. The conflict with Lemaire had to be, at least in part, something the reporters had invented. I thought the true explanation lay elsewhere. It must be something much deeper. I began to think that perhaps Guy Lafleur had lost his faith, the way it sometimes happens to mystics, even the greatest, perhaps especially the greatest, who feel that their contact with God has been broken. Suddenly, no one's there, there is no longer a response, no longer the presence of the other. Maybe that's what happened to Guy. He lost his faith. Or the desire or the joy of playing. Which will probably come back."

"For Guy to give up, he must have been truly heartsick," said Jacques Richard, his old companion from the days of the Remparts. "I saw him on television a while before he announced his retirement. He was still skating very well, but he was hardly allowed on the ice. He wanted to score at any price, so he was aiming at the corners. And every time he blew a goal, he lost even more confidence. There are times like that, in life, when you see everything coming —you have perfect anticipation, everything is clear and orderly and you would say that everything happens the way you imagined or arranged it in your head. And there are other times when you are groping in the dark, you get irritated and enraged, you get bogged down. That's what happened to Guy, he got bogged down."

"I personally think Guy Lafleur was still a good player when he quit," said Maurice Richard. "In any case, he was one of the few who was really playing hockey. He wasn't satisfied always to shoot from the blue line, like everyone else today. He really tried to get inside the enemy zone while keeping control of the puck. But then he would find himself all alone. There was no longer anyone with him. He tried to score all by himself, but that's impossible! One time, back then, I met him and I advised him to try to stay in position. I thought he was struggling for nothing. He was nostalgic for the days when hockey had grace. Unfortunately for him, that wasn't the fashion any more."

Jean Béliveau has always claimed that the good athletes should play as long as possible. According to him, Lafleur's departure was premature.

"Guy arrived in Montreal at the moment when all the authority figures had been turned upside down. The role of veterans within the team was no longer considered important. Youth and instinct were everything. People didn't listen to authority like in the fifties and sixties. I think that made Guy's task much more difficult. There was no longer a definite framework, no leadership. In my view, the problem is located somewhere in that looseness. It isn't just Guy's problem, it's a problem of his generation, a sign of the times. Players used to be disciplined and determined soldiers. They were going into combat. Today, it's every man for himself. Team spirit no longer exists."

"Guy and I have many things in common," said Jacques

Lemaire. "We're both Virgos—Guy was born September 20, 1951, I was born on September 7, 1945—and therefore we are very methodical and earthbound.

"We are also very timid, but timid men with driving ambition. Without drive, you will never be a real hockey player. But Guy, unlike me, charged headlong into everything, always, even off the ice. If you put an obstacle in front of him, it stimulated him.

"I met him in the days of the Modern Hockey School. But the first time I really saw him play was at Verdun, at the time of the Quebec Remparts. He was already a huge star in Quebec and Ontario. But he had been so praised—that's the journalists, you can't do anything about it and ultimately it's good for the club even if it's hard on the player—that it was impossible not to expect him to be even better than he really was. When he came here to join us, in 1971, I was surprised by the slowness of his development. But later, having got to know him better, I understood that he was like that. It was when he realized that the people around him were no longer saying he was a Maurice Richard or a Jean Béliveau or a hockey superstar that he became one, that he became Guy Lafleur. He's always been that way in everything. It's when he realizes that he's about to lose something that he wakes up.

"But the moment came when he no longer had a challenge to meet. I think that's when he started getting tired and losing interest. He had been the greatest. Even today, with Gretzky and Mario Lemieux on the scene, there are still those who say that the best, the most graceful, the finest hockey player they've ever seen is Guy Lafleur. That's what Dick Irvin, Jr., the CBC sports commentator, wrote in his book. Lafleur couldn't be any greater than the greatest. I think he got tired of all that.

"When I got back from Europe, I was amazed to see how low he had sunk. He was no longer the same man. On the ice, he had lost his sense of himself. I spoke with him. I understood he was unable to reconcile himself with no longer being a great goal-scorer. In my opinion that was his mistake. If he had wanted, he could have gone on being a very great player, even if he no longer scored as much. But he wasn't playing hockey any more, he was just trying to score. He let it ruin his life. The game wasn't that way any more. He didn't adapt to the change."

• • •

The role that Guy Lafleur would play in the Canadiens organization was very vaguely defined. It had been announced that he would have a position somewhere in the front office, but nothing more specific was said. There was a possibility that he might replace Jean Béliveau in public relations. Béliveau had begun to talk about retiring. He was fifty-three years old, a grandfather, and had plans to travel with his wife Élise. Aside from his front office job, he had several other responsibilities relating to the Molson Breweries, various vice-presidencies, charitable works and other tasks that required a lot of attention.

But the organization didn't want to entrust its image to Guy Lafleur. He had demonstrated perfect behaviour with his nice speech about retiring, but deep down he still harboured the spirit of a rebel who for years had freely spoken his mind in the face of all authority. Guy Lafleur was far too honest, too direct and spontaneous to be a good public relations executive for the venerable Montreal institution. Moreover, he quickly let his bosses know that he wasn't going to deprive himself of saying what he thought just because he'd hung up his skates.

A few days after the announcement of his retirement, the Expos sold their star player, Gary Carter, to the New York Mets. In less than a week, Montreal had lost its two greatest sports stars. One day, when Lafleur was on his way to the Forum to discuss his new job with Ronald Corey, some journalists asked him what he thought of Carter's leaving. He replied spontaneously:

"The sports organizations are getting rid of all of Montreal's stars. The public is going to miss the big names. I find that very serious, as a social phenomenon. I wonder who the youth are going to identify with from now on."

These words were obviously taken as an unequivocal criticism of the Canadiens' directors, who had not known how to keep Lafleur playing. Once again, Lafleur saw beyond hockey. In his eyes, an organization like the Canadiens or the Expos had a social responsibility. Its job was not only to put together a winning team and put on a good show, but especially to provide role models and heroes.

Corey, a compromiser and a diplomat, quickly understood Lafleur's threat to the organization. Lafleur, no matter what the circumstances, could be faithful to nothing but justice and truth, not to the organization itself. No doubt that is why Corey never gave him a clearly defined role or real responsibility. It also explains why he accompanied him, as an obsequious chaperon, on almost all his official outings. In fact, they wanted to harness the formidable power Guy Lafleur had with the media, but they wanted to do it carefully and without taking chances.

Meanwhile, Corey had prepared a list of places where Guy was supposed to show up. As soon as Guy Lafleur was named to the Canadiens' public relations department, the Forum office was inundated with calls from schools, sports and social clubs, hospitals, prisons, political meetings, university or business conferences—everyone wanted Guy Lafleur for meetings, awards festivities, openings, subscription campaigns and more. But often, all that was wanted of him was to be there, to be somewhere at a given moment. By his presence alone he created an event.

Far from regretting having hung up his skates, for a while he was relieved and excited. New horizons were opening before him. In seeing the interest that he excited everywhere, he regained his self-confidence. He had been wrong when he had thought the people had abandoned him. The people had simply turned away while he was down, as though reluctant to see him decline.

Moreover, he had discovered a new life. For example, on Saturday, December 1, a week after his resignation, he watched the hockey game on television. He was being a normal, well-behaved husband, living tranquilly with his very pregnant wife. He slid gently into a cosy, comfortable life, and it was far from disagreeable. The warrior was in repose.

The following morning, another first in his life, he went to the arena with his son, Martin. Martin played for the Baie d'Urfé Saints. He played well. He was very fast and had an obvious hockey sense. But watching him play, his father thought that it would be very difficult for him to make a career in hockey. What an unbearable pressure he would be under, the son of Guy Lafleur!

Maurice Richard had already talked to him about the problems his children had experienced in minor hockey: people were always taking runs at them and testing them, simply because they were the sons of "the Rocket." If he embarked on a hockey-playing career, Martin Lafleur would spend his whole life fighting his way out of his father's shadow.

Lafleur preferred to imagine his son as a lawyer or a brilliant entrepreneur. He wanted him, one way or another, to get a good education. He realized that he himself had almost taken a great chance in wanting to leave school when he was still very young. He was fortunate Chouine had insisted to his parents that he get his grade eleven certificate. But if he'd had a bad accident—a wrecked knee like Bobby Orr, or lost an eye like Georges Guilbeault—he probably would have lived his whole life in the shadows, unimportant and anonymous.

Throughout his career he had been able to meet interesting people from every milieu—other athletes, artists, actors. He had travelled whenever and wherever he wanted. He had shaken the hand of His Royal Highness, Prince Charles, and of Princess Caroline of Monaco. For twenty years every Canadian prime minister had been eager to meet him in order to praise him. He had been lucky, infinitely lucky.

But when it came to his son, Lafleur did not want to trust to luck. He wanted a future solidly based on certainties. Several years of university; that was the real inheritance Guy wanted to leave his son. Not money. He was convinced that money you have not earned yourself can be very dangerous and can sometimes turn against you.

That day, Lafleur realized that he hardly knew his son. Martin had grown up without his really knowing it.

"I might have been too young when he was born," he said to himself. "Do you know what you're doing at twenty-four? Do you ever know what you're doing in life?"

He had promised himself that it would be different with this new child who was to be born in a few days. He would pamper him, he would play with him, he would take him to the country, fishing, to the movies; he would take care of him more than he had Martin. Martin had been raised by Lise, with almost no help from Guy. From time to time Guy would notice that his son knew how to read, how to count, how to program the VCR, how to skate. But with his father, Martin had remained a small and secretive being, already very independent.

"I was like that at his age. I never said anything to anyone."

He was thinking that morning of the day his father had come to see him play for the first time. It was at the Rockland arena, during the International Mosquito Tournament. Guy was nine or ten years old and playing with the Thurso Mosquitos. They were in the middle of the second period when he saw his father standing against the boards, near the players' bench. He was with Jean-Paul Danis, Ti-Paul Meloche, Brother Léo and some of the other Thurso men.

For a moment, Guy had been unable to breathe, and completely lost track of what was happening on the ice. He looked to his left, his right, in front and behind him. He couldn't find the puck anywhere. But the players were skating madly all around him. And the crowd was shouting loudly. The puck must be somewhere. The players wouldn't be skating like that for nothing. *Puck, where are you? Puck, where are you hiding?*

Then he thought he heard his father's voice, very near, soft and perfectly clear despite the immense racket in the arena, as though he had been whispering in his ear.

"Behind you, my boy. Get it, it's behind you."

He gathered in the puck and shot it with all his strength at the opposing net; the goalie took it right in the chest, fell backwards and saw the puck roll behind him to the back of the net. Guy turned towards his father. He saw his smile and the pride in his eyes.

Was Martin already a good player, like his father at the same age? Martin also searched out his father's eyes that morning. But every time he saw him, someone was talking to him. The parents and friends of the other players had come to greet the great Guy Lafleur, praise him, ask him for autographs and ask him how he felt since he had retired, inquire after his plans and Lise's pregnancy. What he wanted to do was watch his son play. But he couldn't do anything about it. The people were so nice, so considerate.

Martin scored a goal that he didn't even see. There was a roar; Guy raised his head and understood, from the disappointed look that Martin gave him, that his son had noticed he wasn't following the play. As always he had been busy elsewhere, with other people. Then Martin turned away and for the rest of the game didn't look at him any more, even after pulling off some spectacular rushes.

Lise often told her husband that his son was just like him. From her, this was the ultimate compliment. She loved her men deeply. They were her whole life. To Guy, it seemed that Martin really did resemble him; he had the same gestures, his vocal intonations, his laugh, his expressions, his tastes.

"But he couldn't have got all that from me," Lafleur would say to himself. "I haven't seen him enough."

Then it occurred to him that Lise had made Martin in his image. Women do that. They model their sons on the men they love.

That same Sunday evening, five days after the announcement of his retirement, Guy Lafleur made his first official appearance at the Montreal Forum. When he arrived behind the Canadiens' bench in his dark brown suit, his striped Canadiens tie, and sat next to the president,

Ronald Corey, the crowd exploded. At a signal from Corey, Guy stood up and raised his arms. But the cheering didn't stop. The whole Forum was shaking with noise. Claude Mouton, the official (and bilingual) voice of the Forum had to wait a full five minutes before announcing that there would be a ceremony that night paying tribute to the longest-serving employees of the Forum. When Lafleur stepped out on the red carpet at the first intermission to give Monsieur Fournier a plaque commemorating his fifty years of good and loyal service, there was another explosion, shouts and tears. And the choir was heard, in perfect harmony, even though no conductor directed it, singing out their magnificent symphony: "Guy! Guy! Guy!"

Obviously, none of this had been expected. Corey had announced that later in the season, in January or February, there would be a big celebration in Guy's honour, but the people had chosen this first occasion to show their hero the grandeur of the passion they felt for him. This spontaneous tribute was a way of saying that Lafleur didn't really belong to the Canadiens organization; he belonged to the people. "And you'll see," could be heard through the applause, "that he won't let himself be taken advantage of. Lafleur will be the fox in the henhouse."

On December 20, Lise gave birth to a big baby boy. "My retirement present," trumpeted his father. That same day, Guy saw in a magazine that the German mark was a strong currency. He had the idea of naming his son after it, Mark, with a k, Mark Lafleur. Lise thought this was an excellent idea. Once again, as at the moment of Martin's birth, Lafleur realized that everything in his life was taking on new meaning. What he had dreamed of had finally been granted: a new life was being offered to him. And for a while he truly believed that he would be happy. Or seemed to believe it.

On February 16, 1985, Lafleur was given a sumptuous party in the Montreal Forum, which was jammed full of emotional fans. More than two hundred reporters, photographers and cameramen had been drawn to the event. The crowd had all been given helmets decorated with an image of Lafleur in red and the Canadiens' logo.

At seven-thirty that evening, the Canadiens and the Buffalo Sabres took their benches. The Sabres, in blue and gold, were on the east side of the Forum. The Canadiens were in their magnificent white uniform which, at that time, they wore when they were playing at home. A strange murmur ran through the Forum crowd. The cameras were trained on the ice surface and on the dark corridor leading to the Canadiens' dressing room. A red carpet had been stretched out, like a floating bridge, towards the centre of the ice. And then suddenly, from everywhere at once, the fans began to call their hero, softly to begin with—"Guy! Guy! Guy!"—then louder and louder, building to a crescendo, until it had become a cry, a prayer, an irresistible incantation: "Guy! Guy! Guy!" Then the hero appeared.

He was wearing the red Canadiens uniform, the one they wore on the road. For the last time he skated around the rink, carrying his stick but without a puck. He skated slowly, his face turned towards the crowd. It had been announced that Lafleur's sweater, number 10, would be retired, like number 2 (Doug Harvey), number 4 (Jean Béliveau), number 7 (Howie Morenz), number 9 (Maurice Richard) and number 16 (Elmer Lach and Henri Richard).

Meanwhile, his wife, his son, his parents and the woman he called his second mother, Madame Baribeau, advanced across the red carpet until they reached centre ice.

From the other side of the rink the Sabres' manager, Roger Crozier, had climbed up to stand on his players' bench. All the players standing up behind him had taken off their helmets and were applauding along with everyone else. Then the Canadiens' players began to hit their sticks against the boards. The Sabres followed suit. It made an incredible racket, savage and grandiose, magnificently moving. The only players ever to receive such a tribute were Howie Morenz, who had died from an injury received on the ice, and Maurice Richard when he retired. All rivalries were forgotten and the players rendered a final tribute to the man who had been the best among them.

Lafleur went to the Canadiens' bench and shook the hands of each of his former teammates. Several had tears in their eyes. Some, who wanted to tell him something, had to hug him and speak right into his ear because the crowd was making so much noise. He stopped for several seconds in front of Larry Robinson, Mario Tremblay, Bob Gainey. Then he spoke to Lemaire and shook his hand.

Next he turned towards the Buffalo Sabres, who were still standing on the other side of the rink. He seemed to hesitate for a moment. He waved at them. Then, to thunderous applause, cries, weeping, shouts of laughter, in a sort of apotheosis, a delirium, he crossed the rink and shook their hands as well. Gilbert Perreault, the veteran, his beloved rival from Junior A days, leaned towards Lafleur and talked to him for a long time, while cameras flashed all around them.

Then he went back to his family at centre ice. It was as though he were going back into private life. After having belonged to the public for almost his whole life, he had finally been given back to his family. It was profoundly moving, and a bit terrifying. He had the clear impression that he was enjoying this voluptuous sensation for the last time. Afterwards, starting tomorrow, he would become a sort of ghost. He had travelled through a country filled with marvellous things and arrived at the other side, at the border of a country unknown to him. That evening, in front of the crowd, he was suddenly aware of it. For the first time in his life, he was facing the unknown.

Guy Lafleur felt that something was escaping him. His life contained all the elements of happiness—a woman who loved him, two children, money—and in spite of all that, he felt once more enveloped in boredom and worry. Everything that happened to him, all these tributes that were offered to him everywhere he went, gave him great pleasure. But his future was still uncertain. Not financially. For almost ten years he had lived exclusively on his advertising earnings; his hockey salary had been placed in trust by the club. Until he was fifty he would get almost $250,000 a year. His worry had nothing to do with money, but rather with the role he would play within the organization. Corey was still being very evasive, and Lafleur was beginning to wonder if he was being manipulated once again. He had been told so many times that he was naive, and he had so often allowed himself to be taken in.

The Canadiens organization had never been very generous towards him. For several years he had been the league's outstanding star, but despite that he'd had to fight to be decently paid. He scored fifty goals a year and earned less than certain players who were hardly able to get half a dozen.

He wondered if Savard and Corey hadn't painted his front office career in glowing terms in order to get him off the ice. So long as he stayed on the ice, he was a master. But in management, with a smooth-talker like Ronald Corey who was used to the world of business, the organization could handle him easily. He knew all that, but he didn't want to think about it too much. He was trying to be positive.

The organization sent him to take courses in marketing. He convinced himself that it was extremely interesting, once more applying Roger Barré's principles of positive thinking. He would have liked to understand how everything at the Forum worked, how the system, the organization, breathed and worked. And he would have liked to have a part to play in it. Talking with Jean Béliveau, he understood that he would have to make a place for himself. But all that made him weary, and even a bit angry. After having battled for years to get a bit of playing time, he would once again have to fight and argue endlessly to win a place within the organization. Sometimes his enthusiasm faltered and he wondered anxiously if what he was doing really made any sense.

In March, the official 1984–85 photo of the Montreal Canadiens was taken. For the first time in fourteen years, Guy Lafleur was there in suit and tie. That year there were a lot of suits, all new, each with a title in brackets just after the name. Yvon Bélanger (physical therapy), Jean Béliveau (public affairs), Serge Savard (managing director), Jacques Lemaire (head coach). Guy Lafleur was in the second row, between Pierre Mondou and Jean Perron (assistant coaches). Beside his name: nothing. Guy Lafleur-nothing. All the men in street clothes had always had a precise function clearly attached to them (trainer, head coach, president). Not Guy Lafleur. It was a first. Guy Lafleur - nothing. His exile had begun. Lafleur had lost his country, his ice, his place. And also his smile. The one he wore in the photograph was obviously borrowed.

In the first three months he spent in the Canadiens organization he made little headway. He quickly realized that he was living on his past accomplishments. He was sought out not for what he was but for what he had been. He felt confusedly that the stock of charisma he had accumulated over the years was not inexhaustible. Going to banquets, presiding over fund-raising campaigns, all that was fine and good. But he didn't want to become a jewel, a decoration, a mascot for the Canadiens.

They had finally assigned him an office and leased a car for him, but he still did not have a clearly defined function or any responsibilities. He was like a trophy on a shelf, a curiosity, the official freak. In fact, there was no place for him there. He felt that he was wasting his time, losing his soul. He had really let himself be taken. They had integrated him into the organization in order to neutralize him. The worst thing was that he had been stupid enough to help them. He had gone and sat himself on the bench.

One day, at his friend Quenneville's house, he saw the fine book Jean-Marie Pellerin had written on Maurice Richard, *L'idole d'un peuple* (*The Idol of a People*). When Richard had retired on September 15, 1960, after tears and pious speeches, it had been announced that he would be "assistant to the president, David Molson," and he had been named goodwill ambassador for the Canadiens club.

He travelled the country from coast to coast, signing autographs, shaking hands, greeting crowds, presiding over banquets. His salary, which had never been very high, was cut in half. Nevertheless, he stayed with the organization, saying that he wanted to participate in the development and administration of his former team. He was installed in a small office where he read the newspapers and practised blowing smoke rings. He was never invited to a single meeting. In no way was his knowledge of hockey ever called upon. They were content simply to exhibit him.

On August 30, 1965, defeated and humiliated, Richard announced his resignation from the position of vice-president of the Canadiens. In 1972, when he became coach of the Nordiques, his season tickets were taken away from him. He had been unfaithful to the Canadiens, an organization that had never shown him any gratitude and had shamelessly exploited him.

Reading Pellerin's book, Lafleur realized that he was reliving Richard's experience. But while the club had formerly been run exclusively by anglophones, it was now in the hands of francophones, his former companions in arms, his own brothers.

When the series against the Nordiques began, it was strongly recommended to Lafleur that he take a holiday in Florida with his wife. They didn't want him to interfere in any way with this potentially explosive situation. Lafleur had already let it be known that he liked the personality and mentality of the Nordiques team, and that he believed it was in many ways superior to the Canadiens. It was true, but no one wanted to listen to him.

Lafleur then began to understand that he had no choice but to leave the organization for good. But how? To go where? To do what?

That summer he enjoyed playing with the Canadiens' softball team. It was a pleasure tinged with sadness and nostalgia. He realized how much he liked playing with a team. But he also realized that what he liked best in the world (running after some kind of ball or a puck) was an activity more or less reserved for the young. Most men his age no longer played anything but golf or tennis, one- or two-person sports, sports that were purely social. And they didn't seem to long for the team sports they had played all through their childhood and youth.

This understanding depressed him. He felt himself growing older. The best part of his life, it seemed to him, was already behind him. He felt that he had not quite taken advantage of it, that he was letting himself be manipulated.

He had never consciously provoked the big changes in his life. But he knew how to be attentive. Sooner or later, something would come up. He was waiting.

• • •

In August, Guy ran into Yves Tremblay. Tremblay, as always, had half a dozen "projects of the century" to propose to him, each one more exciting and profitable than the last—an instructional hockey video, a sports trivia game, a television quiz, an anthology of his career's greatest moments, commercials, a biography, a film, subscription and promotional campaigns.

Yves Tremblay, who Lafleur called "the Kid," always had a new entrepreneurial scheme. His most recent venture had been in the world of show business, and it had fallen flat. He had invested more than he had in a disco singer, and as soon as her career began to take off she had replaced him with an American agent, leaving Tremblay an artist's agent without an artist, crippled with debts. But he wouldn't let himself be beaten. On the contrary, he always gave the impression that he was exploding with new plans. Every day he wrote down new ideas, injecting them with massive doses of blind faith, fervour and sincerity.

Lafleur was very fond of Tremblay. Not only because the Kid had always offered him his limitless admiration, but also because he knew that, deep down, he was honest, generous and would never try to manipulate him. The Kid had worked for years in the public relations department of the Forum, then had been let go with no explanation. Consequently he was not enamoured of the current organization. He amused himself by dreaming of the day when a well-managed coup would make Guy Lafleur president in place of Ronald Corey.

Meanwhile, he suggested to his friend Lafleur that they make a hockey video. Tremblay pictured demonstrations of skating and stickhandling, giving and receiving passes, shooting, checking and feinting, with some outstanding images from the career of the Blond Demon—two or three memorable rushes, the great farewell scene, the five-hundredth goal, awards ceremonies, some footage from his days with the Remparts, the Idéal and the Boomers. Then they would have a product that was both promotional and instructional, like the ones Jack Nicklaus and Martina Navratilova had already put on the market. It would be simple. It could be done quickly and cheaply, and there was a good chance it would make a lot of money.

The scenario was rapidly sketched out. A team was put together. Alain Montpetit, the host, and Pierre Ladouceur, a journalist, both hockey fans, would serve as teammates and commentators. The Kid pre-sold the package to Steinbergs and Simpsons, who promised to buy twenty thousand copies of the video. He also got a filming location, Les Quatre Glaces, a huge sporting complex in Ville-Brossard. But a few days before filming was to begin in mid-September, Guy's career took a turn that would radically change the course of his life.

Lafleur spent an evening with Guy Cloutier. Better than anyone, Cloutier knew what people in Quebec liked and wanted. Whether it be games, models, stars or myths, he usually managed to give it—or sell it—to them. He had often hinted to Lafleur that he would like to be his agent. But Lafleur didn't take the bait. Cloutier, aware that insisting might destroy their friendship, hadn't pursued it. But he thought it was a shame that Lafleur's enormous charismatic potential had not been properly harnessed. The Canadiens, he was sure, had failed to make the best use of Guy Lafleur.

That evening, in a Rue Crescent bar, he offered Guy Lafleur an impressive lesson about himself, showing him his place in the Quebec socio-cultural scene, clearly demonstrating to him that he had misdirected his career and that to work as a bureaucrat or clerk following the orders of a Ronald Corey was really not the thing to do.

"You're worth more than that, Guy. You're bigger than that."

Lafleur thought he was obviously worth more than the $75,000 a year the organization was paying him. Moreover, he had insisted on meeting Eric Molson, the owner of the Canadiens, to politely tell him that he had had enough of being club mascot and that he wanted to participate more fully in the organization. Molson had listened to him carefully, but let him know that, although he might be the owner, he could not go over the heads of Savard and Corey.

Savard and Corey still did not trust Lafleur. Guy began to wonder if they hadn't rushed to celebrate his departure and retire his number in order to rid him of any idea of making a comeback.

"They've done everything but bury my skates in cement," Lafleur said to himself.

Cloutier told Guy once again that he was still the most famous star in Quebec, and that a star should shine and show itself.

"You have immense potential. But so long as you stay locked up in the Forum, you won't be able to show your real value."

Lafleur knew all that. But hearing it said by someone like Cloutier gave him the courage to carry out his own plan of self-emancipation.

A few days later, early in the morning, Bertrand Raymond was in his office at *Le Journal de Montréal* when he saw Guy Lafleur coming into the editorial room. He was doing a promotion for Weston Foods, giving out bread and cakes to the employees of various newspapers and radio stations. How could the Canadiens give such jobs to Guy Lafleur? Politely, he was allowing himself to be photographed with the secretaries, pressmen and reporters.

Seeing Bertrand Raymond, Guy came over to say hello. A sports columnist since 1971, Raymond had followed Lafleur's entire career closely. He understood Guy's thoughts and feelings. They shut themselves up in an interview room, and Lafleur confided to Raymond that he was thinking of contacting Marcel Aubut of the Quebec Nordiques to offer to play hockey for him. He wanted to know what Raymond thought of the idea.

Raymond was amazed. Lafleur, still under contract to the Canadiens, had no right to contact other clubs. Moreover, these other clubs, if they were said to have tampered or raided, would automatically lose their first choice at the next draft.

"Marcel Aubut can't respond to you, Guy. Even if he wants you, he doesn't have the right to take you on without going through Serge Savard. And even if you manage to reach an agreement with Aubut without going through Savard, he would be able to annul the transaction whenever he wanted. Legally, you can't do anything without Savard's consent."

"In other words, I'm a prisoner of the organization. Because the last thing I can hope for from Savard is an okay for anything. Except, maybe, if I ask his permission to disappear."

And, as always, Guy began to say what he really felt: that he wasn't happy on his shelf and that he had no intention of staying there long. "I'm not going to spend my life playing office clerk for $75,000 a year."

He was deeply humiliated. The tasks he had been given (handing out little cakes, going to the opening of a tavern or service station, going through the stores of a shopping centre or attending boring dinners) no longer had any value in his eyes.

Bertrand Raymond was disturbed. When Lafleur left, he consulted his colleagues about whether he should publish Lafleur's disclosures. After thinking it over, he decided that he would say nothing about these hints of a comeback, but that he would write about Lafleur's inner conflicts, his great sadness, his dissatisfaction. He would say that Lafleur thought the organization had manipulated him and that he was being left to rot on a shelf, the way he had been left on the bench as a player. His column would appear the next morning, and it was the detonator that would set off another explosion.

This time, Savard and Corey decided that they had had enough. Lafleur himself, when he found out what Bertrand Raymond had written, understood that he might have gone too far and perhaps should have kept quiet for once. Lise especially was angry and worried. In her eyes, her husband had lacked judgment, and Bertrand Raymond had betrayed his confidence.

The next day, Sunday, at eight in the morning, the Kid woke Lafleur and read him the newspapers over the telephone. Ronald Corey had replied to Lafleur through the newspapers. Rather than calling him directly and asking him to explain himself or make a retraction, he was communicating through the media in order to settle things. His statements regarding Lafleur were very tough. This time it was total war, a fight to the finish between Guy Lafleur and the Canadiens organization.

The Kid was over-excited, and so was Guy. He didn't dare admit it to his wife, but deep down he was extremely happy about what was happening. Finally there was some action, intense and rapid. He had a feeling that over the next few days there would be a whole stream of events and that his life would take a new direction. And he liked new directions. They were exciting, and afterwards everything was new.

Monday morning, September 24, 1985, exactly ten months after he had hung up his skates, four days after his thirty-fourth birthday, Guy Lafleur started to make his video at Les Quatre Glaces. They had placed a camera in a corner of the rink. He shot a series of backhands: high, low, short, sharply angled, from the left and from the right. Then he passed pucks back and forth with Pierre Ladouceur, passing from both sides of his stick, backwards and forwards. It was amusing and relaxing. Child's play.

Towards the middle of the afternoon, the arena receptionist came to inform him that Ronald Corey was looking for him.

"He's waiting for me on the telephone?"

"No. Someone from the Forum called to tell you that Corey wants to speak with you."

Lafleur telephoned the Forum and asked for Ronald Corey. The secretary told him that the president was in a meeting, but that he had something to discuss with him. Lafleur changed, got into his car and went back downtown. He had no idea what he would say to Corey. He certainly found it regrettable that Bertrand Raymond had published what he had said in confidence. But he had no need to make a retraction, for the good and simple reason that what he had said and everything that had appeared in black and white in *Le Journal de Montréal* was the truth, every word of it. Corey knew it himself. Lafleur had told the same story to him numerous times, as well as to Savard and even to Eric Molson. But he was certain that what irritated Ronald Corey was that these truths had been offered to the public. For Corey, the image of the Canadiens was sacred and untouchable. If it had been tarnished and soiled, it must never be said, or even noticed.

At the Forum he found his office locked. He asked the secretary what was going on. She replied that Corey had given the order that Lafleur was not to be allowed in. He went to see Corey who let him know, very laconically, that he was dismissed. "You're not wanted here any more, Guy. Go away." Lafleur was tempted to ask why he hadn't said that to him over the telephone. What was the idea of making someone come from one end of the city to the other just to tell him to go away? But he left the office, leaving the door open. The atmosphere was highly charged. The only thing he heard, until he got to the door at the top of the stairs, was the sound of his own footsteps. He walked past the secretaries, the receptionists, a messenger. No one dared look at him. But no one was working. You might have said they were all stopped dead in their tracks, living statues, like in a science-fiction movie.

At five in the afternoon he was outside, on the street. He no longer belonged to the Canadiens organization. He felt a soft euphoria growing in him. Feeling serene, he drove home to Baie d'Urfé. He called his wife from his car. He had

nothing new to tell her because she knew what had
happened. A brief communiqué put out by the organization
had already been broadcast. On all the radio stations, they
talked of nothing else. Lise was floored. She was stunned
and in tears, but Guy told her:

"You'll see, Lise. It's the best thing that could have
happened to me."

The next morning he went back to Les Quatre Glaces.
Fifty journalists were waiting with cameras, spotlights and
microphones. Once again, Guy Lafleur was making
headlines. And once again, calmly, he spoke as a free man,
without holding back.

"When the Canadiens offered me a lifetime contract, it
was to buy my silence. To make themselves look good. But it
became obvious they didn't want me. If they kept me within
their organization, it was to get me safely out of the
way."

That same evening, Bertrand Raymond was sitting
nervously in front of his television. Pierre Nadeau asked
Guy Lafleur whether he held the journalist who had
reported his statements in *Le Journal de Montréal* responsible
for the irreparable conflict that now existed between him
and the management of the Canadiens. Certain radio
commentators had implied that Raymond had distorted
Lafleur's remarks and put words in his mouth. Lafleur
hesitated for a long moment—or what seemed like a long
moment to Bertrand Raymond. If Lafleur replied yes to
Nadeau's question, Raymond was finished. Lafleur was so
strong and powerful, so popular, that he could destroy his
credibility as a sports columnist. In the public's opinion,
Bertrand Raymond could never be in the right against Guy
Lafleur. To his great relief, Lafleur replied to Nadeau:

"Not at all. Bertrand Raymond faithfully reported my
words."

In fact, Lafleur was a bit angry at Raymond. Had
Nadeau asked him if Raymond had abused his confidence,
he might have said yes. But that was not the question, and
Guy Lafleur never replied to questions he wasn't asked. In
addition, he had always felt friendship and respect towards

journalists, even those who sometimes let him down. He understood their profession. Like them, he had a passion for making things known, for revealing what others had an undue desire to hide. He firmly believed that the truth should always be spoken.

● ● ●

Guy Lafleur no longer had a role to play with the Montreal Canadiens organization. In truth, he had never had one; the only difference was that from now on it would be official. However, he was still not a free man. As a player, he still belonged to the Montreal team. He could not work in any way whatsoever for another hockey team until the three-year contract he signed in 1984 had expired. Unless the Canadiens gave him permission.

He didn't have to ask Serge Savard if he could come back to play with the Canadiens. The press had taken on the task of posing this question. The answer was no. A large, categorical and definitive no. And elsewhere? Could he offer his services to the Rangers or the Capitals or the Canucks? Savard had been evasive, but it was clear he would do nothing to make it easy for Lafleur to join another team.

The idea that his future, his happiness, even his life were totally dependent on Serge Savard and Ronald Corey sometimes threw Lafleur into outbursts of despair and rage. He was entirely at their mercy. He coped with his anger by launching, mostly for his own benefit, a campaign of disinformation. He had no other choice. He had to convince himself thoroughly that he no longer had any desire to play hockey.

That was certainly what he told the press and his friends when his video was put on the market at the end of the fall. That day, during a screening, he found himself standing beside his longtime friend, Richard Morency, sports director for radio station CKAC. In silence they watched the famous goal Lafleur had scored against the Boston Bruins in the Stanley Cup semi-finals of 1979. It had been 4 to 3 for the Bruins, with two minutes left in the game. They saw the smiling face of the Boston coach, Don Cherry, who believed that his team's victory was assured. Then they saw

Lafleur skate along the boards, extend his arms to Lemaire's long lead pass, cross the Bruins' blue line alone, fake out a defenceman, come back towards the centre, turn towards the net, get past the other defenceman and put the puck in the net behind the goalie, Gilles Gilbert.

"Now you see why I retired," Lafleur said to Morency.

"What do you mean?"

"I retired because I realized that I couldn't do that sort of thing any more, those fakes and rushes."

"But of course you still can!" Morency returned. "Why do you say that?"

"Listen, Richard, I know better than you. Ask any player here."

"But I still don't see your logic. You can play hockey without making rushes like the one we just saw."

"Everyone will tell you that after thirty-two or thirty-three, you aren't as fast, your wind isn't as good, you're not as strong."

But while he was talking this way, a voice inside was asking, "Why are you saying this, you idiot? What's got into you? You know very well that it's not true. You can still play like that." He had to stifle that voice. And he heard himself telling Morency and the others who were there that he had retired at the right time, that he was satisfied with his decision. He wanted to project the image of a happy man who has made the right decisions in his life.

His disinformation campaign didn't work. He was tortured by the desire to play again. While he was making that video at Les Quatre Glaces, he had rediscovered the pleasures of skating, of holding a stick in his hands, of feeling the weight of the puck, of shooting, of evading an opponent. And he realized that he still had good hockey in him, and that probably the best thing he could do was to put on his skates and start playing again. He was in excellent condition; after nine months away from the rink he still weighed the same, almost to the pound. He could easily play again. But where? On what rink? With what team? He was sure he still liked playing and that, sooner or later, unless he wanted to go crazy, he'd have to take the step, gather his courage and play again. Nevertheless, he waited a long time.

It wasn't until the end of the following summer that he decided to call Savard, who gave him permission to test the waters. He contacted the New York Rangers, the Pittsburgh Penguins and the Los Angeles Kings. In New York, where he could have rejoined Pierre Larouche, the team was in a transitional phase. The club was rebuilding with young players. "No place for an old player like Lafleur," was the reply. Pittsburgh hesitated. Twenty-year-old Mario Lemieux, who had become an imposing star in his first NHL season (43 goals, 57 assists), had said he would like to play with Lafleur. But the Penguins' boss, Eddie de Bartolo, refused, for reasons he would not disclose.

Los Angeles also refused. Nevertheless, the club wasn't doing very well and everyone said that a player like Lafleur could help at the box office. Lafleur had often let it be known that he would enjoy living there, in that other world far from the huge pressure that the Quebec public and media placed on its players. But the timing was wrong. The managing director of the Kings was Rogie Vachon, the man Lafleur had once named the best goalie in the NHL. Vachon had certainly not forgotten this. But that didn't keep him from being a close friend of Serge Savard's. Had Savard advised him not to take on Lafleur?

In October, the twenty-one NHL teams had completed their line-ups. Guy Lafleur was not to be found. Serge Savard had changed his mind. He had put Lafleur on the Canadiens' protected list, which meant that Lafleur was no longer a free agent and consequently could not be drafted directly by another team. If some organization wanted to acquire him, they would have to go through Serge Savard, who could then exercise his rights of ownership, accepting or refusing offers made to Guy Lafleur without even consulting him.

Lafleur took this gesture of the managing director as a low form of revenge. But "the Senator," who was not above twisting the truth to his own advantage, explained to the press that if he had not protected Lafleur, any team at all could have claimed him. He might have been forced to agree to play for a second-class club. And after all he had meant to the Montreal Canadiens, it would have been shameful for him to end his career like that.

Total impasse. In the whole NHL there was no longer a single bit of ice for Guy Lafleur.

During the winter he started to look elsewhere. Was there anything else in life to interest him? Was there life after hockey? Georges Guilbeault and Léo Drolet, the makers of Sherwood hockey sticks, proposed a business partnership to him. They wanted to get into the marketing of a wide range of sporting goods, and Lafleur was an expert in this field. As a professional athlete he had followed the development of sports equipment. In addition, he had several times been the representative of big brand names like Koho, Sherwood and Bauer. He knew the markets for these products and how to pitch them.

Guilbeault's and Drolet's plans were sufficiently interesting to Lafleur that he thought about moving to the Eastern Townships. Lise was not so taken with the idea, but she knew Guy's life needed a big change. He had already talked about selling the Baie d'Urfé house; he wanted to change everything—house, car, friends, habits. Guy himself was changing. Lise saw him sinking into a deep depression. Sometimes he drank alone, in the dark. When the telephone rang he almost always said, "Whoever it is, I'm not home." He didn't seem to be interested in anything any more.

Lise herself had been depressed since Mark had been born. She often cried. "It's the baby blues," she would tell herself. But worst of all was this unbearable feeling that everything had disintegrated. Guy had made a mess of his exit from hockey. Their relationship had gradually deteriorated to the point where they were no longer able to talk to each other. Contact had been broken. Two solitudes.

One winter evening, when they were at Georges Guilbeault's house in Sherbrooke, Guilbeault told them something terrible.

"Twice, Serge Savard has told me that he's heard rumours that you're taking drugs, Guy. It's also being said that you drink too much, and that the reason your career took such a bad turn is because of drugs and drinking."

The problem of drugs in professional sports was then beginning to be a controversial topic. Two years earlier, John Ziegler, the NHL president, had suspended Ric Nattress for forty games because he had been caught smoking marijuana. The punishment had been considered excessive, but Ziegler had wanted to set an example, and the other important powers in the league had agreed with his strategy. People were beginning to talk about drugs and to be afraid of them. Professional athletes, rich and in good physical condition, were dangerously exposed to the plague and were suspected by the sports writers, always eager for sensation and scandal, of over-participation in sex, drugs and alcohol. The hockey world was filled with all sorts of rumours, which, one by one, tainted all the best-known players in the league.

For his part, Lafleur might often have had his share of drink, but he had always stayed clear of drugs, which he associated with a whole set of values that he rejected.

"When did Savard say that?"

"The first time we were down south, in Bermuda I think. The other time was here at Sherbrooke, in front of the people from the Junior Canadiens organization."

"And what did they say?"

"Nothing. But I don't think it was the first time they'd heard that kind of thing."

"What do you mean?" asked Lise.

"I mean Savard wasn't making it up on the spot."

"So, according to you, these rumours are well-founded!" Big tears rolled down her cheeks.

"I didn't say that. I said Savard was only referring to rumours that had been around for a long time."

Lafleur was astounded. Lise sobbed loudly. She got up and went to the guest room, where her husband soon joined her. He wanted to take her in his arms. She pushed him away violently.

"I never want you to touch me again. You've deceived me again. You've lied to me the way you've lied to everyone. I don't want to live with a man who lies."

Lafleur was as amazed by her reaction as he had been by Guilbeault's revelations. Despite the fact that he swore up and down that he had never taken drugs, Lise wouldn't believe anything he said. She was lying face down, stretched out on the bed, her head buried in the pillow and her body shaking with sobs.

"You're smart enough to see that this whole thing is one of Savard's schemes. He's the liar, Lise."

She didn't respond. She had spontaneously given credence to the rumours Savard had talked about. The fragile trust her husband had re-established with her since his escapades and separations had just crumbled again. It was true that sometimes he drank too much. And sometimes he spent hours alone in the dark! Does a man in a normal state do that kind of thing? Does a happy man feel the need to go out every evening and come back at five or six in the morning?

Until then, Lise had never believed her husband was capable of taking drugs. Claude Quenneville, who she totally trusted, had reassured her. Several years ago Quenneville had given up alcohol, tobacco, all drugs. But before this reform he had often gone to bars and discos with Guy. Often, at parties, he'd seen Lafleur turn down drugs, without hesitation: "He never accepted anything, not even a joint. Guy allows himself to be influenced in a lot of things, but never about drugs. Never."

In addition, it was said that cocaine reduced the appetite. If there was one thing Guy Lafleur never lacked, it was appetite. Morning, noon and night he always ate a lot, often making himself a sandwich before going to sleep when he came home late.

Until she heard Savard's rumours, Lise had always believed that Guy always told the truth. But something was breaking down. She suddenly realized just how far he had gone from her. Doubtless he no longer loved her. They never had those long conversations that used to make them feel so close.

What threw Lafleur was that his wife had chosen to believe Savard over him.

"Why can't you see that he's doing this to destroy me, to justify himself in having got rid of me?"

"All I see is that you've lied to me. One more time. And if you lied about that, you could have lied about lots of other things."

"But you know very well that Savard is trying to ruin me."

"I think you're the one, Guy Lafleur, who's trying to ruin yourself."

Lise knew Savard had called Quenneville a few months earlier to ask him directly if Guy Lafleur was taking drugs. Savard knew that the two men had long been close friends. Quenneville, put out that Savard could take him for a potential informer, had nevertheless replied with conviction. In his opinion, Lafleur did not take drugs. There was absolutely no doubt in his mind. Lafleur did not like drugs, and his reasons were very elementary. One was fear. He knew that he was excessive in all things, and so he was afraid that if he started he might not be able to stop in time. It was the same thing that sometimes happened when he drank, or when he drove fast, always pushing his Ferrari or his Harley to the limit until he lost control. He didn't want to do the same thing with drugs; it was too dangerous. Even the most insignificant pills frightened him. When he was hurt, he always refused to take the tranquillizers prescribed by the doctor.

Quenneville thought he had convinced Savard, and Lafleur was persuaded that the suspicions directed towards him had been quashed. But now here was Guilbeault talking about widespread rumours!

Lafleur suspected Savard of being the origin of these rumours, or at the very least of having intentionally spread them. In portraying Lafleur as a drug-user, he would show himself to be justified in having got rid of him. In addition, he was making his association with any other enterprise practically impossible. Who would want to be represented by a notorious drug-user? It was certain that Lafleur's image had been considerably tarnished. In some circles it was already said that Lafleur was a man who bit the hand that fed him.

Fortunately, despite the difficulty of the situation, Guilbeault knew what to do.

"This has to be cleared up," he said.

Guilbeault contacted Mike Pelletier, an RCMP officer who over the summer had been investigating some of the rumours, and found that each one, as he tried to pin it down, disappeared as though by magic.

"Yes, Lafleur takes drugs," he was sometimes told.

"Have you seen him taking drugs?"

"No. But I know someone who knows someone who . . ."

Pelletier went to see Savard, who was very annoyed by the importance that the whole affair had taken on. He began by denying any responsibility for the rumours. But Guilbeault was a credible witness: he might have lost an eye playing hockey, but he still had both his ears. Savard finally had to admit that he had called Lafleur a drug-user, but without, he protested, really thinking about it. He claimed there were many such rumours making the rounds, and that this was not surprising since, according to him, Lafleur associated with the shady world of scalpers and pushers, hung out with artistic types, went to disreputable bars and discos. "He hasn't done anything to help himself," he said to Pelletier.

Lafleur thought about suing. But who? For what? And it might have just made things worse without serving any purpose. He preferred to forget the whole business. Nevertheless, he remained convinced that Savard had resolved to ruin him. Now he no longer had a single friend within the organization. Brian Travers, his faithful ally, had overnight become *persona non grata* at the Forum even though for years he had come and gone as he pleased, night and day.

Guy Lafleur had become an undesirable, a pariah. For a while he accepted this sad fate, and even tried to make himself a comfortable life in retirement, without dreams or hopes.

• • •

Towards the end of that summer of 1986, Richard Morency, Guy's friend from radio station CKAC, happened to see him interviewed on television. It was a long time since he had seen Lafleur. During the previous months, Guy had made himself scarce. No more commercials, promotions, shocking revelations. Nevertheless, within sports circles, he was still a favourite topic of conversation. A day never passed without Morency hearing about him in one way or another, or without his station's listeners calling to find out what was happening with the famous retired player.

On the television screen he seemed to be in fine form; he was tanned, confident, laughed easily. But listening to him, Morency gradually began to feel doubts. Lafleur had begun to proclaim the joys of golf; he had even gone so far as to say that it was an agreeable form of relaxation. Now Morency happened to know that Guy Lafleur had never truly liked golf. If he had nothing better to do than to convince himself that he did, then things were perhaps not going so well. Moreover, when the interviewer asked him his plans, he told her that he hadn't any, and that he would be happy to spend the next year taking care of his sons.

To help raise his children was certainly a worthy ambition, but that would not prevent a man of Lafleur's calibre from having other activities. Morency knew Lafleur well enough, for long enough, to know that Lafleur was once again deluding himself and was trying desperately to believe that he was happy.

The next morning Morency telephoned Guy and invited him to lunch. They met at the Latini, on Dorchester. Lafleur was beaming with the ostentatious but superficial good humour Morency had seen the night before. For a while Lafleur kept repeating how happy he was in his new life, that he regretted nothing, that he was relieved to no longer be under pressure. Just the same, he did finally admit that, despite everything, he sometimes got bored, and that he might not mind having some sort of job.

"What hurts the most is when Martin tells me he doesn't know what to tell his friends when they ask him what his father does."

"Do something, then. You have a choice, don't you?"

The truth was that he had so many choices that he didn't know which to take. He was rich and healthy, still young, free. He could have gone into business, bought a restaurant, a bar, teamed up with Guilbeault and Drolet at Sherwood or with his brother-in-law Pierre Barré, an automobile dealer. He could have travelled, left on an expedition to the end of the world, gone up the Amazon or the Zambezi Rivers, climbed Annapurna or Kilimanjaro, crossed the Kalahari or the Sahara, seen the ruins of Angkor, Machu Picchu, Mecca . . . But he didn't do anything. He hesitated. He waited.

"You have to do something," Morency told him. "You especially have to stop saying on television that you're not doing anything and that you're no longer interested in anything. People don't want to know that. You still represent a lot for the Québecois people. You have responsibilities."

"But what do you want me to do? All I know how to do is play hockey."

"You know how to talk to people. You are a true communicator. When you talk, people listen. Use that."

Morency sensed that Lafleur was completely lost. He remembered that two years ago Lafleur had told him that the people of Thurso had gone into mourning when he retired.

"It's almost as though I died," he said. "In Thurso, people look at me as though I'm a ghost."

Morency asked himself, that day at the Latini, if Lafleur hadn't ended up thinking of himself as one of the living dead. It was as though he'd accepted his fate, his role as a has-been.

But the next day Lafleur called him at CKAC.

"Did I dream it, or is it true that yesterday at lunch you really offered me a job on the radio?"

"If you're interested, you could learn how to do it. I talked about it with Pierre Arcand, the station director, and he agrees."

"When do I begin?"

"Whenever you want."

At the end of the fall, on a program called "Amateurs de Sports" ("Sports Lovers"), Guy met up with his old friend Pierre Bouchard and was introduced to Danielle Rainville, a brilliant journalist who had succeeded in establishing herself in the men's world of sports journalism. An agreement was struck. Lafleur would be paid little, but money was not the point. He wanted a job and the opportunity to learn a new profession that would allow him to maintain his relationship with the public, which he knew he needed to stay alive. And as he had emphasized to Morency during their lunch at the Latini, he wanted his son to know what to say when he was asked what his father did for a living.

Every morning at eight o'clock, Guy phoned in and delivered his impressions and commentary on the previous night's game, on the performances of this or that player, the tactics of whichever coach. He didn't have the practised ease of a Pierre Bouchard, nor the incomparable talent of a Danielle Rainville; his speech was slow, he often hesitated, he had to search for words. But he had a trump card that even the best communicators sometimes lack: he was already an immense star. Everyone in Quebec recognized the sound of his voice. And when he was on CKAC, wherever they were or whatever he said, everyone listened. Guy Lafleur, the man with the magnetic personality, was speaking.

He was happy. A new career was opening before him. It was not exactly what he had wanted to do; he would have preferred working in a hockey organization. But he told himself that you don't always get to do what you want in life, that you have to know how to pick yourself up after a failure and that sports journalism had great possibilities to offer.

He sold his house at Baie d'Urfé, bought a superb apartment in the Sanctuaire, Montreal's most luxurious condominium development in Mount Royal, bought a new car, changed his habits, stopped drinking alone in the dark, started going to bed early and getting up early. He believed he had truly turned the page on his past and that he had skilfully slid into a new life. But hockey was going to catch him up again in an unexpected way.

In 1985 Lafleur had joined, as a founding member, the Petro-Canada hockey team of former Canadiens players. This was a team of valiant and generous old-timers who, for $175 a game, played against amateur teams in various municipalities to raise money to encourage sports among the young. Spectators paid five dollars to watch their teams being massacred by the ex-NHL stars. The games were always entertaining and enjoyable. But Guy Lafleur, who remained the centre of attention in these events, did not really enjoy playing because the games weren't real hockey.

Of course he had the satisfaction of helping out a good cause. Also, sometimes, he had the opportunity to see old friends again. Even Jacques Lemaire played occasionally, and Lafleur was surprised that he could again enjoy playing with his former boss. Discouraged by life under the unrelenting microscope of the media, Lemaire had given up his position as head coach of the Canadiens. Lemaire, like Lafleur, had been deeply marked by his experience. He, too, had a bruised soul, scars. Between Lemaire and Lafleur there was no longer that beautiful and total harmony that used to exist, but on the ice they left behind their rancour and bitterness. Inevitably, they stole the show.

But the hockey was not real. Slapshots were forbidden, as well as checks and body contact, and the former number 10 couldn't really put his energy into this simulation of hockey. In addition, every time he got ready for one of these games, he was torn by nostalgia. Despite all the efforts he had made over the past two years to convince himself that he had no more hockey left in him, the desire to play kept welling up in him.

One day, in January 1987, the Petro-Canada club was to play against the former Thurso Pee Wees, the ones he'd starred with while winning the international tournaments in Quebec in 1963 and 1964. Except for one man who'd died a few years earlier, they were all there. They had aged, gained weight, their hair was turning white. But they were all happy to be together again, celebrating again, enjoying once more—after almost twenty years—the ceremony of a game of hockey in the little Thurso arena where they used to play, when they had all had the same dream and their whole lives ahead of them.

They played with spirit, but they were defeated by their childhood friend. The next day, however, he played with them against the Petro-Canada club. This time the old Thurso Pee Wees won. Lafleur was happy. At the Hotel Lafontaine where they all went after the games, he rediscovered the warmth of his childhood, these familiar faces, the old jokes. They roared with laughter late into the night. At the same time, somewhere deep inside him, Lafleur could sense his sadness, his inextinguishable sadness, stirring. He was well aware that he was still a great player. Practically single-handedly he had beaten the two clubs, one after the other. He wasn't a has-been like the others. He was still alive and capable, and he didn't really belong among these retired players. Now he knew for sure that he had not left the Forum of his own accord. He could do without his office on the second floor, but he desperately missed playing. He had become a kind of *Canadien errant*, a deportee, a victim of a giant manipulation.

There had been nothing glorious about his retirement, none of the sense of the fitness of things that comes when a faithful veteran who has played out his time and his glory takes his richly deserved rest. What he had experienced was a defeat, a demotion, a demolition. More and more, he felt that he had ruined his exit, and he was obsessed by the thought that he should have done the whole thing differently. He was filled with regret and remorse.

But he was quick to dismiss these dark thoughts, and when anyone asked him if he sometimes thought of playing again, he was quick to say that he never did. It was a white lie, but he had no choice.

On the other hand, he acknowledged that these sad seasons spent far from the ice, from the real ice, had allowed him to think things out about his life. He had grown much closer to Lise; they had taken up their long talks again, the way they used to. Once more his life was rooted in Lise and the children.

For the holidays they decided to take a winter vacation and went to Mont Tremblant for two weeks of skiing. Lise and Martin were excellent skiers but Guy was sure he wouldn't be any good at it. Hockey players are rarely good skiers. First, because their teams, fearing injuries, forbid skiing, but also because the training and psychological conditioning they undergo is incompatible with the sport. They are too tense and nervous, too aggressive, always ready to attack, whereas skiing demands flexibility, a sense of rhythm, a kind of abandon that you never find on the hockey rink.

Much to his surprise, after a few hours on the slopes of Mont Tremblant, Guy Lafleur, amazed by his own performance, had found a new passion, which showed just how detached from hockey he had become.

A sudden thaw ruined the skiing for a few days. Lafleur used the time to drive around the area in the company of Canadian ski champion Peter Duncan, who knew the mountainous country well. It was during one of these outings that Lafleur saw, to the north of the Mont Tremblant highlands, a landscape that went straight to his heart: a field of sparkling snow that extended to a big evergreen woods. "For Sale, 10 Acres." A few weeks later he put in a bid for it and reactivated the old dream he'd had with Lise at Verchères of a well-laid-out property, a super-hobby with which he could amuse himself for years. This was the ideal spot to realize his long-cherished dream.

He would start from zero, from wilderness, and he would fashion it as he pleased. There he would be able to live in perfect independence; there he would be the supreme authority, like Roger Barré or Léo Drolet.

Lise Lafleur was not as carried away by this dream as her husband. She thought the place was too far north, too high in the Laurentians, too bleak and cold in the winter. The summer, with the blackflies and gnats, would be unbearable. And in the spring, the roads would be impassable. Just one thing consoled her: her husband's enthusiasm. He was so happy, so taken with this project, that it was making him forget all his disappointments, his remorse and his bitterness. He was even hoping to bury the hatchet with the Canadiens.

In January, he called Ronald Corey and asked him for a friendly meeting. He wanted to let him know that he was ready once again to work in the organization. They agreed to meet at the Ritz at eight o'clock in the morning. Lafleur, who came half an hour early, waited for Corey in the restaurant. He knew the surroundings well, and certain faces reminded him of his happiest years.

At the agreed-upon time, someone came up to him and discreetly informed him that he was expected in one of the hotel's suites. Lafleur went up, amazed. Corey himself opened the door, polite, nice, sweet as honey. Corey was also nervous, and very ill at ease. They sent for food. When the waiter knocked at the door, Corey seemed panic stricken. Before opening it, he asked Lafleur to hide in the adjoining room. It seemed clear that he did not want them to be seen together. Lafleur thought the whole thing was beginning to turn into a farce. From whom might he be hiding? From reporters, no doubt. Corey probably wanted his meeting with Lafleur, the wolf who had threatened the Canadiens' sheepfold, to be kept secret.

Nevertheless, Lafleur told him the purpose of his visit. He was ready once more to represent the Canadiens and handle promotions.

"But the position you had no longer exists, Guy."

"I know that, Ronald. In fact, between you and me, that

position never really existed. I never knew what you expected of me."

Corey's face was blank, as though he had not heard what Lafleur said.

"You understand that a job couldn't be held open for you forever."

"But Ronald, what job? You know very well I never had a job in the organization."

Then Corey offered him employment on a casual basis, without a contract; he would represent the Canadiens on various occasions when he was asked for.

"But you'll have to wait until after Rendez-Vous '87. For the moment, with O'Keefe in the picture, things are a bit delicate, you understand. I hope I don't need to draw you a picture."

Rendez-Vous '87 was to be the event of the decade in the world of international hockey. Marcel Aubut, president of the Nordiques, had invited the Soviets to Quebec, both the Red Army Chorus and the Red Army hockey team. A few weeks earlier he had announced that Guy Lafleur would be Canada's official ambassador to this event.

Carling O'Keefe Breweries, the owner of the Quebec Nordiques, was the official sponsor of Rendez-Vous '87. And of course the Quebec Nordiques were the sworn enemies of the Montreal Canadiens, owned by Molson Breweries.

It was only after he had left the hotel and got into his car that Lafleur remembered that Serge Savard, managing director of the Canadiens, was himself associated with Rendez-Vous '87, and that Corey did not seem to find that a problem.

In spite of everything, once the Soviets were safely gone he called Corey several times. Corey, always very friendly and each time asking after Lafleur's family and Lise's health, would say, "Unfortunately, I don't have anything for you right now. But please feel free to call me again."

Finally, Lafleur realized that he had only himself to depend on, and that he could never expect to receive any help from the Canadiens.

OVERTIME

●

ON THE EVENING OF May 26, 1988, slumped deep in the armchairs of the luxurious Sanctuaire apartment, their feet propped up on the low Italian marble table, Guy Lafleur and Yves Tremblay were watching television. The Edmonton Oilers had just beaten the Boston Bruins (6 to 3) and for the second consecutive year, the fourth time in five years, won the Stanley Cup.

It was a beautiful, mild evening. Through the wide-open windows they could smell the foliage, the warm fresh air, the breath of the nearby mountain. Like six million other Canadians, they quietly drank their beer and watched the game.

It was something Guy Lafleur had almost never done. Since retiring, he had gradually lost interest in what was happening in the NHL. For a long time he had not even set foot in the Forum. He was afraid it might be too painful for him, and in any case he was not interested any more. For over a year he hadn't even watched a game on television for more than five minutes. He didn't know half the players and knew almost nothing about the new power alignments in the NHL.

That evening—Lise was at her mother's with the children—Yves Tremblay had brought the steaks and the wine. They'd prepared the fries and cooked their steaks on the terrace barbecue. They ate early while working on the list of guests for the Guy Lafleur Golf Tournament in support of Leucan, a charitable organization raising money

407

for cancer research, which was supposed to take place at the beginning of July on Lac Masson in the Laurentians. The guest list was extremely important to Guy because it allowed him to define and position himself within Quebec society. With Lise and the Kid, he had taken great care in choosing the sports and show business personalities he would be asking to come.

At the top of the list were his friends: Jean-Yves Doyon, Narcisse "the Beaver" Charrette, a Baie d'Urfé neighbour with whom he'd stayed in close contact, Richard Morency, Claude Quenneville, Pierre Bruneau, various other people he admired and trusted. In other words, no one from the Montreal Canadiens organization would be on this list.

For three years Lafleur had campaigned for Leucan. Its spokesperson, little Charles Bruneau, had just recently died of cancer. He was eleven years old. Engaging and effective on the media, headstrong and combative, Charles was also a great hockey fan. He had already written to Maurice Filion and Michel Bergeron to tell them that, even though he lived in Boucherville and all his friends were hard-core fans of the Canadiens, he preferred the Nordiques, because it was a team that had to struggle and establish itself.

At their first meetings, Lafleur had been a bit uncomfortable. Charles had been on a course of chemotherapy and had lost all his hair. But gradually, a real friendship grew up between the two. When they were together they laughed a lot. Lafleur would come to see him or telephone him every now and then, and when he was travelling he made sure to send him postcards, always of beautiful, wild landscapes, often of sunrises over the sea, that Charles would put up on the wall of his room.

Charles had an innate sense of public relations. He was the author of the famous slogan that Leucan used for several years: "When I grow up, I'll be cured . . . for life." Charles' life was a great adventure, always at the borders of the unknown. At that time, Lafleur was experiencing some difficult moments, but in Charles' eyes Lafleur was a success.

Lafleur was friends with Charles' father, Pierre Bruneau, a journalist and television news-reader on the TVA network. In the spring, Lafleur noticed Bruneau was no longer on the news at the end of the evening. Worried, he went to Sainte-Justine Hospital, where he found out that Charles had gone into a deep coma. Pushing open the door of the room, he saw Pierre Bruneau sitting in the dark at his son's bedside. Lafleur came up to Bruneau, put his hand on his shoulder and said, as though to excuse himself for being there, "I haven't seen you for three days. I thought Charles must be unwell." They stayed for a moment in the shadow without talking. Then Guy left. An hour later Charles died.

For the Québecois, and even more for Guy Lafleur, who had known him during the most extraordinary and painful moments of his short life, Charles Bruneau had been an example of bravery, of lucidity, of cool-headedness, of faith in life. He died convinced that, sooner or later, a cure would be found for cancer, and that his illness and his efforts had had some purpose. During the last year of his life he had been close to Lafleur, who found his presence both stimulating and reassuring. The fact that he was now gone made the organization of the tournament that much more difficult; Charles had had ideas, energy, audacity.

It was Charles who had pushed Lafleur to call André-Philippe Gagnon to ask him to participate in the tournament and give a show after the banquet. Lafleur didn't dare. He said that Gagnon, one of the biggest show business stars in Canada, would have neither the time nor the desire to participate in a golf tournament, much less to give a performance.

Charles said, "The worst that can happen is that he'll turn you down."

Not only had Gagnon not refused, but he had immediately agreed to provide his services free of charge. Like the young Charles Bruneau, André-Philippe Gagnon was a notorious fan of the Nordiques, the great rivals of the Canadiens. In publicly associating with him, Lafleur was making his position clear. And Gagnon, by teaming up with Lafleur, was putting himself on the side of the lone wolf, the man against the Establishment.

Both André-Philippe Gagnon and his librettist, Stéphane Laporte, were hockey fanatics. Ferociously partisan to the Canadiens, Laporte knew even more about hockey than Claude Mouton, the official historian of the Montreal team. Together, Laporte and Gagnon had mounted some spectacular numbers about certain NHL stars, players, commentators and coaches.

Gagnon had been at the Colisée on November 25, 1985, when Marcel Aubut launched his famous promotional campaign for the Nordiques. A few weeks earlier, after having been the sparkling hit of the 1985 Festival Juste pour Rire (Just for Laughs), Gagnon had appeared on Johnny Carson's "Tonight Show" where he had astounded the American audience by imitating the eighteen singers of "We Are the World," from Bruce Springsteen to Michael Jackson, including Dionne Warwick and Bob Dylan. Before the game at the Colisée began, the image of this unforgettable performance had been projected onto the arena's giant screen. Then Gagnon had appeared with Marcel Aubut, who gave him a complete set of Nordiques' equipment and invited him to speak. In front of the Colisée crowd, Gagnon imitated first Aubut, then the Nordiques' coach, Michel Bergeron.

During the preceding winter both the Canadiens and the Nordiques, then in fierce competition, had poured out veritable reservoirs of charm to win the support of Olympic medallists Gaëtan Boucher and Sylvie Bernier. In getting Gagnon, a star of the first magnitude, Aubut had scored important points. Gagnon's celebrity, his sometimes biting humour, his disarming politeness made him a major coup for a hockey club wanting to give itself a winning image. By inviting him to his tournament, Lafleur was thumbing his nose at the Canadiens organization. He was putting together a huge event in the world of sport, and it was one to which the Canadiens were not invited. At least, not officially. He had invited a few players with whom he had remained friendly, but of course no one from management.

Lafleur and Tremblay worked on their list until about nine, then relaxed in the living room to watch the hockey game. Lafleur had finally let himself be convinced to watch this Stanley Cup final being televised from the Northlands Coliseum in Edmonton. Right from the beginning, listening to the national anthems and watching the players stand at attention on the ice, he realized that he was having an attack of nerves almost as violent and sensuous as if he himself were about to play. He was well aware that he would not be able to watch indifferently, and that all sorts of disturbing memories were about to be stirred up. But as soon as the game began, he focused on the players—their moves, their tactics, their mistakes—with a closeness of attention he had not had for a long time.

The Oilers were clearly superior to the Boston Bruins. Much of this difference was due to the Oilers' Wayne Gretzky, who would once more win the Conn Smythe trophy for his extraordinary performance during the series: 43 points, including 31 assists, in 19 games. Ten years earlier it had been he, Guy Lafleur, who had won all the trophies—the Art Ross, the Conn Smythe, the Lester B. Pearson, as well as the Molson trophies, the Stanley Cup and innumerable other honours. Then he had been the best in the NHL, the strongest, number one. Now it was Gretzky's turn. Guy watched him play, not without a certain sadness. But he couldn't help admiring this twenty-seven-year-old's skill. He was generous, he made things happen, he was the one pulling the strings. He was now the best, the idol of the young, the electrifying number 99, the famous and well-loved Wonder Boy. How lucky the Oilers were to have Gretzky to set up their plays and make the passes!

In the middle of the second period, Lafleur turned to Tremblay and said:

"You know, Kid, the more I watch them play, the more I think I could play just as well. Apart from Gretzky, of course, and two or three others."

For three years he had laboured to banish all thought of making a comeback from his mind, but the idea wouldn't go away. The Kid, who knew that, wanted to say, "If you want to play, Flower, just let people know." But he'd said things like that before and, every time, Lafleur had got angry.

But, just the same, Lafleur's words had not fallen on deaf ears.

The tournament was a success: good weather, good spirits, good show. Lafleur noticed that he still aroused the interest of the media, and that the hockey world held him in great respect. He also realized that, once again, he had nothing to look forward to; he had his past, his good memories, but no plans for the future.

A few days later, Wayne Gretzky married a voluptuous California beauty, Janet Jones. For days, the newspapers and television doted on this royal marriage. A week later, Tom Lapointe, a reporter for *Le Journal de Montréal*, published an incredible scoop: Wayne Gretzky had been sold by the Edmonton Oilers to the Los Angeles Kings for $15 million. Overnight, the continental geography and economy of hockey had been turned upside down. A new era had commenced.

● ● ●

That summer, Lafleur taught stickhandling and playmaking for an obscure travelling hockey school. He enjoyed it. He had always liked the company of young people, their enthusiasm, their energy, their craziness. Almost every time, moreover, he would get caught up in the game, and the course would finish with a real match. A good teacher, he knew how to spot talent and liked to make the young players work. But when he was back in his real life again, without skates, he couldn't help thinking that he was not flying very high. The tournament had been a success, and for a few days there had been a lot of talk about him. Then Gretzky's marriage and the trade had eclipsed everything, and Lafleur had returned to the shadows.

About a week after the famous Oilers–Kings transaction, it was learned that the owner of the Kings, Bruce McNall, wanting to showcase his star appropriately, had made an offer for Mike Bossy. Bossy, considered by some a successor to Maurice Richard, had desperately tried to get himself drafted by the Canadiens in 1977. He went on to make an illustrious career with the New York Islanders, where he had had nine fifty-goal seasons. But because of excruciating back pain, he had retired in the spring of 1987. The press and the hockey world were amazed that someone was trying to take on a player who, by his own admission, was no longer capable of playing well.

Every morning, in his small office at Sportstar, Yves Tremblay read the sports pages. And gradually "the idea" took shape in his mind. At that time, he had another project he had started work on with Lafleur, a trivia game called "Prodigies of Sport" that he wanted to market using the name and personality of Guy Lafleur.

On August 11, a Thursday, Lafleur had a photo session at the studio of Denis Brodeur, a well-known sports photographer. Posters were being prepared for an opening promotion campaign for "Prodigies of Sport." At noon, before the session, Lafleur and Tremblay met at a restaurant called La Dora on Sherbrooke in Montreal's east end. Tremblay was obsessed and excited by his new idea. But the only thing that seemed to interest Lafleur was his Mont Tremblant house, where landscaping, stump-removal and drainage operations had now begun. It was not until the end of the meal that Tremblay could begin to play his cards.

"If Bossy can make a comeback, surely you can too."

To which Lafleur, visibly sad, replied:

"There's no question of that, Kid. It's certain that I could, but they don't want me. I tried, as you know. It's all over."

"You could try again. Things have changed."

"I told you, no. My head is elsewhere now. I'm not really interested any more."

After the photo session, Lafleur left for Mont Tremblant. Yves Tremblay went back to his place, to the Iberville apartments, where Lafleur used to live. He watched the sun set behind Mount Royal and made the decision to act on his own. The next day at noon he called Los Angeles and asked to speak to Bruce McNall, the multi-millionaire Kings owner. McNall was not yet at his office. Tremblay explained himself:

"I'm calling on behalf of Guy Lafleur. He wants to play hockey again."

Tremblay was taken seriously. He was told that he would certainly be called back. Tremblay hung up and called Lafleur at Mont Tremblant. Guy and Lise were having their lunch. Tremblay told him that he'd called Bruce McNall and offered him his services.

"My services?" Lafleur asked.

"Not mine, Guy."

"Have you lost your mind or what?"

But Tremblay could tell that Lafleur was very excited.

"The guy I talked to told me that they'd call me back today. What should I tell them?"

"Ask to speak to Rogie Vachon. He's the managing director. But I don't think we have much of a chance with him. He's a close friend of Serge Savard's."

Then Guy took a few moments to talk with Lise. Tremblay could not hear what they were saying, but he supposed, knowing Lise, that she must be pushing Guy to accept. She had always been very important to Guy, and even more so since his retirement. He always ended up having his way, as with the house in the Laurentians that Lise didn't want, but just the same Guy consulted her on everything. She had always been in favour of his playing again.

After a few minutes, Lafleur came back to the telephone and told the Kid he'd meet him at the Sainmartin about eight o'clock.

Meanwhile, Rogie Vachon, the general manager of the Kings, called Tremblay again at Sportstar. Vachon had been the Canadiens' goaltender for five years, from 1966 to 1971, and had gone on to play in Los Angeles, Detroit and Boston before becoming part of the Los Angeles organization. Lafleur hadn't often met him, but he held him in great respect. For reasons he didn't understand, he'd always had a hard time beating Vachon. When Lafleur had skated up to him, Vachon had almost always been able to distract him. Lafleur had the impression that he could anticipate his moves.

When he called Tremblay, the former Canadiens goalie wanted first of all to know whether Lafleur was in good shape.

"Better than good," Tremblay replied.

"He hasn't got too fat?"

"Believe it or not, he's six pounds under his normal weight."

Most players, especially the large, husky ones, gain a lot of weight as soon as they stop playing. Guy Lafleur, thanks to the numerous games he'd played with the Petro-Canada team, but also because of his exceptional metabolism, had never needed to watch the scales.

Vachon told the Kid that he'd consult his staff and call him back that day.

"Okay," Tremblay said, "but don't talk about this to anyone outside your organization."

"Don't worry about that. I'll call you back."

At nine in the evening Tremblay was still in his office. He'd had no news from Vachon and it seemed obvious that he wouldn't. It was six in Los Angeles, the offices had closed there, too. Just in case, he left the number of the Sainmartin on Vachon's answering machine and went to meet Lafleur.

He found him sitting at one of the tables near the big windows looking out over the Metropolitain highway. No landscape in Montreal was as similar to Los Angeles as the one you saw from the Sainmartin's windows. But the atmosphere there is rustic, barnboard, soft, filtered light, toned-down music. Lafleur and the Kid were at ease there, practically part of the family. In the entrance was a big photo of Guy Lafleur with the owners, two sturdy garage-owners.

Lafleur began by thanking Tremblay for giving him the

kick he'd needed. He was now completely determined to do everything possible to come back. Together they decided that if Rogie didn't respond, they'd look elsewhere first thing in the morning. Los Angeles would certainly be agreeable, though—the climate, the ambience, a whole new world to discover! For all NHL hockey players, the land of the Kings was also that of Hollywood, of luxury, of beauty. Moreover, there was Gretzky.

However, it seemed that Vachon and McNall were in no hurry to reply. They must have contacted Savard and, once again, he must have told them that Lafleur would just complicate their lives.

"Lemaire played with him for the Petro-Canada old-timers and said he was done. Guy Lafleur, the great Guy Lafleur, is no longer." That's what Savard must have said to Rogie.

Lafleur and Tremblay prepared their campaign carefully. New York first. New York, the Big Apple, would be exciting, too. The Rangers also had Michel Bergeron as coach, and Bergeron liked Lafleur. He never missed a chance to say so to anyone who would listen. He had never hidden the fact that he would prefer to work with experienced players than rookies. New York also had Lafleur's friend Chris Nilan, formerly of the Canadiens. And Marcel Dionne, who was within a few days of the same age as Guy Lafleur. What a pleasure it would be to find himself playing with Dionne again, almost a quarter century after the Pee Wee tournaments in Quebec.

The Kid took out his briefcase, his address book, and sketched out on paper their plan of attack, while Lafleur ordered a second bottle of wine.

So, if Los Angeles didn't respond they would call New York. The general manager there, Phil Esposito, a former star player (five fifty-goal seasons) had played until he was over forty years old, and in his last year in the NHL had scored thirty-nine goals for the New York Rangers. If anyone on earth could understand that Guy Lafleur wanted to make a comeback, and that he was capable of it, it would be Phil Esposito.

And if New York wasn't interested, they would contact the Detroit Red Wings, where Jacques Demers, a fellow Québecois, was coach. At Pittsburgh they would call Tony Esposito, Phil's brother; Mario Lemieux, the Penguins' centre, had often declared his great desire to play with Guy Lafleur.

Saturday and Sunday, August 13 and 14, Lafleur stayed at Mont Tremblant. But, once more compelled by his dreams, he had practically abandoned his work on the property.

Monday the 15th, at eight-thirty in the morning, Yves Tremblay called Michel Bergeron at his house in Rye, a suburb north of New York City. Bergeron instantly rose to the bait.

"Give me Guy. I want to talk to him."

"He's up north, at Mont Tremblant."

"Listen. I'm really interested in what you're proposing. Do you hear me?"

"But of course, Bergie, I hear you!"

"Have you been in touch with any other organizations?"

"Vaguely. But this morning, you're the first on our list."

"Good. Give me until three this afternoon to consult my people."

Since his days with the Nordiques, Bergeron often saw Jean-Yves Doyon, Guy's great friend. Doyon had now become the manager of Le Paddock restaurant, a few steps from the Quebec Colisée. Every time they saw each other, Bergeron would ask after Lafleur. But Lafleur had been under contract to the Canadiens, and when he finally became free Marcel Aubut, the Nordiques' president, did not seem interested.

Later, in 1987–88, Bergeron was in charge of the Rangers. Halfway through the season, when six players on his team were hurt, Richard Morency of radio station CKAC had talked to him about Lafleur several times and suggested Bergeron approach him.

"I'm telling you, Bergie, Lafleur is far from finished."

Bergeron had laughed. Not because he really believed Lafleur was finished, but because he thought Lafleur himself believed it and wouldn't want to play again. It was up to Lafleur to know what he wanted and decide his own future. Bergeron had said that you don't get anywhere by disturbing someone when they're asleep.

"If Lafleur wants to play," he said, "he'll wake up by himself."

Now Lafleur had clearly woken up and was saying that he wanted to play.

"I'll speak to Phil Esposito and our money man, Joe Bokino, then I'll call you back."

"Okay. Not a word to anyone."

"Not a word."

Towards eleven o'clock that same Monday morning, just after Lafleur had come into Tremblay's office, the telephone rang. It was a reporter from the *Los Angeles Times* wanting to ask about the rumour that Guy Lafleur was getting ready to make a comeback. Tremblay, totally stupefied, found nothing better to say than that he had someone on the other line, which he said in order to give himself time to think. But even after that he couldn't find anything to say to the *Times* reporter.

"Who told you that?"

"I can't say. I promised."

"In that case, I can't say anything either."

The reporter ended up admitting that he had been informed by someone from the Los Angeles Kings organization.

"McNall?"

"No."

"Vachon?"

"No."

Tremblay finally figured out that it was probably Vachon's secretary, the same one who, apparently, had told *Journal de Montréal* reporter Tom Lapointe about Wayne Gretzky's sale to the Kings.

Finally, Tremblay admitted to the reporter, "Yes, it's true. Guy Lafleur wants to play again."

"In Los Angeles?"

"If the Kings want him, perhaps. But some other clubs have already let us know that they are interested."

Lafleur had grasped the essence of the situation. As soon as the Kid hung up, Lafleur said, "We can't let the news be brought out by someone from Los Angeles. We have to keep control of the scoop."

Guy Lafleur was well versed in the sports media, their practices and their ethics. He therefore knew that the Quebec press would not be too happy to learn that he was getting ready to come back from a Los Angeles daily. While he and the Kid tried to put together a plan, the telephone rang again. It was Michel Bergeron.

"We'll meet you Thursday, August 18, at ten in the morning, at the South Gate Hotel in Manhattan, right opposite the Garden."

In mid-afternoon Rogie Vachon finally called to say that he and McNall had thought things over and that they weren't interested in having Lafleur with their team.

"You don't think very fast," the Kid said sarcastically. "I thought you were supposed to call me Friday afternoon."

"I couldn't, I'm sorry."

"Aside from that, you might have at least respected our confidentiality agreement."

Vachon seemed truly amazed.

"If there was a leak, it had nothing to do with me. I swear it."

"It's not serious. Forget it. In any case, we're already involved elsewhere."

"Where?"

"Guess."

The Kid hung up.

They were still wondering to whom to entrust their scoop when Réjean Tremblay from *La Presse* telephoned. He had doubtless been informed by his *Los Angeles Times* colleague, trying to confirm the rumours. Once again the Kid was taken by surprise.

"I don't have time to talk to you, Réjean. I'll call you back."

And he hung up.

"Call him back," Lafleur said immediately. "He's the one we should tell."

Réjean Tremblay, a prolific and intelligent writer who was well-respected in sports circles, had, in Lafleur's eyes, a very important attribute. Unlike most Montreal journalists, he was not affiliated with Molstar, the Molson Breweries' promotion company. Molstar was in charge of media coverage for hockey games and was responsible, in one way or another, for getting the majority of Montreal sports journalists work as commentators. Tremblay was a close friend of Marcel Aubut, the Nordiques' owner. By choosing Tremblay, Lafleur was sending a derisive message to the Canadiens organization and showing himself more obviously than ever to be a member of the Nordiques' network. In addition, he knew that Réjean would do his job well.

Fifteen minutes later, Réjean Tremblay was at Yves Tremblay's office, accompanied by a French film producer who was working for the television series "He Shoots, He Scores," for which Réjean Tremblay was one of the writers. They told Tremblay the whole story.

The next day, the news of Guy Lafleur's comeback came out in *La Presse* at the same time as in the *Los Angeles Times*. It was Tuesday, August 16. All the radio stations in Canada and the United States were picking up the story, and in Quebec they talked about nothing else.

When the Kid showed up at his office at about nine o'clock, television, radio and newspaper reporters were there with their pens, their microphones, their lights, their notebooks. They wanted to talk to Lafleur.

"Guy? He's gone to Abitibi with his hockey school. He won't be here until the end of the day tomorrow."

That evening, the Kid was seen on all the news shows. He was heard over the radio. He was quoted everywhere. He confirmed the rumour of Guy Lafleur's comeback. But he didn't talk about New York. He was very evasive.

"We've had two or three proposals which we'll take the necessary time to consider."

But the next morning, *Le Journal de Montréal*, doubtless eager to take revenge for the fact that *La Presse* had been favoured with the scoop, published the big page-one headline: "Los Angeles Says No to Lafleur." In addition to being humiliating, this threatened to ruin the carefully planned strategy that Lafleur and the Kid had set in motion.

During the morning the Red Wings called to say that they didn't need a right-winger for their line-up. Jacques Demers even insinuated that he didn't really believe Lafleur could play well again.

Undaunted, Tremblay wanted to get in touch with Tony Esposito, the coach of the Pittsburgh Penguins. In twenty-four hours, the New York Rangers would be making them an offer, and they would be crazy to negotiate with no alternative. Everyone now knew that Los Angeles had said no. Probably reporters were already calling all the NHL teams, one after the other, and it would be known the next morning that Detroit had also refused. If Lafleur wanted to have negotiating leverage with the Rangers, he should have more than one team interested. But Tony Esposito was impossible to find. The Kid called the mother of Mario Lemieux, the Penguins' star player.

"Mario? He's playing golf."

"Where?"

"At Joliette."

Tremblay is a maestro of the telephone. Ten minutes later, he had contacted Lemieux at the eighth hole. Mario knew where Tony Esposito could be found.

By the end of the afternoon, Tremblay finally had him on the phone. But Tony didn't really seem interested.

"Guy Lafleur? How much?"

"Listen, Tony. I can't just discuss that over the telephone. Are you interested, yes or no?"

"You have to give us time to think."

"Okay. Think."

They took the eight o'clock plane for New York; it was their only hope. If they could not reach agreement with the Rangers organization, they would come back empty-handed. Tremblay was well aware that he had led Lafleur into an adventure that might end badly and from which he might emerge bitter and demoralized.

"I don't care," Lafleur said when Tremblay talked to him about this possibility. "I really don't care. And don't worry about it. I'm doing this first and foremost to make things clear in my own mind. At least, afterwards, I'll know where I stand."

At eleven o'clock they met Michel Bergeron, Phil Esposito and Joe Bokino, the New York Rangers' vice-president of finance. Aside from them, the South Gate Hotel restaurant was empty. It was cool and dark, a pleasant contrast to the sweltering heat outdoors.

Phil Esposito was a controversial character. He liked to provoke, to shock, to stir things up. The preceding winter, television reporter Anne-Marie Dussault had gone to New York with a team from the program "Le Point" to do a documentary on Michel Bergeron. Anne-Marie was perfectly bilingual, but unfamiliar with the world and language of hockey. While interviewing Phil, she asked him several times to clarify what he was saying.

"What's that? You don't understand English? Where do you think you are? This is North America, not France. Why do you persist, in Quebec, in refusing to speak English like everyone else?"

With this one outburst he'd made himself some firm enemies in Quebec, and for a little while he could boast of being the man the Québecois most loved to hate. But he didn't really care. It had all been just a game. Esposito was a natural leader and a born troublemaker, a man whose candour was equal to any test and who never let himself be dominated by anyone. Lafleur liked him very much. He had often played against him in the days when, with Bobby Orr, Phil Esposito was the star of the Boston Bruins. He respected Esposito, and he knew that the respect was mutual.

"We'll start working on a contract. You'll come to our

training camp. You'll prove yourself. Afterwards, when we've seen what you're made of, we'll talk again."

• • •

That afternoon, Lafleur and Tremblay visited the Rangers' facilities in Rye, a pleasant and well-to-do suburb just north of Manhattan where almost all the players and members of the Rangers organization lived.

Of course Lafleur found this all very exciting. Worrying, too. He had three weeks to get into condition before the Rangers' training camp which, by good fortune, would be held this year at Trois-Rivières, where coach Michel Bergeron had known his first successes. While driving Lafleur back to the airport, Bergeron advised Lafleur to get to work right away.

"You have to get your stamina and your skating back. So skate, skate, skate. But there's something else. Even though, as I can see, you haven't put on an ounce of fat since you stopped playing, your muscles are surely not as firm as they were. Don't forget, you haven't taken a bodycheck for four years. You'll have to make yourself a new coat of armour. And fast!"

Lafleur said nothing. Day-dreaming, he was looking beyond the tangle of highways to the lights of Manhattan. He desperately wanted what the city could give him, and the desire he could hardly contain was making him deliriously happy. He hadn't felt like this for four years. He recognized it as what he'd missed the most—the desire and appetite to play, and to be alive.

"I don't know if you've followed things closely," Bergeron continued, "but in the last four years the players have become a lot bigger. If you're not ready, you could be in for quite a surprise."

"I'll be ready, Bergie, don't worry."

Back in Montreal, Guy and the Kid went to the Bocca d'Oro on Rue Saint-Mathieu, to take stock and collect themselves. Lafleur phoned Lise, and told her that the trip had been a success. He talked to her particularly about the trip to Rye with Michel Bergeron, how impressed he'd been by the pleasant suburb, with the sea at its doorstep, where the Rangers' players lived, a forty-five-minute drive north of Manhattan. He was so excited that he was already making plans, as though everything had been decided and signed. Now it was more than just the hockey that he wanted; it was also the whole way of life that comes with the game, and the New York lifestyle, Rye, Manhattan, Broadway.

Nonetheless, he asked himself when, where and how he would get that armour Bergeron had talked about. They were having a drink when journalist Réjean Tremblay joined them at the table. He was full of questions, but he also brought an answer.

"You should call George Cherry, the boxing trainer. He works with the Hilton brothers. He might be able to help you."

"Flower, I think that's the best idea we've heard in a long time."

"You're right. Réjean, I think you've just come up with a damned good idea!"

The next morning Lafleur was at the Saint Vincent de Paul arena where he took part in the practice session of the Laval junior team. Ten seconds after he'd joined in the scrimmage, he was convinced that he was not only more experienced, but also much stronger and more creative than all these players twenty years younger than he. It was obvious to everyone watching. But it was his speed that was even more amazing. He skated better than anyone else and, coming and going, outmanoeuvered them all.

In the afternoon, Tremblay came to let him know that he'd arranged for him to work with George Cherry.

"He's expecting you tomorrow morning at nine."

"But tomorrow is Saturday."

"There aren't any days off in your program."

George Cherry was a short, compact man, nervous and muscular, tough as nails. For Lafleur he had prepared an hour and a half of intensive training. It's said that a boxer's training is the most demanding and difficult of all, both physically and mentally. A boxer is a machine for giving and absorbing blows. His land is that of pain and blind, cold hate. He should become a veritable robot, insensitive and pitiless.

Tremblay had prepared a cassette of the soundtrack from *Rocky* for Lafleur, and Lafleur worked out to the sound of this inspirational music. He had recently gone back to see *Rocky III*, the film in which the fallen champion, spoiled by success too easily obtained, makes a painful comeback and gets back his title and his golden belt. A wonderful challenge. But it was hard, hard. For hours, Lafleur hit, danced, always out of breath and at the limit of his strength.

The intensive training went on for three weeks. In the morning he ate lightly (orange juice, coffee, toast) at Labelle, a small restaurant near the Sportstar office. Then he went to George Cherry's place to submit to his daily torture. At about ten o'clock, when he was in the midst of that intoxication brought on by intense physical effort, the journalists would arrive. Every day, without exception, there were some who came to witness his training. They found him streaming with sweat, a faint smile on his lips. Once more he was the centre of attention. Once more he was truly alive.

In Montreal, Guy Lafleur's comeback was one of the great spectacles of the eighties, one to rival the most imaginative pieces of performance art from the most trendy, experimental theatre people. In addition, the Lafleur "happening" had intrigue, suspense, a moral, a fascinating mythology and, of course, a great hero.

One morning during breakfast, two weeks after the beginning of his training regime, Lafleur unexpectedly said, "I wonder if I've done the right thing." On that morning he doubted the success of his undertaking. But not for a second did he hesitate, not for a second did he consider giving up. No more than when he was twelve or thirteen years old, training alone in Thurso, wearing the heavy, steel-filled boots his father had made him. But then he'd had no choice. He had been caught up in a dream he could not resist. That had been the real source of his genius, his real wealth, his real gift from God, his vocation.

But how could he, at thirty-seven, rediscover that intensity, that ardour, that motivation?

There have been many books and movies about the downfall of the successful and satisfied athlete. There lies the ultimate moral of *Rocky III*. Rocky is rich and famous, a world champion, but he finds he is much more vulnerable than he was in the original *Rocky*, when he was a pathetic hopeful, without money or experience. Now his challenger, the terrible Clubber Lang, played by Mr T, has all the hunger and rage to win. He wants not only to become the champion, but also to win and possess, to realize his dreams, to have a car, a house, a mistress . . . Without this desire to win, everything becomes more difficult, more uncertain.

In 1986, for example, when Boris Becker won Wimbledon for the second straight year, his coach, Günther Bosch, began to worry. It was too much, too fast. Boris was only eighteen years old and he had just beaten Ivan Lendl (6–4, 6–3, 7–5), the best tennis player in the world. Had he not climbed too high, too quickly, too easily?

Bosch was afraid his protégé would lose his intensity and his hunger, the raging desire and need to win at all costs that motivates an athlete to be the best. Five months later, in New York, Boris Becker lost to Lendl (4–6, 4–6, 4–6). And three weeks after that, he was eliminated by Wally Masur in the Australian Open in Melbourne. That evening, Bosch talked about his fears. Everything had been too easy.

A few days later, Becker announced to Bosch that he had found a solution to his problem. "I'm dismissing you, that's it." He no longer wanted to be the protégé, always under the watchful eye of this intelligent, devoted and omnipresent coach. He had decided that henceforth he would stop having everything decided for him, everything taken care of; he would no longer have a chauffeur, or let other people do his talking for him; he would never again lead the easy life, because easiness is dangerous and boring, and boredom is the opposite of desire and hunger. "I'm the boss. From now on I do what I want." The young Becker, in dismissing his beloved coach, had voluntarily put himself in danger.

He then undertook to get himself back to the top, on his own.

The challenge facing Lafleur with the Rangers was of a totally different nature. First, Lafleur was almost twice Boris Becker's age. There could be no question of his regaining his position as the leading NHL scorer and getting thirty minutes of ice time every game, as he had in the seventies. In fact, Guy Lafleur had never been a star according to the record books. Even when he was at his peak, he had established few durable records. Many players (Mike Bossy, Bryan Trottier, Wayne Gretzky, Bobby Clarke, Bobby Orr, Maurice Richard and many others, even some obscure players with mediocre clubs) held as many if not more records than he. Lafleur's greatness was not to be measured by his numbers but by his art, his style, his flair. A Lafleur goal was always an event. An assist by Lafleur in an insignificant game was always page-one news. A Lafleur statement was repeated everywhere for days.

In taking on Lafleur, Esposito and Bokino were hoping to get the Rangers out of the limbo in which they had long been stranded. In fact, they had become one of the least exciting teams in the NHL. With Lafleur in their ranks, they would certainly get themselves talked about, and would once more be part of what was happening in the league. It wouldn't necessarily lead them to the Stanley Cup (which they hadn't won since 1939), but they would at least get some attention, an audience, some intensity.

Of course, Lafleur got talked about even more than the Rangers. The Trois-Rivières Colisée where they held their training camp at the beginning of September was besieged by the North American sporting press. Lafleur's performances soon convinced everyone, including Esposito and Bokino.

Less than an hour before the game that was to mark the camp's closing, Esposito had Lafleur called to his small office in the Colisée. Bokino and Jack Diller, the vice-president of the Rangers and of Madison Square Garden, were there, and welcomed Lafleur with open arms.

They wanted him to sign the contract they had prepared right away. Lafleur refused categorically.

"I don't want to sign anything without Georges Guilbeault being here. I don't even want to see your contract."

"If you don't sign, you don't play this evening," Jack Diller then said to him.

"That's fine with me," Lafleur said. "I won't play."

The Rangers' managers were staggered. Until then, they had believed that Lafleur would accept almost any conditions, that he was almost ready to pay for the privilege of playing. After all, it was he who had approached them and asked them for the chance to play.

But it wasn't just for the glory and the chance to play that Lafleur had trained so hard for three weeks, and was risking this dangerous and stressful comeback. His main objective was to rid himself of a doubt that had haunted him for three years. He was obsessed by the idea that he had allowed his retirement to be imposed on him, and that he had been both the victim and co-author of a manipulation whose objective had been to push him aside. He wanted finally to understand what had happened in 1984, and to find out if he could still comport himself with honour on an NHL rink. He had no intention of compromising his experience by offering himself at a sale price.

The next day, in Trois-Rivières, they began work on the contract. Georges Guilbeault had come from Sherbrooke to discuss the terms. Lafleur received a good salary, $400,000 a year, and the contract was for two years with an option. That same evening, at the end of the exhibition game, it was officially announced that Guy Lafleur was back in the NHL.

For the sporting press, Lafleur's comeback was the event of the year. In the newspapers, over the radio, all over the country, people were talking about other great comebacks. Jacques Plante had come back, in 1969, after three years away from the rinks and had won the Vezina trophy at the age of thirty-nine. In 1966, "Boom Boom" Geoffrion had come back to play for the New York Rangers after two and a half years of inactivity, and scored nineteen goals. After two years of retirement, Gordie Howe had come back to play for the Houston Astros of the WHA. He was forty-three, and his return lasted nine years, ending in 1980 with the Hartford Whalers. In his last season he had scored fifteen goals and made twenty-six assists. Outside of hockey there was also Pelé, the gifted Brazilian soccer player, one of the century's great stars, who in 1975, after having led his team to the World Cup in the biggest stadiums of America and Europe, signed a three-year contract with the New York Cosmos for several million dollars.

Guy Lafleur was no longer the *Canadien errant*. Now he had become the unpredictable Stranger. Each of his deeds had a special significance. Even if this comeback were later seen as a disaster, it would still hold a lesson, a message: it is necessary to try, to go to the limit; so long as there is life there is hope. Lafleur had become even more important than the athlete he had been. He was an athlete with a moral; he had become a hero.

● ● ●

Once again, Quebec had begun to contemplate the actions and gestures of Guy Lafleur. Poets, athletes, artists, politicians, businessmen, everyone was drawing lessons from Lafleur's experience.

"Lafleur has been unusual in having the courage to go against the trend of his era," Gilles Vigneault pointed out. "Today, there are many players with no particular aspirations, and they stop playing while they're still young. Lafleur has given them the desire to get going, to get to work, to get back into condition. He has invented and set an extraordinary example. In a world where everything is ephemeral, he has chosen to endure. That's the biggest challenge of all."

His great courage was also much discussed. He had been brave enough to take a chance. He knew he was able to play again, but there had been no assurance that anyone would want him. Many people, some of them very important in Lafleur's eyes, had not believed in him. But he had persisted just the same. With humility. Even if New York had refused

him after Los Angeles, Detroit and Pittsburgh, even if all of
America had said that he was finished, it would not have
mattered. For a while he stood alone, but he held on
tight.

Maurice Richard himself wrote that he did not believe
Lafleur could acquit himself honourably on the new NHL
rinks. Jacques Lemaire, who during the preceding months
had played on the same line as Lafleur with the
Petro-Canada team, affirmed that he was finished. Nor did
Mario Tremblay believe that he could come out of
retirement; he had even bet that Lafleur would not last
the season.

A *Journal de Montréal* poll revealed the total incredulity
of the public. "Lafleur is burned-out," people said. "He
won't get far in the new NHL." "He is too old." "He can
never recover his former intensity." "He's going to
be crushed."

Strangely enough, most of the positive statements came
from the young players, those from whom Lafleur thought
he had everything to fear. For the first time in the
seventy-five-year history of the NHL, the average age of
players was under twenty-five. While the population of
Canada and the United States as a whole was ageing at a
terrifying rate, the population of the NHL was growing
younger. Now, according to Mario Lemieux, the most
promising of the young players, they were beginning to
suffer from an overdose of youth; they needed, more than
ever, experienced, veteran players. Lemieux made it very
clear that he was delighted by Lafleur's return.

"It will be good for him and for all of us. Playing either
with or against Guy Lafleur can only be enriching.
Everyone will be better off."

The wise old men of hockey like Paul Dumont or Ti-Paul
Meloche knew that Lafleur was physically capable of
making a successful comeback. This extraordinarily gifted
athlete was obviously still in peak condition, strong, supple
and fast. But could he re-establish his mental conditioning
and, especially, would he be able to deal with the
formidable psychological pressure and the nervous tension?

That was the real challenge; by overcoming the mental hurdles he could show himself to be more than just a great athlete, but a great man.

Questioned daily by the reporters, Lafleur pursued, aloud and publicly, his meditations on the meaning of life, happiness, the passage of time:

"I have a message for young people. I want to tell them to follow things to the end and not to give up."

"Above all, I was so eager to make this comeback because I wanted to rid myself of doubt. It's impossible to live with a heart full of regrets."

"When I see people doubting that I can come back, I tell myself they are the fearful ones and I think—'You don't know me.' Me, I am unpredictable. I have stayed unpredictable. Therein lies my strength."

Life is a hockey game. It has its periods, its intermissions, its penalties. There are winners and there are losers. There are those who never let go, like Guy Lafleur. Now he is in overtime. He can still win.

● ● ●

On June 13, 1988, some time before he began thinking of playing again, Guy Lafleur was inducted into the Hall of Fame. He rented a luxury car to bring to Toronto, at his own expense, all his guests, relatives and friends. The celebration was magnificent, but also a little sad. Lafleur had the sense of being put into his tomb. His elegy was delivered, the high points of his career recounted, his portrait unveiled hanging among those glorious players of the past on the wall of the Pantheon. Onto the wall had been fastened one of his old autographed sticks, the puck from his five-hundredth goal, an old pair of skates, a few relics, a sweater. Thus everything was officially closed for him. Exit Guy Lafleur.

In deciding to make a comeback two months later, he caused a violent disturbance among the archivists and statisticians who had, quite properly, closed the book on him the day of the grand ceremony. He had also aggravated the Canadiens organization. It was customary for a team to give a player a party when he was enthroned in the Hall of

Fame. The Canadiens thus found themselves in the peculiar position of paying tribute to an opponent.

But they had no choice. Ronald Corey, who preferred compromise to confrontation, told himself that this would be a good opportunity to bury the hatchet. Arrangements were even made with the New York Rangers so that they could also honour the great man.

On December 17, 1988, the Rangers were to play against the Canadiens at the Forum. For the first time since November 1984, Lafleur would be on the Forum ice. This would be the perfect time. Alas, a few days before the game he injured his ankle. Thus it was without his uniform or skates, limping a little, that he advanced along the red carpet stretched out to the centre of the rink. But the ceremony was no less colourful and emotional.

When he appeared, greeted by the immense roar of the crowd, he was still wondering what he would do and say. He couldn't help glancing quickly upwards, across the light that floated above the rink, to the Canadiens' box where Savard, Corey and Lemaire must be. No doubt they would be standing up like all the others who were applauding him.

After the usual speeches, Kelly Kisio, the Rangers' captain, came to hand him a Rangers' sweater, number 10. The protocol had provided for Lafleur to say a few words, wave to the crowd, politely receive his applause and then quietly leave the rink through the visitors' gate. Lafleur gave the short speech he had prepared, duly waved to the crowd and gave his thanks. As the spectators began to cheer, he looked once more to the Canadiens' box. Then he began putting on his New York Rangers' sweater. From all over the arena people began to roar. During the brief moment when he was blinded, as he was pulling the sweater over his head, he thought hard about those men—Lemaire, Corey and Savard—who had once so cruelly deprived him of playing time and who had convinced him that he was finished. When his head came out he raised his arms slowly, held them high, then turned towards the Canadiens' box.

The crowd exploded. Then a kind of intoxicating torpor seemed to descend on the Forum, as though time had grown thick, almost stopped. The crowd was screaming and crying. Every head had turned towards the Canadiens' box. Ronald Corey himself had begun to clap, along with Serge Savard and even Jacques Lemaire; they were carried away by the frenzy of the crowd that was cheering "Guy! Guy! Guy!" They must have been a bit uncomfortable, but they could not help admiring the courage of this man, his innate sense of spectacle and event. Once again, he had stolen the spotlight and added to his own legend. They knew, as everyone did that night, that this event would live on as one of the most spectacular moments of the decade. They recognized that from now on they would seem to have acted a bit crazily; they would play the fools in this saga in which Lafleur had appropriated the starring, heroic role.

In carrying off his comeback in such a masterly fashion, Lafleur had in fact provided irrefutable proof that he had been badly used and badly treated by the Canadiens organization. Consequently the theory that held that he had been forced into retirement gained credence. For two months he'd been seen setting up beautiful plays in every game, executing spectacular rushes, bringing crowds all across the continent to their feet. He had won. He was happy, as were Lise and the children.

The family had never spent so much time together. They would go to see Broadway shows, shop on Fifth Avenue, stroll along the nearby seashore or in Central Park; they visited the World Trade Center and the Sea Air Space Museum. Everything was new and fascinating. It was a new beginning.

In Montreal, Lafleur had hardly ever gone out. The adoration of his public had become too stifling. He felt as though he might implode at any moment. Then, after he retired, he became antisocial and taciturn. In New York, he felt as though he was being reborn. Suddenly he was interested in everything; he talked about buying a boat, wanted to study Italian, had even started sharing the cooking with Lise. He sometimes had the impression that he had just come back to earth after a long space voyage, and that he was finally beginning to make himself a life as a real human being. He hadn't just started playing hockey again, he had also started to live again.

He learned to enjoy and feel at home in the New York jungle as much as in the forest of his childhood. In one as in the other, he knew how to orient himself, how to get along, how to relax. When friends came to visit from Quebec, he would talk about and show them the new and fascinating country he now possessed. During the fourteen seasons he had spent in the NHL, he had come regularly to New York, but he had never known much about it. Although they travel endlessly through the big cities in North America, hockey players usually confine their explorations to one or two hotels and the arena where they play.

For two months he lived in a motel for businessmen in Armonk, north of Manhattan. It was a replay of the year of his arrival in Montreal, when he had found himself alone, far from his loved ones. But this time, instead of feeling lost, he had the euphoric feeling of having discovered a new world where everything was marvellous and magical. He had agreed with Lise that he would take two months to find a house. He spent his free time travelling the area— Armonk, Rye, Westchester, Eastchester, Mamaroneck, Harrison—those handsome suburban villages just north of the Bronx, between salt water and fresh, between the Hudson River and the jagged and spectacular Atlantic coast.

At the beginning of December, Lise and the children came to live with him in the big house he had rented in Rye; it was in the heart of white America, opulent and happy, everything neat and trim, the American Dream. They had completely transformed the scenery and the script of their dreams. The house in the Laurentians had now been pushed far into the background. What they wanted now, what they were desperately hoping for, was that Guy would have a good season, and that the Rangers would renew his contract in a way that made him part of their organization. Then he would apply for his green card and they would establish themselves, perhaps permanently, in the United States. Lafleur was confident; he had played well. At the beginning of the regular season, October 16, 1988, he had scored his first NHL goal since October 25, 1984. Despite the injury to his ankle in December, he was among the leading scorers that season.

On the ice, there were some things he had been struck by. First of all, the players were indeed much younger and bigger than before. The pace was also quicker. There was more hooking, sticks were often raised, but, everything considered, the game was less violent. The time of the furious madmen and fighters was over.

But the most significant changes he noticed were in himself: his approach to the game, his way of being on the ice and in the locker room, his attitude—all these were new and different. His position and his role within the team had changed. Bergeron had repeated to him that he was counting on him to create a strong and exciting team spirit.

During those last years with the Canadiens, when everything was going so badly for him, he had been asked to assume the role of veteran, and he had bluntly refused. No doubt because at the time he had not wanted to admit that he had aged and that his most useful role was other than on the firing line. Now he saw things in a totally different way. This season now beginning might be his last. He knew it, and he often thought about it—with a dash of nostalgia, of course, but also with great serenity and a sort of joyous understanding.

"This time, when it's over, it will be over once and for all," he said. "I'll never play hockey again. I realized, with the Petro-Canada team, that hockey is something I can't play halfway or as an amateur. Jacques Lemaire wasn't wrong when he said I played sloppily. But what he couldn't understand was that I wasn't interested in that little game. When I play hockey, real hockey, it's my whole life. When I don't play any more, my life will be something else."

He had just made an extraordinary discovery. Imagine!

You think you're through, your obituary has been written by all the specialists. People say, "You're finished, my friend. Hang up your skates and accept it." Some are even happy about it, others weep a little. Everyone says their farewell. Everyone tells you, "We've had some good times together, but it's over now. Go. We won't soon forget you." And you're at the bottom of the abyss, all alone. People won't even look at you any more. The lights are turned off and everyone goes home.

Suddenly, looking somewhere deep down inside yourself, what do you discover but a new life, fresh and vibrant, impatient to be born. It's infinitely more welcome than a billion dollars. And that is what Guy Lafleur, he who probably didn't believe in it any more than anyone else, discovered, by chance, in the summer of 1988. It was nothing less than a new beginning. He intended to use it wisely.

Guy and Lise had once more begun to look around for a house to buy. They would take the Boston Post Road, one of the oldest highways in the United States, and drive through the attractive countryside for hours. They both had very conservative taste in houses. They liked them old and surrounded by trees, in grey stone or red brick, with ivy and a slate roof. Their new life together had brought them much closer and, as they did years ago, they would talk to each other for hours.

Lafleur had never felt so free in all his life. The New York reporters were not so curious and persistent as those in Montreal. They followed the Rangers from a distance and were somewhat indifferent, thinking only of what happened on the ice. Everything else—the players' private lives, conflicts with the organization or with their wives—seemed of no interest. They hardly ever came to see what was happening in the dressing room, never questioned the politics of the organization or the strategies of the coach. Lafleur found a freedom and pleasure in living that he'd never experienced. His only remaining desire was to have a position in the organization. Phil Esposito couldn't guarantee anything, but Guy had grounds to be hopeful.

On February 4, 1989, for the first time since November 24, 1984, Guy Lafleur played at the Montreal Forum. For the first time in his life, in this place he had so loved and where he had experienced, over thirteen years, his greatest moments of glory, he had become the enemy. He changed in the visitors' dressing room on the east side of the Forum, a place where he had hardly ever set foot. As usual, he put on his uniform and went onto the ice to warm up. When his teammates arrived, a bit later—Nilan, Rochefort, Deblois, Dionne—they found him deep in the dreams of the solitary skater. He seemed down. They talked to him, but he hardly responded.

In the dressing room, when Chris Nilan asked if he felt nervous, Lafleur of course said that he did not. Lafleur always denied fear at the moment he felt it. But fear takes over, like a poison. It is omnipresent—in the body, in the thoughts and even in the nerves and muscles. If you don't want to think about it, you have to think about nothing. You have to hide in that kind of numbness in which Lafleur had now buried himself.

As always, as soon as he got onto the ice, his attack of nerves dissipated. He once more heard that familiar and unforgettable voice, the intoxicating voice of the Montreal fans, the best fans in the world of hockey. They had begun to chant his name. The magic still worked. Montreal had not forgotten Guy Lafleur.

While the American national anthem was being sung, Lafleur heard his heart beating. He struggled for the words of the Lord's Prayer and Hail Mary. Opposite him, on the other side of the rink, the Canadiens were standing with their helmets under their arms, their sticks resting on the ice. Robinson, Carbonneau, Gainey, his former allies, his friends, looked at him furtively. He could also feel the television cameras aimed at him. He imagined that the commentators—Lionel Duval, Richard Garneau, Mario and Gilles Tremblay, Dick Irvin, all of them, English and French, Canadian and American—would be talking about him, about the nervousness he must be feeling. He knew that everywhere, in Quebec homes, people watching television must be wondering how he felt. That familiar feeling of pressure once more descended on him—an intense, stimulating, demanding companion.

The crowd was also nervous. And emotionally torn. With all its heart it wanted Lafleur to play well. But it still didn't want the Canadiens to lose. As things turned out, it got what it wanted. Once more they saw Lafleur at his peak, the unpredictable genius, the Blond Demon, who for long, unforgettable moments had perfect control of the puck, made unheard-of moves, about-faces, incredible rushes, and proved that no one had really replaced him, no one had his grace, his innate sense of theatre, his magic.

Hollywood's best writers could not have written a better script for the evening. The public wanted the Canadiens to win; the Canadiens won. They wanted Lafleur to play a good game; he scored two goals.

Nevertheless, the Rangers weren't doing well. Halfway through the season they were in last place in the Patrick Division. Lafleur, as he had done in Montreal, continued to say what he thought and what he knew. He criticized certain of his teammates for their egotism. Each was playing for himself and trying to score goals, not to make the team win but to build a good point total.

In May, Georges Guilbeault, now Lafleur's agent and negotiator, came to New York to meet Phil Esposito. Esposito had committed some serious blunders, but was still at the helm of the team. On April 1, with only four games left in the regular season, he had fired Michel Bergeron and decided to coach the Rangers himself. It was a monumental mistake! He had lost the last four games and his club had been quickly eliminated from the playoffs.

Despite the ankle injury that had kept him off the ice for three weeks, Lafleur had managed a good season: 18 goals, 27 assists, for a respectable total of 45 points. In February he had even scored a hat trick in a game against Wayne Gretzky and the Los Angeles Kings. Lafleur had eclipsed Gretzky that night, establishing himself right from the beginning of the game as the uncontested master of the ice.

But Guy had done more than just score points. Because it was Guy Lafleur's team, people in the hockey world had talked about the Rangers all year. New Yorkers, who hadn't seen the Stanley Cup since 1939, were excited again. Lafleur was thus within his rights to expect a good contract from the team.

He asked for one or two years more as an active player, then two or more years as a member of the Rangers organization. Knowing that sooner or later he would have to leave the NHL rinks once and for all, he had begun to look for new territory to occupy. And what could be more natural for an ex-hockey player than to work within a team organization? He wasn't necessarily eager to be in public relations. He could more easily see himself working as an adviser regarding the acquisition and training of players. During his retirement, and then with the Rangers, he had discovered that he got great pleasure from working with young players.

Guilbeault's meeting with Esposito was very positive. Esposito was very fond of Lafleur, and considered him a useful player both on the rink and in the dressing room.

But right at the beginning of the summer, there was another revolution in the Rangers organization. Phil Esposito, who had sadly failed in his attempt to set the Rangers on their feet, was fired. Lafleur had no ally among the new bosses. In June they let him know that he was still wanted as a player, for a season or perhaps two, but there was no question of keeping him on as a member of the new organization.

A beautiful dream had just collapsed. He had to begin all over again. He started looking elsewhere, to other teams in the league. He would have to find another house, a school for Martin, a kindergarten for Mark, a new life for Lise, all somewhere else in an unknown city. But Lafleur told himself that the world of hockey was big, and that he'd be able to find a way to make a place for himself somewhere. He believed that this time it wouldn't be as hard.

The future would prove him wrong. Guy Lafleur's next

challenge would be the most serious a celebrated hockey veteran can confront.

• • •

Once again Quebec was witness to a suspenseful drama. During June 1989, hundreds of questions were posed daily in the newspapers and on the radio. As soon as Michel Bergeron was named coach of the Nordiques, replacing Jean Perron, a rumour began to circulate that he would hire the indefatigable Blond Demon. But another rumour had Guy Lafleur going to Los Angeles to play alongside Wayne Gretzky.

Quebec, as in all things, was deeply divided over the fate of its hero. Some thought a return to Quebec would be pure madness. Why expose oneself to the ravages of winter when the sunny Pacific was available? Why deliver oneself to the most voracious media machine in the world when one could take it easy in the land of movie stars and big dollars? There were others, however, who thought that by agreeing to play in Los Angeles, Lafleur was running the risk of having it said of him, forever, that he had been cowardly and satisfied to tag along behind Gretzky, that he had fled the heavy responsibilities he knew would await him in Quebec.

Some gave in to unbridled poetry and compared Lafleur to the spawning salmon who swims upstream through torrents and rivers to find the place of her birth. Only to die there? the others said. Why would Lafleur want to end his days in Quebec?

On July 11, during the Guy Lafleur Golf Tournament for Leucan, a small army of reporters went to the Lachute Golf and Country Club to try to solve the mystery. Everyone was trying, with various degrees of subtlety, to get Bergeron and Lafleur to talk. But they were evasive: Bergeron said that Lafleur was a free man and would make up his mind for himself, and Lafleur preferred to talk about Leucan, about children with cancer, about the research that was being carried out in this area and the hopes for a cure.

Three days after the Lachute tournament, it was learned that Guy Lafleur would be joining the Quebec Nordiques.

The date was July 14, 1989, the two-hundredth anniversary of the storming of the Bastille. Sports columnists were reminded of another very significant date, twenty years ago, June 24, 1969, Saint-Jean-Baptiste Day, when Guy Lafleur had signed with the Quebec Remparts. As in 1969, Guy Lafleur was joining a Quebec team that was in the midst of serious problems. In fact, the Nordiques were in full retreat. A few weeks earlier, the citizens of Quebec City had organized a parody of a Stanley Cup parade, dragging through the streets of the Old Capital a symbolic float on which were perched twenty turkeys.

This time Lafleur's mission was different. In 1969 he had been a great goal-scorer; in 1989, his contribution would have to be at another level. Bergeron and Aubut wanted to revamp the image of the Nordiques, create a good team spirit and, especially, revive Quebec's desire to encourage and support their team. Lafleur would be able to fulfil this mandate without even putting on his skates. In a few days, immediately after it had been announced that he would be part of the Nordiques' line-up, four hundred season tickets were sold at roughly one thousand dollars each, a total equivalent to Lafleur's annual salary. Mission accomplished! But for Lafleur, the most difficult task remained. Now he would have to fulfil the hopes that the public had for him.

After the idyllic season he had spent in New York, he was once more going to experience the enormous pressure of a public that was avid, pressing and demanding. A few days after he'd signed his contract, while strolling along Quebec's Grande-Allée, he had created a real stir on the terraces and in the cafés. People came out to the street to shake his hand, praise him, thank him. The welcome he received was warm, but also excessive and frightening.

In fact, the territory that Lafleur now proposed to reconquer, in the summer of 1989, was infinitely more dangerous than the one he had faced the year before. In New York, all things considered, everything had been very easy. It had been exciting and morale-building, restful as well, and practically without danger. In New York it would have been difficult for him to disappoint. He'd had much to gain and nothing to lose.

In Quebec, just the opposite was true. He was coming back to the place where he'd known his most glorious moments, the most exciting of his career. In this confrontation with himself, or rather with the self he had been, much was at stake; he might not only disappoint, but be disappointed.

An amazing encounter Lafleur had then gave him a better understanding of the adventure on which he had embarked.

It was the end of August. At the time, he was living alone in Quebec, in the Château Bonne-Entente. The children were in Thurso with his parents, and Lise was busy closing the Mont Tremblant chalet and putting the Sanctuaire apartment up for sale. One day, Guy got a call from a woman from Sarrazin House, a nursing home just outside of the city. An important businessman about sixty years old had asked to see Guy Lafleur. Guy went there the same day.

"I just wanted to shake your hand before I died," he said. "I have great admiration for what you're doing. For years I've followed your hockey career. Now, it's your own personal career that interests me. In my opinion, you've carried yourself well. I think you were especially brave to come back to play here. I never thought you'd agree."

"To be honest," said Lafleur, "I had no other choice. They didn't want me in Los Angeles."

"You could have done nothing!"

"I tried that already. I'm incapable of it."

"You are like me."

And the man began to talk about the business projects he'd had to give up: the creation of a giant herd of Charolais cattle in the Nicolet region, the establishment of a mill in the Bois-Francs, the construction of an office building in Quebec and a condominium development near Tampa, Florida. He talked about these projects he would never realize with such intensity and pleasure that Lafleur forgot he was with a man at death's door. They sat down on a wide terrace, facing the river and the sun. For an hour, while having a drink and smoking cigarillos, the man talked about the life he had led, his children, the reversals of fortune he had experienced, some mistakes he had made, the women he had loved. He told how he had played the banjo when he was young, that he had been a good skater and dancer and that he used to enjoy drinking.

His features were drawn, he was frightfully thin, and sometimes his voice faltered. Then he would stop for a moment, to catch his breath and find the right words, before picking up his story. There was something almost childlike about him, especially in his eyes—a sense of wonder, a flame. When all was said and done, life seemed to have been very generous to him; he had lived without holding back and burned the candle at both ends, with no regrets. Roger Barré, Lise's father, had been that way at the end, still immersed in his business and his loves. Alive! And even though he knew everything would soon be over for him, he still believed in his plans, in his ideas, in life.

"Why do you say that it takes courage for me to come back here?"

"You know as well as I that they'll never leave you alone. That's the way we are in Quebec. You must know that. When we love someone, we try to devour him. But the most difficult thing for you is that you'll have to behave perfectly. I hope you're not planning to start playing around on your wife again, or crashing into highway barriers at three in the morning, because here, everyone ends up knowing everything. You won't even need to go to confession. Everything you do, people will know."

"Do you think they'll give me absolution?"

"Of course. But I know how they are. They'll feel obliged to impose a penance on you and teach you a lesson. If I can give you a piece of advice, it's this: mind your own business."

"What do you mean?"

"Do what you really want to do. That way, you can't make a mistake."

"The problem is, I don't always know what I really want to do."

"After a certain age, which is more or less your age, there's no excuse for not knowing that."

Lafleur had thought he would be offering comfort; instead he was getting advice and a lesson about life.

"When you get to the other side," Guy said as he was leaving, "will you help me to skate?"

"I promise."

Two weeks later, as he was on his way to the Colisée for the Nordiques' morning practice, Lafleur heard André Arthur, Quebec radio's compulsive moralist and bigmouth, ridiculing him for having agreed to make a hair-replacement commercial. When Bobby Hull had appeared in an ad for a Toronto wig-maker, the entire Canadian sporting press had made fun of him.

In spite of that, when Yves Tremblay came to tell Lafleur that he was being offered $100,000 and a free hair graft for a commercial that would take one or two days to film, Lafleur accepted right away. First of all, because, according to Guy, you can't just turn down $100,000, unless you're a bit dishonest with yourself. Second, because he wanted the hair replacement. And finally, and most especially, because he knew that he would be doing a favour to Tremblay, who got a share in this kind of advertising deal. Lafleur held Tremblay responsible for the fact that he was playing hockey again, and in his gratitude he forgave him many things. Tremblay was sometimes very pushy, often taking things on without consulting Guy, or making promises that would fall through. But Yves had great heart; he was totally honest and devoted. Most of all, he was there when Lafleur needed him.

Listening to André Arthur's idiocies, Lafleur thought again about the man from Sarrazin House and what he'd told him: that the Québecois would always be wanting to teach him a lesson, and that every one of his words and deeds would be closely examined, chewed up and devoured. And for a while he was seized by an uncontrollable attack of nerves.

This anxiety would not disappear until Guy was on the ice for the Nordiques' practices. He put his whole heart into them and then, when he started to warm up, he would finally relax.

From the beginning of training camp he had understood that things were not going well. The team was terribly weak, poorly balanced, fragile and awkward. Only young Joe Sakic and the veteran Peter Stastny seemed really animated. By the beginning of November it was clear that the season would be, at best, a disaster comparable to that of the year before. Later, when Lafleur, their second leading scorer, left the line-up with another ankle injury, people began to fear the worst for the Nordiques. When Guy started playing again at Christmas, matters were worse and worse.

After the holidays, Guy was hurt again, this time more seriously, requiring a longer recuperation. For a long time he was unable either to worry about the fate of the Nordiques, the laziness of certain players, or the organization's flagrant errors in judgment. His wife was not happy in Quebec City. She didn't know anyone there any more. Even her mother now lived in Montreal. Guy spent a lot of time with Lise, trying to interest her in his plans.

They wanted to buy a house, or have one built. They had even sent for the plans for a small château that he'd seen in an American magazine. Meanwhile, Lafleur had bought a big maple sugar operation at Saint-Augustin with 6,000 maple trees and a 150-seat restaurant, whose management he'd entrusted to his old friend Jean-Yves Doyon.

In spite of his injuries and the setbacks of his team, Lafleur's spirits remained high. He had played well and truly given his best. Everyone said so, and it was true. The season was a disaster but the future was bright.

The Nordiques had to start working right away on rebuilding the team. The job would be long and painful, but fascinating. That was what really interested Guy Lafleur now: working at creating a new hockey team, starting from almost nothing, building it from the ground up.

In coming to Quebec, he had signed a four-year

contract with the Nordiques, stipulating two years as a player and then two more as a member of the organization. In 1990 he discovered that this organization would be facing a truly creative challenge over the next few years, and he decided to be part of it.

What could be better, after being a hero, than to become a creator, an author?

One evening in January, coming home from dinner with some friends, Lafleur left his wife at the Château Bonne-Entente and went to Saint-Augustin, to the maple sugar business. He wanted to be alone, far from anyone, far from everything. He went into his office, lit some candles and started to put his thoughts on paper.

It was very late when he came back to the hotel. When Lise woke up in the morning, he had already left. She found a poem on the refrigerator door. Just as he had in the early days of their love, her husband had shared his thoughts with her:

Candle,
By your light you make us dream
In your glow we lose our cares
Tell me why you don't burn always?
Tell me why we don't always take the time to light
    you?

To shine, you need shadow
You give us thoughts of greatness
When you are here, the truth cannot be hidden
You are the one who sees all, says all
I would love to be like you
Always burning with the flame of truth
Always knowing how to choose
Between the shadow and the light.

Epilogue

IT IS MARCH 30, 1991. The Quebec Nordiques are at the Forum to play the Montreal Canadiens. Even from the depth of the visitors' dressing room, the deafening noise of the crowd can be heard. The Nordiques change silently, waiting for the television producers to let them know everything is ready for the big ceremony.

Usually before a game, especially against the Canadiens, the team is over-excited, nervous and noisy. Some of the players gather around Lafleur, now affectionately known as "the Old Man," "the Patriarch" or even "the Ancestor." Lafleur makes them laugh, reassures them, helps them calm down.

But tonight the players aren't nervous. The season has been a disaster, and it no longer matters if they win or lose. With two games left, the Nordiques are once again deep in the cellar of the NHL. Tonight has been set aside for something other than hockey. In a few minutes, the Blond Demon will, one more time, one last time, find himself before the huge crowd that is now loudly calling for him. The players aren't speaking to Lafleur. It's as though they are giving him time to gather himself before he has to confront the millions of eyes that will soon be focused on him, one more time, one last time, carefully inspecting his face to read his emotions, his thoughts, his future.

They all leave the dressing room together. They all carry their helmets under their arms. Except for Lafleur, of course. Claude Mouton, the master of ceremonies and the official voice of the Montreal Forum, is waiting in the corridor. He waves Lafleur over. He reminds Lafleur, who is only half-listening, how the farewell ceremony will proceed.

"First it will be announced that the Montreal Canadiens wish to recognize the retirement of a great player. Then you'll leap onto the ice. The people will clap and cheer. Let them keep going for a while. Two minutes, perhaps three. Long enough to skate slowly twice round the rink, stopping now and then to wave. Like the other times, Guy. Nothing to worry about. And then Maurice Richard is going to offer you a gift on behalf of the Canadiens. You'll say a few words, whatever you want. And that's it."

When the players appear, the brightly lit Forum is filled with a single cry: "Guy! Guy! Guy!" Lafleur wants it to be over quickly. This kind of thing is certainly agreeable. It is enriching, it adds to your stature, it is something money cannot buy. But at the moment it is happening, you can hardly experience it; it is so violent, so disturbing, so upsetting. There are so many spotlights, you can't see. So many voices, you can't hear. So many emotions, you can't feel.

Nevertheless, he has begun to get used to these big displays and excessive ovations. Twice already, he has been given this kind of grand farewell. The first was on February 15, 1985, a little while after he first retired. What a terribly sad celebration that was! He never said so, but his heart felt as though it were broken. Despite the enormous affection the crowd poured out to him, he felt as though he was at his own funeral, as though he was being buried under all the applause and the praise.

Guy couldn't help thinking that his retirement was terrible. Four years wasted soaking in his own bitterness. He had truly allowed himself to be taken advantage of; that was why he bore a grudge for so long against Lemaire, Savard and Corey. They had convinced him he was finished when he was not. And he had proved it, later, almost too much later, by making his comeback. If they had fired him, traded him or sold him, that would have been all right. He could have recovered quickly. But what they did was worse. They played with his mind and with his soul.

Tonight, Lise is still very bitter. Just a few days ago, she again made sensational statements to the press, denouncing the Canadiens organization, and especially Serge Savard. She said that she could not and did not want to forgive or forget the way Savard had allowed rumours to circulate about Guy, rumours that had almost destroyed their marriage. And if there is one person in the world whose opinions Guy Lafleur respects, it is Lise, his wife.

Nevertheless, tonight at the Forum Guy wishes everything could be perfect and forgotten. He has thought a lot about that these last few days. Of how happy he will be to retire, finally of his own volition, leaving neither rancour nor hate behind him. He even wonders if he might not shake Corey's hand tonight. Corey is in his usual place, behind the Canadiens' bench. Certainly, a reconciliation with the Canadiens would make the Montreal public happy, and on this evening, Guy Lafleur has an intense desire to gratify his fans. This past week he has been offered so many bouquets and compliments that he feels the need to give something in return.

When the voice of Claude Mouton finally echoes through the Forum and the television producer signals Lafleur to leap onto the ice, he no longer knows what he is going to do. Bobby Orr, the player Lafleur admired so much, always said that hockey was a game of chance and luck. You have to be ready for anything, and, above all, you have to know how to improvise.

In fact, this evening reminds him of December 17, 1988, when Guy found himself on the ice at the Forum for the first time in four years, once again receiving the tribute of the fans.

He would never forget it. Like this evening, he hadn't really known what he would do, until the moment when he pulled on his New York Rangers sweater, number 10, and raised his arms in victory. That happy memory made him think of his father, who had been so proud of him that evening. The next morning he had even phoned to say, "My boy, I'm really proud of you. You got your revenge."

That evening had indeed been sweet for Guy Lafleur. But he had not been seeking revenge. He didn't like that word. He had not revenged himself. He had done better. They had thrown him on the scrap heap, and he had emerged.

This evening, March 30, 1991, he bears no malice. The only person he has perhaps not quite forgiven is himself. He still sometimes blames himself for allowing himself to be taken, but during his retirement he has learned a lot. He knows now that never again can his strength or his faith be taken away.

He is tired—happy, gratified, but tired. The last few days have been hard. He has gone everywhere. He has been on all the television and radio shows. Every day, in all the newspapers, there have been big articles about him. Every day for a week *La Presse* has been publishing hundreds of letters from admirers, poems, drawings, messages from ordinary people stating their gratitude to him, or tributes from big corporations that have bought full pages to honour him. And more! Réjean Tremblay, the reporter, told him only the best letters had been chosen. There were thousands of others. There were enough to make a book of at least a thousand pages. Good!

While waiting for the ceremony to begin, he has already made two circuits of the rink. He has stopped for a moment in front of the Nordiques' bench, then in front of the Canadiens', where his eyes caught Corey's. He has waved left and right to the crowd, he has looked at the people way up in the blues, he has smiled at the cameras. The noise has become so strong that it is hard to move. Before, these cries carried him, they pushed him, they gave him wings. But this evening is different. This evening, what is happening is more than hockey.

He skates slowly in circles. He feels a tingling in his left ankle, an old, familiar injury that sometimes comes back, a moment of lightning pain, then nothing. When he turns around, his back to the spotlights, he sees the Forum plunged into a deep blue shadow. And all the ice is his

alone, as it used to be in Thurso, when he went to the arena
early Saturday mornings. In those days he dreamed of
becoming a great hockey player, like Jean Béliveau. And it
happened. He was a great player, a legend, a man beyond
the ordinary, the most admired and the most loved of his
generation.

But this evening he is at the end of the dream—on the
other side of the dream. He realizes that for a long time he
has not even been a real hockey player, because he is no
longer possessed by that strange passion he used to have. He
no longer feels the same desire to carry the puck like a
madman, attacking head down, thinking of nothing, seeing
nothing, expecting nothing, wanting only one thing, to put
the puck in the net, to score, to win.

This winter, in Vancouver, in New York, in Winnipeg,
there were a few times when he was swept away by the old
whirlwind of energy. And a few last times he awoke the fans
and their cries of "Guy! Guy! Guy!" But it wasn't like it
used to be. Something of his passion had been lost. That was
a little painful, but not too much. Perhaps that was what it
meant to be growing old. Growing old isn't only something
that happens to the body; a lot of it has to do with the mind,
the heart. And that isn't entirely bad. On the contrary. You
simply want to experience something different, live another
way.

As he passes, he looks at the young players on the
Nordiques' bench. To tell the truth, he would not want to be
in their place this evening. Certainly, he might envy them
their youth—it is always good to be twenty years old. But he
thinks of all the work it will take them to get where he is, to
travel to the other side of the dream. He thinks of those
famous lines of poetry written on the walls of the Canadiens
players' room: "To you from failing hands we throw/The
torch; be yours to hold it high!" His failing hands? Not
really. He is still in good condition, strong and supple. He
knows it, he feels it. He often says he has been lucky to have
been paid millions of dollars to keep himself in shape. Of
course, he still hasn't been able to stop smoking, but that's

one of his plans for when he retires. Seriously! He's going to stop smoking. It will make Lise and the children happy.

Another project, his real project, is to work to create a good and well-balanced team for Quebec. So much needs to be done: the tradition must be re-established, confidence regained, the public won over. There is everything to win and nothing to lose. Even though the two years he spent in Quebec were disastrous, Lafleur ended up with a real feeling for the team. He knows that one day, sooner or later, the club will improve, because the fans want it, and Lafleur believes that public support is the main element that ensures a strong and winning team. He knows it will happen, and he wants to work towards it. Because the Nordiques are finishing this year at the bottom of the league, at the next draft they will be able to get a good player, the first choice overall. With luck and a lot of work, the team will be able to extricate itself from the quagmire they've been wallowing in these past few years.

Once again, the Blond Demon waves to the crowd. This afternoon someone said to him, "You might as well enjoy it, Guy. It could be the last time." And he immediately thought, "The last time? Maybe not."

In fact, you never know. The time could come, long after the year 2000, somewhere around 2031 for instance, the year of his eightieth birthday, when there might be some big celebration bringing together all the veterans. All the old quarrels will finally be forgotten, and time will have smoothed everything over. There could be celebrations, like tonight's, to commemorate, to salute. And he intends to be there. Aurèle Joliat, a few years ago, at eighty-four years of age, came to greet the fans at the Forum. Why can't he, Guy Lafleur, come back one more time when he's eighty years old? Even at ninety, if he's invited. These days you can stay fit indefinitely. You never know, one day they might find out how to make people live well beyond a hundred. How great it would be to be here, the day of his hundredth birthday, for the start of the hockey season. Why not? George Burns, the American actor that he likes so much, ninety-six years old and still surrounded by beautiful girls, with a cigar in his mouth and a smile on his lips, says that on his hundredth birthday, in 1995, he will put on a show in New York. Why can't he, Guy Lafleur, hope to be on his skates at that age?

For the moment, he is alone amid the clamour of the fans who, no doubt realizing that the Blond Demon, their beloved Blond Demon, will soon disappear for good, have now all risen to their feet and begun to howl even more loudly. And they show no sign of stopping. He has now been alone on the ice for more than five minutes, imprisoned by the cone of light that follows him everywhere. He has already twice signalled Claude Mouton to start talking, but each time Mouton begins to say "Ladies and gentle-men . . ." the crowd cries more loudly and drowns out his voice. And Mouton raises his arms helplessly and looks at Lafleur, who has no choice but to return to his strange meditation.

The evening before, on CJMS, a special program was dedicated to him. For three hours dozens of people took turns paying tribute to him. It was almost frightening, all that praise, compliments, almost too much. Ti-Paul Meloche was there, Claude Quenneville, the Canadiens old-timers, former Remparts. Marius Fortier, Gilles Lupien, Pierre Bouchard, who made everyone laugh, Yvan "Roadrunner" Cournoyer, tanned as always, Mario Tremblay of course, and many others. A world of men, the men of his life. John Ziegler, the president of the NHL, the same man who in April had ruled that Lafleur could not play in the League all-star game, also telephoned, his voice sweet and unctuous, to congratulate him. But he didn't even take the trouble to say a single word in French—not even *"felicitations"* or *"merci."* Guy felt like saying something rude back to him. But what was the point? Everyone was being so nice. Everyone laughed. He no longer wanted to argue. Later, at the end of the show, when it was time for him to express his thanks, he said to the host, Mario Tremblay, "You have truly given me a lot. You've gone so far that I don't think there will be anything left to add when I die."

Of course he has been thinking about his death these past few days. You can't retire without thinking of the passing of time and the fact that one day it will all be over. In the meantime, life continues to go well for Guy Lafleur. He finally has the house of his dreams. He found it in an architecture magazine when he was living in New York. It is a huge, grey stone house, with ivy and turrets, surrounded by trees. He bought the plans and had them adapted to his—and Lise's—taste by a Quebec architect. To build it he bought three adjoining lots in Quebec City's new exclusive district, Mesnil, in the foothills of the Laurentians. While the house was being constructed, people were always dropping by to watch the work progress, say hello to Guy, get excited with him, share his joy. Lafleur loves Quebec, its people, its countryside, its seasons. He loves the way the Québecois are with him. Warm, simple, like himself.

Tomorrow evening, Easter Sunday, he'll be playing his last game, at the Colisée. Luck, his own luck, his friendly luck, has once again arranged things to suit him. The last two games of his NHL career are being played against the Montreal Canadiens, at the Forum and the Colisée. He knows that tonight he won't lack for ice time. On the contrary, he'll get as much as he can take. And the boys will do everything possible to get him a goal. He knows that the opportunity will come. He is going to score. He wants to score. A goal. Just one. The final point, the point to mark the end of his career.

The ovation has now lasted almost six minutes. Lafleur signals the crowd for silence and goes to the boards. In spite of the noise, Maurice Richard comes to present him with the gift of the Canadiens organization, a fishing outfit—tackle, rods, lines, flies, lures, etc. No surprise, but he is happy. He waves to the crowd. And in the near silence he has managed to impose, he starts towards the exit. The players from both clubs come onto the ice. Guy is about to arrive at his bench when, once more, his eyes meet Corey's. Without even thinking, he goes towards him. He holds out his hand. The Canadiens president leans forward and embraces him. And as the fans cry out, Lafleur knows he has just made a worthwhile point. Once again, without planning, he has found the memorable gesture. He has won.

It is time for the face-off. The game has begun. And it has finished. Once again, one last time, Guy Lafleur will play hockey. And after? After tomorrow, Monday, April 1, 1991, there will be nothing left except life, the real life that is waiting for him. In fact, a double life: that of a forty-year-old man, living in Quebec, husband, father, businessman and consultant, hockey executive in the administrative offices of the Colisée; and that of a ghost, in Montreal, the most uncontrollable, the most engaging, the most alive of all the Forum's ghosts.

Also available from Penguin Books

David Cruise & Alison Griffiths

NET WORTH

In December 1990, about fifty NHL old-timers — including Gordie Howe, Bobby Hull, Carl Brewer and Bobby Orr — gathered at a hotel in Toronto to debate whether or not to sue the NHL. Their reason: after decades of frustration, they felt they had been deprived by the League and their own players' association of millions of dollars.

The shocking story of greed and abuse goes back decades to the '30s, when "Big Jim" Norris, a Chicago magnate, illegally owned three of the six NHL teams of the day and ran them as a private fiefdom. His style set a precedent that, to some extent, is still with us: owners who conceal enormous profits and pay their players low salaries, all the while complaining that player demands are going to kill the game; infighting among general managers and owners who worry more about settling their own feuds than about the good of the game; disorganization that has lost the League and the players millions in TV and other revenue; and All-Star players who find that their much-lauded pension plan doesn't pay them enough to live on after retirement.

In *Net Worth*, David Cruise and Alison Griffiths expose the colourful characters and backroom deals that have made the NHL what it is today. Meet Eddie Shore, a minor league owner so brutal his players finally rose up against him and changed pro hockey forever; the little-known 1957 player rebellion led by Ted Lindsay and Doug Harvey; the "Young Lions", a group of brilliant Maple Leaf players who laid the groundwork for the present players' association, out of which came the man who seems to be everywhere in hockey — Alan Eagleson.

This book is both a tribute to the men who have made the game great and a searing indictment of those who have turned it into a highly profitable private empire.

Kelly Gruber & Kevin Boland

KELLY: AT HOME ON THIRD

The story of the Blue Jays' 1990 Most Valuable Player and most popular star.

From Texas to Toronto by way of Cleveland and a dozen other towns in between — that's the trail third baseman Kelly Gruber of the Toronto Blue Jays has blazed to superstardom in the decade since he left home at the age of 18 to become a professional ballplayer.

And what a cast of characters there were to help him along the way:

> How about Dirty Al Gallagher, one of Gruber's toughest managers in the minor leagues, who could chew tobacco, smoke a cigar and snore up a storm all at the same time?

> How about Bob Quinn, the architect of the 1990 World Series Champion Cincinnati Reds, whose 1983 blunder allowed the Blue Jays to swipe Gruber from the Cleveland Indians?

> Then there's Jimy Williams, the nice guy who got no respect as manager of the Blue Jays; his hot-tempered predecessor Bobby Cox; and cool-as-a-cucumber Cito Gaston, who manages the team today.

And of course there is the stellar third baseman himself. In *Kelly: At Home on Third* we hear of the ballplayer's dog days in the minors, including his fight to hit the breaking ball and rescue his career from dismal statistics. Kelly discusses how he plays today, sharing the secrets of his impressive batting technique and of how he sizes up the guys on the mound. We learn how Kelly's personal life fits into his life in the leagues: his family in Texas, his Canadian wife Lynn and their son Kody, and his strongly held Christian faith.

As open and earthy as his home turf of Texas, Kelly offers opinions on all the fun, feuds and scandals that are packed into the 162-game season.

Robert Olver

THE MAKING OF CHAMPIONS

A boy sits in the rookie dressing-room of the Saskatoon Blades,

"and in spite of himself begins thinking of all the things he would prefer to be doing at this instant instead of...savouring the smell of sweat and loneliness. Part of him, make no mistake, wants to be here, is excited at the prospect that this is his chance to break into Junior A hockey, last step before the National Hockey League. He has to be here, he wants to be here, because that is the one thing he shares with all the others in the room — this dream of someday playing in the NHL."

But the boy is just 16, and a very long way from home. The daunting reality for the six dreamers profiled here in *The Making of Champions* is that they are alone, strangers in a land of physical and emotional risk.

Based on the young men's own diaries and interviews, *The Making of Champions* is an engrossing account of how Junior A players cope with life on and off the ice. Many hockey books celebrate the glories of the sport, but few examine the costs of such a career. This is the first look at both the exhilaration and the rigors of junior hockey and its effect on young men and their families.

"*Champions* embodies the essence of junior hockey: endless bus rides, homesickness and, above all, intensely competitive and emotional hockey....A champion work...which becomes infectious upon reading."

Metro One